* **PIONEER SOCIOLOGIST**
* **REVISIONIST HISTORIAN**
* **NOVELIST AND POET**
* **CRUSADING EDITOR**
* **CIVIL RIGHTS MILITANT**
* **POLITICAL RADICAL**

W. E. B. Du Bois was all of these—and more. As a superb scholar and trailblazing investigator, he illumined the racial situation in 20th-century America as has no other writer, black or white. As a tireless leader and eloquent voice of protest, he offered his people an activist alternative to a policy of gradualism that had proved itself illusory.

The writings in this volume address an enormous range of topics and problems. *But they speak with the voice of a single man—one of the most remarkable figures our country has ever produced.*

SIGNET and MENTOR Titles
of Related Interest

The Selected Writings of
W. E. B. Du Bois

Edited by WALTER WILSON

With an Introduction by
STEPHEN J. WRIGHT

A MENTOR BOOK from
NEW AMERICAN LIBRARY
TIMES MIRROR
New York and Toronto
The New English Library Limited, London

MENTOR TRADEMARK REG. U.S. PAT. OFF. AND FOREIGN COUNTRIES
REGISTERED TRADEMARK—MARCA REGISTRADA
HECHO EN CHICAGO, U.S.A.

SIGNET, SIGNET CLASSICS, MENTOR AND PLUME BOOKS
are published in the United States by
The New American Library, Inc.,
1301 Avenue of the Americas, New York, New York 10019,
in Canada by The New American Library of Canada Limited,
295 King Street East, Toronto 2, Ontario,
in the United Kingdom by The New English Library Limited,
Barnard's Inn, Holborn, London, E.C. 1, England

FIRST PRINTING, JUNE, 1970

PRINTED IN THE UNITED STATES OF AMERICA

CREDO*

. . . . I believe in the Prince of Peace. I believe that War is Murder. I believe that armies and navies are at bottom the tinsel and braggadocio of oppression and wrong, and I believe that the wicked conquest of weaker and darker nations by nations whiter and stronger but foreshadows the death of that strength.

I believe in Liberty for all men: the space to stretch their arms and their souls, the right to breathe and the right to vote, the freedom to choose their friends, enjoy the sunshine, and ride on the railroads, uncursed by color; thinking, dreaming, working as they will in a kingdom of beauty and love.

I believe in the Training of Children, black even as white; the leading out of little souls into the green pastures and beside the still waters, not for pelf or peace, but for life lit by some large vision of beauty and goodness and truth; lest we forget, and the sons of the fathers, like Esau, for mere meat barter their birthright in a mighty nation.

Finally, I believe in Patience—patience with the weakness of the Weak and the strength of the Strong, the prejudice of the Ignorant and the ignorance of the Blind; patience with the tardy triumph of Joy and the mad chastening of Sorrow —patience with God!

INDEPENDENT MAGAZINE, OCTOBER, 1904

* This essay was later used in *Darkwater* and elsewhere.

CONTENTS

INTRODUCTION

When William Edward Burghardt Du Bois died in Accra, Ghana on August 27, 1963, at age 95—the day before the great Civil Rights March on Washington—he had written 19 books and literally hundreds of editorials, articles, and pamphlets. His published writings spanned some 60 years—longer than most men live. These writings include sociological research, history, poetry, short stories, novels, autobiography, but above all crusading editorials. Nearly all of his writings deal directly or indirectly with the racial problem. In his later years, he became concerned with world peace.

But Du Bois was more than a writer. He founded and edited four periodicals: *The Crisis, Horizon, The Brownies' Book,* and *Phylon.* He was a founder of the Niagara Movement, the NAACP and the Pan-African Movement. Yet he was more than an organizer. For over 30 years, he was undoubtedly the most articulate, fearless, and widely read spokesman for the equal rights of Negroes in America. Moreover, at one time or another he was a college professor, a researcher, an editor, an able espouser of the cause of peace, and a Pan-Africanist. He was a self-confident—some would say vain and arrogant—sensitive, stubborn, individualistic, indefatigable, and innovative man. His training, experience and perhaps basic character combined to make him, preeminently, the right man, in the right places at the right times in the first half of the twentieth century history of Negroes in America. In a sense, he was the bridge between the militant Frederick Douglass who died in 1895 and the current movement for racial justice and equality.

Background and Education

Du Bois was greatly influenced by both his New England background and his formal education. Born in Great Barrington, Massachusetts in 1868 and educated in its public schools, he entered Fisk University in 1885 and was graduated in 1888. Fisk, then as now dedicated to education in the liberal arts, prepared him to enter Harvard, from which he was graduated, *cum laude,* in 1890, with another baccalaureate degree. Five years later, he received the degree of Doctor of Philosophy from Harvard, having spent two years studying in Germany as was the custom for doctoral students at the time. His thesis, *The Suppression of the African Slave Trade to the United States of America, 1638 to 1870,* in which he took lasting pride, is Volume I in the Harvard University Historical Series. His doctoral degree was the first to be conferred by Harvard on an American Negro and the fifth to be conferred upon a Negro by an American University.

Du Bois' teachers at Harvard included some of the greatest teachers of that time or any other time—among them were Albert Bushnell Hart, William James, George Santayana, Josiah Royce, and George Lyman Kittredge.

Thus, the education with which Du Bois began his career was as good as could be obtained at the time and this, to be sure, contributed to his poise and self-confidence—qualities which he never lost. It was also the type of education that led him, almost instinctively, to know that the "industrial" education advocated by Booker T. Washington was far too limited for a race of people.

Du Bois' career may be divided into five periods:

1. Researcher and university instructor, 1895–1910
2. Editor of the NAACP's *The Crisis,* 1910–1934
3. Second period as university instructor, 1934–1944
4. Second period with the NAACP, 1944–1948
5. International years, 1948–1963

The Early Researcher and University Instructor

Following a year of service as Professor of the Classics at Wilberforce University, Du Bois accepted an appointment as Assistant Instructor at the University of Pennsylvania, having as his assignment the conducting of a special investigation of the condition of Negroes in Philadelphia. The results of this investigation were published in 1899 under the title *The Philadelphia Negro: A Social Study*— the first scientific study of the Negro and the first scientific sociological study in the United States. Gunnar Myrdal, 45 years later, said of this study: "We cannot close this description of what a study of a Negro community should be without calling attention to the study which best meets our requirements, a study which is now all but forgotten. We refer to W. E. B. Du Bois', *The Philadelphia Negro,* published in 1899."[1]

Du Bois spent 13 years, 1897–1910, as Professor of History and Economics at Atlanta University. These years were among his most productive as a scholar, editor, and writer. During this period the following were among his major publications:

1. *The Atlanta University Publications*—i.e., 3–18 inclusive (15–18 co-edited with Augustus G. Dill), 1898 to 1914. They represent the best data available on Negroes for the 16-year period covered in these studies.
2. *The Souls of Black Folk: Essays and Sketches* has had 27 editions. It included the famous essay, "Of Mr. Booker T. Washington and Others," and began the historic Washington–Du Bois controversy on the education of the Negro, stating in blunt, unequivocal language his position on the rights of Negroes.
3. *Horizon; A Journal of the Color Line* was the first of the four periodicals founded and edited by Du Bois. His editorials were a forerunner of the column "As the Crow Flies," which appeared later in *The Crisis.*
4. *John Brown.*

The Editorship of The Crisis, *1910–1934*

In 1910, Du Bois became editor of *The Crisis,* the official organ of the NAACP, a position which he held until 1934 —24 exciting years. At its peak, its circulation reached 104,000 and his column, "As the Crow Flies," was read avidly by thousands of Negroes. His vituperative attacks on injustices done to Negroes and his powerful advocacy of equal rights for Negroes combined to make him, following the death of Booker T. Washington, the best known Negro in America. But more importantly, he became the philosopher of the Negro protest.

During this period he found time to publish two novels: *The Quest of the Silver Fleece* and *Dark Princess,* as well as a pageant, "The Star of Ethiopia." In a more scholarly vein, he published *The Negro, Darkwater,* and *The Gift of Black Folk.*

[1] Gunnar Myrdal, *An American Dilemma* (New York: Harper and Brothers, 1944), p. 1132.

Not only did Du Bois reach Negro audiences, but his incisive articles were accepted by the most prestigious periodicals in the nation during this time: *The Annals of the American Academy of Political and Social Science; The American Historical Review; Outlook; Independent; The Atlantic Monthly;* etc.

One of the most interesting and perceptive of his efforts was the founding and editing of *The Brownies' Book,* a monthly magazine for Negro children. Its purpose, according to Du Bois, was "To make colored children realize that being colored is a normal, beautiful thing, to make them familiar with the history and achievements of the Negro race, to make them know that other colored children have grown into beautiful, useful, famous persons. . . ." In this endeavor, he anticipated "Black is Beautiful" and "Black Studies" by more than 40 years.

It was also during this period that Du Bois became interested in Pan-Africanism, initiated the Movement and later became the moving spirit of the five Pan-African Congresses.

Second Period as a University Instructor, 1934–1944

Breaking with the NAACP over the editorial policy of *The Crisis,* Du Bois ended his editorship by resigning in 1934. He returned to Atlanta University as Professor of Sociology and began, almost immediately, one of the most productive periods of his life. Beginning at age 65, he wrote *Black Reconstruction; Black Folk, Then and Now; Dusk of Dawn* (an autobiography); and *Color and Democracy.* In addition, he founded and edited *Phylon: The Atlanta University Review of Race and Culture* (1940), a journal of high quality and continuing importance.

Second Period with the NAACP, 1944–1948

At age 76, but against his will, Du Bois was retired in 1944 from Atlanta University. Later that year he accepted an invitation to rejoin the staff of the NAACP. His duties, responsibilities, and conditions of service were apparently unclear. According to Du Bois, he was to revive the Pan-African Movement and concern himself with the international aspects of the race problem. In any event, Du Bois was accredited by the NAACP in 1945, along with Walter White, the executive secretary, as a consultant to the founding convention of the United Nations. He also presided over the Fifth Pan-African Congress the same year.

Du Bois' second period with the NAACP was, however, not a pleasant one for him. Differences between him and Walter White over such matters as office space, secretarial assistance, and more importantly over the role Du Bois was to play in the affairs of the NAACP became increasingly antagonistic. In 1948, White accused Du Bois of "leaking" to the press a memorandum in which he charged that the NAACP was supporting President Truman's election to the detriment of the larger Negro cause and that White's appointment to the American Delegation to the United Nations General Assembly in Paris was a political payoff.

White, thereupon, asked the board of the NAACP to dismiss Du Bois. To Du Bois' surprise, it did. Thus, at age 80, Du Bois' career had reached another turning point.

The International Years, 1948–1963

As Du Bois became advanced in years, he became more interested in socialism, Marxism, world peace, and Africa.

Following his dismissal from the NAACP in 1948, he became co-chairman with Paul Robeson of the Council on African Affairs. In 1949, he helped to organize the Cultural and Scientific Conference for World Peace held in New York City and, later that year, he attended both the Paris and Moscow peace conferences. The following year, he became chairman of the Peace Information Center which later involved him in one of the most traumatic experiences of his life.

The Center, according to Du Bois, had as its major purpose informing citizens of the United States about the efforts other nations were making toward world peace and, in the pursuit of this objective, it engaged in two activities:[2]

1. The publication of "Peacegrams" through which the peace efforts of other nations were disseminated to citizens of the United States.
2. Securing signatures for the "Stockholm Appeal," calling for the abolition of the atomic bomb. According to Du Bois, the Center succeeded in collecting some 2,500,000 signatures for the "Stockholm Appeal."

In February, 1951, Du Bois and the other officers of the

---

[2] W. E. B. Du Bois, "A Soliloquy on Viewing My Life from the Last Decade of Its First Century," *The Autobiography of W. E. B. Du Bois* (New York: International Publishers, 1968), pp. 356–357.

Center were indicted for failure to register as agents of a foreign principal. The trial was held in November, 1951; Du Bois' reaction to it is best stated in his own words: "I have faced during my life many unpleasant experiences: the growl of a mob; the personal threat of murder; the scowling distaste of an audience. But nothing has so cowed me as that day, November 8, 1951, when I took my seat in a Washington courtroom as an indicted criminal."[3] Fortunately, the judge granted a motion for a judgment of acquittal on the ground that the evidence did not permit the conclusion of guilt beyond a reasonable doubt. Du Bois tells the story in his book *In Battle for Peace*.

Several years following this ordeal, Du Bois traveled extensively in the U.S.S.R. and China. In 1961, he joined the Communist Party of the United States, and later that year he accepted the invitation of President Nkrumah to come to Ghana as Director of the *Encyclopedia Africana* project. Two years later, in 1963, he became a citizen of Ghana and he died there on August 27 of that year.

Roy Wilkins, announcing Du Bois' death before the huge March on Washington Crowd on August 28, 1963, stated that the spirit of Du Bois had marched with them on that historic day.

The Influence of Du Bois

Sometime before his death, Du Bois prepared his last message to the world and entrusted his wife, Shirley Graham Du Bois, with its dissemination upon his death. The statement reads, in part:

> *I have loved my work, I have loved people and my play, but always I have been uplifted by the thought that What I have done well will live long and justify my life; that which I have done ill or never finished can now be handed over to others for endless days to be finished, perhaps better than I could have done.*[4]

The question that must be asked of the life of Du Bois or of any other meaningful life is: "What did he do so well that it will live long and justify his life?"

In the case of Du Bois, the total answer varies, depending

---

[3] Du Bois, *op. cit.* p. 379.
[4] *Freedomways* (W. E. B. Du Bois Memorial Issue), Winter, 1965, p. 206.

on whether he was known personally or vicariously through his writings and the writings about him. The consensus is, I believe, that he wrote much that will live long and justify his life.

Most would agree that while he wrote novels, he was not a great novelist; that while he wrote poetry—some of it passionate—he was not a great poet; that while he wrote history and was an adequate historian, he was not a great historian. But he was a historian with a great cause. They would also agree, as he himself admitted in *Dusk of Dawn*, that he did not possess the warmth and the charismatic personality to become a great popular leader. He was warm, witty, and charming with his intimate friends, but to those outside this privileged circle he could be, and often was, aloof, cold, abrupt, impatient, and devastating in his criticisms. He was a gadfly, an innovator, an imaginative interpreter of facts, a master of the English language, an able, passionate espouser of the Negro cause, and a prophet.

Most would agree that among the things he did superbly and which, therefore, will live long and justify his life are the following:

1. His scholarly writings on racial problems in America. He set the pace and the pattern. His *The Philadelphia Negro*, his *Atlanta University Publications*, and, in a sense, his *Black Reconstruction* are his monuments in this area.

2. For more than 40 years, he was the uncompromising philosopher of the Negro's Struggle for Equality in America. He provided the intellectual basis for the Negro's protest and he not only influenced and inspired thousands of Negroes, but he alerted liberal white Americans to the dimensions of the problem. His crusading editorials in *The Crisis*, his *The Souls of Black Folk*, and his *Credo* are among his monuments in this area.

3. He was, at the time it counted most, the most articulate and relevant spokesman for the nature of the education needed by Negro Americans. He possessed an unshakable faith in liberal education and, perhaps more than any other single person in the nation, he helped to counteract the Booker T. Washington notion of "industrial" education for the great masses of the Negro people. His essays "Of Mr. Booker T. Washington and Others," "The College Bred Negro," "The Talented Tenth," and

"Of the Training of Black Men" are among his monuments in this area.

4. By the emulative example he set, he led other talented young Negroes to believe that study and research in their history and culture were worthy of their best scholarly endeavors. *Gift of Black Folk in the Making of America* and *Phylon* are among his monuments in this area.

5. He planted the seeds of Pan-Africanism which may yet bear fruit. In the Pan-African congresses, he touched the hearts and minds of many of the men who now lead the new African nations. His essays "Black Africa Tomorrow" and "Pan-Africa: A Mission in My Life and the Pan-African Movement" are among his monuments in this area.

The publication of a Du Bois Reader is especially appropriate at this point in the racial struggle in America. It should help to put many of the issues and problems in perspective and also suggest the lateness of the hour. The recently released six-year study of race relations in Britain stated that: "The dominant question of our century is whether men of all races and colors whom advances in science and technology have made near neighbors can live together in peace and harmony." Prophet that he was, Du Bois asserted more than 40 years ago that the dominant problem of the twentieth century was "the color line."

While there will undoubtedly be disagreements with the choice of selections, the readers—especially the younger readers—will be introduced to the mind, thought and character of one of the Olympian figures of this century.

STEPHEN J. WRIGHT
Teaneck, New Jersey

From THE PHILADELPHIA NEGRO

In 1899, at the age of 31, Du Bois published, under the auspices of the University of Pennsylvania, his second important book The Philadelphia Negro. *With this work he moved, as one of the few pioneers, into the young field of sociology. The book was such a success that it is still considered a model in the field of race and urban studies. Although he received less than $1,000 in salary, Du Bois personally conducted most of the research, including the interviewing of 5,000 people.*

Gunnar Myrdal, author of the classic study of the American Negro, An American Dilemma, *once wrote about the need for further study of the subject and said, "We cannot close this description of what a study of a Negro community should be without calling attention to the study which best meets our requirements. We refer to W. E. B. Du Bois'* The Philadelphia Negro, *published in 1899." He also commented that this study "is now all but forgotten." That is not entirely true, for scholars and students, whenever possible, are continuing to use the Du Bois book. Of course it was out of print and almost unobtainable but in 1967 a new edition was published.*

Du Bois has indicated how he came to write the book and that the subject held a peculiar fascination for him. He said that he had arrived at a point when "The Negro problem in my mind was a matter of systematic investigation and intelligent understanding." He thought the "ultimate evil was stupidity." (Actually in all of his work he was documenting, consciously or unconsciously, the theory of economic determinism and class struggle, the theory he espoused for most of his life and particularly in his later years.) Without regard for the pitiful compensation he received for the job, he eagerly undertook the task. He knew what was expected of him. He wrote about it in Dusk of Dawn:

The fact was that the city of Philadelphia at that time had a theory; and that theory was that this great, rich, and famous municipality was going to the dogs because of the crime and venality of its Negro citizens who lived largely centered in the slum at the lower end of the seventh ward. Philadelphia wanted to prove this by figures and I was the man to do it. Of this theory back of the plan, I neither knew or cared. I saw only here a chance to study a historical group of black folk and show exactly what their place was in the community.

Du Bois, the sociologist, completed his work and commented, "It revealed the Negro group, and not an inert, sick body of crime; as a long historic development and not a transient occurrence."

Du Bois' findings on a number of topics were far from flattering to "the City of Brotherly Love." He even dared investigate and report on interracial sex and intermarriage and found no natural antipathy (otherwise how explain the mulatto population?), and he boldly said the matter of intermarriage was of concern only to the parties involved. He accused Philadelphia whites of judging all members of the black race for the acts of the worst elements of its population. Though there were, of course, some vicious Negroes, crime as a generalization was caused by environment— discrimination, lack of opportunity and poverty. Many other topics were explored in depth. In the end, The Philadelphia Negro reported that the Negro problem was a problem of the poor and dispossessed and had nothing to do with inherent inferiority.

This sampling from The Philadelphia Negro consists of excerpts from the findings on topics such as intermarriage, crime, education, housing, living conditions, attitude of whites, role of the Christian church, and race prejudice.

The Contact of the Races

COLOR PREJUDICE—Incidentally throughout this study the prejudice against the Negro has been again and again mentioned. It is time now to reduce this somewhat indefinite term to something tangible. Everybody speaks of the matter, everybody knows that it exists, but in just what form it shows itself or how influential it is few agree. In the Negro's mind, color prejudice in Philadelphia is that widespread feeling of dislike for his blood, which keeps him and his children out of decent employment, from certain public conveniences and amusements, from hiring houses in many sections, and in general, from being recognized as a man. Negroes regard this prejudice as the chief cause of their present unfortunate condition. On the other hand most white people are quite unconscious of any such powerful and vindictive feeling; they regard color prejudice as the easily explicable feeling that intimate social intercourse with a lower race is not only undesirable but impracticable if our present standards of culture are to be maintained; and although they are aware that some people feel the aversion more intensely than others, they cannot see how such a feeling has much influence on the real situation or alters the social condition of the mass of Negroes.

As a matter of fact, color prejudice in this city is something between these two extreme views: it is not to-day responsible for all, or perhaps the greater part of the Negro problems, or of the disabilities under which the race labors; on the other hand it is a far more powerful social force than most Philadelphians realize. The practical results of the attitude of most of the inhabitants of Philadelphia toward persons of Negro descent are as follows:

1. As to getting work:

No matter how well trained a Negro may be, or how fitted for work of any kind, he cannot in the ordinary course of competition hope to be much more than a menial servant.

He cannot get clerical or supervisory work to do save in exceptional cases.

He cannot teach save in a few of the remaining Negro schools.

He cannot become a mechanic except for small transient jobs, and cannot join a trades union.

A Negro woman has but three careers open to her in this city: domestic service, sewing, or married life.

2. As to keeping work:

The Negro suffers in competition more severely than white men.

Change in fashion is causing him to be replaced by whites in the better paid positions of domestic service.

Whim and accident will cause him to lose a hard-earned place more quickly than the same things would affect a white man.

Being few in number compared with the whites the crime or carelessness of a few of his race is easily imputed to all, and the reputations of the good, industrious and reliable suffer thereby.

Because Negro workmen may not often work side by side with white workmen, the individual black workman is rated not by his own efficiency, but by the efficiency of a whole group of black fellow workmen which may often be low.

Because of these difficulties which virtually increase competition in his case, he is forced to take lower wages for the same work than white workmen.

3. As to entering new lines of work:

Men are used to seeing Negroes in inferior positions; when, therefore, by any chance a Negro gets in a better position, most men immediately conclude that he is not fitted for it, even before he has a chance to show his fitness.

If, therefore, he set up a store, men will not patronize him.

If he is put into public position men will complain.

If he gain a position in the commercial world, men will quietly secure his dismissal or see that a white man succeeds him.

4. As to his expenditure:

The comparative smallness of the patronage of the Negro, and the dislike of other customers makes it usual to increase the charges or difficulties in certain directions in which a Negro must spend money.

He must pay more house-rent for worse houses than most white people pay.

He is sometimes liable to insult or reluctant service in some restaurants, hotels and stores, at public resorts, theatres and places of recreation; and at nearly all barber shops.

5. As to his children:

The Negro finds it extremely difficult to rear children in such an atmosphere and not have them either cringing or impudent: if he impresses upon them patience with their lot, they may grow up satisfied with their condition; if he inspires them with ambition to rise, they may grow to despise their own people, hate the whites and become embittered with the world.

His children are discriminated against, often in public schools.

They are advised when seeking employment to become waiters and maids.

They are liable to species of insult and temptation peculiarly trying to children.

6. As to social intercourse:

In all walks of life the Negro is liable to meet some objection to his presence or some discourteous treatment; and the ties of friendship or memory seldom are strong enough to hold across the color line.

If an invitation is issued to the public for any occasion, the Negro can never know whether he would be welcomed or not; if he goes he is liable to have his feelings hurt and get into unpleasant altercation; if he stays away, he is blamed for indifference.

If he meet a lifelong white friend on the street, he is in a dilemma; if he does not greet the friend he is put down as boorish and impolite; if he does greet the friend he is liable to be flatly snubbed.

If by chance he is introduced to a white woman or man, he expects to be ignored on the next meeting, and usually is.

White friends may call on him, but he is scarcely expected to call on them, save for strictly business matters.

If he gain the affections of a white woman and marry her he may invariably expect that slurs will be thrown on her reputation and on his, and that both his and her race will shun their company.[1]

When he dies he cannot be buried beside white corpses.

7. The result:

Any one of these things happening now and then would not be remarkable or call for especial comment; but when one group of people suffer all these little differences of treatment and discriminations and insults continually, the result is either discouragement, or bitterness, or over-sensitiveness, or recklessness. And a people feeling thus cannot do their best.

Presumably the first impulse of the average Philadelphian would be emphatically to deny any such marked and blighting discrimination as the above against a group of citizens in this metropolis. Every one knows that in the past color prejudice in the city was deep and passionate; living men can remember when a Negro could not sit in a street car or

[1] Cf. Section 49, The Intermarriage of the Races.

walk many streets in peace. These times have passed, however, and many imagine that active discrimination against the Negro has passed with them. Careful inquiry will convince any such one of his error. To be sure a colored man to-day can walk the streets of Philadelphia without personal insult; he can go to theatres, parks and some places of amusement without meeting more than stares and discourtesy; he can be accommodated at most hotels and restaurants, although his treatment in some would not be pleasant. All this is a vast advance and augurs much for the future. And yet all that has been said of the remaining discrimination is but too true. . . .

THE INTERMARRIAGE OF THE RACES—For years much has been said on the destiny of the Negro with regard to intermarriage with the whites. To many this seems the difficulty that differentiates the Negro question from all other social questions which we face, and makes it seemingly insoluble; the questions of ignorance, crime and immorality, these argue, may safely be left to the influence of time and education; but will time and training ever change the obvious fact that the white people of the country do not wish to mingle socially with the Negroes or to join blood in legal wedlock with them? This problem is, it must be acknowledged, difficult. Its difficulty arises, however, rather from an ignorance of surrounding facts than from the theoretic argument. Theory in such case is of little value; the white people as members of the races now dominant in the world naturally boast of their blood and accomplishments, and recoil from an alliance with a people which is to-day represented by a host of untrained and uncouth ex-slaves. On the other hand, whatever his practice be, the Negro as a free American citizen must just as strenuously maintain that marriage is a private contract, and that given two persons of proper age and economic ability who agree to enter into that relation, it does not concern any one but themselves as to whether one of them be white, black or red. It is thus that theoretical argument comes to an unpleasant standstill, and its further pursuit really settles nothing, nay, rather unsettles much, by bringing men's thoughts to a question that is, at present at least, of little practical importance. For in practice the matter works itself out: the average white person does not marry a Negro; and the average Negro, despite his theory, himself marries one of his race, and frowns darkly on his fellows unless they do likewise. In those very circles of Negroes who have a large infusion of white blood, where the freedom of marriage is most strenuously advocated, white wives have always been treated with a disdain bordering on insult, and white husbands never received on any terms of social recognition.

Notwithstanding theory and the practice of whites and Negroes in general, it is nevertheless manifest that the white and black races have mingled their blood in this country to a vast extent. Such facts puzzle the foreigner and are destined to puzzle the future historian. A serious student of the subject gravely declares in one chapter that the races are separate and distinct and becoming more so, and in another that by reason of the intermingling of white blood the "original type of the African has almost completely disappeared"; here we have reflected the prevailing confusion in the popular mind. Race amalgamation is a fact, not a theory; it took place, however, largely under the institution of slavery and for the most part, though not wholly, outside the bonds of legal marriage. . . .

CRIME AND ENVIRONMENT—It would, of course, be idle to assert that most of the Negro crime was caused by prejudice; the violent economic and social changes which the last fifty years have brought to the American Negro, the sad social history that preceded these changes, have all contributed to unsettle morals and pervert talents. Nevertheless it is certain that Negro prejudice in cities like Philadelphia has been a vast factor in aiding and abetting all other causes which impel a half-developed race to recklessness and excess. Certainly a great amount of crime can be without doubt traced to the discrimination against Negro boys and girls in the matter of employment. Or to put it differently, Negro prejudice costs the city something.

The connection of crime and prejudice is, on the other hand, neither simple nor direct. The boy who is refused promotion in his job as porter does not go out and snatch somebody's pocketbook. Conversely the loafers at Twelfth and Kater streets, and the thugs in the county prison are not usually graduates of high schools who have been refused work. The connections are much more subtle and dangerous; it is the atmosphere of rebellion and discontent that unrewarded merit and reasonable but unsatisfied ambition make. The social environment of excuse, listless despair, careless indulgence and lack of inspiration to work is the growing force that turns black boys and girls into gamblers, prostitutes and rascals. And this social environment has been built up slowly out of the disappointments of deserving men and the sloth of the unawakened. How long can a city say to a part of its citizens, "It is useless to work; it is fruitless to deserve well of men; education will gain you nothing but disappointment and humiliation"? How long can a city teach its black children that the road to success is to have a white face? How long can a city do this and escape the inevitable penalty? . . .

Negro Treatment: Philadelphia's Disgrace

After referring to some of his findings Du Bois said:

Such a situation is a disgrace to the city—a disgrace to its Christianity, to its spirit of justice, to its common sense; what can be the end of such a policy but increased crime and increased excuse for crime? Increased poverty and more reason to be poor? Increased political serfdom of the mass of black voters to the bosses and rascals who divide the spoils? Surely here lies the first duty of a civilized city.

Secondly, in their efforts for the uplifting of the Negro the people of Philadelphia must recognize the existence of the better class of Negroes and must gain their active aid and co-operation by generous and polite conduct. Social sympathy must exist between what is best in both races and there must no longer be the feeling that the Negro who makes the best of himself is of least account to the city of Philadelphia, while the vagabond is to be helped and pitied. This better class of Negro does not want help or pity, but it does want a generous recognition of its difficulties, and a broad sympathy with the problem of life as it presents itself to them. It is composed of men and women educated and in many cases cultured; with proper co-operation they could be a vast power in the city, and the only power that could successfully cope with many phases of the Negro problems. But their active aid cannot be gained for purely selfish motives, or kept by churlish and ungentle manners; and above all they object to being patronized. . . .

THE DUTY OF THE NEGROES—That the Negro race has an appalling work of social reform before it need hardly be said. Simply because the ancestors of the present white inhabitants of America went out of their way barbarously to mistreat and enslave the ancestors of the present black inhabitants gives those blacks no right to ask that the civilization and morality of the land be seriously menaced for their benefit. Men have a right to demand that the members of a civilized community be civilized; that the fabric of human culture, so laboriously woven, be not wantonly or ignorantly destroyed. Consequently a nation may rightly demand, even of a people it has consciously and intentionally wronged, not indeed complete civilization in thirty or one hundred years, but at least every effort and sacrifice possible on their part toward making themselves fit members of the community within a reasonable length of time; that thus they may early become a source of strength and help instead of a national burden. Modern society has too many problems of its own, too much proper anxiety as to its own ability to survive under its present organization, for it lightly to shoulder all the burdens of a less advanced people, and it can rightly demand that as far as possible and as rapidly as possible the Negro bend his energy to the solving of his own social problems—contributing to his poor, paying his share of the taxes and supporting the schools and public administration. For the accomplishment of this the Negro has a right to demand freedom for self-development, and no more aid from without than is really helpful for furthering that development. Such aid must of necessity be considerable. . . .

THE DUTY OF THE WHITES—. . . Again, the white people of the city must remember that much of the sorrow and bitterness that surrounds the life of the American Negro comes from the unconscious prejudice and half-conscious actions of men and women who do not intend to wound or annoy. One is not compelled to discuss the Negro question with every Negro one meets or to tell him of a father who was connected with the Underground Railroad; one is not compelled to stare at the solitary black face in the audience as though it were not human; it is not necessary to sneer, or be unkind or boorish, if the Negroes in the room or on the street are not all the best behaved or have not the most elegant manners; it is hardly necessary to strike from the dwindling list of one's boyhood and girlhood acquaintances or school-day friends all those who happen to have Negro blood, simply because one has not the courage now to greet them on the street. The little decencies of daily intercourse can go on, the courtesies of life be exchanged even across the color line without any danger to the supremacy of the Anglo-Saxon or the social ambition of the Negro. Without doubt social differences are facts not fancies and cannot lightly be swept aside; but they hardly need to be looked upon as excuses for downright meanness and incivility.

A polite and sympathetic attitude toward these striving thousands; a delicate avoidance of that which wounds and embitters them; a generous granting of opportunity to them; a seconding of their efforts, and a desire to reward honest success—all this, added to proper striving on their part, will go far even in our day toward making all men, white and black, realize what the great founder of the city meant when he named it the City of Brotherly Love. . . .

THE DUTY OF BOTH RACES—. . . If in the hey-day of the greatest of the world's civilizations, it is possible for one people ruthlessly to steal another, drag them helpless across the water, enslave them, debauch them, and then slowly murder them by economic and social exclusion until they disappear from the face of the earth—if the consummation of such a crime be possible in the twentieth century, then our civilization is vain and the republic is a mockery and a farce.

But this will not be; first, even with the terribly adverse circumstances under which Negroes live, there is not the slightest likelihood of their dying out; a nation that has endured the slave-trade, slavery, reconstruction, and present prejudice three hundred years, and under it increased in numbers and efficiency, is not in any immediate danger of extinction. Nor is the thought of voluntary or involuntary emigration more than a dream of men who forget that there are half as many Negroes in the United States as Spaniards in Spain. If this be so then a few plain propositions may be laid down as axiomatic:

1. The Negro is here to stay.

2. It is to the advantage of all, both black and white, that every Negro should make the best of himself.

3. It is the duty of the Negro to raise himself by every effort to the standards of modern civilization and not to lower those standards in any degree.

4. It is the duty of the white people to guard their civilization against debauchment by themselves or others; but in order to do this it is not necessary to hinder and retard the efforts of an earnest people to rise, simply because they lack faith in the ability of that people.

5. With these duties in mind and with a spirit of self-help, mutual aid and co-operation, the two races should strive side by side to realize the ideals of the republic and make this truly a land of equal opportunity for all men.

From THE SOULS OF BLACK FOLK

By the end of the nineteenth century, black America had been beaten back toward slavery and despair. The black people in the South were virtually no longer citizens. They were often denied mobility, suffrage, the right to own desirable land, and be self-employed. The opportunity for meaningful education, the right to bear arms, the right to serve on juries and the right to testify against whites were also denied to them. In short, the black man no longer had any rights a white man was bound to respect. Violence against Negroes, including thousands of lynchings often under official protection, was commonplace.

The United States Supreme Court had struck down the early state and Federal civil rights laws which attempted to make real the promises of the Negro "Magna Carta"— the 13th, 14th, and 15th amendments. Special laws, modeled on the infamous Black Codes, had been carefully reformulated and reenacted in the Southern states to hold the blacks under the system of forced labor substituted for chattel slavery. Under these laws, at the whim of an employer or hostile white, a Negro man, woman, or child could be conscripted into the chain gang, which was an invention of the "redeemers" for the dual purpose of obtaining cheap convict labor and for social control. Naturally, wherever there was a need for forced labor, a Negro "crime wave" ensued.

By the time The Souls of Black Folk appeared, the propaganda victory concerning the Civil War had been conceded to the Southern apologists. By that time the ideals of the Civil War and the great abolitionists like Charles Sumner, William Lloyd Garrison, and Thaddeus Stevens had been repudiated by the dominant forces in America. The Lost Cause had been found and was being extolled throughout the land in books, songs, articles, sermons, and Fourth-of-July orations. Monuments with appropriate Northern approval were being erected in Washington to leaders of the Rebellion and the Ku Klux Klan. Historian propagandists entrenched in Northern universities furnished the proof that the Southern colonels and belles best represented American civilization and that the black race was inferior.

What courage, what confidence, what arrogance must have filled the body of the black youth who stepped into the 20th century to challenge this situation. In 1903, W. E. B. Du Bois did something which won him almost instantaneous recognition as a worthy champion of the black race and American democracy. In The Souls of Black Folk, Du Bois confronted the evils of white greed, hatred, violence, and racism and asserted that "The problem of the Twentieth Century is that of the color line." The Souls of Black Folk contained 14 brief essays or stories. But each contained an idea "whose time had come." Since 1903, the book has gone into more than 30 editions. Yet the age of Du Bois is just beginning.

A white critic, Irving Howe, called the essay that opened the Du Bois–Booker T. Washington controversy one of the most important of this century. But The Souls of Black Folk was best appreciated by those Negro intellectuals and civil rights leaders who were inspired by it. Saunders Redding wrote, "The Souls of Black Folk may be seen as fixing that moment in history when the American Negro began to reject the idea of the world belonging to white people." James Weldon Johnson said it had "greater effect upon and within the Negro race in America than any other single book published in this country since Uncle Tom's Cabin." Roy Wilkins said of Du Bois, "The Souls of Black Folk established him as the voice of the twentieth century civil rights movement." There is a consensus that this volume symbolized the rise of Du Bois as the great twentieth-century prophet, educator, activist, and spokesman of the colored races of America and the world.

For the W. E. B. Du Bois Reader we have selected four of his pieces from The Souls of Black Folk. We have used in full "Of Mr. Booker T. Washington and Others," and we have excerpted "Of the Training of Black Men," "Of Our Spiritual Strivings," and "Of the Sons of Master and Man." A fifth selection, a short story, "Of the Coming of John," is to be found in the chapter on the creative works of Dr. Du Bois.

Of Mr. Booker T. Washington
and Others

FROM BIRTH TILL DEATH ENSLAVED; IN WORD, IN DEED,
  UNMANNED!
HEREDITARY BONDSMEN! KNOW YE NOT
WHO WOULD BE FREE THEMSELVES MUST STRIKE THE BLOW!
                                              BYRON.

Easily the most striking thing in the history of the American Negro since 1876 is the ascendancy of Mr. Booker T. Washington. It began at the time when war memories and ideals were rapidly passing; a day of astonishing commercial development was dawning: a sense of doubt and hesitation overtook the freedmen's sons—then it was that his leading began. Mr. Washington came, with a single definite programme, at the psychological moment when the nation was a little ashamed of having bestowed so much sentiment on Negroes, and was concentrating its energies on Dollars. His programme of industrial education, conciliation of the South, and submission and silence as to civil and political rights, was not wholly original; the Free Negroes from 1830 up to war-time had striven to build industrial schools, and the American Missionary Association had from the first taught various trades; and Price and others had sought a way of honorable alliance with the best of the Southerners. But Mr. Washington first indissolubly linked these things; he put enthusiasm, unlimited energy, and perfect faith into this programme, and changed it from a by-path into a veritable Way of Life. And the tale of the methods by which he did this is a fascinating study of human life.

It startled the nation to hear a Negro advocating such a programme after many decades of bitter complaint; it startled and won the applause of the South, it interested and won the admiration of the North; and after a confused murmur of protest, it silenced if it did not convert the Negroes themselves.

To gain the sympathy and coöperation of the various elements comprising the white South was Mr. Washington's first task; and this, at the time Tuskegee was founded, seemed, for a black man, well-nigh impossible. And yet ten years later it was done in the words spoken at Atlanta: "In all things purely social we can be as separate as the five fingers, and yet one as the hand in all things essential to mutual progress." This "Atlanta Compromise" is by all odds the most notable thing in Mr. Washington's career. The South interpreted it in different ways: the radicals received it as a complete surrender of the demand for civil and political equality; the conservatives, as a generously conceived working basis for mutual understanding. So both approved it, and to-day its author is certainly the most distinguished Southerner since Jefferson Davis, and the one with the largest personal following.

Next to this achievement comes Mr. Washington's work in gaining place and consideration in the North. Others less shrewd and tactful had formerly essayed to sit on these two stools and had fallen between them; but as Mr. Washington knew the heart of the South from birth and training, so by singular insight he intuitively grasped the spirit of the age which was dominating the North. And so thoroughly did he learn the speech and thought of triumphant commercialism, and the ideals of material prosperity, that the picture of a lone black boy poring over a French grammar amid the weeds and dirt of a neglected home soon seemed to him the acme of absurdities. One wonders what Socrates and St. Francis of Assisi would say to this.

And yet this very singleness of vision and thorough oneness with his age is a mark of the successful man. It is as though Nature must needs make men narrow in order to give them force. So Mr. Washington's cult has gained unquestioning followers, his work has wonderfully prospered, his friends are legion, and his enemies are confounded. To-day he stands as the one recognized spokesman of his ten million fellows, and one of the most notable figures in a nation of seventy millions. One hesitates, therefore, to criticise a life which, beginning with so little, has done so much. And yet the time is come when one may speak in all sincerity and utter courtesy of the mistakes and shortcomings of Mr. Washington's career, as well as of his triumphs, without being thought captious or envious, and without forgetting that it is easier to do ill than well in the world.

The criticism that has hitherto met Mr. Washington has not always been of this broad character. In the South especially has he had to walk warily to avoid the harshest judgments—and naturally so, for he is dealing with the one subject of deepest sensitiveness to that section. Twice—once when at the Chicago celebration of the Spanish-American War he alluded to the color-prejudice that is "eating away the vitals of the South," and once when he dined with President Roosevelt—has the resulting Southern criticism been violent enough to threaten seriously his popularity. In the North the feeling has several times forced itself into words, that Mr. Washington's counsels of submission overlooked certain elements of true manhood, and that his educational programme was unnecessarily narrow. Usually, however, such criticism has not found open expression, although, too, the spiritual sons of the Abolitionists have not been prepared to acknowledge that the schools founded before Tuskegee, by men of broad ideals and self-sacrificing spirit, were wholly failures or worthy of ridicule. While, then, criticism has not failed to follow Mr. Washington, yet the prevailing public opinion of the land has been but too willing to deliver the solution of a wearisome problem into his hands, and say, "If that is all you and your race ask, take it."

Among his own people, however, Mr. Washington has encountered the strongest and most lasting opposition, amounting at times to bitterness, and even to-day continuing strong and insistent even though largely silenced in outward expression by the public opinion of the nation. Some of this opposition is, of course, mere envy; the disappointment of displaced demagogues and the spite of narrow minds. But aside from this, there is among educated and thoughtful colored men in all parts of the land a feeling of deep regret, sorrow, and apprehension at the wide currency and ascendancy which some of Mr. Washington's theories have gained. These same men admire his sincerity of purpose, and are willing to forgive much to honest endeavor which is doing something worth the doing. They coöperate with Mr. Washington as far as they conscientiously can; and, indeed, it is no ordinary tribute to this man's tact and power that, steering as he must between so many diverse interests and opinions, he so largely retains the respect of all.

But the hushing of the criticism of honest opponents is a dangerous thing. It leads some of the best of the critics to unfortunate silence and paralysis of effort, and others to burst into speech so passionately and intemperately as to lose listeners. Honest and earnest criticism from those whose interests are most nearly touched—criticism of writers by readers, of government by those governed, of leaders by those led—this is the soul of democracy and the safeguard of modern society. If the best of the American Negroes receive by outer pressure a leader whom they had not recognized before, manifestly there is here a certain palpable gain. Yet there is also irreparable loss—a loss of that peculiarly valuable education which a group receives when by search and criticism it finds and commissions its own leaders. The way in which this is done is at once the most elementary and the nicest problem of social growth. History is but the record of such group-leadership; and yet how infinitely changeful is its type and character! And of all types and kinds, what can be more instructive than the leadership of a group within a group?—that curious double movement where real progress may be negative and actual advance be relative retrogression. All this is the social student's inspiration and despair.

Now in the past the American Negro has had instructive experience in the choosing of group leaders, founding thus a peculiar dynasty which in the light of present conditions is worth while studying. When sticks and stones and beasts form the sole environment of a people, their attitude is largely one of determined opposition to and conquest of natural forces. But when to earth and brute is added an environment of men and ideas, then the attitude of the imprisoned group may take three main forms—a feeling of revolt and revenge; an attempt to adjust all thought and action to the will of the greater group; or, finally, a determined effort at self-realization and self-development despite environing opinion. The influence of all of these attitudes at various times can be traced in the history of the American Negro, and in the evolution of his successive leaders.

Before 1750, while the fire of African freedom still burned in the veins of the slaves, there was in all leadership or attempted leadership but the one motive of revolt and revenge—typified in the terrible Maroons, the Danish blacks, and Cato of Stono, and veiling all the Americas in fear of insurrection. The liberalizing tendencies of the latter half of the eighteenth century brought, along with kindlier relations between black and white, thoughts of ultimate adjustment and assimilation. Such aspiration was especially voiced in the earnest songs of Phyllis, in the martyrdom of Attucks, the fighting of Salem and Poor, the intellectual accomplishments of Banneker and Derham, and the political demands of the Cuffes.

Stern financial and social stress after the war cooled much of the previous humanitarian ardor. The disappointment and impatience of the Negroes at the persistence of slavery and serfdom voiced itself in two movements. The slaves in the South, aroused undoubtedly by vague rumors of the Haytian revolt, made three fierce attempts at insurrection— in 1800 under Gabriel in Virginia, in 1822 under Vesey in Carolina, and in 1831 again in Virginia under the terrible Nat Turner. In the Free States, on the other hand, a new and curious attempt at self-development was made. In Philadelphia and New York color-prescription led to a withdrawal of Negro communicants from white churches and the formation of a peculiar socio-religious institution among the Negroes known as the African Church—an organization still living and controlling in its various branches over a million of men.

Walker's wild appeal against the trend of the times showed how the world was changing after the coming of the cotton-gin. By 1830 slavery seemed hopelessly fastened on the South, and the slaves thoroughly cowed into submission. The free Negroes of the North, inspired by the mulatto immigrants from the West Indies, began to change the basis of their demands; they recognized the slavery of slaves, but insisted that they themselves were freemen, and sought assimilation and amalgamation with the nation on the same terms with other men. Thus, Forten and Purvis of Philadelphia, Shad of Wilmington, Du Bois of New Haven, Barbadoes of Boston, and others, strove singly and together as men, they said, not as slaves; as "people of color," not as "Negroes." The trend of the times, however, refused them recognition save in individual and exceptional cases, considered them as one with all the despised blacks, and they soon found themselves striving to keep even the rights they formerly had of voting and working and moving as freemen. Schemers of migration and colonization arose among them; but these they refused to entertain, and they eventually turned to the Abolition movement as a final refuge.

Here, led by Remond, Nell, Wells-Brown, and Douglass, a new period of self-assertion and self-development dawned. To be sure, ultimate freedom and assimilation was the ideal before the leaders, but the assertion of the manhood rights of the Negro by himself was the main reliance, and John Brown's raid was the extreme of its logic. After the war and emancipation, the great form of Frederick Douglass, the greatest of American Negro leaders, still led the host. Self-assertion, especially in political lines, was the main programme, and behind Douglass came Elliot, Bruce, and Langston, and the Reconstruction politicians, and, less conspicuous but of greater social significance Alexander Crummell and Bishop Daniel Payne.

Then came the Revolution of 1876, the suppression of the Negro votes, the changing and shifting of ideals, and the seeking of new lights in the great night. Douglass, in his old age, still bravely stood for the ideals of his early manhood—ultimate assimilation *through* self-assertion, and on no other terms. For a time Price arose as a new leader, destined, it seemed, not to give up, but to re-state the old ideals in a form less repugnant to the white South. But he passed away in his prime. Then came the new leader. Nearly all the former ones had become leaders by the silent suffrage of their fellows, had sought to lead their own people alone, and were usually, save Douglass, little known outside their race. But Booker T. Washington arose as essentially the leader not of one race but of two—a compromiser between the South, the North, and the Negro. Naturally the Negroes resented, at first bitterly, signs of compromise which surrendered their civil and political rights, even though this was to be exchanged for larger chances of economic development. The rich and dominating North, however, was not only weary of the race problem, but was investing largely in Southern enterprises, and welcomed any method of peaceful coöperation. Thus, by national opinion, the Negroes began to recognize Mr. Washington's leadership; and the voice of criticism was hushed.

Mr. Washington represents in Negro thought the old attitude of adjustment and submission; but adjustment at such a peculiar time as to make his programme unique. This is an age of unusual economic development, and Mr. Washington's programme naturally takes an economic cast, becoming a gospel of Work and Money to such an extent as apparently almost completely to overshadow the higher aims of life. Moreover, this is an age when the more advanced races are coming in closer contact with the less developed races, and the race-feeling is therefore intensified; and Mr. Washington's programme practically accepts the alleged inferiority of the Negro races. Again, in our own land, the reaction from the sentiment of war time has given impetus to race-prejudice against Negroes, and Mr. Washington withdraws many of the high demands of Negroes as men and American citizens. In other periods of intensified prejudice all the Negro's tendency to self-assertion has been called forth; at this period a policy of submission is advocated. In the history of nearly all other races and peoples the doctrine preached at such crises has been that manly self-respect is worth more than lands and houses, and that a people who voluntarily surrender such respect, or cease striving for it, are not worth civilizing.

In answer to this, it has been claimed that the Negro can survive only through submission. Mr. Washington distinctly asks that black people give up, at least for the present, three things—

First, political power,

Second, insistence on civil rights,

Third, higher education of Negro youth—

and concentrate all their energies on industrial education, the accumulation of wealth, and the conciliation of the South. This policy has been courageously and insistently advocated for over fifteen years, and has been triumphant for perhaps ten years. As a result of this tender of the palm-branch, what has been the return? In these years there have occurred:

1. The disfranchisement of the Negro.

2. The legal creation of a distinct status of civil inferiority for the Negro.

3. The steady withdrawal of aid from institutions for the higher training of the Negro.

These movements are not, to be sure, direct results of Mr. Washington's teachings; but his propaganda has, without a shadow of doubt, helped their speedier accomplishment. The question then comes: Is it possible, and probable, that nine millions of men can make effective progress in economic lines if they are deprived of political rights, made a servile caste, and allowed only the most meagre chance for developing their exceptional men? If history and reason give any distinct answer to these questions, it is an emphatic *No.* And Mr. Washington thus faces the triple paradox of his career:

1. He is striving nobly to make Negro artisans business men and property-owners; but it is utterly impossible, under modern competitive methods, for workingmen and property-owners to defend their rights and exist without the right of suffrage.

2. He insists on thrift and self-respect, but at the same time counsels a silent submission to civic inferiority such as is bound to sap the manhood of any race in the long run.

3. He advocates common-school and industrial training, and depreciates institutions of higher learning; but neither the Negro common-schools, nor Tuskegee itself, could remain open a day were it not for teachers trained in Negro colleges, or trained by their graduates.

This triple paradox in Mr. Washington's position is the object of criticism by two classes of colored Americans. One class is spiritually descended from Toussaint the Savior, through Gabriel, Vesey, and Turner, and they represent the attitude of revolt and revenge; they hate the white South blindly and distrust the white race generally, and so far as they agree on definite action, think that the Negro's only hope lies in emigration beyond the borders of the United States. And yet, by the irony of fate, nothing has more effectually made this programme seem hopeless than the recent course of the United States toward weaker and darker peoples in the West Indies, Hawaii, and the Philippines—for where in the world may we go and be safe from lying and brute force?

The other class of Negroes who cannot agree with Mr. Washington has hitherto said little aloud. They deprecate the sight of scattered counsels, of internal disagreement; and especially they dislike making their just criticism of a useful and earnest man an excuse for a general discharge of venom from small-minded opponents. Nevertheless, the questions involved are so fundamental and serious that it is difficult to see how men like the Grimkes, Kelly Miller, J. W. E. Bowen, and other representatives of this group, can much longer be silent. Such men feel in conscience bound to ask of this nation three things:

1. The right to vote.
2. Civic equality.
3. The education of youth according to ability.

They acknowledge Mr. Washington's invaluable service in counselling patience and courtesy in such demands; they do not ask that ignorant black men vote when ignorant whites are debarred, or that any reasonable restrictions in the suffrage should not be applied; they know that the low social level of the mass of the race is responsible for much discrimination against it, but they also know, and the nation knows, that relentless color-prejudice is more often a cause than a result of the Negro's degradation; they seek the abatement of this relic of barbarism, and not its systematic encouragement and pampering by all agencies of social power from the Associated Press to the Church of Christ. They advocate, with Mr. Washington, a broad system of Negro common schools supplemented by thorough industrial training; but they are surprised that a man of Mr. Washington's insight cannot see that no such educational system ever has rested or can rest on any other basis than that of the well-equipped college and university, and they insist that there is a demand for a few such institutions throughout the South to train the best of the Negro youth as teachers, professional men, and leaders.

This group of men honor Mr. Washington for his attitude of conciliation toward the white South; they accept the "Atlanta Compromise" in its broadest interpretation, they recognize, with him, many signs of promise, many men of high purpose and fair judgment, in this section; they know that no easy task has been laid upon a region already tottering under heavy burdens. But, nevertheless, they insist that the way to truth and right lies in straightforward honesty, not in indiscriminate flattery; in praising those of the South who do well and criticising uncompromisingly those who do ill; in taking advantage of the opportunities at hand and urging their fellows to do the same, but at the same time in remembering that only a firm adherence to their higher ideals and aspirations will ever keep those ideals within the realm of possibility. They do not expect that the free right to vote, to enjoy civic rights, and to be educated, will come in a moment; they do not expect to see the bias and prejudices of years disappear at the blast of a trumpet; but they are absolutely certain that the way for a people to gain their reasonable rights is not by voluntarily throwing them away and insisting that they do not want them; that the way for a people to gain respect is not by continually belittling and ridiculing themselves; that, on the contrary, Negroes must insist continually, in season and out of season, that voting is necessary to modern manhood, that color discrimination is barbarism, and that black boys need education as well as white boys.

In failing thus to state plainly and unequivocally the legitimate demands of their people, even at the cost of opposing an honored leader, the thinking classes of American Negroes would shirk a heavy responsibility—a responsibility to themselves, a responsibility to the struggling masses, a responsibility to the darker races of men whose future depends so largely on this American experiment, but especially a responsibility to this nation—this common Fatherland. It is wrong to encourage a man or a people in evil-doing; it is wrong to aid and abet a national crime simply because it is unpopular not to do so. The growing spirit of kindliness and reconciliation between the North and South after the frightful difference of a generation ago ought to be a source of deep congratulation to all, and especially to those whose mistreatment caused the war; but if that reconciliation is to be marked by the industrial slavery and civic death of those same black men, with permanent legislation into a position of inferiority, then those black men, if they are really men, are called upon by every consideration of patriotism and loyalty to oppose such a course by all civilized methods, even though such opposition involves disagreement with Mr. Booker T. Washington. We have no right to sit silently by while the inevitable seeds are sown for a harvest of disaster to our children, black and white.

First, it is the duty of black men to judge the South discriminatingly. The present generation of Southerners are not responsible for the past, and they should not be blindly hated or blamed for it. Furthermore, to no class is the indiscriminate endorsement of the recent course of the South toward Negroes more nauseating than to the best thought of the South. The South is not "solid"; it is a land in the ferment of social change, wherein forces of all kinds are fighting for supremacy; and to praise the ill the South is to-day perpetrating is just as wrong as to condemn the good. Discriminating and broad-minded criticism is what the South needs—needs it for the sake of her own white sons and daughters, and for the insurance of robust, healthy mental and moral development.

To-day even the attitude of the Southern whites toward the blacks is not, as so many assume, in all cases the same; the ignorant Southerner hates the Negro, the workingmen fear his competition, the money-makers wish to use him as a laborer, some of the educated see a menace in his upward development, while others—usually the sons of the masters —wish to help him to rise. National opinion has enabled this last class to maintain the Negro common schools, and to protect the Negro partially in property, life, and limb. Through the pressure of the money-makers, the Negro is in danger of being reduced to semi-slavery, especially in the country districts; workingmen, and those of the educated who fear the Negro, have united to disfranchise him, and some have urged his deportation; while the passions of the ignorant are easily aroused to lynch and abuse any black man. To praise this intricate whirl of thought and prejudice is nonsense; to inveigh indiscriminately against "the South" is unjust; but to use the same breath in praising Governor Aycock, exposing Senator Morgan, arguing with Mr. Thomas Nelson Page, and denouncing Senator Ben Tillman, is not only sane, but the imperative duty of thinking black men.

It would be unjust to Mr. Washington not to acknowledge that in several instances he has opposed movements in the South which were unjust to the Negro; he sent memorials to the Louisiana and Alabama constitutional conventions, he has spoken against lynching, and in other ways has openly or silently set his influence against sinister schemes and unfortunate happenings. Notwithstanding this, it is equally true to assert that on the whole the distinct impression left by Mr. Washington's propaganda is, first, that the South is justified in its present attitude toward the Negro because of the Negro's degradation; secondly, that the prime cause of the Negro's failure to rise more quickly is his wrong education in the past; and, thirdly, that his future rise depends primarily on his own efforts. Each of these propositions is a dangerous half-truth. The supplementary truths must never be lost sight of: first, slavery and race-prejudice are potent if not sufficient causes of the Negro's position; second, industrial and common-school training were necessarily slow in planting because they had to await the black teachers trained by higher institutions—it being extremely doubtful if any essentially different development was possible, and certainly a Tuskegee was unthinkable before 1880; and, third, while it is a great truth to say that the Negro must strive and strive mightily to help himself, it is equally true that unless his striving be not simply seconded, but rather aroused and encouraged, by the initiative of the richer and wiser environing group, he cannot hope for great success.

In his failure to realize and impress this last point, Mr. Washington is especially to be criticised. His doctrine has tended to make the whites, North and South, shift the burden of the Negro problem to the Negro's shoulders and stand aside as critical and rather pessimistic spectators; when in fact the burden belongs to the nation, and the hands of none of us are clean if we bend not our energies to righting these great wrongs.

The South ought to be led, by candid and honest criticism, to assert her better self and do her full duty to the race she has cruelly wronged and is still wronging. The North—her co-partner in guilt—cannot salve her conscience by plastering it with gold. We cannot settle this problem by diplomacy and suaveness, by "policy" alone. If worse comes to worst, can the moral fibre of this country survive the slow throttling and murder of nine millions of men?

The black men of America have a duty to perform, a duty stern and delicate—a forward movement to oppose a part of the work of their greatest leader. So far as Mr. Washington preaches Thrift, Patience, and Industrial Training for the masses, we must hold up his hands and strive with him, rejoicing in his honors and glorying in the strength of this Joshua called of God and of man to lead the headless host. But so far as Mr. Washington apologizes for injustice, North or South, does not rightly value the privilege and duty of voting, belittles the emasculating effects of caste distinctions, and opposes the higher training and ambition of our brighter minds—so far as he, the South, or the Nation, does this—we must unceasingly and firmly oppose them. By every civilized and peaceful method we must strive for the rights which the world accords to men, clinging unwaveringly to those great words which the sons of the Fathers would fain forget: "We hold these truths to be self-evident: That all men are created equal; that they are endowed by their Creator with certain unalienable rights; that among these are life, liberty, and the pursuit of happiness."

INDUSTRIAL VS. LIBERAL ARTS
EDUCATION

Of the Training of Black Men

. . . To-day we have climbed to heights where we would open at least the outer courts of knowledge to all, display its treasures to many, and select the few to whom its mystery of Truth is revealed, not wholly by birth or the accidents of the stock market, but at least in part according to deftness and aim, talent and character. This programme, however, we are sorely puzzled in carrying out through that part of the land where the blight of slavery fell hardest, and where we are dealing with two backward peoples. To make here in human education that ever necessary combination of the permanent and the contingent—of the ideal and the practical in workable equilibrium—has been there, as it ever must be in every age and place, a matter of infinite experiment and frequent mistakes.

In rough approximation we may point out four varying decades of work in Southern education since the Civil War. From the close of the war until 1876, was the period of uncertain groping and temporary relief. There were army schools, mission schools, and schools of the Freedmen's Bureau in chaotic disarrangement seeking system and coöperation. Then followed ten years of constructive definite effort toward the building of complete school systems in the South. Normal schools and colleges were founded for the freedmen, and teachers trained there to man the public schools. There was the inevitable tendency of war to underestimate the prejudices of the master and the ignorance of the slave, and all seemed clear sailing out of the wreckage of the storm. Meantime, starting in this decade yet especially developing from 1885 to 1895, began the industrial revolution of the South. The land saw glimpses of a new destiny and the stirring of new ideals. The educational system striving to complete itself saw new obstacles and a field of work ever broader and deeper. The Negro colleges, hurriedly founded, were inadequately equipped, illogically distributed, and of varying efficiency and grade; the normal and high schools were doing little more than common-school work, and the common schools were training but a third of the children who ought to be in them, and training these too often poorly. At the same time the white South, by reason of its sudden conversion from the slavery ideal, by so much the more became set and strengthened in its racial prejudice, and crystallized it into harsh law and harsher custom; while the marvellous pushing forward of the poor white daily threatened to take even bread and butter from the mouths of the heavily handicapped sons of the freedmen. In the midst, then, of the larger problem of Negro education sprang up the more practical question of work, the inevitable economic quandary that faces a people in the transition from slavery to freedom, and especially those who make that change amid hate and prejudice, lawlessness and ruthless competition.

The industrial school springing to notice in this decade, but coming to full recognition in the decade beginning with 1895, was the proffered answer to this combined educational and economic crisis, and an answer of singular wisdom and timeliness. From the very first in nearly all the schools some attention had been given to training in handiwork, but now was this training first raised to a dignity that brought it in direct touch with the South's magnificent industrial development, and given an emphasis which reminded black folk that before the Temple of Knowledge swing the Gates of Toil.

Yet after all they are but gates, and when turning our eyes from the temporary and the contingent in the Negro problem to the broader question of the permanent uplifting and civilization of black men in America, we have a right to inquire, as this enthusiasm for material advancement mounts to its height, if after all the industrial school is the final and sufficient answer in the training of the Negro race; and to ask gently, but in all sincerity, the ever-recurring query of the ages, Is not life more than meat, and the body more than raiment? And men ask this to-day all the more eagerly because of sinister signs in recent educational movements. The tendency is here, born of slavery and quickened to renewed life by the crazy imperialism of the day, to regard human beings as among the material resources of a land to be trained with an eye single to future dividends. Race-prejudices, which keep brown and black men in their "places," we are coming to regard as useful allies with such a theory, no matter how much they may dull the ambition and sicken the hearts of struggling

human beings. And above all, we daily hear that an education that encourages aspiration, that sets the loftiest of
ideals and seeks as an end culture and character rather than
bread-winning, is the privilege of white men and the danger
and delusion of black.

Especially has criticism been directed against the former
educational efforts to aid the Negro. In the four periods
I have mentioned, we find first, boundless, planless enthusiasm and sacrifice; then the preparation of teachers for a
vast public-school system; then the launching and expansion
of that school system amid increasing difficulties; and finally
the training of workmen for the new and growing industries.
This development has been sharply ridiculed as a logical
anomaly and flat reversal of nature. Smoothly we have been
told that first industrial and manual training should have
taught the Negro to work, then simple schools should have
taught him to read and write, and finally, after years, high
and normal schools could have completed the system, as
intelligence and wealth demanded.

That a system logically so complete was historically impossible, it needs but a little thought to prove. Progress in
human affairs is more often a pull than a push, a surging
forward of the exceptional man, and the lifting of his duller
brethren slowly and painfully to his vantage-ground. Thus
it was no accident that gave birth to universities centuries
before the common schools, that made fair Harvard the first
flower of our wilderness. So in the South: the mass of the
freedmen at the end of the war lacked the intelligence so
necessary to modern workingmen. They must first have
the common school to teach them to read, write, and cipher;
and they must have higher schools to teach teachers for the
common schools. The white teachers who flocked South
went to establish such a common-school system. Few held
the idea of founding colleges; most of them at first would
have laughed at the idea. But they faced, as all men since
them have faced, that central paradox of the South—the
social separation of the races. At that time it was the sudden
volcanic rupture of nearly all relations between black and
white, in work and government and family life. Since then
a new adjustment of relations in economic and political
affairs has grown up—an adjustment subtle and difficult
to grasp, yet singularly ingenious, which leaves still that
frightful chasm at the color-line across which men pass at
their peril. Thus, then and now, there stand in the South
two separate worlds; and separate not simply in the higher
realms of social intercourse, but also in church and school,

on railway and street-car, in hotels and theatres, in streets and city sections, in books and newspapers, in asylums and jails, in hospitals and graveyards. There is still enough of contact for large economic and group coöperation, but the separation is so thorough and deep that it absolutely precludes for the present between the races anything like that sympathetic and effective group-training and leadership of the one by the other, such as the American Negro and all backward peoples must have for effectual progress.

This the missionaries of '68 soon saw; and if effective industrial and trade schools were impracticable before the establishment of a common-school system, just as certainly no adequate common schools could be founded until there were teachers to teach them. Southern whites would not teach them; Northern whites in sufficient numbers could not be had. If the Negro was to learn, he must teach himself, and the most effective help that could be given him was the establishment of schools to train Negro teachers. This conclusion was slowly but surely reached by every student of the situation until simultaneously, in widely separated regions, without consultation or systematic plan, there arose a series of institutions designed to furnish teachers for the untaught. Above the sneers of critics at the obvious defects of this procedure must ever stand its one crushing rejoinder: in a single generation they put thirty thousand black teachers in the South; they wiped out the illiteracy of the majority of the black people of the land, and they made Tuskegee possible.

Such higher training-schools tended naturally to deepen broader development: at first they were common and grammar schools, then some became high schools. And finally, by 1900, some thirty-four had one year or more of studies of college grade. This development was reached with different degrees of speed in different institutions: Hampton is still a high school, while Fisk University started her college in 1871, and Spelman Seminary about 1896. In all cases the aim was identical—to maintain the standards of the lower training by giving teachers and leaders the best practicable training; and above all, to furnish the black world with adequate standards of human culture and lofty ideals of life. It was not enough that the teachers of teachers should be trained in technical normal methods; they must also, so far as possible, be broadminded, cultured men and women, to scatter civilization among a people whose ignorance was not simply of letters, but of life itself.

It can thus be seen that the work of education in the

South began with higher institutions of training, which threw off as their foliage common schools, and later industrial schools, and at the same time strove to shoot their roots ever deeper toward college and university training. That this was an inevitable and necessary development, sooner or later, goes without saying; but there has been, and still is, a question in many minds if the natural growth was not forced, and if the higher training was not either overdone or done with cheap and unsound methods. Among white Southerners this feeling is widespread and positive. . . .

While most fair-minded men would recognize this as extreme and overdrawn, still without doubt many are asking, Are there a sufficient number of Negroes ready for college training to warrant the undertaking? Are not too many students prematurely forced into this work? Does it not have the effect of dissatisfying the young Negro with his environment? And do these graduates succeed in real life? Such natural questions cannot be evaded, nor on the other hand must a Nation naturally skeptical as to Negro ability assume an unfavorable answer without careful inquiry and patient openness to conviction. We must not forget that most Americans answer all queries regarding the Negro *a priori*, and that the least that human courtesy can do is to listen to evidence.

The advocates of the higher education of the Negro would be the last to deny the incompleteness and glaring defects of the present system: too many institutions have attempted to do college work, the work in some cases has not been thoroughly done, and quantity rather than quality has sometimes been sought. But all this can be said of higher education throughout the land; it is the almost inevitable incident of educational growth, and leaves the deeper question of the legitimate demand for the higher training of Negroes untouched. And this latter question can be settled in but one way—by a first-hand study of the facts. If we leave out of view all institutions which have not actually graduated students from a course higher than that of a New England high school, even though they be called colleges; if then we take the thirty-four remaining institutions, we may clear up many misapprehensions by asking searchingly, What kind of institutions are they? what do they teach? and what sort of men do they graduate?

And first we may say that this type of college, including Atlanta, Fisk, and Howard, Wilberforce and Claflin, Shaw, and the rest, is peculiar, almost unique. Through the shining trees that whisper before me as I write, I catch glimpses of a boulder of New England granite, covering a grave, which graduates of Atlanta University have placed there—

> GRATEFUL MEMORY OF THEIR
> FORMER TEACHER AND FRIEND
> AND OF THE UNSELFISH LIFE
> HE LIVED, AND THE NOBLE
> WORK HE WROUGHT; THAT
> THEY, THEIR CHILDREN, AND
> THEIR CHILDREN'S CHILDREN
> MIGHT BE BLESSED.

This was the gift of New England to the freed Negro: not alms, but a friend; not cash, but character. It was not and is not money these seething millions want, but love and sympathy, the pulse of hearts beating with red blood—a gift which to-day only their own kindred and race can bring to the masses, but which once saintly souls brought to their favored children in the crusade of the sixties, that finest thing in American history, and one of the few things untainted by sordid greed and cheap vainglory. The teachers in these institutions came not to keep the Negroes in their place, but to raise them out of the defilement of the places where slavery had wallowed them. The colleges they founded were social settlements; homes where the best of the sons of the freedmen came in close and sympathetic touch with the best traditions of New England. They lived and ate together, studied and worked, hoped and harkened in the dawning light. In actual formal content their curriculum was doubtless old-fashioned, but in educational power it was supreme, for it was the contact of living souls.

From such schools about two thousand Negroes have gone forth with the bachelor's degree. The number in itself is enough to put at rest the argument that too large a proportion of Negroes are receiving higher training. If the ratio to population of all Negro students throughout the land, in both college and secondary training, be counted, Commissioner Harris assures us "it must be increased to five times its present average" to equal the average of the land.

Fifty years ago the ability of Negro students in any appreciable numbers to master a modern college course would have been difficult to prove. To-day it is proved by the fact that four hundred Negroes, many of whom have been reported as brilliant students, have received the bachelor's degree from Harvard, Yale, Oberlin, and seventy other leading colleges. Here we have, then, nearly twenty-five hundred Negro graduates, of whom the crucial query must be made, How far did their training fit them for life? It is of course extremely difficult to collect satisfactory data on such a point—difficult to reach the men, to get trustworthy testimony, and to gauge that testimony by any generally acceptable criterion of success. In 1900, the Conference at Atlanta University undertook to study these graduates, and published the results. First they sought to know what these graduates were doing, and succeeded in getting answers from nearly two-thirds of the living. The direct testimony was in almost all cases corroborated by the reports of the colleges where they graduated, so that in the main the reports were worthy of credence. Fifty-three per cent of these graduates were teachers—presidents of institutions, heads of normal schools, principals of city school-systems, and the like. Seventeen per cent were clergymen; another seventeen per cent were in the professions, chiefly as physicians. Over six per cent were merchants, farmers, and artisans, and four per cent were in the government civil-service. Granting even that a considerable proportion of the third unheard from are unsuccessful, this is a record of usefulness. Personally I know many hundreds of these graduates, and have corresponded with more than a thousand; through others I have followed carefully the life-work of scores; I have taught some of them and some of the pupils whom they have taught, lived in homes which they have builded, and looked at life through their eyes. Comparing them as a class with my fellow students in New England and in Europe, I cannot hesitate in saying that nowhere have I met men and women with a broader spirit of helpfulness, with deeper devotion to their life-work, or with more consecrated determination to succeed in the face of bitter difficulties than among Negro college-bred men. They have, to be sure, their proportion of ne'er-do-wells, their pedants and lettered fools, but they have a surprisingly small proportion of them; they have not that culture of manner which we instinctively associate with university men, forgetting that in reality it is the heritage from cultured homes, and that no people a generation removed from slavery can escape a certain unpleasant rawness and *gaucherie*, despite the best of training.

With all their larger vision and deeper sensibility, these men have usually been conservative, careful leaders. They have seldom been agitators, have withstood the temptation to head the mob, and have worked steadily and faithfully in a thousand communities in the South. As teachers, they have given the South a commendable system of city schools and large numbers of private normal-schools and academies. Colored college-bred men have worked side by side with white college graduates at Hampton; almost from the beginning the backbone of Tuskegee's teaching force has been formed of graduates from Fisk and Atlanta. And to-day the institute is filled with college graduates, from the energetic wife of the principal down to the teacher of agriculture, including nearly half of the executive council and a majority of the heads of departments. In the professions, college men are slowly but surely leavening the Negro church, are healing and preventing the devastations of disease, and beginning to furnish legal protection for the liberty and property of the toiling masses. All this is needful work. Who would do it if Negroes did not? How could Negroes do it if they were not trained carefully for it? If white people need colleges to furnish teachers, ministers, lawyers, and doctors, do black people need nothing of the sort?

If it is true that there are an appreciable number of Negro youth in the land capable by character and talent to receive that higher training, the end of which is culture, and if the two and a half thousand who have had something of this training in the past have in the main proved themselves useful to their race and generation, the question then comes, What place in the future development of the South ought the Negro college and college-bred man to occupy? That the present social separation and acute race-sensitiveness must eventually yield to the influences of culture, as the South grows civilized, is clear. But such transformation calls for singular wisdom and patience. If, while the healing of this vast sore is progressing, the races are to live for many years side by side, united in economic effort, obeying a common government, sensitive to mutual thought and feeling, yet subtly and silently separate in many matters of deeper human intimacy—if this unusual and dangerous development is to progress amid peace and order, mutual respect and growing intelligence, it will call for social surgery at once the delicatest and nicest in modern history. It will demand broad-minded, upright men, both white and black, and in its final accomplishment American civilization will triumph. So far as white men are concerned, this fact is to-day being recognized in the South, and a happy renaissance of university education seems imminent. But the very voices that cry hail to this good work are, strange to relate, largely silent or antagonistic to the higher education of the Negro.

Strange to relate! for this is certain, no secure civilization can be built in the South with the Negro as an ignorant, turbulent proletariat. Suppose we seek to remedy this by making them laborers and nothing more: they are not fools, they have tasted of the Tree of Life, and they will not cease to think, will not cease attempting to read the riddle of the world. By taking away their best equipped teachers and leaders, by slamming the door of opportunity in the faces of their bolder and brighter minds, will you make them satisfied with their lot? or will you not rather transfer their leading from the hands of men taught to think to the hands of untrained demagogues? We ought not to forget that despite the pressure of poverty, and despite the active discouragement and even ridicule of friends, the demand for higher training steadily increases among Negro youth: there were, in the years from 1875 to 1880, 22 Negro graduates from Northern colleges; from 1885 to 1890 there were 43, and from 1895 to 1900, nearly 100 graduates. From Southern Negro colleges there were, in the same three periods, 143, 413, and over 500 graduates. Here, then, is the plain thirst for training; by refusing to give this Talented Tenth the key to knowledge, can any sane man imagine that they will lightly lay aside their yearning and contentedly become hewers of wood and drawers of water?

No. The dangerously clear logic of the Negro's position will more and more loudly assert itself in that day when increasing wealth and more intricate social organization preclude the South from being, as it so largely is, simply an armed camp for intimidating black folk. Such waste of energy cannot be spared if the South is to catch up with civilization. And as the black third of the land grows in thrift and skill, unless skillfully guided in its larger philosophy, it must more and more brood over the red past and the creeping, crooked present, until it grasps a gospel of revolt and revenge and throws its new-found energies athwart the current of advance. Even to-day the masses of the Negroes see all too clearly the anomalies of their position and the moral crookedness of yours. You may marshal strong indictments against them, but their counter-cries, lacking though they be in formal logic, have burning truths within them which you may not wholly ignore, O Southern Gentlemen! If you deplore their presence here, they ask, Who brought us? When you cry, Deliver us from the vision of intermarriage, they answer that legal marriage is infinitely better than systematic concubinage and prostitution and if in just fury you accuse their vagabonds of violating women, they also in fury quite as just may reply: The rape which your gentlemen have done against helpless black women in defiance of your own laws is written on the foreheads of two millions of mulattoes, and written in ineffaceable blood. And finally, when you fasten crime upon this race as its peculiar trait, they answer that slavery was the arch-crime, and lynching and lawlessness its twin abortion; that color and race are not crimes, and yet it is they which in this land receive most unceasing condemnation, North, East, South, and West.

I will not say such arguments are wholly justified—I will not insist that there is no other side to the shield; but I do say that of the nine millions of Negroes in this nation, there is scarcely one out of the cradle to whom these arguments do not daily present themselves in the guise of terrible truth. I insist that the question of the future is how best to keep these millions from brooding over the wrongs of the past and the difficulties of the present, so that all their energies may be bent toward a cheerful striving and coöperation with their white neighbors toward a larger, juster, and fuller future. That one wise method of doing this lies in the closer knitting of the Negro to the great industrial possibilities of the South is a great truth. And this the common schools and the manual training and trade schools are working to accomplish. But these alone are not enough. The foundations of knowledge in this race, as in others, must be sunk deep in the college and university if we would build a solid, permanent structure. Internal problems of social advance must inevitably come—problems of work and wages, of families and homes, of morals and the true valuing of the things of life; and all these and other inevitable problems of civilization the Negro must meet and solve largely for himself, by reason of his isolation; and can there be any possible solution other than by study and thought and an appeal to the rich experience of the past? Is there not, with such a group and in such a crisis, infinitely more danger to be apprehended from half-trained minds and shallow thinking than from over-education and over-refinement? Surely we have wit enough to found a Negro college so manned and equipped as to steer successfully between the *dilettante* and the fool. We shall hardly induce black men to believe that if their stomachs be full, it matters little about their brains. They already dimly perceive that the paths of peace winding between honest toil and dignified manhood call for the guidance of skilled thinkers, the loving, reverent comradeship between the black lowly and the black men emancipated by training and culture.

The function of the Negro college, then, is clear: it must maintain the standards of popular education, it must seek the social regeneration of the Negro, and it must help in the solution of problems of race contact and coöperation. And finally, beyond all this, it must develop men. Above our modern socialism, and out of the worship of the mass, must persist and evolve that higher individualism which the centres of culture protect; there must come a loftier respect for the sovereign human soul that seeks to know itself and the world about it; that seeks a freedom for expansion and self-development; that will love and hate and labor in its own way, untrammeled alike by old and new. Such souls aforetime have inspired and guided worlds, and if we be not wholly bewitched by our Rhinegold, they shall again. Herein the longing of black men must have respect: the rich and bitter depth of their experience, the unknown treasures of their inner life, the strange rendings of nature they have seen, may give the world new points of view and make their loving, living, and doing precious to all human hearts. And to themselves in these the days that try their souls, the chance to soar in the dim blue air above the smoke is to their finer spirits boon and guerdon for what they lose on earth by being black.

I sit with Shakespeare and he winces not. Across the color line I move arm in arm with Balzac and Dumas, where smiling men and welcoming women glide in gilded halls. From out the caves of evening that swing between the strong-limbed earth and the tracery of the stars, I summon Aristotle and Aurelius and what soul I will, and they come all graciously with no scorn nor condescension. So, wed with Truth, I dwell above the Veil. Is this the life you grudge us, O knightly America? Is this the life you long to change into the dull red hideousness of Georgia? Are you so afraid lest peering from this high Pisgah, between Philistine and Amalekite, we sight the Promised Land?

———————

Of Our Spiritual Strivings

. . . Between me and the other world there is ever an unasked question: unasked by some through feelings of delicacy; by others through the difficulty of rightly framing it. All, nevertheless, flutter round it. They approach me in a half-hesitant sort of way, eye me curiously or compassionately, and then, instead of saying directly, How does it feel to be a problem? they say, I know an excellent colored man in my town; or, I fought at Mechanicsville; or, Do not these Southern outrages make your blood boil? At these I smile, or am interested, or reduce the boiling to a simmer, as the occasion may require. To the real question, How does it feel to be a problem? I answer seldom a word.

And yet, being a problem is a strange experience—peculiar even for one who has never been anything else, save perhaps in babyhood and in Europe. . . .

Why did God make me an outcast and a stranger in mine own house? The shades of the prison-house closed round about us all: walls strait and stubborn to the whitest, but relentlessly narrow, tall, and unscalable to sons of night who must plod darkly on in resignation, or beat unavailing palms against the stone, or steadily, half hopelessly, watch the streak of blue above.

After the Egyptian and Indian, the Greek and Roman, the Teuton and Mongolian, the Negro is a sort of seventh son, born with a veil, and gifted with second-sight in this American world—a world which yields him no true self-consciousness, but only lets him see himself through the revelation of the other world. It is a peculiar sensation, this double-consciousness, this sense of always looking at one's self through the eyes of others, of measuring one's soul by the tape of a world that looks on in amused contempt and pity. One ever feels his twoness—an American, a Negro; two souls, two thoughts, two unreconciled strivings; two warring ideals in one dark body, whose dogged strength alone keeps it from being torn asunder.

The history of the American Negro is the history of this strife—this longing to attain self-conscious manhood, to merge his double self into a better and truer self. In this merging he wishes neither of the older selves to be lost. He would not Africanize America, for America has too much to teach the world and Africa. He would not bleach his Negro soul in a flood of white Americanism, for he knows that Negro blood has a message for the world.

He simply wishes to make it possible for a man to be both a Negro and an American, without being cursed and spit upon by his fellows, without having the doors of Opportunity closed roughly in his face.

This, then, is the end of his striving; to be a co-worker in the kingdom of culture, to escape both death and isolation, to husband and use his best powers and his latent genius. These powers of body and mind have in the past been strangely wasted, dispersed, or forgotten. The shadow of a mighty Negro past flits through the tale of Ethiopia the Shadowy and of Egypt the Sphinx. Throughout history, the powers of single black men flash here and there like falling stars, and die sometimes before the world has rightly gauged their brightness. Here in America, in the few days since Emancipation, the black man's turning hither and thither in hesitant and doubtful striving has often made his very strength to lose effectiveness, to seem like absence of power, like weakness. And yet it is not weakness—it is the contradiction of double aims. The double-aimed struggle of the black artisan—on the one hand to escape white contempt for a nation of mere hewers of wood and drawers of water, and on the other hand to plough and nail and dig for a poverty-stricken horde—could only result in making him a poor craftsman, for he had but half a heart in either cause. By the poverty and ignorance of his people, the Negro minister or doctor was tempted toward quackery and demagogy; and by the criticism of the other world, toward ideals that made him ashamed of his lowly tasks. The would-be black *savant* was confronted by the paradox that the knowledge his people needed was a twice-told tale to his white neighbors, while the knowledge which would teach the white world was Greek to his own flesh and blood. The innate love of harmony and beauty that set the ruder souls of his people a-dancing and a-singing raised but confusion and doubt in the soul of the black artist; for the beauty revealed to him was the soul-beauty of a race which his larger audience despised, and he could not articulate the message of another people. This waste of double aims, this seeking to satisfy two unreconciled ideals, has wrought sad havoc with the courage and faith and deeds of ten thousand thousand people—has sent them often wooing false gods and invoking false means of salvation, and at times has even seemed about to make them ashamed of themselves. . . .

The Nation has not yet found peace from its sins; the freedman has not yet found in freedom his promised land. Whatever of good may have come in these years of change, the shadow of a deep disappointment rests upon the Negro people—a disappointment all the more bitter because the unattained ideal was unbounded save by the simple ignorance of a lowly people.

The first decade was merely a prolongation of the vain search for freedom, the boon that seemed ever barely to elude their grasp—like a tantalizing will-o'-the-wisp, maddening and misleading the headless host. The holocaust of war, the terrors of the Ku Klux Klan, the lies of carpetbaggers, the disorganization of industry, and the contradictory advice of friends and foes, left the bewildered serf with no new watchword beyond the old cry for freedom. As the time flew, however, he began to grasp a new idea. The ideal of liberty demanded for its attainment powerful means, and these the Fifteenth Amendment gave him. The ballot, which before he had looked upon as a visible sign of freedom, he now regarded as the chief means of gaining and perfecting the liberty with which war had partially endowed him. And why not? Had not votes made war and emancipated millions? Had not votes enfranchised the freedmen? Was anything impossible to a power that had done all this? A million black men started with renewed zeal to vote themselves into the kingdom. So the decade flew away, the revolution of 1876 came, and left the half-free serf weary, wondering but still inspired. Slowly but steadily, in the following years, a new vision began gradually to replace the dream of political power—a powerful movement, the rise of another ideal to guide the unguided, another pillar of fire by night after a clouded day. It was the ideal of "book-learning"; the curiosity, born of compulsory ignorance, to know and test the power of the cabalistic letters of the white man, the longing to know. Here at last seemed to have been discovered the mountain path to Canaan; longer than the highway of Emancipation and law, steep and rugged, but straight, leading to heights high enough to overlook life.

Up the new path the advance guard toiled, slowly, heavily, doggedly; only those who have watched and guided the faltering feet, the misty minds, the dull understandings, of the dark pupils of these schools know how faithfully, how piteously, this people strove to learn. It was weary work. The cold statistician wrote down the inches of progress here and there, noted also where here and there a foot had slipped or some one had fallen. To the tired climbers, the horizon was ever dark, the mists were often cold, the Canaan was always dim and far away. If, however, the vistas disclosed as yet no goal, no resting-place, little but flattery and criticism, the journey at least gave leisure for reflection and self-examination; it changed the child of Emancipation to the youth with dawning self-consciousness, self-realization, self-respect. In those sombre forests of his striving his own soul rose before him, and he saw himself— darkly as through a veil; and yet he saw in himself some faint revelation of his power, of his mission. He began to have a dim feeling that, to attain his place in the world, he must be himself, and not another. For the first time he sought to analyze the burden he bore upon his back, that dead-weight of social degradation partially masked behind a half-named Negro problem. He felt his poverty; without a cent, without a home, without land, tools, or savings, he had entered into competition with rich, landed, skilled neighbors. To be a poor man is hard, but to be a poor race in a land of dollars is the very bottom of hardships. He felt the weight of his ignorance—not simply of letters, but of life, of business, of the humanities; the accumulated sloth and shirking and awkwardness of decades and centuries shackled his hands and feet. Nor was his burden all poverty and ignorance. The red stain of bastardy, which two centuries of systematic legal defilement of Negro women had stamped upon his race, meant not only the loss of ancient African chastity, but also the hereditary weight of a mass of corruption from white adulterers, threatening almost the obliteration of the Negro home.

A people thus handicapped ought not to be asked to race with the world, but rather allowed to give all its time and thought to its own social problems. But alas! while sociologists gleefully count his bastards and his prostitutes, the very soul of the toiling, sweating black man is darkened by the shadow of a vast despair. Men call the shadow prejudice, and learnedly explain it as the natural defence of culture against barbarism, learning against ignorance, purity against crime, the "higher" against the "lower" races. To which the Negro cries Amen! and swears that to so much of this strange prejudice as is founded on just homage to civilization, culture, righteousness, and progress, he humbly bows and meekly does obeisance. But before that nameless prejudice that leaps beyond all this he stands helpless, dismayed, and well-nigh speechless; before that personal disrespect and mockery, the ridicule and systematic humiliation, the distortion of fact and wanton license of fancy, the cynical ignoring of the better and the boisterous welcoming of the worse, the all-pervading desire to inculcate disdain for everything black, from Toussaint to the devil—before this there rises a sickening despair that would disarm and discourage any nation save that black host to whom "discouragement" is an unwritten word.

But the facing of so vast a prejudice could not but bring the inevitable self-questioning, self-disparagement, and lowering of ideals which ever accompany repression and breed in an atmosphere of contempt and hate. Whispering and portents came borne upon the four winds: Lo! we are diseased and dying, cried the dark hosts; we cannot write, our voting is vain; what need of education, since we must always cook and serve? And the Nation echoed and enforced this self-criticism, saying: Be content to be servants, and nothing more; what need of higher culture for half-men? Away with the black man's ballot, by force or fraud—and behold the suicide of a race! Nevertheless, out of the evil came something of good—the more careful adjustment of education to real life, the clearer perception of the Negroes' social responsibilities, and the sobering realization of the meaning of progress.

So dawned the time of *Sturm und Drang:* storm and stress to-day rocks our little boat on the mad waters of the world-sea; there is within and without the sound of conflict, the burning of body and rending of soul; inspiration strives with doubt, and faith with vain questionings. The bright ideals of the past—physical freedom, political power, the training of brains and the training of hands—all these in turn have waxed and waned, until even the last grows dim and overcast. Are they all wrong—all false? No, not that, but each alone was over-simple and incomplete—the dreams of a credulous race-childhood, or the fond imaginings of the other world which does not know and does not want to know our power. To be really true, all these ideals must be melted and welded into one. The training of the schools we need to-day more than ever—the training of deft hands, quick eyes and ears, and above all the broader, deeper, higher culture of gifted minds and pure hearts. The power of the ballot we need in sheer self-defence—else what shall save us from a second slavery? Freedom, too, the long-sought, we still seek—the freedom of life and limb, the freedom to work and think, the freedom to love and aspire. Work, culture, liberty—all these we need, not singly but together, not successively but together, each growing and aiding each, and all striving toward that vaster ideal that swims before the Negro people, the ideal of human brotherhood, gained through the unifying ideal of Race; the ideal of fostering and developing the traits and talents of the Negro, not in opposition to or contempt for other races, but rather in large conformity to the greater ideals of the American Republic, in order that some day on American soil two world-races may give each to each those characteristics both so sadly lack. We the darker ones come even now not altogether empty-handed: there are to-day no truer exponents of the pure human spirit of the Declaration of Independence than the American Negroes; there is no truer American music but the wild sweet melodies of the Negro slave; the American fairy tales and folk-lore are Indian and African; and, all in all, we black men seem the sole oasis of simple faith and reverence in a dusty desert of dollars and smartness. Will America be poorer if she replace her brutal dyspeptic blundering with light-hearted but determined Negro humility? or her coarse and cruel wit with loving jovial good-humor? or her vulgar music with the soul of the Sorrow Songs?

Merely a concrete test of the underlying principles of the great republic is the Negro Problem, and the spiritual striving of the freedmen's sons is the travail of souls whose burden is almost beyond the measure of their strength, but who bear it in the name of an historic race, in the name of this the land of their fathers' fathers, and in the name of human opportunity.

And now what I have briefly sketched in large outline let me on coming pages tell again in many ways, with loving emphasis and deeper detail, that men may listen to the striving in the souls of black folk.

Of the Sons of Master and Man

... It is, then, the strife of all honorable men of the twentieth century to see that in the future competition of races the survival of the fittest shall mean the triumph of the good, the beautiful, and the true; that we may be able to preserve for future civilization all that is really fine and noble and strong, and not continue to put a premium on greed and impudence and cruelty. To bring this hope to fruition, we are compelled daily to turn more and more to a conscientious study of the phenomena of race-contact—to a study frank and fair, and not falsified and colored by our wishes or our fears. And we have in the South as fine a field for such a study as the world affords—a field, to be sure, which the average American scientist deems somewhat beneath his dignity, and which the average man who is not a scientist knows all about, but nevertheless a line of study which by reason of the enormous race complications with which God seems about to punish this nation must increasingly claim our sober attention, study, and thought, we must ask, what are the actual relations of whites and blacks in the South? and we must be answered, not by apology or fault-finding, but by a plain, unvarnished tale.

In the civilized life of to-day the contact of men and their relations to each other falls in a few main lines of action and communication: there is, first, the physical proximity of homes and dwelling-places, the way in which neighborhoods group themselves, and the contiguity of neighborhoods. Secondly, and in our age chiefest, there are the economic relations—the methods by which individuals coöperate for earning a living, for the mutual satisfaction of wants, for the production of wealth. Next, there are the political relations, the coöperation in social control, in group government, in laying and paying the burden of taxation. In the fourth place there are the less tangible but highly important forms of intellectual contact and commerce, the interchange of ideas through conversation and conference, through periodicals and libraries; and, above all, the gradual formation for each community of that curious *tertium quid* which we call public opinion. Closely allied with this come the various forms of social contact in everyday life, in travel, in theatres, in house gatherings, in marrying and giving in marriage. Finally, there are the varying forms of religious enterprise, of moral teaching and benevolent endeavor. These are the principle ways in which men living in the same communities are brought into contact with each other. It is my present task, therefore, to indicate, from my point of view, how the black race in the South meet and mingle with the whites in these matters of everyday life.

First, as to physical dwelling. It is usually possible to draw in nearly every Southern community a physical color-line on the map, on the one side of which whites dwell and on the other Negroes. The winding and intricacy of the geographical color line varies, of course, in different communities. I know some towns where a straight line drawn through the middle of the main street separates nine-tenths of the whites from nine-tenths of the blacks. In other towns the older settlement of whites has been encircled by a broad band of blacks; in still other cases little settlements or nuclei of blacks have sprung up amid surrounding whites. Usually in cities each street has its distinctive color, and only now and then do the colors meet in close proximity. Even in the country something of this segregation is manifest in the smaller areas, and of course in the larger phenomena of the Black Belt.

All this segregation by color is largely independent of that natural clustering of social grades common to all communities. A Negro slum may be in dangerous proximity to a white residence quarter, while it is quite common to find a white slum planted in the heart of a respectable Negro district. One thing, however, seldom occurs: the best of the whites and the best of the Negroes almost never live in anything like close proximity. It thus happens that in nearly every Southern town and city, both whites and blacks see commonly the worst of each other. This is a vast change from the situation in the past, when, through the close contact of master and house-servant in the patriarchal big house, one found the best of both races in close contact and sympathy, while at the same time the squalor and dull round of toil among the field-hands was removed from the sight and hearing of the family. One can easily see how a person who saw slavery thus from his father's parlors, and sees freedom on the streets of a great city, fails to grasp or comprehend the whole of the new picture. On the other hand, the settled belief of the mass of the Negroes that the Southern white people do not have the black man's best interests at heart has been intensified in later years by this continual daily contact of the better class of blacks with the worst representatives of the white race. . . .

The average American can easily conceive of a rich land awaiting development and filled with black laborers. To him the Southern problem is simply that of making efficient workingmen out of this material, by giving them the requisite technical skill and the help of invested capital. The problem, however, is by no means as simple as this, from the obvious fact that these workingmen have been trained for centuries as slaves. They exhibit, therefore, all the advantages and defects of such training; they are willing and good-natured, but not self-reliant, provident, or careful. If now the economic development of the South is to be pushed to the verge of exploitation, as seems probable, then we have a mass of workingmen thrown into relentless competition with the workingmen of the world, but handicapped by a training the very opposite to that of the modern self-reliant democratic laborer. What the black laborer needs is careful personal guidance, group leadership of men with hearts in their bosoms, to train them to foresight, carefulness, and honesty. Nor does it require any fine-spun theories of racial differences to prove the necessity of such group training after the brains of the race have been knocked out by two hundred and fifty years of assiduous education in submission, carelessness, and stealing. After Emancipation, it was the plain duty of some one to assume this group leadership and training of the Negro laborer. I will not stop here to inquire whose duty it was—whether that of the white ex-master who had profited by unpaid toil, or the Northern philanthropist whose persistence brought on the crisis, or the National Government whose edict freed the bondsmen; I will not stop to ask whose duty it was, but I insist it was the duty of some one to see that these workingmen were not left alone and unguided, without capital, without land, without skill, without economic organization, without even the bald protection of law, order, and decency —left in a great land, not to settle down to slow and careful internal development, but destined to be thrown almost immediately into relentless and sharp competition with the best of modern workingmen under an economic system where every participant is fighting for himself, and too often utterly regardless of the rights or welfare of his neighbor. . . .

Left by the best elements of the South with little protection or oversight, [the Negro] has been made in law and custom the victim of the worst and most unscrupulous men in each community. The crop-lien system which is depopulating the fields of the South is not simply the result of shiftlessness on the part of Negroes, but is also the result of cunningly devised laws as to mortgages, liens, and misdemeanors, which can be made by conscienceless men to entrap and snare the unwary until escape is impossible, further toil a farce, and protest a crime. I have seen, in the Black Belt of Georgia, an ignorant, honest Negro buy and pay for a farm in installments three separate times, and then in the face of law and decency the enterprising American who sold it to him pocketed money and deed and left the black man landless, to labor on his own land at thirty cents a day. I have seen a black farmer fall in debt to a white storekeeper, and that storekeeper go to his farm and strip it of every single marketable article—mules, ploughs, stored crops, tools, furniture, bedding, clocks, looking-glass—and all this without a sheriff or officer, in the face of the law for homestead exemptions, and without rendering to a single responsible person any account or reckoning. And such proceedings can happen, and will happen, in any community where a class of ignorant toilers are placed by custom and race-prejudice beyond the pale of sympathy and race-brotherhood. So long as the best elements of a community do not feel in duty bound to protect and train and care for the weaker members of their group, they leave them to be preyed upon by these swindlers and rascals. . . .

In the attitude of the American mind toward Negro suffrage can be traced with unusual accuracy the prevalent conceptions of government. In the [eighteen-]fifties we were near enough to the echoes of the French Revolution to believe pretty thoroughly in universal suffrage. We argued, as we thought then rather logically, that no social class was so good, so true, and so disinterested as to be trusted wholly with the political destiny of its neighbors; that in every state the best arbiters of their own welfare are the persons directly affected; consequently that it is only by arming every hand with a ballot—with the right to have a voice in the policy of the state—that the greatest good to the greatest number could be attained. To be sure, there were objections to these arguments, but we thought we had answered them tersely and convincingly; if some one complained of the ignorance of voters, we answered, "Educate them." If another complained of their venality, we replied, "Disfranchise them or put them in jail." And, finally, to the men who feared demagogues and the natural perversity of some human beings we insisted that time and bitter experience would teach the most hardheaded. . . .

Can we establish a mass of black laborers and artisans and landholders in the South who, by law and public opinion, have absolutely no voice in shaping the laws under which they live and work? Can the modern organization of industry, assuming as it does free democratic government and the power and ability of the laboring classes to compel respect for their welfare—can this system be carried out in the South when half its laboring force is voiceless in the public councils and powerless in its own defence? To-day the black man of the South has almost nothing to say as to how much he shall be taxed, or how those taxes shall be expended; as to who shall execute the laws, and how they shall do it; as to who shall make the laws, and how they shall be made. It is pitiable that frantic efforts must be made at critical times to get law-makers in some States even to listen to the respectful presentation of the black man's side of a current controversy. Daily the Negro is coming more and more to look upon law and justice, not as protecting safeguards, but as sources of humiliation and oppression. The laws are made by men who have little interest in him; they are executed by men who have absolutely no motive for treating the black people with courtesy or consideration; and, finally, the accused lawbreaker is tried, not by his peers, but too often by men who would rather punish ten innocent Negroes than let one guilty one escape. . . .

Moreover, the political status of the Negro in the South is closely connected with the question of Negro crime. There can be no doubt that crime among Negroes has sensibly increased in the last thirty years, and that there has appeared in the slums of great cities a distinct criminal class among the blacks. In explaining this unfortunate development, we must note two things: (1) that the inevitable result of Emancipation was to increase crime and criminals, and (2) that the police system of the South was primarily designed to control slaves. As to the first point, we must not forget that under a strict slave system there can scarcely be such a thing as crime. But when these variously constituted human particles are suddenly thrown broadcast on the sea of life, some swim, some sink, and some hang suspended, to be forced up or down by the chance currents of a busy hurrying world. So great an economic and social revolution as swept the South in [18]63 meant a weeding out among the Negroes of the incompetents and vicious, the beginning of a differentiation of social grades. Now a rising group of people are not lifted bodily from the ground like an inert solid mass, but rather stretch upward like a living plant with its roots still clinging in the mould. The appearance, therefore, of the Negro criminal was a phenomenon to be awaited; and while it causes anxiety, it should not occasion surprise.

Here again the hope for the future depended peculiarly on careful and delicate dealing with these criminals. Their offences at first were those of laziness, carelessness, and impulse, rather than of malignity or ungoverned viciousness. Such misdemeanors needed discriminating treatment, firm but reformatory, with no hint of injustice, and full proof of guilt. For such dealing with criminals, white or black, the South had no machinery, no adequate jails or reformatories;

its police system was arranged to deal with blacks alone, and tacitly assumed that every white man was *ipso facto* a member of that police. Thus grew up a double system of justice, which erred on the white side by undue leniency and the practical immunity of redhanded criminals, and erred on the black side by undue severity, injustice, and lack of discrimination. For, as I have said, the police system of the South was originally designed to keep track of all Negroes, not simply of criminals; and when the Negroes were freed and the whole South was convinced of the impossibility of free Negro labor, the first and almost universal device was to use the courts as a means of reënslaving the blacks. It was not then a question of crime, but rather one of color, that settled a man's conviction on almost any charge. Thus Negroes came to look upon courts as instruments of injustice and oppression, and upon those convicted in them as martyrs and victims. . . .

But the chief problem in any community cursed with crime is not the punishment of the criminals, but the preventing of the young from being trained to crime. And here again the peculiar conditions of the South have prevented proper precautions. I have seen twelve-year-old boys working in chains on the public streets of Atlanta, directly in front of the schools, in company with old and hardened criminals; and this indiscriminate mingling of men and women and children makes the chain-gangs perfect schools of crime and debauchery. . . .

It is the public schools, however, which can be made, outside the homes, the greatest means of training decent self-respecting citizens. We have been so hotly engaged recently in discussing trade-schools and the higher education that the pitiable plight of the public-school system in the South has almost dropped from view. Of every five dollars spent for public education in the State of Georgia, the white schools get four dollars and the Negro one dollar; and even then the white public-school system, save in the cities, is bad and cries for reform. If this is true of the whites, what of the blacks? I am becoming more and more convinced, as I look upon the system of common-school training in the South, that the national government must soon step in and aid popular education in some way. To-day it has been only by the most strenuous efforts on the part of the thinking men of the South that the Negro's share of the school fund has not been cut down to a pittance in some half-dozen States; and that movement not only is not dead, but in many communities is gaining strength. What in the name of reason does this nation expect of a people, poorly trained and hard pressed in severe economic competition, without political rights, and with ludicrously inadequate common-school facilities? What can it expect but crime and listless-ness, offset here and there by the dogged struggles of the fortunate and more determined who are themselves buoyed by the hope that in due time the country will come to its senses? . . .

From JOHN BROWN

W. E. B. Du Bois once wrote some bitter lines about white friends of the black people: "I do not believe any people ever had so many 'friends,' and may the good God deliver him from most of them, for they are like to lynch his soul." But Du Bois was no chauvinist and on his list of many white heroes the name of John Brown is near the top. He considered Brown one of the men who most influenced American race relations.

Du Bois' appreciation of John Brown was shown best in two major efforts. The second of the annual meetings of the Niagara Movement, the militant civil rights group organized by Du Bois in 1906 which merged with the NAACP in 1910, was held at Harpers Ferry to honor John Brown. In 1909, Du Bois wrote a biography-eulogy of Brown which he called "a record and a tribute to the man who of all white Americans has perhaps come nearest to touching the real souls of black folk." This biography the great Negro educator always considered one of his finest creations.

Possibly the most important chapter was "The Legacy of John Brown," included here. The main theme of the book, a theme to which Du Bois returned often throughout his life, is: "The cost of liberty is less than the price of repression."

John Brown, written sixty years ago, was reissued for the first time in 1962. Time has not dated it: its history and prophecy are just as relevant now as when the book was written in 1909. Du Bois could have been writing about today's racial problems when he wrote in the concluding chapter of John Brown:

John Brown taught us that the cheapest price to pay for liberty is its cost today. The building of barriers against the advance of Negro-Americans hinders but in the end cannot altogether stop their progress. The excuse of benevolent tutelage cannot be urged, for that tutelage is not benevolent that does not prepare for

65

free responsible manhood. Nor can the efficiency of greed as an economic developer be proven—it may hasten development but it does so at the expense of solidity of structure, smoothness of motion, and real efficiency. Nor does selfish exploitation help the undeveloped; rather it hinders and weakens them.

It is now *a full century* since this white-haired old man lay weltering in the blood which he spilled for broken and despised humanity. Let the nation which he loved and the South to which he spoke reverently listen again today to those words, as prophetic now as then:

"You had better—all you people of the South—prepare yourselves for a settlement of this question. It must come up for settlement sooner than you are prepared for it, and the sooner you commence that preparation, the better for you. You may dispose of me very easily—I am nearly disposed of now; but this question is still to be settled—this Negro question, I mean. The end of that is not yet."

The Legacy of John Brown

"I, John Brown, am quite certain that the crimes of this guilty land will never be purged away but with blood. I had, as I now think vainly, flattered myself that without very much bloodshed it might be done."[1]

These were the last written words of John Brown, set down the day he died—the culminating of that wonderful message of his forty days in prison, which all in all made the mightiest Abolition document that America has known. Uttered in chains and solemnity, spoken in the very shadow of death, its dramatic intensity after that wild and puzzling raid, its deep earnestness as embodied in the character of the man, did more to shake the foundations of slavery than any single thing that ever happened in America. . . .

To his family he hands down the legacy of his faith and works: "I beseech you all to live in habitual contentment with moderate circumstances and gains of worldly store, and earnestly to teach this to your children and children's children after you, by example as well as precept." And again: "Be sure to remember and follow my advice, and my example too, so far as it has been consistent with the holy religion of Jesus Christ, in which I remain a most firm and humble believer. Never forget the poor, nor think anything you bestow on them to be lost to you, even though they may be black as Ebedmelech, the Ethiopian eunuch, who cared for Jeremiah in the pit of the dungeon; or as black as the one to whom Philip preached Christ. Be sure to entertain strangers. . . . Remember them that are in bonds as bound with them."[2]

Of his own merit and desert he is modest but firm: "The great bulk of mankind estimate each other's actions and motives by the measure of success or otherwise that attends them through life. By that rule, I have been one of the worst and one of the best of men. I do not claim to have been one of the latter, and I leave it to an impartial tribunal to decide whether the world has been the worse or the better for my living and dying in it."[3]

He has no sense of shame for his action: "I feel no consciousness of guilt in that matter, nor even mortification on account of my imprisonment and irons; I feel perfectly sure

---

[1] Letter to D. R. Tilden in Sanborn, pp. 609–610. [Benjamin Franklin Sanborn, *The Life and Letters of John Brown*. 1885.]

[2] Letters to his family, 1859, in Sanborn, pp. 579–580, 613–615.

[3] Letter to D. R. Tilden in Sanborn, pp. 609–610.

that very soon no member of my family will feel any possible disposition to blush on my account."[1]

"I do not feel conscious of guilt in taking up arms; and had it been in behalf of the rich and powerful, the intelligent, the great (as men count greatness), or those who form enactments to suit themselves and corrupt others, or some of their friends, that I interfered, suffered, sacrificed, and fell, it would have been doing very well. But enough of this. These light afflictions, which endure for a moment, shall but work for me a far more exceeding and eternal weight of glory."[2] . . .

"I think I feel as happy as Paul did when he lay in prison. He knew if they killed him, it would greatly advance the cause of Christ; that was the reason he rejoiced so. On that same ground 'I do rejoice, yea, and will rejoice.' Let them hang me; I forgive them, and may God forgive them, for they know not what they do. I have no regret for the transaction for which I am condemned. I went against the laws of men, it is true, but 'whether it be right to obey God or men, judge ye.' "[3]

"When and in what form death may come is but of small moment. I feel just as content to die for God's eternal truth and for suffering humanity on the scaffold as in any other way; and I do not say this from disposition to 'brave it out.' No; I would readily own my wrong were I in the least convinced of it. I have now been confined over a month, with a good opportunity to look the whole thing as 'fair in the face' as I am capable of doing; and I feel it most grateful that I am counted in the least possible degree worthy to suffer for the truth."[4]

"I can trust God with both the time and the manner of my death, believing, as I now do, that for me at this time to seal my testimony for God and humanity with my blood will do vastly more toward advancing the cause I have earnestly endeavored to promote, than all I have done in my life before."[5]

"My whole life before had not afforded me one-half the opportunity to plead for the right. In this, also, I find much to reconcile me to both my present condition and my immediate prospect."[6]

[1] Letter to his family, 1859, in Sanborn, pp. 579–580.
[2] Letter to a friend, 1859, in Sanborn, pp. 582–583.
[3] Letter to Mr. McFarland, 1859, in Sanborn, pp. 598–599.
[4] Letter to his younger children, 1859, in Sanborn, pp. 596–597.
[5] Letter to his wife and children in Sanborn, pp. 585–587.
[6] Letter to D. R. Tilden in Sanborn, pp. 609–610.

Against slavery his face is set like flint: "There are no ministers of Christ here. These ministers who profess to be Christian, and hold slaves or advocate slavery, I cannot abide them. My knees will not bend in prayer with them, while their hands are stained with the blood of souls."[1] He said to one Southern clergyman: "I will thank you to leave me alone; your prayers would be an abomination to God." To another he said, "I would not insult God by bowing down in prayer with any one who had the blood of the slave on his skirts."

And to a third who argued in favor of slavery as "a Christian institution," John Brown replied impatiently: "My dear sir, you know nothing about Christianity; you will have to learn its A, B, C; I find you quite ignorant of what the word Christianity means. . . . I respect you as a gentleman, of course; but it is as a heathen gentleman."[2]

To his children he wrote: "Be determined to know by experience, as soon as may be, whether Bible instruction is of divine origin or not. Be sure to owe no man anything, but to love one another. John Rogers wrote his children, 'Abhor that arrant whore of Rome.' John Brown writes to his children to abhor, with undying hatred also, that sum of all villanies—slavery."[3]

And finally he rejoiced: "Men cannot imprison, or chain, or hang the soul. I go joyfully in behalf of millions that 'have no rights' that this great and glorious, this Christian republic 'is bound to respect.' Strange change in morals, political as well as Christian, since 1776."[4]

"No formal will can be of use," he wrote on his doomsday, "when my expressed wishes are made known to my dutiful and beloved family."[5]

This was the man. His family is the world. What legacy did he leave? It was soon seen that his voice was a call to the great final battle with slavery.

In the spring of 1861 the Boston Light Infantry was sent to Fort Warren in Boston harbor to drill. A quartette was formed among the soldiers to sing patriotic songs and for them was contrived the verses,

---

[1] Letter to Mr. McFarland, 1859, in Sanborn, pp. 598–599.

[2] Redpath, pp. 382–383. [James Redpath, author of *Echoes of Harper's Ferry*, 1860.]

[3] Last letter to his family, 1859, in Sanborn, pp. 614–615.

[4] Letter to F. B. Musgrave, 1859, in Sanborn, p. 593.

[5] Report: Reports of Senate Committees, 36th Congress, 1st Session, No. 278; Testimony of Joshua R. Giddings, pp. 147–156.

"John Brown's body lies a-mouldering in the grave,
His soul is marching on," etc.

This was set to the music of an old camp-meeting tune—possibly of Negro origin—called, "Say, Brother, Will You Meet Us?" The regiment learned it and first sang it publicly when it came up from Fort Warren and marched past the scene where Crispus Attucks fell.[1] Gilmore's Band learned and played it and thus "the song of John Brown was started on its eternal way!"

Was John Brown simply an episode, or was he an eternal truth? And if a truth, how speaks that truth to-day? John Brown loved his neighbor as himself. He could not endure therefore to see his neighbor, poor, unfortunate or oppressed. This natural sympathy was strengthened by a saturation in Hebrew religion which stressed the personal responsibility of every human soul to a just God. To this religion of equality and sympathy with misfortune, was added the strong influence of the social doctrines of the French Revolution with its emphasis on freedom and power in political life. And on all this was built John Brown's own inchoate but growing belief in a more just and a more equal distribution of property. From this he concluded—and acted on that conclusion—that all men are created free and equal, and that the cost of liberty is less than the price of repression. . . .

Those that stepped into the pathway marked by men like John Brown faltered and large numbers turned back. They said: He was a good man—even great, but he has no message for us to-day—he was a "belated Covenanter," an anachronism in the age of Darwin, one who gave his life to lift not the unlifted but the unliftable. We have consequently the present reaction—a reaction which says in effect, Keep these black people in their places, and do not attempt to treat a Negro simply as a white man with a black face; to do this would mean the moral deterioration of the race and the nation—a fate against which a divine racial prejudice is successfully fighting. This is the attitude of the larger portion of our thinking people.

It is not, however, an attitude that has brought mental rest or social peace. On the contrary, it is to-day involving a degree of moral strain and political and social anomaly that gives the wisest pause. The chief difficulty has been that the natural place in which by scientific law the black

---

[1] [Attucks was a Negro killed by the British at the Boston Massacre; first casualty in the American Revolution.]

race in America should stay, cannot easily be determined. To be sure, the freedmen did not, as the philanthropists of the [eighteen-]sixties apparently expected, step in forty years from slavery to nineteenth-century civilization. Neither, on the other hand, did they, as the ex-masters confidently predicted, retrograde and die. Contrary to both these views, they chose a third and apparently quite unawaited way. From the great, sluggish, almost imperceptibly moving mass, they sent off larger and larger numbers of faithful workmen and artisans, some merchants and professional men, and even men of educational ability and discernment. They developed no world geniuses, no millionaires, no great captains of industry, no artists of the first rank; but they did in forty years get rid of the greater part of their total illiteracy, accumulate a half-billion dollars of property in small homesteads, and gain now and then respectful attention in the world's ears and eyes. It has been argued that this progress of the black man in America is due to the exceptional men among them and does not measure the ability of the mass. Such an admission is, however, fatal to the whole argument. If the doomed races of men are going to develop exceptions to the rule of inferiority, then no rule, scientific or moral, should or can proscribe the race as such.

To meet this difficulty in racial philosophy, a step has been taken in America fraught with the gravest social consequences to the world, and threatening not simply the political but the moral integrity of the nation: that step is denying in the case of black men the validity of those evidences of culture, ability, and decency which are accepted unquestionably in the case of other people; and by vague assertions, unprovable assumptions, unjust emphasis, and now and then by deliberate untruth, aiming to secure not only the continued proscription of all these people, but, by caste distinction, to shut in the faces of their rising classes many of the paths to further advance.

When a social policy, based on a supposed scientific sanction, leads to such a moral anomaly, it is time to examine rather carefully the logical foundations of the argument. And as soon as we do this many things are clear: First, assuming the truth of the unproved dictum that there are stocks of human beings whose elimination the best welfare of the world demands, it is certainly questionable if these stocks include the majority of mankind; and it is indefensible and monstrous to pretend that we know to-day with any reasonable assurance which these stocks are. We can point to degenerate individuals and families here and there among all races, but there is not the slightest warrant for assuming that there do not lie among the Chinese and Hindus, the African Bantus and American Indians as lofty possibilities of human culture as any European race has ever exhibited. It is, to be sure, puzzling to know why the Soudan should linger a thousand years in culture behind the valley of the Seine, but it is no more puzzling than the fact that the valley of the Thames was miserably backward as compared with the banks of the Tiber. Climate, human contact, facilities of communication and what we call accident, have played a great part in the rise of culture among nations: to ignore these and assert dogmatically that the present distribution of culture is a fair index of the distribution of human ability and desert, is to make an assertion for which there is not the slightest scientific warrant. . . .

What now does the present hegemony of the white races threaten? It threatens by means of brute force a survival of some of the worst stocks of mankind. It attempts to people the best parts of the earth and put in absolute authority over the rest, not usually (and indeed not mainly) the culture of Europe but its greed and degradation—not only some representatives of the best stocks of the West End of London, upper New York and the Champs Elysées, but also, in as large if not larger numbers, the worst stocks of Whitechapel, the East Side and Montmartre; and it essays to make the slums of white society in all cases and under all circumstances the superior of any colored group, no matter what its ability or culture. To be sure, this outrageous program of wholesale human degeneration is not outspoken yet, save in the backward civilizations of the Southern United States, South Africa and Australia. But its enunciation is listened to with respect and tolerance in England, Germany, and the Northern states by those very persons who accuse philanthropy with seeking to degrade holy white blood by an infiltration of colored strains. And the average citizen is voting ships and guns to carry out this program. . . .

Even armed with this morality of the club, and every advantage of modern culture, the white races have been unable to possess the earth. Many signs of degeneracy have appeared among them: their birth-rate is falling, their average ability is not increasing, their physical stamina is impaired, and their social condition is not reassuring. Lacking the physical ability to take possession of the world, they are to-day fencing in America, Australia, and South Africa and declaring that no dark race shall occupy or develop the land which they themselves are unable to use. And all this on the plea that their stock is threatened with deterioration from without, when in reality its most dangerous threat is deterioration from within.

We are, in fact, to-day repeating in our intercourse between races all the former evils of class distinction within the nation: personal hatred and abuse, mutual injustice, unequal taxation and rigid caste. Individual nations outgrew these fatal things by breaking down the horizontal barriers between classes. We are bringing them back by seeking to erect vertical barriers between races. Men were told that abolition of compulsory class distinction meant leveling down, degradation, disappearance of culture and genius and the triumph of the mob. As a matter of fact, it has been the salvation of European civilization. Some deterioration and leveling there was but it was more than balanced by the discovery of new reservoirs of ability and strength. So to-day we are told that free racial contact—or "social equality" as Southern *patois* has it—means contamination of blood and lowering of ability and culture. It need mean nothing of the sort. Abolition of class distinction did not mean universal intermarriage of stocks, but rather the survival of the fittest by peaceful, personal and social selection—a selection all the more effective because free democracy and equality of opportunity allow the best to rise to their rightful place. The same is true in racial contact. Vertical race distinctions are even more emphatic hindrances to human evolution than horizontal class distinctions, and their tearing away involves fewer chances of degradation and greater opportunities of human betterment than in case of class lines. On the other hand, persistence in racial distinction spells disaster sooner or later. The earth is growing smaller and more accessible. Race contact will become in the future increasingly inevitable not only in America, Asia, and Africa but even in Europe. The color line will mean not simply a return to the absurdities of class as exhibited in the sixteenth and seventeenth centuries, but even to the caste of ancient days. This, however, the Japanese, the Chinese, the East Indians and the Negroes are going to resent in just such proportion as they gain the power; and they are gaining the power, and they cannot be kept from gaining more power. The price of repression will then be hypocrisy and slavery and blood.

This is the situation to-day. Has John Brown no message —no legacy, then, to the twentieth century? He has and it is this great word: the cost of liberty is less than the price of repression. The price of repressing the world's darker races is shown in a moral retrogression and an economic waste unparalleled since the age of the African slave-trade. What would be the cost of liberty? what would be the cost of giving the great stocks of mankind every reasonable help and incentive to self-development—opening the avenues of opportunity freely, spreading knowledge, suppressing war and cheating, and treating men and women as equals the world over whenever and wherever they attain equality? It would cost something. It would cost something in pride and prejudice, for eventually many a white man would be blacking black men's boots; but this cost we may ignore—its greatest cost would be the new problems of racial intercourse and intermarriage which would come to the front. Freedom and equal opportunity in this respect would inevitably bring some intermarriage of whites and yellows and browns and blacks. This might be a good thing and it might not be. We do not know. Our belief on the matter may be strong and even frantic, but it has no adequate scientific foundation. If such marriages are proven inadvisable, how could they be stopped? Easily. We associate with cats and cows, but we do not fear intermarriage with them, even though they be given all freedom of development. So, too, intelligent human beings can be trained to breed intelligently without the degradation of such of their fellows as they may not wish to breed with. In the Southern United States, on the contrary, it is assumed that unwise marriages can be stopped only by the degradation of the blacks—the classing of all darker women with prostitutes, the loading of a whole race with every badge of public isolation, degradation and contempt, and by burning offenders at the stake. Is this civilization? No. The civilized method of preventing ill-advised marriage lies in the training of mankind in the ethics of sex and child-bearing. We cannot ensure the survival of the best blood by the public murder and degradation of unworthy suitors, but we can substitute a civilized human selection of husbands and wives which shall ensure the survival of the fittest. Not the methods of the jungle, not even the careless choices of the drawing-room, but the thoughtful selection of the schools and laboratory is the ideal of future marriage. This will cost something in ingenuity, self-control and toleration, but it will cost less than forcible repression.

Not only is the cost of repression to-day large—it is a continually increasing cost: the procuring of coolie labor, the ruling of India, the exploitation of Africa, the problem of the unemployed, and the curbing of the corporations, are a tremendous drain on modern society with no near end in sight. The cost is not merely in wealth but in social progress and spiritual strength, and it tends ever to explosion, murder, and war. All these things but increase the difficulty of beginning a régime of freedom in human growth and development—they raise the cost of liberty. Not only that but the very explosions, like the Russo-Japanese War, which bring partial freedom, tend in the complacent current philosophy to prove the wisdom of repression. "Blood will tell," men say. "The fit will survive; stop up the tea-kettle and eventually the steam will burst the iron," and therefore only the steam that bursts is worth the generating; only organized murder proves the fitness of a people for liberty. This is a fearful and dangerous doctrine. It encourages wrong leadership and perverted ideals at the very time when loftiest and most unselfish striving is called for—as witness Japan after her emancipation, or America after the Civil War. Conversely, it leads the shallow and unthinking to brand as demagogue and radical every group leader who in the day of slavery and struggle cries out for freedom.

For such reasons it is that the memory of John Brown stands to-day as a mighty warning to his country. He saw, he felt in his soul the wrong and danger of that most daring and insolent system of human repression known as American slavery. He knew that in 1700 it would have cost something to overthrow slavery and establish liberty; and that by reason of cowardice and blindness the cost in 1800 was vastly larger but still not unpayable. He felt that by 1900 no human hand could pluck the vampire from the body of the land without doing the nation to death. He said, in 1859, "Now is the accepted time." Now is the day to strike for a free nation. It will cost something—even blood and suffering, but it will not cost as much as waiting. And he was right. Repression bred repression—serfdom bred slavery, until in 1861 the South was farther from freedom than in 1800.

The edict of 1863 was the first step in emancipation and its cost in blood and treasure was staggering. But that was not all—it was only a first step. There were other bills to pay of material reconstruction, social regeneration, mental training and moral uplift. These the nation started to meet in the Fifteenth Amendment, the Freedmen's Bureau, the crusade of school-teachers and the Civil Rights Bill. But the effort was great and the determination of the South to pay no single cent or deed for past error save by force, led in the revolution of 1876 to the triumph of reaction. Reaction meant and means a policy of state, society and individual, whereby no American of Negro blood shall ever come into the full freedom of modern culture. In the carrying out of this program by certain groups and sections, no pains have been spared—no expenditure of money, ingenuity, physical or moral strength. The building of barriers around these black men has been pushed with an energy so desperate and unflagging that it has seriously checked the great outpouring of benevolence and sympathy that greeted the freedman in 1863. It has come to so swathed and gowned in graciousness as to disarm philanthropy and chill enthusiasm. It has used double-tongued argument with deadly effect. Has the Negro advanced? Beware his further strides. Has the Negro retrograded? It is his fate, why seek to help him? Thus has the spirit of repression gained attention, complacent acquiescence, and even coöperation. To be sure, there still stand staunch souls who cannot yet believe the doctrine of human repression, and who pour out their wealth for Negro training and freedom in the face of the common cry. But the majority of Americans seem to have forgotten the foundation principles of their government and the recklessly destructive effect of the blows meant to bind and tether their fellows. We have come to see a day here in America when one citizen can deprive another of his vote at his discretion; can restrict the education of his neighbors' children as he sees fit; can with impunity load his neighbor with public insult on the king's highway; can deprive him of his property without due process of law; can deny him the right of trial by his peers, or of any trial whatsoever if he can get a large enough group of men to join him; can refuse to protect or safeguard the integrity of the family of some men whom he dislikes; finally, can not only close the door of opportunity in commercial and social lines in a fully competent neighbor's face, but can actually count on the national and state governments to help and make effective this discrimination.

Such a state of affairs is not simply disgraceful; it is deeply and increasingly dangerous. Not only does the whole nation feel already the loosening of joints which these vicious blows on human liberty have caused—lynching, lawlessness, lying and stealing, bribery and divorce—but it can look for darker deeds to come.

And this not merely because of the positive harm of this upbuilding of barriers, but above all because within these bursting barriers are men—human forces which no human hand can hold. It is human force and aspiration and endeavor which are moving there amid the creaking of timbers and writhing of souls. It is human force that has already done in a generation the work of many centuries. . . . These proscribed millions have given America music, inspired art and literature, made its bread, dug its ditches, fought its battles, and suffered in its misfortunes. The great mass of these men is becoming daily more thoroughly organized, more deeply self-critical, more conscious of its power. Threatened though it has been naturally, as a proletariat, with degeneration and disease, it is to-day reducing its death-rate and beginning organized rescue of its delinquents and defectives. The mass can still to-day be called ignorant, poor and but moderately efficient, but it is daily growing better trained, richer and more intelligent. And as it grows it is sensing more and more the vantage-ground which it holds as a defender of the right of the freedom of human development for black men in the midst of a centre of modern culture. It sees its brothers in yellow, black and brown held physically at arms' length from civilization lest they become civilized and less liable to conquest and exploitation. It sees the world-wide effort to build an aristocracy of races and nations on a foundation of darker half-enslaved and tributary peoples. It knows that the last great battle of the West is to vindicate the right of any man of any nation, race, or color to share in the world's goods and thoughts and efforts to the extent of his effort and ability.

Thus to-day the Negro American faces his destiny and doggedly strives to realize it. He has his tempters and temptations. There are ever those about him whispering: "You are nobody; why strive to be somebody? The odds are overwhelming against you—wealth, tradition, learning and guns. Be reasonable. Accept the dole of charity and the cant of missionaries and sink contentedly to your place as humble servants and helpers of the white world." If this has not been effective, threats have been used: "If you continue to complain, we will withdraw all aid, boycott your labor, cease to help support your schools and let you die and disappear from the land in ignorance, crime and disease." Still the black man has pushed on, has continued to protest, has refused to die out and disappear, and to-day stands as physically the most virile element in America, intellectually among the most promising, and morally the most tremendous and insistent of the social problems of the New World. Not even the silence of his friends, or of those who ought to be the friends of struggling humanity, has silenced him. Not even the wealth of modern Golconda has induced him to believe that life without liberty is worth living.

On the other side heart-searching is in order. It is not well with this land of ours: poverty is certainly not growing less, wealth is being wantonly wasted, business honesty is far too rare, family integrity is threatened, bribery is poisoning our public life, theft is honeycombing our private business, and voting is largely unintelligent. Not that these evils are unopposed. There are brave men and women striving for social betterment, for the curbing of the vicious power of wealth, for the uplift of women and the downfall of thieves. But their battle is hard, and how much harder because of the race problem—because of the calloused conscience of caste, the peonage of black labor hands, the insulting of black women, and the stealing of black votes? How far are business dishonesty and civic degradation in America the direct result of racial prejudice?

Well do I know that many persons defend their treatment of undeveloped peoples on the highest grounds. They say, as Jefferson Davis intimated, that liberty is for the full-grown, not for children. It was during Senator Mason's inquisition after the hanging of John Brown, whereby the Southern leader hoped to entrap the Abolitionists. Joshua R. Giddings, keen, impetuous and fiery, was on the rack. Senator Davis, pale, sallow and imperturbable, with all the aristocratic poise and dignity built on the unpaid toil of two centuries of slaves, said:

"Did you, in inculcating, by popular lectures, the doctrine of a law higher than that of the social compact, make your application exclusively to Negro slaves, or did you also include minors, convicts, and lunatics, who might be restrained of their liberty by the laws of the land?"

Mr. Giddings smiled. "Permit me," he said, ". . . with all due deference, to suggest, so that I may understand you, do you intend to inquire whether those lectures would indicate whether your slaves of the slave states had a right at all times to their liberty?"

"I will put the question in that form if you like it," answered Davis, and then Giddings flashed:

"My lectures, in all instances, would indicate the right of every human soul in the enjoyment of reason, while he is charged with no crime or offense, to maintain his life, his liberty, the pursuit of his own happiness; that this has reference to the enslaved of all the states as much as it had reference to our own people while enslaved by the Algerines in Africa."

But Mr. Davis suavely pressed his point: "Then the next question is, whether the same right was asserted for minors and apprentices, being men in good reason, yet restrained of their liberty by the laws of the land."

Giddings replied. "I will answer at once that the proposition or comparison is conflicting with the dictates of truth. The minor is, from the law of nature, under the restraints of parental affection for the purposes of nurture, of education, of preparing him to secure and maintain the very rights to which I refer."[1]

This debate is not yet closed. It was not closed by the Civil War. Men still maintain that East Indians and Africans and others ought to be under the restraint and benevolent tutelage of stronger and wiser nations for their own benefit. Well and good. Is the tutelage really benevolent? Then it is training in liberty. Is it training in slavery? Then it is not benevolent. Liberty trains for liberty. Responsibility is the first step in responsibility.

Even the restraints imposed in the training of men and children are restraints that will in the end make greater freedom possible. Is the benevolent expansion of to-day of such a character? Is England trying to see how soon and how effectively the Indians can be trained for self-government or is she willing to exploit them just so long as they can be cajoled or quieted into submission? Is Germany trying to train her Africans to modern citizenship or to modern "work without complaint"? Is the South trying to make the Negroes responsible, self-reliant freemen of a republic, or the dumb driven cattle of a great industrial machine?

No sooner is the question put this way than the defenders of modern caste retire behind a more defensible breastwork. They say: "Yes, we exploit nations for our own advantage purposely—even at times brutally. But only in that way can the high efficiency of the modern industrial process be maintained, and in the long run it benefits the oppressed even more than the oppressor." This doctrine is as widespread as it is false and mischievous. It is true that the bribe of greed will artificially hasten economic development, but it does so at fearful cost, as America itself can testify. We have here a wonderful industrial machine, but a machine quickly rather than carefully built, formed of forcing rather than of growth, involving sinful and unnecessary expense. Better smaller production and more equitable distribution; better fewer miles of railway and more honor, truth, and

[1] Report: Reports of Senate Committees, 36th Congress, 1st Session, No. 278; Testimony of Joshua R. Giddings, pp. 147–156.

liberty; better fewer millionaires and more contentment. So it is the world over, where force and fraud and graft have extorted rich reward from writhing millions. Moreover, it is historically unprovable that the advance of undeveloped peoples has been helped by wholesale exploitation at the hands of their richer, stronger, and more unscrupulous neighbors. This idea is a legend of the long exploded doctrine of inevitable economic harmonies in all business life. True it is that adversity and difficulties make for character, but the real and inevitable difficulties of life are numerous enough for genuine development without the aid of artificial hindrances. The inherent and natural difficulties of raising a people from ignorant unmoral slavishness to self-reliant modern manhood are great enough for purposes of character-building without the aid of murder, theft, caste, and degradation. Not because of but in spite of these latter hindrances has the Negro-American pressed forward.

This, then, is the truth: the cost of liberty is less than the price of repression, even though that cost be blood. Freedom of development and equality of opportunity is the demand of Darwinism and this calls for the abolition of hard and fast lines between races, just as it called for the breaking down of barriers between classes. Only in this way can the best in humanity be discovered and conserved, and only thus can mankind live in peace and progress. The present attempt to force all whites above all darker peoples is a sure method of human degeneration. The cost of liberty is thus a decreasing cost, while the cost of repression ever tends to increase to the danger point of war and revolution. . . .

From DARKWATER

Darkwater: Voices from Within the Veil *was written in 1920. It is surely one of the most significant books ever written on racial prejudice and exploitation. Yet it is relatively unknown, having been reprinted only in 1969 and virtually unobtainable except in some of the larger libraries.*

Several of the ten well-reasoned and informative essays were highly controversial—for some, they were inflammatory—but none more so than the chapter entitled "The Souls of White Folk." In this, Du Bois relentlessly lays bare the record of white racism in America and the hypocritical camouflage under which the aggressions against blacks were committed. Likewise, he castigates and ridicules "white folks" souls in his great essay "The Damnation of Women" (which is in part the sordid story of how white men fulfilled their need for black women by coercion or even rape and in part a tribute to the beauty, courage and strength of black women).

Two of the several brief creative works in Darkwater *are his famous "Credo" (first published in 1904) and his much-quoted poem "A Litany at Atlanta," in which he attacked the anti-Negro pogroms of 1906 and dared question the objective fairness of the white God who permitted such things. (Both of these works appear in this volume under "Creative Works.") "Work and Wealth" and "Of the Ruling of Men" were chapters exposing the economics and methods of race prejudice and racist policies promulgated by the white power structure in America, North and South.*

But of all the essays in Darkwater *that disturbed the souls of white folk, none raised such a cry of horror and outrage as "The Souls of White Folk," and nothing in that was so shocking as a brief paragraph containing another of Du Bois' many prophecies:*

But what of the darker world that watches? Most men belong to this world. With Negro and Negroids, East Indian, Chinese and Japanese they form two-thirds of the population of the world. A belief in humanity is a belief in colored men. . . . What, then, is this dark world thinking? It is thinking that as wild and awful as this shameful war was [World War I] IT IS NOTHING TO COMPARE WITH THAT FIGHT FOR FREEDOM WHICH BLACK AND BROWN AND YELLOW MEN MUST AND WILL MAKE UNLESS THEIR OPPRESSION AND INSULT AT THE HANDS OF THE WHITE WORLD CEASE. THE DARK WORLD IS GOING TO SUBMIT TO ITS PRESENT TREATMENT JUST AS LONG AS IT MUST AND NOT ONE MOMENT LONGER. [Du Bois' emphasis.]

The socialist, publicist, and humanitarian Charles Edward Russell, one of the principal founders of the NAACP, did a long review of Darkwater *when it appeared in 1920 and recommended it to every literate black. He also said, "I wish every intelligent white man in the United States could be compelled to read it." For he said: "Of all the penned indictments of the white man for his treatment of his dark-skinned brother this extraordinary book is* certainly the most powerful." *[Editor's emphasis.]*

Russell was especially impressed by the essay on black women as the victims of white men. "The greatest chapter in the whole great book is probably the 'Damnation of Women.' I think few white men can read without shame that record of the evil wrought by their kind." In concluding his own essay Russell compared Du Bois' writings to those of Swift and said, "This man has all the material of the skilled observer and all the wit and faultless vision of the great satirists."

Du Bois' two timeless essays: "The Souls of White Folk" and "The Damnation of Women" are included here.

The Souls of White Folk

. . . I know many souls that toss and whirl and pass, but none there are that intrigue me more than the Souls of White Folk.

Of them I am singularly clairvoyant. I see in and through them. I view them from unusual points of vantage. Not as a foreigner do I come, for I am native, not foreign, bone of their thought and flesh of their language. Mine is not the knowledge of the traveler or the colonial composite of dear memories, words and wonder. Nor yet is my knowledge that which servants have of masters, or mass of class, or capitalist of artisan. Rather I see these souls undressed and from the back and side. I see the working of their entrails. I know their thoughts and they know that I know. This knowledge makes them now embarrassed, now furious! They deny my right to live and be and call me misbirth! My word is to them mere bitterness and my soul, pessimism. And yet as they preach and strut and shout and threaten, crouching as they clutch at rags of facts and fancies to hide their nakedness, they go twisting, flying by my tired eyes and I see them ever stripped—ugly, human.

The discovery of personal whiteness among the world's peoples is a very modern thing—a nineteenth and twentieth century matter, indeed. The ancient world would have laughed at such a distinction. The Middle Age regarded skin color with mild curiosity; and even up into the eighteenth century we were hammering our national manikins into one, great, Universal Man, with fine frenzy which ignored color and race even more than birth. Today we have changed all that, and the world in a sudden, emotional conversion has discovered that it is white and by that token, wonderful!

This assumption that of all the hues of God whiteness alone is inherently and obviously better than brownness or tan leads to curious acts; even the sweeter souls of the dominant world as they discourse with me on weather, weal, and woe are continually playing above their actual words an obligato of tune and tone, saying:

"My poor, un-white thing! Weep not nor rage. I know, too well, that the curse of God lies heavy on you. Why? That is not for me to say, but be brave! Do your work in your lowly sphere, praying the good Lord that into heaven above, where all is love, you may, one day, be born—white!"

I do not laugh. I am quite straight-faced as I ask soberly:

"But what on earth is whiteness that one should so desire it?" Then always, somehow, some way, silently but clearly, I am given to understand that whiteness is the ownership of the earth forever and ever, Amen!

Now what is the effect on a man or a nation when it comes passionately to believe such an extraordinary dictum as this? That nations are coming to believe it is manifest daily. Wave on wave, each with increasing virulence, is dashing this new religion of whiteness on the shores of our time. Its first effects are funny: the strut of the Southerner, the arrogance of the Englishman amuck, the whoop of the hoodlum who vicariously leads your mob. Next it appears dampening generous enthusiasm in what we once counted glorious; to free the slave is discovered to be tolerable only in so far as it freed his master! Do we sense somnolent writhings in black Africa or angry groans in India or triumphant banzais in Japan? "To your tents, O Israel!" These nations are not white!

After the more comic manifestations and the chilling of generous enthusiasm come subtler, darker deeds. Everything considered, the title to the universe claimed by White Folk is faulty. It ought, at least, to look plausible. How easy, then, by emphasis and omission to make children believe that every great soul the world ever saw was a white man's soul; that every great thought the world ever knew was a white man's thought; that every great deed the world ever did was a white man's deed; that every great dream the world ever sang was a white man's dream. In fine, that if from the world were dropped everything that could not fairly be attributed to White Folk, the world would, if anything, be even greater, truer, better than now. And if all this be a lie, is it not a lie in a great cause?

Here it is that the comedy verges to tragedy. The first minor note is struck, all unconsciously, by those worthy souls in whom consciousness of high descent brings burning desire to spread the gift abroad—the obligation of nobility to the ignoble. Such sense of duty assumes two things: a real possession of the heritage and its frank appreciation by the humble-born. So long, then, as humble black folk, voluble with thanks, receive barrels of old clothes from lordly and generous whites, there is much mental peace and moral satisfaction. But when the black man begins to dispute the white man's title to certain alleged bequests of the

Fathers in wage and position, authority and training; and when his attitude toward charity is sullen anger rather than humble jollity; when he insists on his human right to swagger and swear and waste—then the spell is suddenly broken and the philanthropist is ready to believe that Negroes are impudent, that the South is right, and that Japan wants to fight America.

After this the descent to Hell is easy. On the pale, white faces which the great billows whirl upward to my tower I see again and again, often and still more often, a writing of human hatred, a deep and passionate hatred, vast by the very vagueness of its expressions. Down through the green waters, on the bottom of the world, where men move to and fro, I have seen a man—an educated gentleman—grow livid with anger because a little, silent, black woman was sitting by herself in a Pullman car. He was a white man. I have seen a great, grown man curse a little child, who had wandered into the wrong waiting-room, searching for its mother: "Here, you damned black——." He was white. In Central Park I have seen the upper lip of a quiet, peaceful man curl back in a tigerish snarl of rage because black folk rode by in a motor car. He was a white man. We have seen, you and I, city after city drunk and furious with ungovernable lust of blood; mad with murder, destroying, killing, and cursing; torturing human victims because somebody accused of crime happened to be of the same color as the mob's innocent victims and because that color was not white! We have seen—Merciful God! in these wild days and in the name of Civilization, Justice, and Motherhood— what have we not seen, right here in America, of orgy, cruelty, barbarism, and murder done to men and women of Negro descent.

Up through the foam of green and weltering waters wells this great mass of hatred, in wilder, fiercer violence, until I look down and know that today to the millions of my people no misfortune could happen—of death and pestilence, failure and defeat—that would not make the hearts of millions of their fellows beat with fierce, vindictive joy! Do you doubt it? Ask your own soul what it would say if the next census were to report that half of black America was dead and the other half dying.

Unfortunate? Unfortunate. But where is the misfortune? Mine? Am I, in my blackness, the sole sufferer? I suffer. And yet, somehow, above the suffering, above the shackled anger that beats the bars, above the hurt that crazes there surges in me a vast pity—pity for a people imprisoned and enthralled, hampered and made miserable for such a cause, for such a phantasy!

Conceive this nation, of all human peoples, engaged in a crusade to make the "World Safe for Democracy"! Can you imagine the United States protesting against Turkish atrocities in Armenia, while the Turks are silent about mobs in Chicago and St. Louis; what is Louvain compared with Memphis, Waco, Washington, Dyersburg, and Estill Springs? In short, what is the black man but America's Belgium, and how could America condemn in Germany that which she commits, just as brutally, within her own borders?

A true and worthy ideal frees and uplifts a people; a false ideal imprisons and lowers. Say to men, earnestly and repeatedly: "Honesty is best, knowledge is power; do unto others as you would be done by." Say this and act it and the nation must move toward it, if not to it. But say to a people: "The one virtue is to be white," and the people rush to the inevitable conclusion, "Kill the 'nigger'!"

Is not this the record of present America? Is not this its headlong progress? Are we not coming more and more, day by day, to making the statement "I am white," the one fundamental tenet of our practical morality? Only when this basic, iron rule is involved is our defense of right nation-wide and prompt. Murder may swagger, theft may rule and prostitution may flourish and the nation gives but spasmodic, intermittent and lukewarm attention. But let the murderer be black or the thief brown or the violator of womanhood have a drop of Negro blood, and the righteousness of the indignation sweeps the world. Nor would this fact make the indignation less justifiable did not we all know that it was blackness that was condemned and not crime.

In the awful cataclysm of World War, where from beating, slandering, and murdering us the white world turned temporarily aside to kill each other, we of the Darker Peoples looked on in mild amaze. . . .

Consider our chiefest industry—fighting. Laboriously the Middle Ages built its rules of fairness—equal armament, equal notice, equal conditions. What do we see today? Machine-guns against assegais; conquest sugared with religion; mutilation and rape masquerading as culture—all this, with vast applause at the superiority of white over black soldiers!

War is horrible! This the dark world knows to its awful cost. But has it just become horrible, in these last days, when under essentially equal conditions, equal armament, and equal waste of wealth white men are fighting white men, with surgeons and nurses hovering near? . . .

Behold little Belgium and her pitiable plight, but has the world forgotten Congo? What Belgium now suffers is not half, not even a tenth, of what she has done to black Congo since Stanley's great dream of 1880. . . .

Harris declares that King Leopold's régime meant the death of twelve million natives, "but what we who were behind the scenes felt most keenly was the fact that the real catastrophe in the Congo was desolation and murder in the larger sense. The invasion of family life, the ruthless destruction of every social barrier, the shattering of every tribal law, the introduction of criminal practices which struck the chiefs of the people dumb with horror—in a word, a veritable avalanche of filth and immorality overwhelmed the Congo tribes. . . ."

Here is a civilization that has boasted much. Neither Roman nor Arab, Greek nor Egyptian, Persian nor Mongol ever took himself and his own perfectness with such disconcerting seriousness as the modern white man. We whose shame, humiliation, and deep insult his aggrandizement so often involved were never deceived. We looked at him clearly, with world-old eyes, and saw simply a human thing, weak and pitiable and cruel, even as we are and were.

These super-men and world-mastering demi-gods listened, however, to no low tongues of ours, even when we pointed silently to their feet of clay. Perhaps we, as folk of simpler soul and more primitive type, have been most struck in the welter of recent years by the utter failure of white religion. We have curled our lips in something like contempt as we have witnessed glib apology and weary explanation. Nothing of the sort deceived us. A nation's religion is its life, and as such white Christianity is a miserable failure.

Nor would we be unfair in this criticism: We know that we, too, have failed, as you have, and have rejected many a Buddha, even as you have denied Christ; but we acknowledge our human frailty, while you, claiming super-humanity, scoff endlessly at our shortcomings. . . .

Yet the fields of Belgium laughed, the cities were gay, art and science flourished; the groans that helped to nourish this civilization fell on deaf ears because the world round about was doing the same sort of thing elsewhere on its own account.

As we saw the dead dimly through rifts of battlesmoke and heard faintly the cursings and accusations of blood brothers, we darker men said: This is not Europe gone mad;

this is not aberration nor insanity; this *is* Europe; this seeming Terrible is the real soul of white culture—back of all culture—stripped and visible today. . . .

Europe has never produced and never will in our day bring forth a single human soul who cannot be matched and over-matched in every line of human endeavor by Asia and Africa. . . .

Why, then, is Europe great? Because of the foundations which the mighty past have furnished her to build upon: the iron trade of ancient, black Africa, the religion and empire-building of yellow Asia, the art and science of the "dago" Mediterranean shore, east, south, and west, as well as north. And where she has builded securely upon this great past and learned from it she has gone forward to greater and more splendid human triumph; but where she has ignored this past and forgotten and sneered at it, she has shown the cloven hoof of poor, crucified humanity—she has played, like other empires gone, the world fool!

If, then, European triumphs in culture have been greater, so, too, may her failures have been greater. How great a failure and a failure in what does the World War betoken? . . . What is that breath of life, thought to be so indispensable to a great European nation? Manifestly it is expansion overseas; it is colonial aggrandizement which explains, and alone adequately explains, the World War. How many of us today fully realize the current theory of colonial expansion, of the relation of Europe which is white, to the world which is black and brown and yellow? Bluntly put, that theory is this: It is the duty of white Europe to divide up the darker world and administer it for Europe's good.

This Europe has largely done. The European world is using black and brown men for all the uses which men know. Slowly but surely white culture is evolving the theory that "darkies" are born beasts of burden for white folk. It were silly to think otherwise, cries the cultured world, with stronger and shriller accord. The supporting arguments grow and twist themselves in the mouths of merchant, scientist, soldier, traveler, writer, and missionary; Darker peoples are dark in mind as well as in body; of dark, uncertain, and imperfect descent; of frailer, cheaper stuff; they are cowards in the face of mausers and maxims; they have no feelings, aspirations, and loves; they are fools, illogical idiots—"half-devil and half-child."

Such as they are civilization must, naturally, raise them, but soberly and in limited ways. They are not simply dark white men. They are not "men" in the sense that Europeans are men. To the very limited extent of their shallow capacities lift them to be useful to whites, to raise cotton, gather rubber, fetch ivory, dig diamonds—and let them be paid what men think they are worth—white men who know them to be well-nigh worthless.

Such degrading of men by men is as old as mankind and the invention of no one race or people. Ever have men striven to conceive of their victims as different from the victors, endlessly different, in soul and blood, strength and cunning, race and lineage. It has been left, however, to Europe and to modern days to discover the eternal world-wide mark of meanness—color! . . .

This theory of human culture and its aims has worked itself through warp and woof of our daily thought with a thoroughness that few realize. Everything great, good, efficient, fair, and honorable is "white"; everything mean, bad, blundering, cheating, and dishonorable is "yellow"; a bad taste is "brown"; and the devil is "black." The changes of this theme are continually rung in picture and story, in newspaper heading and moving-picture, in sermon and school book, until, of course, the King can do no wrong—a White Man is always right and a Black Man has no rights which a white man is bound to respect.

There must come the necessary despisings and hatreds of these savage half-men, this unclean *canaille* of the world—these dogs of men. All through the world this gospel is preaching. It has its literature, it has its priests, it has its secret propaganda and above all—it pays!

There's the rub—it pays. Rubber, ivory, and palm-oil; tea, coffee, and cocoa; bananas, oranges, and other fruit; cotton, gold, and copper—they, and a hundred other things which dark and sweating bodies hand up to the white world from their pits of slime, pay and pay well, but of all that the world gets the black world gets only the pittance that the white world throws it disdainfully.

Small wonder, then, that in the practical world of things-that-be there is jealousy and strife for the possession of the labor of dark millions, for the right to bleed and exploit the colonies of the world where this golden stream may be had, not always for the asking, but surely for the whipping and shooting. It was this competition for the labor of yellow, brown, and black folks that was the cause of the World War. Other causes have been glibly given and other contributing causes there doubtless were, but they were subsidiary and subordinate to this vast quest of the dark world's wealth and toil.

Colonies, we call them, these places where "niggers" are cheap and the earth is rich; they are those outlands where like a swarm of hungry locusts white masters may settle to be served as kings, wield the lash of slave-drivers, rape girls and wives, grow as rich as Croesus and send homeward a golden stream. . . .

The cause of war is preparation for war; and of all that Europe has done in a century there is nothing that has equaled in energy, thought, and time her preparation for wholesale murder. The only adequate cause of this preparation was conquest and conquest, not in Europe, but primarily among the darker peoples of Asia and Africa; conquest, not for assimilation and uplift, but for commerce and degradation. For this, and this mainly, did Europe gird herself at frightful cost for war. . . .

Thus the world market most wildly and desperately sought today is the market where labor is cheapest and most helpless and profit is most abundant. This labor is kept cheap and helpless because the white world despises "darkies." If one has the temerity to suggest that these workingmen may walk the way of white workingmen and climb by votes and self-assertion and education to the rank of men, he is howled out of court. They cannot do it and if they could, they shall not, for they are the enemies of the white race and the whites shall rule forever and forever and everywhere. Thus the hatred and despising of human beings from whom Europe wishes to extort her luxuries has led to such jealousy and bickering between European nations that they have fallen afoul of each other and have fought like crazed beasts. Such is the fruit of human hatred.

But what of the darker world that watches? Most men belong to this world. With Negro and Negroid, East Indian, Chinese, and Japanese they form two-thirds of the population of the world. A belief in humanity is a belief in colored men. If the uplift of mankind must be done by men, then the destinies of this world will rest ultimately in the hands of darker nations.

What, then, is this dark world thinking? It is thinking that as wild and awful as this shameful war was, *it is nothing to compare with that fight for freedom which black and brown and yellow men must and will make unless their oppression and humiliation and insult at the hands of the White World cease. The Dark World is going to submit to its present treatment just as long as it must and not one moment longer.*

Let me say this again and emphasize it and leave no room for mistaken meaning: The World War was primarily the jealous and avaricious struggle for the largest share in exploiting darker races. As such it is and must be but the prelude to the armed and indignant protest of these despised and raped peoples. . . .

If Europe hugs this delusion, then this is not the end of world war—it is but the beginning. . . .

For two or more centuries America has marched proudly in the van of human hatred—making bonfires of human flesh and laughing at them hideously, and making the insulting of millions more than a matter of dislike—rather a great religion, a world war-cry: Up white, down black; to your tents, O white folk, and world war with black and particolored mongrel beasts!

Instead of standing as a great example of the success of democracy and the possibility of human brotherhood America has taken her place as an awful example of its pitfalls and failures, so far as black and brown and yellow peoples are concerned. . . .

I will not believe that all that was must be, that all the shameful drama of the past must be done again today before the sunlight sweeps the silver seas.

If I cry amid this roar of elemental forces, must my cry be in vain, because it is but a cry—a small and human cry amid Promethean gloom?

Back beyond the world and swept by these wild, white faces of the awful dead, why will this Soul of White Folk—this modern Prometheus—hang bound by his own binding, tethered by a fable of the past? I hear his mighty cry reverberating through the world, "I am white!" Well and good, O Prometheus, divine thief! Is not the world wide enough for two colors, for many little shinings of the sun? Why, then, devour your own vitals if I answer even as proudly, "I am black!"

The Damnation of Women

. . . As I remember through memories of others, backward among my own family, it is the mother I ever recall—the little, far-off mother of my grandmother who sobbed her life away in song, longing for her lost palm-trees and scented waters; the tall and bronzed grandmother, with beaked nose and shrewish eyes, who loved and scolded her black and laughing husband as he smoked lazily in his high oak chair; above all, my own mother, with all her soft brownness—the brown velvet of her skin, the sorrowful black-brown of her eyes, and the tiny brown-capped waves of her midnight hair as it lay new parted on her forehead. All the way back in these dim distances it is mothers and mothers of mothers who seem to count, while fathers are shadowy memories.

Upon this African mother-idea, the westward slave trade and American slavery struck like doom. In the cruel exigencies of the traffic in men and in the sudden, unprepared emancipation the great pendulum of social equilibrium swung from a time, in 1800—when America had but eight or less black women to every ten black men—all too swiftly to a day, in 1870—when there were nearly eleven women to ten men in our Negro population. This was but the outward numerical fact of social dislocation; within lay polygamy, polyandry, concubinage, and moral degradation. They fought against all this desperately, did these black slaves in the West Indies, especially among the half-free artisans; they set up their ancient household gods, and when Toussaint and Christophe founded their kingdom in Haiti, it was based on old African tribal ties and beneath it was the mother-idea.

The crushing weight of slavery fell on black women. Under it there was no legal marriage, no legal family, no legal control over children. To be sure, custom and religion replaced here and there what the law denied, yet one has but to read advertisements like the following to see the hell beneath the system:

> One hundred dollars reward will be given for my two fellows, Abram and Frank. Abram has a wife at Colonel Stewart's, in Liberty County, and a mother at Thunderbolt, and a sister in Savannah.
>
> WILLIAM ROBERTS.

> Fifty dollars reward—Ran away from the subscriber a Negro girl named Maria. She is of a copper color, between thirteen and fourteen years of age—bareheaded and barefooted. She is small for her age—very sprightly and very likely. She stated she was going to see her mother at Maysville.
>
> SANFORD THOMPSON.

Fifty dollars reward—Ran away from the subscriber his Negro man Pauladore, commonly called Paul. I understand General R. Y. Hayne has purchased his wife and children from H. L. Pinckney, Esq., and has them now on his plantation at Goose Creek, where, no doubt, the fellow is frequently lurking.

T. DAVIS.

The Presbyterian synod of Kentucky said to the churches under its care in 1835: "Brothers and sisters, parents and children, husbands and wives, are torn asunder and permitted to see each other no more. These acts are daily occurring in the midst of us. The shrieks and agony often witnessed on such occasions proclaim, with a trumpet tongue, the iniquity of our system. There is not a neighborhood where these heartrending scenes are not displayed. There is not a village or road that does not behold the sad procession of manacled outcasts whose mournful countenances tell that they are exiled by force from all that their hearts hold dear."

A sister of a president of the United States declared: "We Southern ladies are complimented with the names of wives, but we are only the mistresses of seraglios."

Out of this, what sort of black women could be born into the world of to-day? There are those who hasten to answer this query in scathing terms and who say lightly and repeatedly that out of black slavery came nothing decent in womanhood; that adultery and uncleanness were their heritage and are their continued portion.

Fortunately so exaggerated a charge is humanly impossible of truth. The half-million women of Negro descent who lived at the beginning of the 19th century had become the mothers of two and one-fourth million daughters at the time of the Civil War and five million granddaughters in 1910. Can all these women be vile and the hunted race continue to grow in wealth and character? Impossible. Yet to save from the past the shreds and vestiges of self-respect has been a terrible task. I most sincerely doubt if any other race of women could have brought its fineness up through so devilish a fire.

Alexander Crummell once said of his sister in the blood: "In her girlhood all the delicate tenderness of her sex has been rudely outraged. In the field, in the rude cabin, in the press-room, in the factory she was thrown into the companionship of coarse and ignorant men. No chance was given her for delicate reserve or tender modesty. From her childhood she was the doomed victim of the grossest passion. All the virtues of her sex were utterly ignored. If the instinct of chastity asserted itself, then she had to fight like a tiger for the ownership and possession of her own person and ofttimes had to suffer pain and lacerations for her virtuous self-assertion. When she reached maturity, all the tender instincts of her womanhood were ruthlessly violated. At the age of marriage—always prematurely anticipated under slavery—she was mated as the stock of the plantation were mated, not to be the companion of a loved and chosen husband, but to be the breeder of human cattle for the field or the auction block."

Down in such mire has the black motherhood of this race struggled—starving its own wailing offspring to nurse to the world their swaggering masters; welding for its children chains which affronted even the moral sense of an unmoral world. Many a man and woman in the South have lived in wedlock as holy as Adam and Eve and brought forth their brown and golden children, but because the darker woman was helpless, her chivalrous and whiter mate could cast her off at his pleasure and publicly sneer at the body he had privately blasphemed.

I shall forgive the white South much in its final judgment day: I shall forgive its slavery, for slavery is a world-old habit; I shall forgive its fighting for a well-lost cause, and for remembering that struggle with tender tears; I shall forgive its so-called "pride of race," the passion of its hot blood, and even its dear, old, laughable strutting and posing; but one thing I shall never forgive, neither in this world nor the world to come: its wanton and continued and persistent insulting of the black womanhood which it sought and seeks to prostitute to its lust. I cannot forget that it is such Southern gentlemen into whose hands smug Northern hypocrites of today are seeking to place our women's eternal destiny—men who insist upon withholding from my mother and wife and daughter those signs and appellations of courtesy and respect, which elsewhere he withholds only from bawds and courtesans.

The result of this history of insult and degradation has been both fearful and glorious. It has birthed the haunting prostitute, the brawler, and the beast of burden; but it has also given the world an efficient womanhood, whose strength lies in its freedom and whose chastity was won in the teeth of temptation and not in prison and swaddling clothes.

To no modern race does its women mean so much as to the Negro nor come so near to the fulfilment of its meaning. As one of our women writes: "Only the black woman can say 'when and where I enter, in the quiet, undisputed dignity of my womanhood, without violence and without suing or special patronage, then and there the whole Negro race enters with me.'"

They came first, in earlier days, like foam flashing on dark, silent waters—bits of stern, dark womanhood here and there tossed almost carelessly aloft to the world's notice. First and naturally they assumed the panoply of the ancient African mother of men, strong and black, whose very nature beat back the wilderness of oppression and contempt. Such a one was that cousin of my grandmother, whom western Massachusetts remembers as "Mum Bett."[1] Scarred for life by a blow received in defense of a sister, she ran away to Great Barrington and was the first slave, or one of the first, to be declared free under the Bill of Rights of 1780. The son of the judge who freed her writes:

Even in her humble station, she had, when occasion required it, an air of command which conferred a degree of dignity and gave her an ascendancy over those of her rank, which is very unusual in persons of any rank or color. Her determined and resolute character, which enabled her to limit the ravages of Shays' mob, was manifested in her conduct and deportment during her whole life. She claimed no distinction, but it was yielded to her from her superior experience, energy, skill, and sagacity. Having known this woman as familiarly as I knew either of my parents, I cannot believe in the moral or physical inferiority of the race to which she belonged. The degradation of the African must have been otherwise caused than by natural inferiority. . . .

From such spiritual ancestry came two striking figures of war-time—Harriet Tubman and Sojourner Truth.

For eight or ten years previous to the breaking out of the Civil War, Harriet Tubman was a constant attendant at anti-slavery conventions, lectures, and other meetings; she was a black woman of medium size, smiling countenance, with her upper front teeth gone, attired in coarse

---

[1] [Real name Elizabeth Freeman. According to tradition, Jacob Burghardt's second wife.]

but neat clothes, and carrying always an old-fashioned reticule at her side. Usually as soon as she sat down she would drop off in sound sleep.

She was born a slave in Maryland, in 1820, bore the marks of the lash on her flesh; and had been made partially deaf, and perhaps to some degree mentally unbalanced by a blow on the head in childhood. Yet she was one of the most important agents of the Underground Railroad and a leader of fugitive slaves. She ran away in 1849 and went to Boston in 1854, where she was welcomed into the homes of the leading abolitionists and where every one listened with tense interest to her strange stories. She was absolutely illiterate, with no knowledge of geography, and yet year after year she penetrated the slave states and personally led North over three hundred fugitives without losing a single one. A standing reward of $10,000 was offered for her, but she said: "The whites cannot catch us, for I was born with the charm, and the Lord has given me the power." She was one of John Brown's closest advisers and only severe sickness prevented her presence at Harper's Ferry.

When the war cloud broke, she hastened to the front, flitting down along her own mysterious paths, haunting the armies in the field, and serving as guide and nurse and spy. She followed Sherman in his great march to the sea and was with Grant at Petersburg, and always in the camps the Union officers silently saluted her.

The other woman belonged to a different type—a tall, gaunt, black, unsmiling sybil, weighted with the woe of the world. She ran away from slavery and giving up her own name took the name of Sojourner Truth. She says: "I can remember when I was a little, young girl, how my old mammy would sit out of doors in the evenings and look up at the stars and groan, and I would say, 'Mammy, what makes you groan so?' And she would say, 'I am groaning to think of my poor children; they do not know where I be and I don't know where they be. I look up at the stars and they look up at the stars!' "

Her determination was founded on unwavering faith in ultimate good. Wendell Phillips says that he was once in Faneuil Hall, when Frederick Douglass was one of the chief speakers. Douglass had been describing the wrongs of the Negro race and as he proceeded he grew more and more excited and finally ended by saying that they had no hope of justice from the whites, no possible hope except in their own right arms. It must come to blood! They must fight for themselves. Sojourner Truth was sitting, tall and dark, on the very front seat facing the platform, and in the hush of feeling when Douglass sat down she spoke out in her deep, peculiar voice, heard all over the hall:

"Frederick, is God dead?"

Such strong, primitive types of Negro womanhood in America seem to some to exhaust its capabilities. They know less of a not more worthy, but a finer type of black woman wherein trembles all of that delicate sense of beauty and striving for self-realization, which is as characteristic of the Negro soul as is its quaint strength and sweet laughter. George Washington wrote in grave and gentle courtesy to a Negro woman, in 1776, that he would "be happy to see" at his headquarters at any time, a person "to whom nature has been so liberal and beneficial in her dispensations." This child, Phillis Wheatley, sang her trite and halting strain to a world that wondered and could not produce her like. Measured today her muse was slight and yet, feeling her striving spirit, we call to her still in her own words:

"Through thickest glooms look back, immortal shade."

Perhaps even higher than strength and art loom human sympathy and sacrifice as characteristic of Negro womanhood. Long years ago, before the Declaration of Independence, Kate Ferguson was born in New York. Freed, widowed, and bereaved of her children before she was twenty, she took the children of the streets of New York, white and black, to her empty arms, taught them, found them homes, and with Dr. Mason of Murray Street Church established the first modern Sunday School in Manhattan.

Sixty years later came Mary Shadd up out of Delaware. She was tall and slim, of that ravishing dream-born beauty—that twilight of the races which we call mulatto. Well-educated, vivacious, with determination shining from her sharp eyes, she threw herself singlehanded into the great Canadian pilgrimage when thousands of hunted black men hurried northward and crept beneath the protection of the lion's paw. She became teacher, editor, and lecturer; tramping afoot through winter snows, pushing without blot or blemish through crowd and turmoil to conventions and meetings, and finally becoming recruiting agent for the United States government in gathering Negro soldiers in the West.

After the war the sacrifice of Negro women for freedom and uplift is one of the finest chapters in their history. Let one life typify all: Louise De Mortie, a free-born Virginia girl, had lived most of her life in Boston. Her high forehead, swelling lips, and dark eyes marked her for a woman of feeling and intellect. She began a successful career as a public reader. Then came the War and the Call. She went to the orphaned colored children of New Orleans—out of freedom into insult and oppression and into the teeth of the yellow fever. She toiled and dreamed. In 1887 she had raised money and built an orphan home and that same year, in the thirty-fourth year of her young life, she died, saying simply: "I belong to God."

As I look about me today in this veiled world of mine, despite the noisier and more spectacular advance of my brothers, I instinctively feel and know that it is the five million women of my race who really count. Black women (and women whose grandmothers were black) are today furnishing our teachers; they are the main pillars of those social settlements which we call churches; and they have with small doubt raised three-fourths of our church property. If we have today, as seems likely, over a billion dollars of accumulated goods, who shall say how much of it has been rung from the hearts of servant girls and washerwomen and women toilers in the fields? As makers of two million homes these women are today seeking in marvelous ways to show forth our strength and beauty and our conception of the truth. . . .

What is today the message of these black women to America and to the world? The uplift of women is, next to the problem of the color line and the peace movement, our greatest modern cause. When, now, two of these movements—woman and color—combine in one, the combination has deep meaning.

In other years women's way was clear: to be beautiful, to be petted, to bear children. Such has been their theoretic destiny and if perchance they have been ugly, hurt, and barren, that has been forgotten with studied silence. In partial compensation for this narrowed destiny the white world has lavished its politeness on its womankind—its chivalry and bows, its uncoverings and courtesies—all the accumulated homage disused for courts and kings and craving exercise. The revolt of white women against this preordained destiny has in these latter days reached splendid proportions, but it is the revolt of an aristocracy of brains and ability—the middle class and rank and file still plod on in the appointed path, paid by the homage, the almost mocking homage, of men.

From black women of America, however (and from some others, too, but chiefly from black women and their daughters' daughters), this gauze has been withheld and without semblance of such apology they have been frankly trodden under the feet of men. They are and have been objected to, apparently for reasons peculiarly exasperating to reasoning human beings. When in this world a man comes forward with a thought, a deed, a vision, we ask not, how does he look—but what is his message? It is of but passing interest whether or not the messenger is beautiful or ugly—the *message* is the thing. This, which is axiomatic among men, has been in past ages but partially true if the messenger was a woman. The world still wants to ask that a woman primarily be pretty and if she is not, the mob pouts and asks querulously, "What else are women for?" Beauty "is its own excuse for being," but there are other excuses, as most men know, and when the white world objects to black women because it does not consider them beautiful, the black world of right asks two questions: "What is beauty?" and, "Suppose you think them ugly, what then? If ugliness and unconventionality and eccentricity of face and deed do not hinder men from doing the world's work and reaping the world's reward, why should it hinder women?"

Other things being equal, all of us, black and white, would prefer to be beautiful in face and form and suitably clothed; but most of us are not so, and one of the mightiest revolts of the century is against the devilish decree that no woman is a woman who is not by present standards a beautiful woman. This decree the black women of America have in large measure escaped from the first. Not being expected to be merely ornamental, they have girded themselves for work, instead of adorning their bodies only for play. Their sturdier minds have concluded that if a woman be clean, healthy, and educated, she is as pleasing as God wills and far more useful than most of her sisters. If in addition to this she is pink and white and straight-haired, and some of her fellow-men prefer this, well and good; but if she is black or brown and crowned in curled mists (and this to us is the most beautiful thing on earth), this is surely the flimsiest excuse for spiritual incarceration or banishment.

The very attempt to do this in the case of Negro Americans has strangely over-reached itself. By so much as the defective eyesight of the white world rejects black women as beauties, by so much the more it needs them as human beings—an enviable alternative, as many a white woman knows. Consequently, for black women alone, as a group, "handsome is that handsome does" and they are asked to be no more beautiful than God made them, but they are asked to be efficient, to be strong, fertile, muscled, and able to work. If they marry, they must as independent workers be able to help support their children, for their men are paid on a scale which makes sole support of the family often impossible. . . .

What does this mean? It forecasts a mighty dilemma which the whole world of civilization, despite its will, must one time frankly face: the unhusbanded mother or the childless wife. God send us a world with woman's freedom and married motherhood inextricably wed, but until He sends it. I see more of future promise in the betrayed girl-mothers of the black belt than in the childless wives of the white North, and I have more respect for the colored serv-ant who yields to her frank longing for motherhood than for her white sister who offers up children for clothes. Out of a sex freedom that today makes us shudder will come in time a day when we will no longer pay men for work they do not do, for the sake of their harem; we will pay women what they earn and insist on their working and earning it; we will allow those persons to vote who know enough to vote, whether they be black or female, white or male; and we will ward race suicide, not by further burden-ing the over-burdened, but by honoring motherhood, even when the sneaking father shirks his duty.

"Wait till the lady passes," said a Nashville white boy.

"She's no lady; she's a nigger," answered another.

So some few women are born free, and some amid insult and scarlet letters achieve freedom; but our women in black had freedom thrust contemptuously upon them. With that freedom they are buying an untrammeled independence and dear as is the price they pay for it, it will in the end be worth every taunt and groan. Today the dreams of the mothers are coming true. We have still our poverty and degradation, our lewdness and our cruel toil; but we have, too, a vast group of women of Negro blood who for strength of character, cleanness of soul, and unselfish devotion of purpose, is today easily the peer of any group of women in the civilized world. And more than that, in the great rank and file of our five million women we have the up-working of new revolutionary ideals, which must in time have vast influence on the thought and action of the land.

For this, their promise, and for their hard past, I honor

the women of my race. Their beauty—their dark and mysterious beauty of midnight eyes, crumpled hair, and soft, full-featured faces—is perhaps more to me than to you, because I was born to its warm and subtle spell; but their worth is yours as well as mine. No other women on earth could have emerged from the hell of force and temptation which once engulfed and still surrounds black women in America with half the modesty and womanliness that they retain. I have always felt like bowing myself before them in all abasement, searching to bring some tribute to these long-suffering victims, these burdened sisters of mine, whom the world, the wise, white world, loves to affront and ridicule and wantonly to insult. I have known the women of many lands and nations—I have known and seen and lived beside them, but none have I known more sweetly feminine, more unswervingly loyal, more desperately earnest, and more instinctively pure in body and in soul than the daughters of my black mothers. This, then—a little thing—to their memory and inspiration.

From THE CRISIS

Much work has yet to be done before it is possible to make a final evaluation of the influence of W. E. B. Du Bois as editor of The Crisis magazine, which he founded in November 1910 to serve both as the organ of the young National Association for the Advancement of Colored People and as his own sounding board. But we do know that for almost 25 years The Crisis as the voice of Du Bois was the clarion to black America.

As editor, Du Bois encouraged young Negro writers, artists, musicians, actors, and teachers, and he published many of their works. But it was his own prodigious labors—essays, criticism, editorials, columns, stories, poems—that made the magazine and gave it so much impact that it was certainly one of the best edited and most powerful publications the country has known. The contents of The Crisis under Du Bois are still relevant to our times.

The editor's pen seemed to be tireless and to touch effectively almost every topic of interest to struggling humanity. In The Crisis observe that he wrote about education, civil rights, Africa, lynching, chain gangs, intermarriage, history, sociology, drama, the class struggle, the Soviet Union, politics, organized labor, the foreign born, women's suffrage, the League of Nations, war, peace, the church, morality, children, nature, and more.

Du Bois' colleagues in the NAACP were in a better position to judge his influence than anyone else. In June 1934 when Du Bois resigned as editor of The Crisis, after a controversy involving both issues and personalities, the NAACP board still felt that it had to pay Du Bois a debt and did in part pay it in the following tribute:

He founded THE CRISIS without a cent of capital, and for many years made it completely self-supporting, reaching a maximum circulation at the end of World War I of 100,000. This is an unprecedented achievement in American journalism, and in itself worthy of a distinguished tribute. But the ideas which he propounded in it and in his books and essays transformed the Negro world as well as a large portion of the liberal white world. . . . He created, what never existed before, a Negro intelligentsia. . . . Without him, the Association could never have been what it was and is.

A recent Du Bois biographer, Francis L. Broderick, points out that to the Negro world Dr. Du Bois was the symbol of The Crisis *and* The Crisis *was the symbol of the NAACP. Broderick asserts that Du Bois'* "best writing appeared in his monthly editorials, in which he clothed his facts with wit, paradox, indignation, and a call to arms. His editorials, with their brevity, luster, and pungency, are his lasting literary monument." *Truman Nelson, referring to Du Bois'* work on The Crisis, *concluded that when Du Bois* "began his grand design," *as editor of* The Crisis, "to unify the black intellectual community . . . he was as dangerous as Karl Marx."

The report of the 16th annual NAACP convention in 1925 said: "When The Crisis *has thundered the truth, it is no idle boast to say that thieves have gone to jail, impostors have disappeared, colleges have reorganized, governments have stood at attention and Klans have scurried to cover."*

Others have testified to the influence of The Crisis *on their lives and the lives of their colleagues. One of these is Dr. Horace Mann Bond, head of the education department of Atlanta University, and father of Georgia legislator Julian Bond. Dr. Bond says,* "I was an avid reader of The Crisis *from my earliest literature days . . . Through* The Crisis *Du Bois helped shape my inner world to a degree impossible to imagine. . . . I believe he was the teacher, likewise, of a host of other persons in this country, and throughout the world. For me, and for others, he was the Great Revelator."* *One could quote hundreds in like vein.*

Roughly 10,000,000 copies of The Crisis *were distributed annually under the editorship of Du Bois. The first editorial in the first issue of* The Crisis, *November 1910, defined the intentions of the magazine on truth and honesty. This gave the guidance which the editor religiously followed for 25 years. Our selections are divided roughly into three parts:*

1. CREDO OF MAN AND EDITOR
2. THE STATE OF DEMOCRACY—AMERICAN RACISM
3. A CRUSADE AND "CREDO" FOR BLACK FOLK

CREDO OF MAN AND EDITOR

DU BOIS' PERSONAL CREDO

Du Bois developed the habit of checking up on his own work and ideals by restating over the years what he called his personal credo. There were many such statements from his early school days until his death, several of which appeared in The Crisis. *Those quoted here are typical.*

A Philosophy for 1913

I am by birth and law a free black American citizen.

As such I have both rights and duties.

If I neglect my duties my rights are always in danger.

If I do not maintain my rights I cannot perform my duties.

I will listen, therefore, neither to the fool who would make me neglect the things I ought to do, nor to the rascal who advises me to forget the opportunities which I and my children ought to have, and must have, and will have.

Boldly and without flinching, I will face the hard fact that in this, my fatherland, I must expect insult and discrimination from persons who call themselves philanthropists and Christians and gentlemen. I do not wish to meet this despicable attitude by blows; sometimes I cannot even protest by words; but may God forget me and mine if in time or eternity I ever weakly admit to myself or the world that wrong is not wrong, that insult is not insult, or that color discrimination is anything but an inhuman and damnable shame.

Believing this with my utmost soul, I shall fight race prejudice continually. If possible, I shall fight it openly and decidedly by word and deed. When that is not possible I will give of my money to help others to do the deed and say the word which I cannot. This contribution to the greatest of causes shall be my most sacred obligation.

Whenever I meet personal discrimination on account of

my race and color I shall protest. If the discrimination is old and deep seated, and sanctioned by law, I shall deem it my duty to make my grievance known, to bring it before the organs of public opinion and to the attention of men of influence, and to urge relief in courts and legislatures.

I will not, because of inertia or timidity or even sensitiveness, allow new discriminations to become usual and habitual. To this end I will make it my duty without ostentation, but with firmness, to assert my right to vote, to frequent places of public entertainment and to appear as a man among men. I will religiously do this from time to time, even when personally I prefer the refuge of friends and family.

While thus fighting for Right and Justice, I will keep my soul clean and serene. I will not permit cruel and persistent persecution to deprive me of the luxury of friends, the enjoyment of laughter, the beauty of sunsets, or the inspiration of a well-written word. Without bitterness (but also without lies), without useless recrimination (but also without cowardly acquiescence), without unnecessary heartache (but with no self-deception), I will walk my way, with uplifted head and level eyes, respecting myself too much to endure without protest studied disrespect from others, and steadily refusing to assent to the silly exaltation of a mere tint of skin or curl of hair.

In fine, I will be a man and know myself to be one, even among those who secretly and openly deny my manhood, and I shall persistently and unwaveringly seek by every possible method to compel all men to treat me as I treat them.

JANUARY, 1913

I Am Resolved

I am resolved in this New Year to play the man—to stand straight, look the world squarely in the eye, and walk to my work with no shuffle or slouch.

I am resolved to be satisfied with no treatment which ignores my manhood and my right to be counted as one among men.

I am resolved to be quiet and law abiding, but to refuse to cringe in body or in soul, to resent deliberate insult, and to assert my just rights in the face of wanton aggression.

I am resolved to defend and assert the absolute equality of the Negro race with any and all other human races and its divine right to equal and just treatment.

I am resolved to be ready at all times and in all places to bear witness with pen, voice, money and deed against the horrible crime of lynching, the shame of "Jim Crow" legislation, the injustice of all color discrimination, the wrong of disfranchisement for race or sex, the iniquity of war under any circumstances and the deep damnation of present methods of distributing the world's work and wealth.

I am resolved to defend the poor and the weak of every race and hue, and especially to guard my mother, my wife, my daughter and all my darker sisters from the insults and aggressions of white men and black, with the last strength of my body and the last suffering of my soul.

For all these things, *I am resolved* unflinchingly to stand, and if this resolve cost me pain, poverty, slander and even life itself, I will remember the Word of the Prophet, how he sang:

> *"Though Love repine and Reason chafe,*
> *There came a Voice, without reply,*
> *'Tis man's Perdition to be safe*
> *When for the Truth he ought to die!"*

JANUARY, 1915

THE CREDO OF *THE CRISIS*

All through the years of his editorship of The Crisis, *Du Bois repeatedly emphasized the magazine's high standards and devotion to courage, education, honesty, fairness, truth, and literacy. Four sample editorials which might be called the credo of* The Crisis *and of Du Bois the editor follow:*

The First Editorial in the First Crisis

The object of this publication is to set forth those facts and arguments which show the danger of race prejudice, particularly as manifested to-day toward colored people. It takes its name from the fact that the editors believe that this is a critical time in the history of the advancement of men. Catholicity and tolerance, reason and forbearance can to-day make the world-old dream of human brotherhood approach realization; while bigotry and prejudice, emphasized race consciousness and force can repeat the awful history of the contact of nations and groups in the past. We strive for this higher and broader vision of Peace and Good Will.

The policy of THE CRISIS will be simple and well defined.

It will, first and foremost, be a newspaper: it will record important happenings and movements in the world which bear on the great problem of interracial relations, and especially those which affect the Negro American.

Secondly, it will be a review of opinion and literature, recording briefly books, articles and important expressions of opinions in the white and colored press on the race problem.

Thirdly, it will publish a few short articles.

Finally, its editorial page will stand for the rights of men, irrespective of color or race, for the highest ideals of American democracy, and for reasonable but earnest and persistent attempt to gain these rights and realize these ideals. The magazine will be the organ of no clique or party and will avoid personal rancor of all sorts. In the absence of proof to the contrary it will assume honesty of purpose on the part of all men, North and South, white and black.

NOVEMBER, 1910

The Gall of Bitterness

Many people object to the policy of THE CRISIS because, as they usually put it, THE CRISIS is "bitter." Some add that our news is depressing or that we are determined to look on the dark side, and so forth.

It may be acknowledged at the outset that THE CRISIS does not try to be funny. Not that we object to fun: our office is a cheerful place, with bits of sunshine and eager young lives and high joyful purpose. But our stock in trade is not jokes. We are in earnest. This is a newspaper. It tries to tell the Truth. It will not consciously exaggerate in any way, but its whole reason for being is the revelation of the facts of racial antagonism now in the world, and these facts are not humorous.

True it is that this country has had its appetite for facts on the Negro problem spoiled by sweets. In earlier days the Negro minstrel who "jumped Jim Crow" was the typical black man served up to the national taste. It was the balmy day when slaves were "happy" and "preferred" slavery to all other possible states. Then came the sobering of abolition days and war, when for one horrified moment the world gazed on the hell of slavery and knew it for what it was.

In the last fifteen years there has come another campaign of Joy and Laughter to degrade black folk. We have been told that all was well or if aught was wrong the wrong was with the colored man. We have had audiences entertained with "nigger" stories, tales of pianos in cabins, and of the general shiftlessness of the freedman, and concerted effort to make it appear that the wrongs of color prejudice are but incidental and trivial, while the shortcomings of black men are stupendous, if not fatal.

This is the lie which THE CRISIS is here to refute. It is a lie, a miserable and shameful lie, which some black men have helped the white South to spread and been well paid for their pains.

It is not easy to impress the real truth after this debauch of defamation, but we must try. In so trying we realize that the mere statement of the facts does not always carry its message. Often the lighter touch, the insinuation and the passing reference are much more effective. We know this, and yet so often the grim awfulness of the bare truth is so insistent we feel it our duty to state it. Take those stark and awful corpses, men murdered by lynch law, in last month's issue: it was a gruesome thing to publish, and yet—could the tale have been told otherwise? Can the nation otherwise awaken to the enormity of this beastly crime of crimes, this rape of law and decency? Could a neat joke or a light allusion make this nation realize what 2,500 murders such as these look like?

We trust that the Gall of Bitterness will not spoil the pages of THE CRISIS or make its readers to shudder at ill-timed frankness. But God forbid that mere considerations of pleasantry and sweetness should ever make us withhold insistence, in season and out, upon that which a Southern white correspondent of ours calls "the barbarous treatment accorded an unfortunate people by the strong and arrogant Caucasian. When Truth shall have come into her own, through the medium of education, the color line will be swept into oblivion of a dark and disgraceful past. Men will shudder at the deeds of their fathers, even as we shudder at the horrors of the Inquisition."

FEBRUARY, 1912

Except by Silence!

Who ever tried harder than the Negro and his "friends" to use the lie for social betterment? We have lied about the South so strenuously that this may account for the persistent blackness of our faces. Oh, yes: the South is the true, tried friend of Negroes; the South wants them educated; the South detests lynching; the South loves black mammies and buries them handsomely; the little playful antics of mobs are but ebullitions of Anglo-Saxon energy or at worst the faults of "poor white trash," who do not count. Moreover, those who dispute these statements are either meddling white Northerners or impudent Negroes who want to marry white women.

All of this we black folk and our "friends" have been saying glibly and frequently. We were lying, and we knew we were lying, *to make the "falsehood come true";* but did the world know this? Did we not lull this nation to false security and fatuous insensibility? And is the uneasiness of our friends at the plain talk of THE CRISIS the cause of ugly feeling or the necessary result of ridiculous lies? How far may we indeed meddle with the truth? . . .

Humanity is progressing toward an ideal; but not, please God, solely by help of men who sit in cloistered ease, hesitate from action and seek sweetness and light; rather we progress today, as in the past, by the soul-torn strength of those who can never sit still and silent while the disinherited and the damned clog our gutters and gasp their lives out on our front porches.

These are the men who go down in the blood and dust of battle. They say ugly things to an ugly world. They spew the lukewarm fence straddlers out of their mouths, like God of old; they cry aloud and spare not; they shout from the housetops, and they make this world so damned uncomfortable with its nasty burden of evil that it tries to get good and does get better.

Evolution is evolving the millennium, but one of the unescapable factors in evolution are the men who hate wickedness and oppression with perfect hatred, who will not equivocate, will not excuse, and will be heard. With the sainted spirits of such as these THE CRISIS would weakly but earnestly stand and cry in the world's four corners of the way; and it claims no man as friend who dare not stand and cry with it.

MAY, 1914

The Philosophy of Mr. Dole

... "Don't antagonize, don't be bitter; say the conciliatory thing; make friends and do not repel them; insist on and emphasize the cheerful and good and dwell as little as possible on wrong and evil."

THE CRISIS does not believe in this policy so far as the present status of the American Negro problem is concerned. We could imagine many social problems, and many phases in a particular problem, when the watchful waiting, the tactfully conciliatory attitude would be commendable and worth while. At other times it would be suicidal and this, in our opinion, is one of the times. . . .

For now nearly twenty years we have made of ourselves mudsills for the feet of this Western world. We have echoed and applauded every shameful accusation made against 10,000,000 victims of slavery. Did they call us inferior half-beasts? We nodded our simple heads and whispered: "We is." Did they call us women prostitutes and our children bastards? We smiled and cast a stone at the bruised breasts of our wives and daughters. Did they accuse of laziness 4,000,000 sweating, struggling laborers, half paid and cheated out of much of that? We shrieked: "Ain't it so?" We laughed with them at our color, we joked at our sad past, and we told chicken stories to get alms.

And what was the result? We got "friends." I do not believe any people ever had so many "friends" as the American Negro today! He has nothing but "friends" and may the good God deliver him from most of them, for they are like to lynch his soul.

What is it to be a friend of the Negro? It is to believe in anything for him except, perhaps, total and immediate annihilation. Short of that, good and kind friends of colored folk believe that he is, in Mr. Dooley's charming phrase, "aisily lynched," and ought to be occasionally. Even if 2,662 accused black people have been publicly lynched, burned and mutilated in twenty-eight years (not to mention the murder of perhaps 10,000 other black folk), our friends think we ought not to disturb the good President of these United States because *the wonder is that there is so little killing!*

It is the old battle of the better and the best. The worst foes of Negro manhood today are those compromising friends who are willingly satisfied with even less than half a loaf. They want the Negro educated; but the South objects to Negro colleges. Oh, very well, then, high schools; but the South objects to "literary" training for "niggers!" Dear, dear! Then "industrial" training; but the South objects to training any considerable number of Negroes for industry; it wants them for menial service. Very well, train them as servants and field hands—anything as long as it is "education!" Then we and THE CRISIS rise and say: *"But—"* Our friends raise deprecating hands; they adjust the sofa pillows, shade the light, and say: "Now, now! *Give them the benefit of the doubt!"*

Or we clamor for the right to vote. "Of course you should vote," say our friends. "But," says the South, "they are too ignorant and inexperienced; we will vote for them." "Excellent," cry our friends, "vote for them and guard them in their civil rights." "What's this?" asks the South. "We mean their economic rights," say our friends glibly, "their right to work and get property." "Yes," answers the South calmly, "the right to work, and we'll work them." "But—" cries THE CRISIS and the black man who has been worked long enough. "Sh!" answer our friends. *"You'll halt the procession!"*

That's precisely what we intend to do. For twenty-five years we have let the procession go by until the systematic denial of manhood rights to black men in America is the crying disgrace of the century. We have wrongs, deep and bitter wrongs. There are local and individual exceptions; there are some mitigating circumstances; there is much to be excused; there is much to be said; and yet for the great mass of 10,000,000 Americans of Negro descent these things are true:

We are denied education.

We are driven out of the Church of Christ.

We are forced out of hotels, theatres and public places.

We are publicly labeled like dogs when we travel.

We can seldom get decent employment.

We are forced down to the lowest wage scale.

We pay the highest rent for the poorest homes.

We cannot buy property in decent neighborhoods.

We are held up to ridicule in the press and on the platform and stage.

We are disfranchised.

We are taxed without representation.

We are denied the right to choose our friends or to be chosen by them, but must publicly announce ourselves as social pariahs or be suggestively kicked by the *Survey*.

In law and custom our women have no rights which a white man is bound to respect.

We cannot get justice in the courts.

We are lynched with impunity.

We are publicly, continuously and shamefully insulted from the day of our birth to the day of our death.

And yet we are told not to be "self-conscious"; to lie about the truth in order to make it "come true"; to grapple with the "philosophy of evolution"; and not to make people "feel ugly" by telling them "ugly facts." . . .

MAY, 1914

THE STATE OF DEMOCRACY—
AMERICAN RACISM.

Through experience, observation, and long and careful study Du Bois became entirely familiar with the essentially racist character of his country and its private, public, and quasi-public institutions. From a vast inventory of information about the United States he was able to write many powerful and persuasive essays and editorials in The Crisis *exposing racism, exploitation, and injustice. These undoubtedly helped to create the mood, methods, and aims of the modern civil rights movement.*

THE "LYNCHING INDUSTRY"

Du Bois probably devoted more space to lynching than to any other evil. He saw it as a source of American lawlessness and violence and as a club to enforce social control. In addition to reporting the atrocities as they occurred, he published an annual summary of lynchings.

Crime and Lynching

A favorite argument with shallow thinkers is: Stop crime and lynching will cease. Such a statement is both historically and logically false. Historically, lynching leads to lynching, burning to burning; and lynching for great crimes to lynching for trivial offenses. Moreover, lynching as practised to-day in the United States is not the result of crime—it is a cause of crime, on account of the flagrant, awful injustice it inflicts in so many cases on innocent men. . . .

What now must be the feeling of the Negroes . . . ? Are they appalled at their own wickedness? Do they see that the wages of sin is death? Not they. They despise the white man's justice, hate him, and whenever they hear of Negro "crime" in the future they will say: "It's a white man's lie."

113

Not only this, but these people know how criminals are made and they pity rather than condemn them. Take, for instance, the cries throughout the South against "vagrants." It means the call for the State enslavement of any man who does not work for a white man at the white man's price. The most outrageous laws and arrests are made under the excuse of vagrancy. In Atlanta, on October 15, thirty-seven laborers were arrested at night in their lodging house as "vagrants." In Texas five laborers were arrested as vagrants and proved their hard, steady jobs. "But," remarks the Galveston Tribune chirpily:

"The State chose to prosecute under a different portion of the law, alleging loitering about houses of ill-fame. The court explained, as he has done before, that a person can be a vagrant yet be steadily employed, the law being general in its effect and covering many points upon which a conviction can be had on a charge of vagrancy."

Suppose now a mischievous boy or a loiterer or a laborer out of work is thrown into jail as a vagrant, what happens to him?

From a thousand examples, let us choose but one from a Texas report on a local "chain gang":

"The day's program was invariably this: Up at 4:30 o'clock in the morning, trot two to five miles to the cane fields, work there in squads until noon, when fifteen to twenty minutes would be allowed for the eating of a cold dinner; driven hard during the afternoon and brought back by starlight at night in the same dog trot they went out in the morning. The weak must keep up with the strong in his work or be punished. Convicts slept in their underclothes or naked, as it happened to rain or shine during the day. If it rained they hung up their clothes to dry and slept without. One convict testified that he had frequently taken his clothes from the nail frozen stiff. One man was on a farm a year, and during that time the bedclothes were not washed and were sunned but twice."

Thus desperate criminals are manufactured and turned out day by day.

Can we stop this by lynching? No. The first step toward stopping crime is to stop lynching. The next step is to treat black men like human beings.

JANUARY, 1912

The Shubuta Lynchings

On Friday night, December 20, four Negroes—Andrew Clark, age 15; Major Clark, age 20; Maggie Howze, age 20; and Alma Howze, age 16, were taken from the little jail at Shubuta, Mississippi, and lynched on a bridge which spans the Chickasawha River near the town. They were suspected of having murdered a Dr. E. L. Johnston, whom the papers stated was "a wealthy retired dentist." These were the meagre facts as given in the press dispatches. The real facts in the case are as follows:

Instead of being an old man Dr. Johnson was thirty-five years of age, a failure at his profession and living at the time of the lynchings on his father's farm where he had with him Maggie Howze whom he had seduced and who was about to bear him a child. On the same farm were Maggie's sister Alma, also a victim of Johnson, and two colored boys, Major and Andrew Clark who were working out a debt of their father's to the Johnsons. Major Clark began going with Maggie and they planned to marry. Dr. Johnson, hearing of this quarreled violently with Major Clark telling him to leave his woman alone. Matters were at this point when the doctor was killed early one morning near his barn.

It is common gossip about Shubuta that the murder was committed by a white man who had his grudge against Johnson and who felt he could safely kill the dentist and have the blame fall on the Negro. At any rate, after subjecting the boy to extreme torture, a confession was secured from Major that he had committed the murder. At this preparations for the lynching began.

Major and Andrew Clark, Maggie and Alma Howze had all been arrested. After Major's "confession" they were taken to Shubuta for trial and placed in a little jail there. The mob secured the keys of the jail from the deputy sheriff in charge of the place without trouble, took out the prisoners, and drove them to the place chosen for their execution, a little covered bridge over the Chickasawha River. Four ropes were produced and four ends were tied to a girder on the under side of the bridge, while the other four ends were made into nooses and fastened securely around the necks of the four Negroes, who were standing on the bridge. Up to the last moment the Negroes protested their innocence and begged the mob not to lynch them. Just as they were about to be killed, Maggie Howze screamed and fought, crying out, "I ain't guilty of killing the doctor and you oughtn't to kill me." In order to silence her cries one of the members of the mob seized a monkey wrench and struck her in the mouth with it, knocking her teeth out. She was also hit across the head with the same instrument, cutting a long gash. The four Negroes, when the ropes had been securely fastened about their necks, were taken bodily by the mob and thrown over the side of the bridge. The younger girl and the two boys were killed instantly. Maggie Howze, however, who was a strong and vigorous young woman, twice caught herself on the side of the bridge, thus necessitating her being thrown over the bridge three times. The third time this was done, she died. In the town the next day, members of the mob told laughingly of how hard it had been to kill "that big black Jersey woman."

The older girl of twenty was to have become a mother in four months, while the younger was to have given birth to a child in two weeks. This sixteen-year-old prospective mother was killed on Friday night and at the time of her burial on Sunday afternoon her unborn baby had not died—one could detect its movements within her womb.

A press despatch from Shubuta the day after the lynching took place reads as follows:

"The theory is advanced that the lynchers acted because of the fact that the next term of the court was not due to be convened until next March. It is hinted that the idea of the county being forced to care for and feed four self-confessed assassins of a leading citizen might have aroused the passion of the mob."

MAY, 1919

The Lynching Industry, 1919

According to THE CRISIS' records, 77 Negroes were lynched during the year 1919, of whom 1 was a colored woman and 11 were soldiers; 4 white persons and 3 Mexicans also were lynched—a total of 84 lynchings.

During the year 1918, 64 Negroes were lynched, 5 of whom were colored women; 4 white men were lynched.

Georgia still leads, with an increase of two lynchings; Mississippi takes second place, instead of Texas, with five more lynchings; Alabama, by an increase of five lynchings, ties with Louisiana.

In methods of torture, burnings have increased from 2 in 1918 to 14 in 1919.

———

According to States

Georgia	22	Missouri	2
Mississippi	12	Colorado	2
Alabama	8	West Virginia	2
Louisiana	8	Nebraska	1
Arkansas	7	Washington	1
Texas	5	Tennessee	1
Florida	5	Kansas	1
North Carolina	4	Sonora (Mexico)	1
South Carolina	2		

By Race

Negro	77	Mexican	3
White	4		

By Sex

Male	83	Female	1

Alleged Crimes

Murder	28	Bandits	3
Rape and attempted rape	19	Unknown	2
Trivial causes	9	Burglary	2
Shooting and assault to murder	7	Labor trouble	1
Insulting women	7	Quarrel	1
Intimacy with women	4	Insurrection	1

Methods of Torture

Hanging	43	Drowning	2
Shooting	23	Beating	1
Burning	14	Cutting	1

Negroes Lynched By Years, 1885–1919

1885	78	1895	112
1886	71	1896	80
1887	80	1897	122
1888	95	1898	102
1889	95	1899	84
1890	90	1900	107
1891	121	1901	107
1892	155	1902	86
1893	154	1903	86
1894	134	1904	83

1905	61	1914	69
1906	64	1915	80
1907	60	1916	55
1908	93	1917	44
1909	73	1918	64
1910	65	1919	77
1911	63		
1912	63	Total	3,052
1913	79		

FEBRUARY, 1920

Lynchings

The recent horrible lynchings in the United States, even the almost incredible burning of human beings alive, have raised not a ripple of interest, not a single protest from the United States Government, scarcely a word from the pulpit and not a syllable of horror or suggestion from the Defenders of the Republic, the 100% Americans, or the propagandists of the army and navy. And this in spite of the fact that the cause of the Louisville, Mississippi, bestiality was, according to the Memphis *Commercial-Appeal*, "widespread indignation at the refusal of the Negroes traveling in slow, second-handed Fords to give road to faster cars." And yet hiding and concealing this barbarism by every resource of American silence, we are sitting in council at Geneva and Peking and trying to make the world believe that we are a civilized nation.

AUGUST, 1927

ORGANIZED LABOR

Du Bois was always a believer in the solidarity among the oppressed of all races, and generally he supported organized labor even though it was often racist in theory and deed. He even supported the American Federation of Labor and had The Crisis published with a union label, though no Negro could belong to the union that printed the paper.

Organized Labor

THE CRISIS believes in organized labor. It realizes that the standard of living among workers has been raised in the last half century through the efforts and sacrifice of laborers banded together in unions, and that all American labor to-day, white, black and yellow, benefits from this great movement.

For such reasons we carry on our front cover the printer's union label to signify that the printing and binding of this magazine is done under conditions and with wages satisfactory to the printers' union.

We do this in spite of the fact, as well known to us as to others, that the "conditions satisfactory" to labor men in this city include the deliberate exclusion from decent-paying jobs of every black man whom white workingmen can exclude on any pretense. We know, and all men know, that under ordinary circumstances no black artisan can to-day work as printer, baker, blacksmith, carpenter, hatter, butcher, tailor, street or railway employee, boilermaker, bookbinder, electrical worker, glass blower, machinist, plumber, telegrapher, electrotyper, textile worker, upholsterer, stone cutter, carriage maker, plasterer, mason, painter —or at any other decent trade, unless he works as a "scab," or unless in some locality he has secured such a foothold that the white union men are not able easily to oust him.

This policy is not always avowed (although there are a dozen unions affiliated with the American Federation of Labor who openly confine admission to "white" men), but it is perfectly well understood. Some unions, like the printers and the carpenters, admit a lone colored man here and there so as to enable them the more easily to turn down the rest. Others, like the masons, admit Negroes in the South where they must, and bar them in the North where they can.

Whatever the tactics, the result is the same for the mass of white workingmen in America; beat or starve the Negro out of his job if you can by keeping him out of the union; or, if you must admit him, do the same thing inside union lines.

What then must be the attitude of the black man in the event of a strike like that of the white waiters of New York?

The mass of them must most naturally regard the union white man as their enemy. They may not know the history of the labor movement, but they know the history of white and black waiters in New York, and when they take back the jobs out of which the white waiters have driven them, they do the natural and sensible thing, howsoever pitiable the necessity of such cutthroat policies in the labor world may be. So long as union labor fights for humanity, its mission is divine; but when it fights for a clique of Americans, Irish or German monopolists who have cornered or are trying to corner the market on a certain type of service, and are seeking to sell that service at a premium, while other competent workmen starve, they deserve themselves the starvation which they plan for their darker and poorer fellows.

JULY, 1912

———

THE AMERICAN LEGION

Du Bois used much anti-American Legion material, accusing the Legion of being a racist body.

Th᠆ American Legion

The American Legion is composed, as President Wilson tells us, of "the men who have served in the Army, Navy and Marine Corps, and who are now banding together to preserve the splendid traditions of that service."

The Legion was formed at preliminary meetings, held in Paris and St. Louis, and sought to settle the inevitable color question by giving all authority as to admitting posts to the state bodies. The South promised faithfully to treat Negroes fairly. As a result, in South Carolina "our committee was told flatly by the Executive Committee of the state organization that it was a white man's organization and that Negroes would not be admitted." In Louisiana, Negroes were also excluded; but Virginia caps the climax by offering to admit Negroes on condition that

Officers of state organization be elected by whites.

Executive Committee be elected by whites.

Time and place of meeting be fixed by whites.

Delegates to national convention to be appointed in "equitable" manner between whites and blacks by the Executive Committee.

Constitution may be amended by two-thirds vote of whites.

This action and other considerations have given impetus to several all-Negro veteran associations—The Grand Army of Americans in Washington, D. C.; The League for Democracy in New York; and The American Alliance in Richmond. There is room and work for such colored bodies, *but every Negro soldier and sailor should fight to join the American Legion.* Do not give up the battle. Organize throughout the North and South. In the North there will be little, if any, opposition. In the South every subterfuge will be sought, but force the fight. Make the Bourbons refuse in writing, and then take the question to the national convention. Do not help the rascals to win by giving up.

SEPTEMBER, 1919

DISCRIMINATION IN MEDICINE

The racist record of the American medical profession was a favorite subject for Du Bois' Crisis editorials.

The Woman's Medical College

The Woman's Medical College of Philadelphia has recently had a most difficult and trying experience, and we are writing to commiserate with it.

You see it was this way: Dr. W. E. Atkins of Hampton, Va., colored, has a daughter, Dr. Lillian Atkins Moore. Dr.

Moore is one of the best students that the Woman's Medical College ever had—which was unfortunate. Colored people ought to be fools and when they are geniuses it makes trouble.

Dr. Moore is the only colored graduate this year and was chosen secretary of the Senior Class. She won the Freshman prize in anatomy with an average of 97, passed the Medical Board with a high average and in general made herself a record most unpleasant for the authorities.

Being about to complete her course with distinction she applied October 12, 1922 for an internship in the hospital. A painful silence ensued. In fact it was not until March 2, 1923, after all internes had been appointed, that Dr. Moore had this letter in answer to a reminder that her application was unanswered:

> *Dear Mrs. Moore: I was a little surprised to get your letter in regard to an internship . . . I had been told that we could not possibly undertake to give you a service here. We are all your good friends and it is a most unpleasant thing to have to tell you that just because you are colored we can't arrange to take you comfortably into the hospital. I am quite sure that most of the internes who come to us next year will not give us as good work as you are capable of doing; and I hope that if I can be of any service to you in helping you to secure an internship that you will let me help.*
>
> *Yours truly,*
> *Jessie W. Pryor, M.D.*
> *Medical Director*
> AUGUST, 1923

THE CHRISTIAN CHURCH

All of his adult life Du Bois challenged and ridiculed the hypocrisy and racism of the white Christian establishment.

The Episcopal Church

In the red blood-guiltiness of the Christian church in America toward black folk the Episcopal Church has undoubtedly larger share than any other group. It was the Episcopal Church that for 250 years made itself the center and bulwark of man stealing and chattel slavery. It was the Episcopal Church that deliberately closed its doors in the face of the praying slave; it was the Episcopal Church that refused after the war to educate the freedmen, and is still refusing. . . . Is not this . . . great institution . . . the church of John Pierpont Morgan and not the church of Jesus Christ?

DECEMBER, 1913

The White Christ

It seems fair to judge the christianity of white folk by two present day developments: the World War and Billy Sunday. As to the widespread and costly murder being waged today by the children of the Prince of Peace comment is unnecessary. It simply spell's christianity's failure.

As to Billy Sunday there is room for opinions. Personally we do not object to him; he is quite natural under the circumstances and a fit expression of his day. He is nearly the same thing as the whirling dervish, the snake dancer and devotee of Mumbo Jumbo. Such methods of appealing to primitive passions and emotions have been usual in the history of the world.

Today they are joined, in the case of Mr. Sunday, to picturesque abuse of the English language, unusual contortions and a curious moral obtuseness which allows Mr. Sunday to appropriate a whole speech belonging to Robert Ingersol and use it as his own. The result has been a large number of converts and widespread demand for Mr. Sunday's services. All this seems necessary. Evidently Mr. Sunday's methods are the only ones that appeal to white Christians. Reason does not appeal. Suffering and poverty does not appeal. The lynching and burning of human beings and torturing of women has no effect. Yet the contortions of Mr. Sunday bring people down the "sawdust" trail.

Selah!

But hereafter let no white man sneer at the medicine men of West Africa or the howling of the Negro revival. The

Negro church is at least democratic. It welcomes everybody. It draws no color-line.

MARCH, 1915

RACE JUSTICE

For 25 years Du Bois used The Crisis *to attack the Southern prison system, which he clearly saw as a double evil: (1) a method of securing forced labor for plantations and public and private exploiters and (2) a merciless club for social control. The fee system, the convict lease system, and their horrors aroused as much compassion in Du Bois as any of the other evils perpetuated by the system.*

Anarchism

THE CRISIS has continually insisted that peonage, false arrest and injustice in the Southern courts were responsible for the mass of so-called Negro crime. The testimony to this comes continually from white Southerners themselves. In nearly every Southern State this has been asserted from time to time in official reports, but perhaps the latest and strongest of these confessions comes from Alabama. The Federal grand jury of Jefferson County says that justices and constables are deliberately enriching themselves by a system of extortion and intimidation:

"For victims, whether male or female, it singles out, in every instance, those too poor or ignorant, too humble or frightened to protect themselves. *A very large majority are Negroes.* Were they not Negroes, but *members of a more resentful race, anarchism would be prevalent.*"

WERE THEY NOT NEGROES!

AUGUST, 1912

Lies

As we have repeatedly intimated, the Bourbon South lies. It lies so repeatedly and openly that most innocent bystanders cannot believe it possible. Take, for instance, this letter in *Life* from a Georgia Congressman:

"In regard to the leasing of convicts by the State of Georgia, I desire to say that above five years ago Georgia did away absolutely with that system. No convicts are leased in Georgia and have not been for about five years."

This is a deliberate attempt to deceive the public. Georgia does lease convicts. The only change made in the law five or six years ago was to let the State pay the guards over the private contractors' camps, and to call those twenty-five or more private camps scattered through the State, under the control of private lessees, the "penitentiary!" Then the State says we do not "lease" our convicts, but does not forget to boast in its own reports:

"The contracts so made will bring into the State treasury annually, for a period of five years, beginning April 1, 1904, the gross sum of $340,000, and after deducting the necessary expenses of this department estimated at $115,000, will leave a net amount of $225,000 per annum, which, under the law, will be divided among those counties not using convict labor upon their public roads, according to population, to be used for school or road purposes."

What, in the long run, can any cause gain by systematic lying?

SEPTEMBER, 1913

Logic

One of the interesting ways of settling the race problem comes to the fore in this period of unemployment among the poor. In Waterloo, Ky., the enterprising chief of police is arresting all unemployed Negroes and putting them in jail, thus securing their labor for the state at the cheapest possible figure. This bright idea did not originate in Kentucky. It is used all through the South and strong sermons and editorials are written against "lazy" Negroes.

Despite this there are people in this country who wonder at the increase of "crime" among colored people.

JANUARY, 1915

Courts and Jails

It is to the disgrace of the American Negro, and particularly of his religious and philanthropic organizations, that they continually and systematically neglect Negroes who have been arrested, or who are accused of crime, or who have been convicted and incarcerated.

One can easily realize the reason for this: ever since Emancipation and even before, accused and taunted with being criminals, the emancipated and rising Negro has tried desperately to disassociate himself from his own criminal class. He has been all too eager to class criminals as outcasts, and to condemn every Negro who has the misfortune to be arrested or accused. He has joined with the bloodhounds in anathematizing every Negro in jail, and has called High Heaven to witness that he has absolutely no sympathy and no known connection with any black man who has committed crime.

All this, of course, is arrant nonsense; is a combination of ignorance and pharisaism which ought to put twelve million people to shame. There is absolutely no scientific proof, statistical, social or physical, to show that the American Negro is any more criminal than other elements in the American nation, if indeed as criminal. Moreover, even if he were, what is crime but disease, social or physical? In addition to this, every Negro knows that a frightful proportion of Negroes accused of crime are absolutely innocent. Nothing in the world is easier in the United States than to accuse a black man of crime. In the South, if any crime is committed, the first cry of the mob is, "Find the Negro!" And while they are finding him, the white criminal comfortably escapes. Nothing is easier, South and North, than for a white man to black his face, saddle a felony upon the Negro, and then go wash his body and his soul. Today, if a Negro is accused, whether he is innocent or guilty, he not only is almost certain of conviction, but of getting the limit of the law. What else is the meaning of the extraordinary fact that throughout the United States the number of Negroes hanged, sentenced for life, or for ten, twenty or forty years, is an amazingly large proportion of the total number?

Meantime, what are we doing about it? Here and there, in a few spectacular cases, we are defending persons, where race discrimination is apparent, and where the poor devil of a victim manages to get into the newspaper. But in most cases, the whole black world is dumb and acquiescent; they will not even visit the detention houses where the accused, innocent and guilty, are herded like cattle. They make few systematic attempts to reform the juvenile delinquent who may be guilty of nothing more than energy and mischief. Only in sporadic cases do we visit the jails and hear the tales of the damned.

For a race which boasts its Christianity, and for a Church which squanders its money upon carpets, organs, stained glass, bricks and stone, this attitude toward Negro crime is the most damning accusation yet made.

MARCH, 1932

OFFICIAL AND MILITARY DISCRIMINATION

Dr. Du Bois for many years exposed the action of the courts in nullifying the verdict of the Civil War as expressed in the Negro "Magna Carta"—the 13th, 14th, and 15th amendments. Under the 14th Amendment, representation in Congress was to be based on actual voters. The "officers of the courts" of the American Bar Association were often upbraided by Du Bois for racism.

The Shifty American Bar

In popular imagination the drawing of the color line is a solemn performance done after grave deliberation by perfectly unselfish men, for lofty purpose and for vast contemplative ends.

In the face of such conception what shall be said at the trickery, lying and chicanery that has marked the drawing of racial lines in the American Bar Association? Why should there be such hiding and deception? Is somebody ashamed of something? Is it a discreditable and disreputable thing to say to a man: "If you are black you cannot join the American Bar Association?" If it is not a nasty and un-worthy discrimination to say this, why not say it flatly and first, instead of:

1. Hushing the matter up.
2. Asking the colored man "quietly" to resign.
3. Seeking to break law and precedent in declaring a member not a member, but a "candidate" for membership.
4. Endless and disingenuous explanations, avowing the broadest charity and highest motives.
5. The sending out of new membership blanks calling for information as to the "race and sex" of candidates before the association had authorized such action.
6. The admission that such blanks were sent without authority, but that the matter would be duly reported when it never was reported.
7. A secret bargain which one of the most prominent lawyers in the United States thus describes: "The resolution was presented by ex-President and ex-Secretary of War Dickinson, seconded by an Illinois man, favored by Wickersham, and then the previous question was instantly moved—all evidently in pursuance of a prearranged plan. I need say no more than that after about fifteen minutes of absolute riot the chairman (Fraser of Indiana, put into the chair by Gregory, as I think, because even Gregory was not willing to do what was about to be done) declared the resolution adopted and declared the meeting adjourned. What was actually said or done in the interval it is impossible to tell. A dozen or twenty men were on their feet constantly yelling for recognition by the chair, and the exclusionist gang was yelling 'question!' 'question!' all over the hall, and it was simply a mob. So far as I could judge, when the question was finally put on the resolution, after I had got recognized for a point of order which the chair conceded but gave us no benefit of, there were about 50 'noes' in a meeting of about 500."

In the name of civilization, what were 450 men so ashamed of that they could not step into the light of day and do frankly and openly that which took three official lies, two infractions of the common law, a corrupt bargain and a "mob" to allow the associated bar of the nation to accomplish?

Does anyone suspect that here, as elsewhere, in this land of the free, a number of eminent gentlemen wished opportunity to do a dirty trick in the dark so as to stand in the light and yell: "We give the black man every chance and yet look at him!"

OCTOBER, 1912

Civil Rights

The sweeping away of the last vestiges of Charles Sumner's civil-rights bill by the Supreme Court leaves the Negro no worse off, but it leaves the nation poor, indeed. Charles Sumner tried to do, right on the heels of emancipation, that which must be done before emancipation is complete. As long as a single American citizen, be he poor or black or ill born, can be publicly insulted by common carriers and public servants, just so long is democracy in the United States a contradiction and a farce.

The civil-rights law has long been a dead letter. First it was declared unconstitutional, as far as the States were concerned, in that series of astounding decisions of the Supreme Court, which turned the Fourteenth Amendment from its true purpose as a protector of men into a refuge for corporations. The law, however, still stood as applying to territories, the District of Columbia and the high seas. In the latest decision this vestige goes, but the Negro is by no means left without civil remedy. He is still a citizen and still has a right under common law, the Constitution and general legislation to appeal against discrimination. Let him neglect no opportunity to do that.

AUGUST, 1913

The Fourteenth Amendment

A correspondent asks us "in view of the explicit and imperative terms of the Fourteenth Amendment is it not the binding duty of Congress to cut down southern representation in apportioning members to Congress to the various states?" We answer, it is. But who is going to make Congress do its duty? We are trying to do this and have tried and will continue to try, but we have not yet succeeded.

MAY, 1915

Reduced Representation in Congress

Friends of Democracy and especially friends of over ten million disfranchised persons—white and black—in the South, are called upon today for clear thinking and a knowledge of the facts.

This nation is putting a *premium* upon oligarchy and a *penalty* upon democracy.

The states *can* and *do* control the conditions under which a citizen may or may not vote. By the 15th and 19th Amendments there are only two checks on their power: They cannot legally disfranchise men for *race* or for *sex*....

Hitherto democracy in the United States has assumed that self interest would keep the number of voters *as large as possible* in the various states. This assumption has *failed* in two respects: It has kept *women* from voting for more than a century and it has kept *Negroes* in the South from voting during the better part of a generation....

We have at present only *one* legal remedy and that lies in the Fourteenth Amendment. Many persons, and especially Negroes, assume that the enforcement of the section of the second section of the 14th Amendment would make the disfranchisement of Negroes legal. *This is absolutely untrue.* As long as the 15th Amendment stands, it is absolutely illegal to disfranchise a person because of "race, color or previous condition of servitude." But it is absolutely legal to disfranchise persons for any number of other reasons. Indeed a state might legally disfranchise a person for having red hair.

But here the 14th Amendment steps in and says: "But when the right to vote at any election . . . is denied to any of the male inhabitants of such state (being 21 years of age and citizens of the United States) or in any way abridged . . . the basis of representation therein shall be reduced in . . . proportion . . ." In other words, if for any *legal* reason a state disfranchises its citizens then the representation of that state in Congress must be proportionately reduced.

The Constitution does not attempt to say that the state may not have perfectly good moral ground for such disfranchisement. In sheer self defense it may be proper, temporarily, for a state to disfranchise the ignorant. It might even defend itself, under a just economic system, in disfranchising the poor. But whatever its motives or justification a *state can disfranchise its citizens for any reason except race and sex.* But if it *does* it is liable to have its representation in Congress reduced, and indeed if it believes in democratic government it ought to be willing and eager for such reduction. . . .

FEBRUARY, 1921

Charles Young[1]

The life of Charles Young was a triumph of tragedy. No one ever knew the truth about the Hell he went through at West Point. He seldom even mentioned it. The pain was too great. Few knew what faced him always in his army life. It was not enough for him to do well—he must always do better; and so much and so conspicuously better, as to disarm the scoundrels that ever trailed him. He lived in the army surrounded by insult and intrigue and yet he set his teeth and kept his soul serene and triumphed. . . .

His second going to Africa, after a terrible attack of black water fever, was suicide. He knew it. His wife knew it. His friends knew it. He had been sent to *Africa* because the Army considered his blood pressure too high to let him go to *Europe!* They sent him there to die. They sent him there because he was one of the very best officers in the service and if he had gone to Europe he could not have been denied the stars of a General. They could not stand a black American General. Therefore they sent him to the fever coast of Africa. . . .

He is dead. But the heart of the Great Black Race, the Ancient of Days—the Undying and Eternal—rises and salutes his shining memory: Well done! Charles Young, Soldier and Man and unswerving Friend.

FEBRUARY, 1922

---

[1] [Colonel Young was highest ranking Negro officer at beginning of World War I.]

SOUTHERN CIVILIZATION

Du Bois never passed up a chance to attack the Southern white power structure. He wrote much in The Crisis *against "the lost cause" and its heirs. He is quoted here on the principles and practices of Southern "civilization."*

The Hurt Hound

The editor has received this news note from a colored friend:

"January 22—Revs. G. H. Burks and P. A. Nichols, returning from Louisville to Paducah, Ky., over the I. C. Railroad, on being detained from 5 p. m. to 2 a. m., by reason of a freight wreck, were ushered into the dining car and given supper without one single word of comment or protest from the whites, who were eating at the same time."

The editor read this and read it yet again. At first he thought it was a banquet given to black men by white; then he thought it charity to the hungry poor; then—then it dawned on his darkened soul: Two decently dressed, educated colored men had been allowed to pay for their unobtrusive meal in a Pullman dining car "WITHOUT ONE SINGLE WORD OF COMMENT OR PROTEST!" No one had cursed them; none had thrown plates at them; they were not lynched! And in humble ecstacy at being treated for once like ordinary human beings they rushed from the car and sent a letter a thousand miles to say to the world: "My God! Look! See!"

What more eloquent comment could be made on the white South? What more stinging indictment could be voiced? What must be the daily and hourly treatment of black men in Paducah, Ky., to bring this burst of applause at the sheerest and most negative decency?

Yet every black man in America has known that same elation—North and South and West. We have all of us felt the sudden relief—the half-mad delight when contrary to fixed expectation we were treated as men and not dogs; and then, in the next breath, we hated ourselves for elation over that which was but due any human being.

This is the real tragedy of the Negro in America: the inner degradation, the hurt hound feeling; the sort of upturning of all values which leads some black men to "rejoice" because "only" sixty-four Negroes were lynched in the year of our Lord 1912. . . .

MARCH, 1913

"Southerners"

We are delighted to learn that Walter H. Page, former editor of the *World's Work* and now Ambassador to Great Britain, is not a "Southerner." This point is definitely settled by the editors of a Southern magazine published in New York for the conversion of the heathen.

We had long suspected this. We have used the term "Southerner" in a restricted sense. It did not refer, for instance, to a person born in the South, otherwise (Heaven forfend!) there would be some 8,000,000 black "Southerners"—an unthinkable thing. "Southerner" means something special, limited, definite. It could not refer to Walter Page. Mr. Page, for instance, has worked for the social uplift of the Negro, he has met Negroes on terms of equality, treating them, indeed, as gentlemen. He believes in the right of black men to vote and aspire.

Now all this we learn . . . precludes Mr. Page from being a "Southerner." A "Southerner," it seems, must be a man who has assimilated no new ideas as to democracy and social classes since 1863; he must be "haughty," intolerant and snobbish. His ancestors must have been "aristocrats" and he must have had a black mammy whom he loved, and as an evidence of this love he now and then lynches her grandchildren. But the "Southerner" has one characteristic above this: he hates Niggers; he pursues them vindictively; he chases a drop of Negro blood like a sleuth. He makes it his chief business in life to hound, oppress and insult black folk, and to tell them personally as often as he can how utterly he despises them—except their women, privately. These he likes. The "Southerner" is intensely religious and set on foreign missions. He especially wishes to convert the heathen in China and the Congo Valley. He is also a familiar friend of God and knows more about the religion of Jesus Christ than any other Christian. . . .

NOVEMBER, 1913

Civilization in the South

An interesting exchange of letters has appeared in the New York *Nation* in which a Canadian has taken the South severely to task for lynching and for its pretended excuses for lynching. A Texan has hotly replied that the culture of the South must not be accused of dishonesty nor made responsible for southern barbarities. To which the Canadian replies: "If 'editors, preachers, lawyers, teachers, indeed, all the professional classes, and all business men of consequence,' are as genuinely indignant as your correspondent supposes, the influence of these persons must be painfully small. . . ."

This brings out the real dilemma of those who would interpret the present South. Is the South a land of barbarism leavened with culture, or a land of culture leavened with barbarism? If we accept the former explanation we can explain lynching. It is a barbaric outburst and survival, and against it the better elements of the South are gradually making headway and gaining strength. But they are not yet strong enough to overcome it. Yet this rational explanation makes the Southerners furious. "No!" they yell, "The South is a center of culture and civilization. It is really one of the most civilized parts of the globe. It is 'pure' in its blood and ideals and suited and able to lead the world." But, if this is so, what about lynching and lawlessness? What sort of a culture is it that cannot control itself in the most fundamental of human relations, that is given over to mobs, reactionary legislation and cruel practices? . . .

MARCH, 1917

The House of Jacob

Where is the chief seat of lawlessness in this land?
The South.
Where is the highest murder rate in the land and the fewest convictions?
In the South.
Where is education at its lowest ebb, school terms shortest, teachers' wages lowest, school children fewest?
In the South.
Where is the percentage of child labor highest and the "age of consent" lowest?
In the South.
Who has defied the Constitution of the United States, the statutes of their own states, and the decalogue?
The South.
Who has disfranchised its citizens by wholesale, and for fifty years lynched, burned, and tortured them?
The South.
Who holds forty-two "rotten borough" seats in Congress,

stolen from black men, and uses them to defeat the will of the voters of the land?

The South.

Who elects the President of the United States, in defiance of the number of votes cast?

The South.

Who hates racial amalgamation so bitterly that it has raised three million mulattoes?

The South.

Who is leading the fight in Congress to stop "lawlessness" and "sedition"?

Southerners.

What do they really want to stop?

Criticism of the South.

Who has a body of intelligent, just, men who know that these things are wrong and foul and that they must be righted?

The South.

Where are these men when they are needed for action?

God knows!

What are YOU going to do about it?

"Cry aloud and spare not, lift up thy voice like a trumpet, and shew my people their transgression and the House of Jacob their sins."

FEBRUARY, 1920

A CRUSADE AND "CREDO" FOR BLACK FOLK

In addition to working out a credo for The Crisis *and a personal credo, Du Bois worked on programs or blueprints for racial justice which might be called a Crusade for Black Folk, along the wide front of suffrage, education, protest, self-defense, social equality, migration, self-segregation, black power, race pride, Negro business cooperatives, equal justice under law. His genius is nowhere more evident than in the scope and passion of the articles urging this Crusade.*

The Immediate Program of the American Negro

The immediate program of the American Negro means nothing unless it is mediate to his great ideal and the ultimate ends of his development. We need not waste time by seeking to deceive our enemies into thinking that we are going to be content with a half loaf, or by being willing to lull our friends into a false sense of our indifference and present satisfaction.

The American Negro demands equality—political equality, industrial equality and social equality; and he is never going to rest satisfied with anything less. He demands this in no spirit of braggadocio and with no obsequious envy of others, but as an absolute measure of self-defense and the only one that will assure to the darker races their ultimate survival on earth.

Only in a demand and a persistent demand for essential equality in the modern realm of human culture can any people show a real pride of race and a decent self-respect. For any group, nation or race to admit for a moment the present monstrous demand of the white race to be the inheritors of the earth, the arbiters of mankind and the sole owners of a heritage of culture which they did not create, nor even improve to any greater extent than the other great division of men—to admit such pretense for a moment is for the race to write itself down immediately as indisputably inferior in judgment, knowledge and common sense.

The equality in political, industrial and social life which modern men must have in order to live, is not to be confounded with sameness. On the contrary, in our case, it is rather insistence upon the right of diversity—upon the right of a human being to be a man even if he does not wear the same cut of vest, the same curl of hair or the same color of skin. Human equality does not even entail, as is sometimes said, absolute equality of opportunity; for certainly the natural inequalities of inherent genius and varying gift make this a dubious phase. But there is a more and more clearly recognized minimum of opportunity and maximum of freedom to be, to move and to think, which the modern world denies to no being which it recognizes as a real man.

These involve both negative and positive sides. They call for freedom on the one hand and power on the other. The Negro must have political freedom; taxation without representation is tyranny. American Negroes of to-day are ruled by tyrants who take what they please in taxes and give what they please in law and administration, in justice, and in injustice; and the great mass of black people must stand helpless and voiceless before a condition which has time and time again caused other peoples to fight and die. . . .

In social intercourse every effort is being made today from the President of the United States and the so-called Church of Christ down to saloons and boot-blacks to segregate, strangle and spiritually starve Negroes so as to give them the least possible chance to know and share civilization.

These shackles must go. But that is but the beginning. The Negro must have power; the power of men, the right to do, to know, to feel and to express that knowledge, action and spiritual gift. He must not simply be free from the political tyranny of white folk, he must have the right to vote and to rule over the citizens, white and black, to the extent of his proven foresight and ability. . . . He must have the right to social intercourse with his fellows. There was a time in the atomic individualistic group when "social intercourse" meant merely calls and tea-parties; to-day social intercourse means theatres, lectures, organizations, churches, clubs, excursions, travel, hotels—it means in short Life; to bar a group from such methods of thinking, living and doing is to bar them from the world and bid them create a new world—a task to which no single group is to-day equal; it is to crucify them and taunt them with not being able to live. . . .

APRIL, 1915

EDUCATION

Du Bois believed that education was synonymous with Negro victory over discrimination. He encouraged Negroes, especially the youth, to make all possible sacrifices to obtain as much schooling as possible. He also developed his theory of the "talented tenth," under which the privileged educated members of the race should devote their talents to racial uplift. One of his principal quarrels with Booker T. Washington was over the type of education Negroes should aspire to—industrial or liberal arts—and the very purposes of education. He encouraged student strikes at Fisk and Hampton to get better standards and to get rid of white administrations. He advocated Negro control of all segregated Negro schools.

Education

. . . Are men to earn a living or simply to live for the sake of working? Is there any justice in making a particular body of men the drudges of society, destined for the worst work under the worst conditions and at the lowest pay, simply because a majority of their fellow men for more or less indefinite and superficial reasons do not like them? Manifestly life, and abundant life, is the object of industry and we teach men to earn a living in order that their industry may administer to their own lives and the lives of their fellows. If, therefore, any human being has large ability it is not only for his advantage but for the advantage of all society that he be put to the work that he can do best. To assume that ability is to be measured by so-called racial characteristics—by color, by hair or by stature is not only ridiculous but dangerous. . . .

The result of limiting the education of Negroes under the mask of fitting them for work is the slow strangulation of the Negro college. Howard to-day is dependent upon the precarious support of the majority in Congress; Fisk has an endowment which looks ridiculous beside that of Hampton and Tuskegee. Atlanta has almost no endowment. None of the five major Negro colleges have today any solid financial prospect for growth and development. Not only that but they are regularly sneered at by men who dare not raise their arguments above a sneer. We hear again and again repeated the usual lie that these colleges are persisting in the curriculum of fifty years ago. As a matter of fact practically all of these colleges are conforming to the standard of education as laid down by the highest authorities in this country. What they are really asked to do is to adopt a course of study which does not conform to modern standards, which no modern system of education will recognize and which condemns the student who takes it to end his education in a blind alley. It is the unforgivable sin of some of the greatest so-called industrial schools that the boy who is induced to take their course is absolutely unfitted thereby from continuing his education at a recognized modern institution. This is a crime against childhood for which any nation ought to be ashamed.

Who are the men who are planning the new Negro curriculum? Are they educational experts learned in the theory and practise of training youth? No, most of them never taught a child or held any responsible place in a school system or gave the subject any serious study. Are they friends of the Negro desiring his best interests and development? No, they are friends of the white South and stand openly committed to any demand of the white South.

The latest attack on Negro education comes from Philadelphia. Very adroitly and cunningly the Negroes have been massed in segregated schools. Now "industrial training" is to be introduced *in the Negro schools* and a representative of a leading southern industrial school is on hand to advise!

Do Negroes oppose this because they are ashamed of having their children trained to work? Certainly not. But they know that if their children are compelled to cook and sew when they ought to be learning to read, write and cipher, they will not be able to enter the high school or go to college as the white children are doing. It is a deliberate despicable attempt to throttle the Negro child before he knows enough to protest.

Even in industrial training the white authorities are persistently dishonest. They will not train our children in good paying trades and respectable vocations. They want them to be servants and menials. The excuse which is continually brought forward, particularly in the North, is that there is "no opening" for them in the higher ranges of the industrial world! For this reason opportunities even for the best industrial training are persistently denied colored students. Trade schools in many of the large cities have the habit of forcing colored students who apply into the courses for domestic service or sewing on the plea that millinery, carpentry and various lines of mechanical work offer no opportunity for colored folk. Surely this reduces the argument for industrial training to rank absurdity and the cause of real, honest industrial training deserves more sensible treatment than this.

In all these arguments and actions there blazes one great and shining light: the persistent army of Negro boys and girls pushing through high school and college continues to increase. Negro mothers and fathers are not being entirely deceived. They know that intelligence and self-development are the only means by which the Negro is to win his way in the modern world. They persist in pushing their children on through the highest courses. May they always continue to do so; and may the bright, fine faces on these pages be inspiration to thousands of other boys and girls in the coming years to resist the contemptible temptation so persistently laid before this race to train its children simply as menials and scavengers.

JULY, 1915

Obituary of Booker T. Washington

The death of Mr. Washington marks an epoch in the history of America. He was the greatest Negro leader since Frederick Douglass, and the most distinguished man, white or black, who has come out of the South since the Civil War. His fame was international and his influence far-reaching. Of the good that he accomplished there can be no doubt: he directed the attention of the Negro race in America to the pressing necessity of economic development; he emphasized technical education and he did much to pave the way for an understanding between the white and darker races.

On the other hand there can be no doubt of Mr. Washington's mistakes and shortcomings: he never adequately grasped the growing bond of politics and industry; he did not understand the deeper foundations of human training and his basis of better understanding between white and black was founded on caste.

We may then generously and with deep earnestness lay on the grave of Booker T. Washington testimony of our thankfulness for his undoubted help in the accumulation of Negro land and property, his establishment of Tuskegee and spreading of industrial education and his compelling of the white South to at least think of the Negro as a possible man.

On the other hand, in stern justice, we must lay on the soul of this man, a heavy responsibility for the consummation of Negro disfranchisement, the decline of the Negro college and public school and the firmer establishment of color caste in this land.

What is done is done. This is no fit time for recrimination or complaint. Gravely and with bowed head let us receive what this great figure gave of good, silently rejecting all else. Firmly and unfalteringly let the Negro race in America, in bleeding Haiti and throughout the world close ranks and march steadily on, determined as never before to work and save and endure, but never to swerve from their great goal: the right to vote, the right to know, and the right to stand as men among men throughout the world. . . .

DECEMBER, 1915

Education

Consider this argument: Education is the training of men for life. The best training is experience, but if we depended entirely upon this each generation would begin where the last began and civilization could not advance.

We must then depend largely on oral and written tradition and on such bits of typical experience as we can arrange for the child's guidance to life.

More than that, children must be trained in the technique of earning a living and doing their part of the world's work.

But no training in technique must forget that the object of education is the child and not the things he makes.

Moreover, a training simply in technique will not do because general intelligence is needed for any trade, and the technique of trades changes.

Indeed, by the careful training of intelligence and ability, civilization is continually getting rid of the hardest and most exhausting toil, and giving it over to machines, leaving human beings freer for higher pursuits and self-development.

Hence, colored people in educating their children should be careful:

First: To conserve and select ability, giving to their best minds higher college training.

Second: They should endeavor to give all their children the largest possible amount of general training and intelligence before teaching them the technique of a particular trade, remembering that the object of all true education is not to make men carpenters, but to make carpenters men. . . .

The caste spirit is rampant in the land; it is laying hold of the public schools and it has the colored public schools by the throat, North, East, South and West. Beware of it, my brothers and dark sisters; educate your children. Give them the broadest and highest education possible; train them to the limit of their ability, if you work your hands to the bone in doing it. See that your child gets, not the highest task, but the task best fitted to his ability, whether it be digging dirt or painting landscapes; remembering that our recognition as common folk by the world depends on the number of men of ability we produce—not great geniuses, but efficient thinkers and doers in all lines. Never forget that if we ever compel the world's respect, it will be by virtue of our heads and not our heels.

FEBRUARY, 1918

Stupidity

Americans are remarkably stupid. They have just completed in Indianapolis a separate high school for Negro students; the first that the city has ever had. And yet the President of the National Education Association at Seattle says that the American school system is the "greatest kindergarten of Democracy ever conceived!"

In the face of such contradictions we blunder ahead. We import millions of slaves and complain because there are Negroes in the United States. We mix black and white blood and shriek for racial purity. We open the doors to foreign immigrants and inveigh against the foreign born. We establish public schools in this democracy and then force the Catholics into separate schools by deliberately misreading all Catholic history; force Italians into Parochial schools by giving them poor accommodations and worse teachers in the public schools; and finally force a whole system of separate public schools upon Negroes because they are socially too weak to resist.

Finally, we work every device to keep Jews, Negroes and foreigners out of the most aristocratic of our colleges. Then, with long faces, we remark that Democracy is a failure. Americans are remarkably stupid.

AUGUST, 1927

ON COMMUNITY CONTROL

Awake

Of all the cities in the South, Charleston is guilty of the meanest act toward colored folks. It keeps in their schools white teachers, teachers who do not want to be there; teachers who despise their work and who work mainly for the money which it brings them. These teachers are Southern whites and they are teaching little colored children, doing the work mechanically and with a cruelty of discipline that is shameful. Openly and persistently the white city gives two and only two reasons for keeping up this farce: first, that they want to teach black folk their place; and, secondly, that they want to supply certain white people with employment.

The colored people of Charleston have stood this long enough. They should awake and stop it. They should tell the white people gently, but firmly, that under present conditions to have Southern white people teaching colored children is as incongruous as it would be to have Turks teaching Armenians. Colored Charleston should register and vote and get rid of this abomination. There are more colored taxpayers in Charleston than white. There are hundreds of colored voters who could register, petition, vote and then, if need be, strike and let every colored child stay at home until teachers were installed who believed them human beings.

APRIL, 1917

SOCIAL EQUALITY—INTERRACIAL SEX AND MARRIAGE

Instead of dodging the most controversial of all racial topics, intermarriage, Du Bois wrote of it in many essays and editorials, beginning with his findings published in The Philadelphia Negro *in 1899. He conducted at least one symposium on the subject in* The Crisis. *He returned constantly to the same two topics: the bodies of Negro women did not belong to white men and all individuals of all races should be free to marry whomever they pleased.*

"Social Equality"

We are with great assiduity collecting practical definitions of "social equality." We say "practical" because the theoretical argument has gone quite insane. Here comes this month, The Missionary Voice, a well-disposed organ of the Southern white Methodists. In reviewing a pamphlet published by Atlanta University the Voice remarks concerning the editor that he is "well known as the leader of those Negroes who desire social equality for their race—a desire which crops out, here and there, through this pamphlet. The fact that no Southern white nor the wisest Southern blacks would sanction this desire for one moment does not lessen the impressiveness of this study of Negro effort to uplift the Negro race."

Here we have a faint clue as to what the South means by "social equality" with black folk. The pamphlet in question is entitled "Efforts for Social Betterment Among Negro Americans." It treats of the charity of church and school, of women's clubs, homes, orphanages and hospitals, nurseries, settlements, etc. This does not look dangerous. Just where social equality "crops out" here it is hard to say, unless the South means by this phrase every effort of black men to be treated like other men.

And this is what the South does mean. Because it means this it plunges into either contradiction or helplessness when Southern religion strikes the color line. In this same magazine, for instance, there occurs the following passage:

"The Methodist Episcopal Church, South, is doing very little directly for the Southern Negro socially, educationally or religiously. The Board of Education appropriates $14,000 annually to the schools of the colored Methodist Episcopal Church, but the only Southern white Methodists that have any personal relation to any of these schools are three teachers in Paine College. Educationally the Negro needs the personal touch of the Christian white man. If we want to do 'social service,' no better place to begin can be found than among the Negroes in our towns and cities."

Does not the Missionary Voice recognize that there can be no true "social service" or "personal touch" without "social equality?" Was it not the fact that Jesus Christ became the social equal of publicans, sinners and prostitutes that made Him the Great Teacher? How much more is social equality with honest laborers who are striving upward absolutely necessary for those who would really uplift? This is the whole movement of the age, and the South is whirling in a back eddy, damming progress and trying at once to avoid hypocrisy and yet teach the black at arm's length with a club in one hand and a Bible in the other.

This Missionary Voice is the voice of earnest, honest people. They are striving toward the light, but they have not reached it, and they are consequently illogical. The only logical folk in the South to-day are the Vardamans and Tillmans. They hold no illusions and know that you cannot treat a man as a man and as a beast at the same time. Therefore, they argue, treat Negroes as beasts. When will logic come to the better South and enable it to arise and say: "I dare despise nothing human. I am not better than my black neighbor."

NOVEMBER, 1911

Divine Right

We would like to know what rights the white people of this land are going to be able to retain? Step by step their dearest and most cherished prerogatives are being invaded, and THE CRISIS wants to say right here and now that it does not countenance oppression of the downtrodden whites by arrogant black folk. A few years ago the right to kick a darky off the sidewalk was unquestioned in the most devout circles, and yet to-day they actually complain at being called by their front names.

Everybody knows that for three hundred years the most jealously guarded right of white men in this land and others has been the right to seduce black women without legal, social or moral penalty. Many white mothers and daughters of the best families have helped to maintain this ancient and honored custom by loading the victims of their fathers' and husbands' lust with every epithet of insult and degradation. Thus has the sweet cleanness of their own race virtue shone holier and higher.

Yet what do we see to-day? The black husbands and brothers are beginning to revolt. In three separate cases, in three consecutive months and in three localities of the southern South have these blind and ignorant fellows actually killed white men who were demanding these ancient rights, and have compelled the chivalry of the land to rise and lynch the black defenders of defenceless virtue; also two strangely illogical black women have been simultaneously killed and a dark and whimpering little girl burned to a quivering crisp.

What does all this mean? Does it portend an unthinkable time when the white man can only get his rights by lynching impudent black husbands and squeamish sweethearts? If so, then, by the Great Jehovah, we can depend on the best friends of the Negro to vindicate the ancient liberties of this land! Anglo-Saxon freedom seems safe at least in the hands of most leaders of Southern society, not to mention the blue blood of Pennsylvania.

Meantime, dear colored brethren, we confess to the error of our ways. We have steadfastly opposed lynching on all occasions, but the South is converting us. We acknowledge our fault. Hereafter we humbly pray that every man, black or white, who is anxious to defend women, will be willing to be lynched for his faith. Let black men especially kill lecherous white invaders of their homes and then take their lynching gladly like men.

It's worth it!

MARCH, 1912

Intermarriage

Few groups of people are forced by their situation into such cruel dilemmas as American Negroes. Nevertheless they must not allow anger or personal resentment to dim their clear vision.

Take, for instance, the question of the intermarrying of white and black folk; it is a question that colored people seldom discuss. It is about the last of the social problems over which they are disturbed, because they so seldom face it in fact or in theory. Their problems are problems of work and wages, of the right to vote, of the right to travel decently, of the right to frequent places of public amusement, of the right to public security.

White people, on the other hand, for the most part profess to see but one problem: "Do you want your sister to marry a Nigger?" Sometimes we are led to wonder if they are lying about their solicitude on this point; and if they are not, we are led to ask why under present laws anybody should be compelled to marry any person whom she does not wish to marry?

This brings us to the crucial question: so far as the present advisability of intermarrying between white and colored people in the United States is concerned, both races are practically in complete agreement. Colored folk marry colored folk and white marry white, and the exceptions are very few.

Why not then stop the exceptions? For three reasons: physical, social and moral.

1. For the *physical* reason that to prohibit such intermarriage would be publicly to acknowledge that black blood is a physical taint—a thing that no decent, self-respecting black man can be asked to admit.

2. For the *social* reason that if two full-grown responsible human beings of any race and color propose to live together as man and wife, it is only social decency not simply to allow, but to compel them to marry. Let those people who have yelled themselves purple in the face over Jack Johnson just sit down and ask themselves this question: Granted that Johnson and Miss Cameron proposed to live together, was it better for them to be legally married or not? We know what the answer of the Bourbon South is. We know that they would rather uproot the foundations of decent society than to call the consorts of their brothers, sons and fathers their legal wives. . . .

3. The *moral* reason for opposing laws against inter-marriage is the greatest of all: such laws leave the colored girl absolutely helpless before the lust of white men. It reduces colored women in the eyes of the law to the position of dogs. Low as the white girl falls, she can compel her seducer to marry her. If it were proposed to take this last defense from poor white working girls, can you not hear the screams of the "white slave" defenders? What have these people to say to laws that propose to create in the United States 5,000,000 women, the ownership of whose bodies no white man is bound to respect?

Note these arguments, my brothers and sisters, and watch your State legislatures. This winter will see a determined attempt to insult and degrade us by such non-intermarriage laws. We must kill them, not because we are anxious to marry white men's sisters, but because we are determined that white men shall let our sisters alone.

FEBRUARY, 1913

"Sex Equality"

The Department of Justice has discovered a new crime—"Sex Equality." This is not as one might presume, equality of men and women, but it is the impudence of a man of Negro descent asserting his right to marry any human being who wants to marry him. With bated breath, Mr. Palmer[1] (who has no power to prevent or punish lynching and who permits peonage to flourish untouched in Arkansas) tells an astonished Senate of this new sign of "Red" propaganda among blacks.

Nonsense! Mr. Palmer is mistaken in assuming that it took a world war to make the Negro conscious of such an elementary right. No Negro with any sense has ever denied his right to marry another human being, for the simple reason that such denial would be frank admission of his own inferiority. For a man to stand up and say: I am not physically or morally or mentally fit to marry this woman, who wishes to marry me, would be a horrible admission. No healthy, decent man—white, black, red, or blue—could for a moment admit so monstrous a fact.

He could, naturally, say: I do not WANT to marry this woman of another race, and this is what 999 black men out of every thousand DO say. Or a woman may say: I do not

---

[1] [A. Mitchell Palmer, then United States Attorney General.]

want to marry this black man, or this red man, or this white man—this she has the absolute and unquestionable right to say. But the impudent and vicious demand that all colored folk shall write themselves down as brutes by a general assertion of their unfitness to marry other decent folk is a nightmare born only in the haunted brain of the bourbon South and transmitted by some astonishing power to the lips of the Attorney General of the United States.

OCTOBER, 1919

Philippine Mulattoes

You will have noticed in the press a delicately worded appeal for funds. It would seem that there are some little children in need in the Philippines. Major General Wood, Governor of the Islands, is speaking in their behalf:

Chief Justice William Howard Taft of the Supreme Court of the United States, former Governor General of the Philippines, W. Cameron Forbes, Major Gen. James G. Harbord, Major Gen. Hugh L. Scott, Martin Egan, Vice-President Charles G. Dawes and dignitaries of the Catholic and Protestant churches are typical of the men who have pledged their support to this drive for funds. General Wood has cabled:

The American people have been so generous in their responses to the cries of children all over the world that I have no hesitation in appealing to them for children of their own blood who are in need of help. Especially do I have profound confidence, as the problem involves the honor of the American nation.

What is all this about? In plain, cold English, the American people in bringing Peace and Civilization to the Philippines have left 18,000 bastards in the islands! Isn't this fine work? Can you not see the Godly White Race struggling under the Black Man's Burden! Can you not see how Americans hate Social Equality with brown women?

Why is America asked to support these illegitimate victims of white men's lust? Because the United States government, the War Department and Governors Wood, Taft and Forbes have somehow let American skunks scuttle from the island and leave their helpless and innocent bastards to beg and perish, and their deserted mothers to starve or serve as prostitutes to white newcomers.

Send, in God's name, America, two million dollars to Mary Frances Kern at 8 West Fortieth Street, New York, now; and send simultaneously two million protests to Washington to lambaste the heads of Congressmen who permit the holding of the Philippines as a house of prostitution for American white men under the glorious stars and stripes.

DECEMBER, 1925

DU BOIS AND SOCIAL REFORM

In addition to his Herculean labors in The Crisis *on behalf of the emancipation of black folk, Dr. Du Bois somehow found time and space to support practically every social reform movement of his time, both at home and abroad, and wrote often on topics ranging from Irish freedom to women's suffrage. He felt the cause of the American Negro was best served by identifying with the oppressed everywhere. He supported the Non-Partisan League, aid to the foreign born, educational reforms, protection for children, prison reform, the I.W.W. (Industrial Workers of the World), the Socialist movement, government ownership of industry, and so on. Here we quote him on women's suffrage, in the fight for which he was a tower of strength.*

Votes for Women

Why should the colored voter be interested in woman's suffrage? There are three cogent reasons. First, it is a great human question. Nothing human must be foreign, uninteresting or unimportant to colored citizens of the world. Whatever concerns half mankind concerns us. Secondly, any agitation, discussion or reopening of the problem of voting must inevitably be a discussion of the right of black folk to vote in America and Africa. Essentially the arguments for and against are the same in the case of all groups of human beings. The world with its tendencies and temptations to caste must ever be asking itself how far may the governed govern? How far can the responsibility of directing, curbing and encouraging mankind be put upon mankind? When we face this vastest of human problems frankly, most of us, despite ourselves and half unconsciously, find ourselves strangely undemocratic, strangely tempted to exclude from participation in government larger and larger numbers of our neighbors. . . .

The same arguments and facts that are slowly but surely opening the ballot box to women in England and America must open it to black men in America and Africa. It only remains for us to help the movement and spread the argument wherever we may.

Finally, votes for women mean votes for black women. There are in the United States three and a third million adult women of Negro descent. Except in the rural South, these women have larger economic opportunity than their husbands and brothers and are rapidly becoming better educated. One has only to remember the recent biennial convention of colored women's clubs with its 400 delegates to realize how the women are moving quietly but forcibly toward the intellectual leadership of the race. The enfranchisement of these women will not be a mere doubling of our vote and voice in the nation, it will tend to stronger and more normal political life, the rapid dethronement of the "heeler" and "grafter" and the making of politics a method of broadest philanthropic race betterment, rather than a disreputable means of private gain. We sincerely trust that the entire Negro vote will be cast for woman suffrage in the coming elections in Ohio, Kansas, Wisconsin and Michigan.

SEPTEMBER, 1912

Hail Columbia!

Hail Columbia, Happy Land! Again the glorious traditions of Anglo-Saxon manhood have been upheld! Again the chivalry of American white men has been magnificently vindicated. Down on your knees, black men, and hear the tale with awestruck faces. Learn from the Superior Race. We do not trust our own faltering pen and purblind sight to describe the reception of the suffragists at the capital of the land. We quote from the Southern reporters of the Northern press:

"Five thousand women, marching in the woman-suffrage pageant yesterday, practically fought their way foot by foot up Pennsylvania Avenue, through a surging mass of humanity that completely defied the Washington police, swamped the marchers, and broke their procession into little companies. The women, trudging stoutly along under great difficulties, were able to complete their march only when troops of cavalry from Fort Myer were rushed into Washington to take charge of Pennsylvania Avenue. . . .

"More than 100 persons, young and old, of both sexes, were crushed and trampled in the uncontrollable crowd in Pennsylvania Avenue yesterday, while two ambulances of the Emergency Hospital came and went constantly for six hours, always impeded and at times actually opposed, so that doctor and driver literally had to fight their way to give succor to the injured.

"Hoodlums, many of them in uniform, leaned forward till their cigarettes almost touched the women's faces while blowing smoke in their eyes, and the police said not a word, not even when every kind of insult was hurled.

"To the white-haired women the men shouted continuously: 'Granny! granny! We came to see chickens, not hens! Go home and sit in the corner!' To the younger women they yelled: 'Say, what you going to do to-night? Can't we make a date?' and the police only smiled. The rowdies jumped on the running boards of the automobiles and snatched the flags from the elderly women, and they attempted to pull the girls from the floats."

Wasn't it glorious? Does it not make you burn with shame to be a mere black man when such mighty deeds are done by the Leaders of Civilization? Does it not make you "ashamed of your race?" Does it not make you "want to be white?" . . .

MARCH, 1913

RACE PRIDE

Du Bois not only taught race pride but coined many of the phrases used by the modern civil rights movement. One of the concepts still evoking action today is that race pride often demands self-segregation. The second essay is one of the many that dwelled on the beauty of being black.

Balls

THE CRISIS noted with exceeding interest last summer four social gatherings; there were doubtless many others, but these came especially under our eye: the balls of the Pythians and Elks at Atlantic City, where some 15,000 colored folk danced on the great Young's Pier; the ball of the National Medical Association at Newark; and of the Sigma Pi Phi fraternity at Philadelphia. For beauty of face and form and robing, for fine fellowship and joy of life it may well be doubted if these gatherings have ever been equalled in the United States. Assemble the nations of earth and say what you will, there is nothing in white Europe or America that can measure up to the wonderful colorings of flesh, grace of movement and rhythm of music such as Black America can furnish. To all this is being subtly added the appropriate richness and color of gown and the gentle manner based on deep, human sympathy. We are discovering at last the long-veiled beauty of our own world.

OCTOBER, 1919

Race Pride

. . . Today Negroes, Indians, Chinese, and other groups are gaining new faith in themselves; they are beginning to "like" themselves; they are discovering that the current theories and stories of "backward" peoples are largely lies and assumptions; that human genius and possibility are not limited by color, race, or blood. What is this new self-consciousness leading to? Inevitably and directly to distrust and hatred of whites; to demands for self-government, separation, driving out of foreigners—"Asia for the Asiatics," "Africa for the Africans," and "Negro officers for Negro troops!"

No sooner do whites see this unawaited development than they point out in dismay the inevitable consequences: "You lose our tutelage," "You spurn our knowledge," "You need our wealth and technique." They point out how fine is the world rôle of Elder Brother.

Very well. Some of the darker brethren are convinced. They draw near in friendship; they seek to enter schools and churches; they would mingle in industry—when lo! "Get out," yells the White World—"You're not our brothers and never will be"—"Go away, herd by yourselves"— "Eternal Segregation in the Lord!"

Can you wonder, Sirs, that we are a bit puzzled by all this and that we are asking gently, but more and more insistently: Choose one or the other horn of the dilemma:

1. Leave the black and yellow world alone. Get out of Asia, Africa, and the Isles. Give us our states and towns and sections and let us rule them undisturbed. Absolutely segregate the races and sections of the world.

Or—

2. Let the world meet as men with men. Give utter Justice to all. Extend Democracy to all and treat all men according to their individual desert. Let it be possible for whites to rise to the highest positions in China and Uganda and blacks to the highest honors in England and Texas.

Here is the choice. Which will you have, my masters?

JANUARY, 1920

VOLUNTARY SEGREGATION

Paradoxically, Du Bois once strongly advocated voluntary self-segregation of Negroes: Negro control of all segregated institutions, including schools and business, as a weapon in ending enforced segregation under the domination of the white power structure. It was largely over this issue that he broke with the NAACP in 1934.

He referred to the Negro minority in America as a "nation within a nation" and as "one of the considerable nations of the world." Today many advocates of this cultural pluralism do not know that Du Bois originated the arguments in favor of it and that he considered this one of his chief weapons in the fight for black power.

The Strength of Segregation

When the American people in their carelessness and impudence have finally succeeded in welding 10,000,000 American Negroes into one great self-conscious and self-acting mass they will realize their mistake.

At present it is still possible to make Negroes essentially Americans with American ideals and instincts. In another generation, however, at the present rate we will have in this country a mass of people of colored blood acting together like one great fist for their own ends, with secret understanding, with pitiless efficiency and with resources for defense which will make their freedom incapable of attack from without.

The actual organization of this group is progressing by leaps and bounds. It needs now but to be knit together into one great unity. This can be done—it is being done. Those who advise "race pride" and "self-reliance" do not realize the Frankenstein which they are evoking. The Negro cannot be beaten in this line by any present methods. The physical intimidation of lynching cannot be kept up; the economic intimidation of exclusion from work cannot, with the present organization of Negro industry, be kept up after ten years. Continual social insult is powerless against those who refuse to be insulted. After this—what? What can America do against a mass of people who move through their world but are not of it and stand as one unshaken group in their battle? Nothing. . . .

DECEMBER, 1913

"Jim Crow"

We colored folk stand at the parting of ways, and we must take counsel. The objection to segregation and "Jim-Crowism" was in other days the fact that compelling Negroes to associate only with Negroes meant to exclude them from contact with the best culture of the day. How could we learn manners or get knowledge if the heritage of the past was locked away from us?

Gradually, however, conditions have changed. Culture is no longer the monopoly of the white nor is poverty and ignorance the sole heritage of the black. Many a colored man in our day called to conference with his own and rather dreading the contact with uncultivated people even though they were of his own blood has been astonished and deeply gratified at the kind of people he has met—at the evidence of good manners and thoughtfulness among his own.

This together with the natural human love of herding like with like has in the last decade set up a tremendous current within the colored race against any contact with whites that can be avoided. They have welcomed separate racial institutions. They have voluntarily segregated themselves and asked for more segregation. The North is full of instances of practically colored schools which colored people have demanded and, of course, the colored church and social organization of every sort are ubiquitous.

Today both these wings of opinion are getting suspicious of each other and there are plenty of whites to help the feeling along. Whites and Blacks ask the Negro who fights separation: "Are you ashamed of your race?" Blacks and Whites ask the Negro who welcomes and encourages separation: "Do you want to give up your rights? Do you acknowledge your inferiority?"

Neither attitude is correct. Segregation is impolitic, because it is impossible. You can not build up a logical scheme of a self-sufficing, separate Negro America inside America or a Negro world with no close relations to the white world. If there are relations between races they must be based on the knowledge and sympathy that come alone from the long and intimate human contact of individuals.

On the other hand, if the Negro is to develop his own power and gifts; if he is not only to fight prejudices and oppression successfully, but also to unite for ideals higher than the world has realized in art and industry and social life, then he must unite and work with Negroes and build a new and great Negro ethos.

Here, then, we face the curious paradox and we remember contradictory facts. Unless we had fought segregation with determination, our whole race would have been pushed into an ill-lighted, unpaved, un-sewered ghetto. Unless we had built great church organizations and manned our own southern schools, we should be shepherdless sheep. Unless we had welcomed the segregation of Fort Des Moines, we would have had no officers in the National Army. Unless we had beaten open the doors of northern universities, we would have had no men fit to be officers.

Here is a dilemma calling for thought and forbearance. Not every builder of racial co-operation and solidarity is a "Jim-Crow" advocate, a hater of white folk. Not every Negro who fights prejudice and segregation is ashamed of his race.

FEBRUARY, 1919

POLITICS

Du Bois always concerned himself with the role of the Negro in politics. In two of these articles he urged Negroes to vote as a bloc, anticipating a form of black power.

The Negro Party

There is for the future one and only one effective political move for colored voters. We have long foreseen it, but we have sought to avoid it. It is a move of segregation, it "hyphenates" us, it separates us from our fellow Americans; but self-defense knows no nice hesitations. The American Negro must either vote as a unit or continue to be politically emasculated as at present.

Miss Inez Milholland, in a recent address, outlined with singular clearness and force a Negro Party on the lines of the recently formed Woman's Party. Mr. R. R. Church, Jr., of Tennessee, and certain leading colored men in New Jersey, Ohio and elsewhere have unconsciously and effectively followed her advice.

The situation is this: At present the Democratic party can maintain its ascendency only by the help of the Solid South. The Solid South is built on the hate and fear of Negroes; consequently it can never, as a party effectively bid for the Negro vote. The Republican party is the party of wealth and big business and, as such, is the natural enemy of the humble working people who compose the mass of Negroes. Between these two great parties, as parties there is little to choose.

On the other hand, parties are represented by individual

candidates. Negroes can have choice in the naming of these candidates and they can vote for or against them. . . .

OCTOBER, 1916

Voting—Then and Now

If there is one thing that should be urged upon colored voters throughout the United States this fall it is independence. No intelligent man should vote one way simply from habit. Only through careful scrutiny of candidates and policies can a man put himself in position to help rule one hundred million people. It is because of the suspicion that colored men are not capable of doing this, or are unwilling to do it, that so many American citizens acquiesce in the nullification of democracy known as disfranchisement.

Let every colored man who can, vote; and whether he vote the Republican or Democratic or Socialist ticket, let him vote it, not because his father did or because he is afraid, but because after intelligent consideration he thinks the success of that ticket is best for his people and his country.

AUGUST, 1912

Politics

The colored voter now stands face to face with the great question of the proper use of his electoral franchise. Under normal conditions 2,000,000 of the 20,000,000 votes which might be cast at a presidential election would belong to the race, and some day, despite every effort of fraud and race prejudice, those votes are going to be cast.

To-day, however, of the 15,000,000 or more votes which will actually be cast for President, some 500,000 will be black men's votes.

What shall we do with these 500,000 ballots?

First of all we must teach ourselves to regard them seriously. The Negro-American is not disfranchised; on the contrary, he is a half million votes this side of disfranchisement and that is a long, long way. There have been but two or three presidential elections since the war which have not been settled by a margin of less than a half million votes, and in every single election since the proslavery compromise of 1850 such a number of votes distributed at strategic points would easily have decided the presidency....

If colored America had long political experience and wide knowledge of men and measures, it would organize the black voters of each State into a solid phalanx. It would say to this phalanx: white and colored voters in this land are selling their votes too cheaply. By the use of a "slush fund" of $3,000,000 Theodore Roosevelt was able almost to split the Republican party. You could easily sell your votes next November for one or two millions of dollars, but that is too cheap. You could easily sell your votes for an Assistant Attorney-General, a Register of the Treasury, a Recorder of Deeds and a few other black wooden men whose duty it is to look pleasant, say nothing and have no opinions that a white man is bound to respect. This also is too cheap—it is dirt cheap.

What price should you ask for 500,000 votes, black America? You should ask this:

1. The abolition of the interstate "Jim Crow" car.

2. The enforcement of the Thirteenth Amendment by the suppression of peonage.

3. The enforcement of the Fourteenth Amendment by cutting down the representation in Congress of the rotten boroughs of the South.

4. National aid to elementary public schools without class or racial discrimination.

Is this price too much to pay for a presidency? It is not if you dare ask it. . . . .

AUGUST, 1912

SELF-DEFENSE

Du Bois did not believe in passive resistance to evil. Here and elsewhere he urged the right and necessity of self-defense.

The Fruit of the Tree

Let no one for a moment mistake that the present increased attack on the Negro along all lines is but the legitimate fruit of that long campaign for subserviency and surrender which a large party of Negroes have fathered now some twenty years. It is not necessary to question the motives of these men nor to deny that their insistence on thrift and saving has had its large and beneficent effect. But, on the other hand, only the blind and foolish can fail to see that a continued campaign in every nook and corner of this land, preaching to people white and colored, that the Negro is chiefly to blame for his condition, that he must not insist on his rights, that he should not take part in politics, that "Jim Crowism" is defensible and even advantageous, that he should humbly bow to the storm until the lordly white man grants him clemency—the fruit of this disgraceful doctrine is disfranchisement, segregation, lynching. . . . Fellow Negroes, is it not time to be men? Is it not time to strike back when we are struck? Is it not high time to hold up our heads and clench our teeth and swear by the Eternal God we will NOT be slaves, and that no aider, abetter and teacher of slavery in any shape or guise can longer lead us?

SEPTEMBER, 1913

Let Us Reason Together

Brothers we are on the Great Deep. We have cast off on the vast voyage which will lead to Freedom or Death.

For three centuries we have suffered and cowered. No race ever gave Passive Resistance and Submission to Evil longer, more piteous trial. Today we raise the terrible weapon of Self-Defense. When the murderer comes, he shall not longer strike us in the back. When the armed lynchers

160

gather, we too must gather armed. When the mob moves, we propose to meet it with bricks and clubs and guns.

But we must tread here with solemn caution. We must never let justifiable self-defense against individuals become blind and lawless offense against all white folk. We must not seek reform by violence. We must not seek Vengeance. "Vengeance is Mine," saith the Lord; or to put it otherwise, only Infinite Justice and Knowledge can assign blame in this poor world, and we ourselves are sinful men, struggling desperately with our own crime and ignorance. We must defend ourselves, our homes, our wives and children against the lawless without stint or hesitation; but we must carefully and scrupulously avoid on our own part bitter and unjustifiable aggression against anybody.

This line is difficult to draw. In the South the Police and Public Opinion back the mob and the least resistance on the part of the innocent black victim is nearly always construed as a lawless attack on society and government. In the North the Police and the Public will dodge and falter, but in the end they will back the Right when the Truth is made clear to them.

But whether the line between just resistance and angry retaliation is hard or easy, we must draw it carefully, not in wild resentment, but in grim and sober consideration; and then back of the impregnable fortress of the Divine Right of Self-Defense, which is sanctioned by every law of God and man, in every land, civilized and uncivilized, we must take our unfaltering stand.

Honor, endless and undying Honor, to every man, black or white, who in Houston, East St. Louis, Washington and Chicago gave his life for Civilization and Order.

If the United States is to be a Land of Law, we would live humbly and peaceably in it—working, singing, learning and dreaming to make it and ourselves nobler and better; if it is to be a Land of Mobs and Lynchers, we might as well die today as tomorrow.

> *"And how can man die better*
> *Than facing fearful odds*
> *For the ashes of his fathers*
> *And the temples of his gods?"*

SEPTEMBER, 1919

MIGRATION

Booker T. Washington told Negroes to "cast down their buckets" where they were, in the South, among their "best friends"—former slave-owners and their sons. Du Bois said, "Brothers, come north!" In many articles and editorials in The Crisis *he reiterated his reasons for encouraging migration: (1) In the long run, there was a better life and hope for Negroes in northern urban areas, and (2) the migration would liberalize the South.*

Migration a Crime in Georgia

The Atlanta, Ga., *Constitution* publishes this extraordinary and matter-of-fact special dispatch from Macon, under the date of October 31 (the italics are ours): "Fearing that the general unrest among the Negroes of the city and the efforts that are being put forth on the part of the authorities *to keep them from being transported from Macon to the North,* may result in a riot which the city authorities will not be able to cope with, Chief of Police, George S. Riley, today recommended to the civil service commission that *forty magazine rifles* be purchased for the police department. At the present time the police *only* have their pistols and clubs.

"Monday morning 1,000 Negroes congregated at the Southern railway depot *expecting* to leave for Michigan in a special train. The police *dispersed them, but had difficulty in making several of them move on.* Several arrests were made. It is said that a surliness now exists among a certain class of the Negroes and the police want to be able to cope with any situation that may arise."

Can you beat this calm defiance of the Thirteenth Amendment?

DECEMBER, 1916

Migration of Negroes

Much has been written of the recent migration of colored people from the South to the North, but there have been very few attempts to give a definite, coherent picture of the whole movement. Aided by the funds of the National Association for the Advancement of Colored People, THE CRISIS has attempted to put into concrete form such knowledge as we have of this movement.

The data at hand are vague and have been collected from

a hundred different sources. While the margin of error is large, the actual information which we have gathered is most valuable.

First, as to the number who have migrated to the North, there is wide difference of opinion. Our own conclusion is that about 250,000 colored workmen have come northward. . . .

As to the reasons of the migration, undoubtedly, the immediate cause was economic, and the movement began because of floods in middle Alabama and Mississippi and because the latest devastation of the boll weevil came in these same districts.

A second economic cause was the cutting off of immigration from Europe to the North and the consequently widespread demand for common labor. . . .

The third reason has been outbreaks of mob violence. . . .

A colored man of Sumter, S. C., says: "The immediate occasion of the migration is, of course, the opportunity in the North, now at last open to us, for industrial betterment. The real causes are the conditions which we have had to bear because there was no escape."

These conditions he sums up as the destruction of the Negroes' political rights, the curtailment of his civil rights, the lack of protection of life, liberty and property, low wages, the Jim Crow car, residential and labor segregation laws, poor educational facilities.

From Oklahoma we learn that Negroes are migrating because of threatened segregation laws and mob violence.

A colored man from Georgia states: "In my opinion the strongest factor in this migration is a desire to escape harsh and unfair treatment, to secure a larger degree of personal liberty, better advantages for children, and a living wage."

The A. M. E. [African Methodist Episcopal] Ministers' Alliance of Birmingham, Ala., names seven causes for the migration: "Prejudice, disfranchisement, Jim Crow cars, lynching, bad treatment on the farms, the boll weevil, the floods of 1916." . . .

It is interesting to note that this migration is apparently a mass movement and not a movement of the leaders. The wave of economic distress and social unrest has pushed past the conservative advice of the Negro preacher, teacher and professional man, and the colored laborers and artisans have determined to find a way for themselves. . . .

JUNE, 1917

Brothers, Come North

The migration of Negroes from South to North continues and ought to continue. The North is no paradise—as East St. Louis, Washington, Chicago, and Omaha prove; but the South is at best a system of caste and insult and at worst a Hell. With ghastly and persistent regularity, the lynching of Negroes in the South continues—every year, every month, every day; wholesale murders and riots have taken place at Norfolk, Longview, Arkansas, Knoxville, and 24 other places in a single year. The outbreaks in the North have been fiercer, but they have quickly been curbed; no attempt has been made to saddle the whole blame on Negroes; and the cities where riots have taken place are today safer and better for Negroes than ever before.

In the South, on the other hand, the outbreaks occurring daily but reveal the seething cauldron beneath—the unbending determination of the whites to subject and rule the blacks, to yield no single inch of their determination to keep Negroes as near slavery as possible.

There are, to be sure, Voices in the South—wise Voices and troubled Consciences; souls that see the utter futility and impossibility of the southern program of race relations in work and travel and human intercourse. But these voices are impotent. . . .

We can vote in the North. We can hold office in the North. As workers in northern establishments, we are getting good wages, decent treatment, healthful homes and schools for our children. Can we hesitate? COME NORTH! Not in a rush—not as aimless wanderers, but after quiet investigation and careful location. The demand for Negro labor is endless. Immigration is still cut off and a despicable and indefensible drive against all foreigners is shutting the gates of opportunity to the outcasts and victims of Europe. Very good. We will make America pay for her Injustice to us and to the poor foreigner by pouring into the open doors of mine and factory in increasing numbers.

Troubles will ensue with white unions and householders, but remember that the chief source of these troubles is rooted in the South; a million Southerners live in the North. These are the ones who by open and secret propaganda fomented trouble in these northern centers and are still at it. They have tried desperately to make trouble in Indianapolis, Cleveland, Pittsburgh, Philadelphia, Baltimore, and New York City.

This is a danger, but we have learned how to meet it by unwavering self-defense and by the ballot.

Meantime, if the South really wants the Negro and wants him at his best, it can have him permanently, on these terms and no others:

1. The right to vote.
2. The abolition of lynching.
3. Justice in the courts.
4. The abolition of "Jim-Crow" cars.
5. A complete system of education, free and compulsory.

JANUARY, 1920

CLASS STRUGGLE

As Martin Luther King, Jr., said shortly before his death, there is no sense in muting the fact that all of his life Du Bois was a radical. Even before he had read Marx or had visited the Soviet Union he was using many of the ideas that Marx popularized, including the economic interpretation of history and the struggle between the classes. He joined the Socialist Party in 1911, and during the remainder of his life considered himself basically a Socialist, advocating a communal system for America, Africa, and the world. This topic received much attention in Du Bois' editorials and essays in The Crisis.

Although Du Bois became an actual member of the Communist Party less than a year before his death at the age of 95, he was often critical of the American Communist movement, as the long editorial on the Scottsboro cases shows. These cases, which became a worldwide cause célèbre in the depression period of the early 1930s, arose out of a charge of rape leveled against several young black boys in Scottsboro, Alabama.

The Negro and Communism

The Scottsboro, Alabama, cases have brought squarely before the American Negro the question of his attitude toward Communism.

The importance of the Russian Revolution can not be gainsaid. It is easily the greatest event in the world since the French Revolution and possibly since the fall of Rome. The experiment is increasingly successful. Russia occupies the center of the world's attention today and as a state it is recognized by every civilized nation, except the United States, Spain, Portugal and some countries of South America.

The challenge to the capitalistic form of industry and to the governments which this form dominates is more and more tremendous because of the present depression. If Socialism as a form of government and industry is on trial in Russia, capitalism as a form of industry and government is just as surely on trial throughout the world and is more and more clearly recognizing the fact. . . .

SEPTEMBER, 1931

The Scottsboro Cases

. . . Advocating the defense of the eight Alabama black boys, who without a shadow of doubt have been wrongly accused of crime, the Communists not only asked to take charge of the defense of these victims, but they proceeded to build on this case an appeal to the American Negro to join the Communist movement as the only solution of their problem.

Immediately, these two objects bring two important problems; first, can the Negroes with their present philosophy and leadership defend the Scottsboro cases successfully? Secondly, even if they can, will such defense help them to solve their problem of poverty and caste?

If the Communistic leadership in the United States had been broadminded and far-sighted, it would have acknowledged frankly that the honesty, earnestness and intelligence of the NAACP during twenty years of desperate struggle proved this organization under present circumstances to be the only one, and its methods the only methods available, to defend these boys and it would have joined capitalists and laborers north and south, black and white in every endeavor to win freedom for victims threatened with judicial murder. Then beyond that and with Scottsboro as a crimson and terrible text, Communists could have proceeded to point out that legal defense alone, even if successful, will never solve the larger Negro problem but that further and more radical steps are needed. . . .

SEPTEMBER, 1931

NAACP and Communists

There is no group of leaders on earth who have so largely made common cause with the lowest of their race as educated American Negroes, and it is their foresight and sacrifice and theirs alone that has saved the American freedman from annihilation and degradation.

This is the class of leaders who have directed and organized and defended black folk in America and whatever their shortcomings and mistakes—and they are legion—their one great proof of success is the survival of the American Negro as the most intelligent and effective group of colored people fighting white civilization face to face and on its own ground, on the face of the earth.

The quintessence and final expression of this leadership is the NAACP. For twenty years it has fought a battle more desperate than any other race conflict of modern times and it has fought with honesty and courage. It deserves from Russia something better than a kick in the back from the young jackasses who are leading Communism in America today. . . .

SEPTEMBER, 1931

Communists and the Color Line

The American Communists have made a courageous fight against the color line among the workers. They have solicited and admitted Negro members. They have insisted in their strikes and agitation to let Negroes fight with them and that the object of their fighting is for black workers as well as white workers. But in this they have gone dead against the thought and desire of the overwhelming mass of white workers, and face today a dead blank wall even in their own school in Arkansas. Thereupon instead of acknowledging defeat in their effort to make white labor abolish the color line, they turn and accuse Negroes of not sympathizing with the ideals of Labor! . . .

American Negroes do not propose to be the shock troops of the Communist Revolution, driven out in front to death, cruelty and humiliation in order to win victories for white workers. They are picking no chestnuts from the fire, neither for capital nor white labor.

Negroes know perfectly well that whenever they try to lead revolution in America, the nation will unite as one fist to crush them and them alone. There is no conceivable idea that seems to the present overwhelming majority of Americans higher than keeping Negroes "in their place."

Negroes perceive clearly that the real interests of the white worker are identical with the interests of the black worker; but until the white worker recognizes this, the black worker is compelled in sheer self-defense to refuse to be made the sacrificial goat.

SEPTEMBER, 1931

Ten Years

It is astonishing to see the determination with which those who believe in the industrial methods of America and Western Europe are spreading misinformation concerning the Russian experiment. The central thing which has happened in Russia is this: the rotten, horrible, inexpressibly brutal and silly tyranny of the Czar has been definitely and finally overthrown. No such travesty on decent government has existed elsewhere in Europe in modern days. It was a stench in the nostrils of humanity. It was flamboyant and impudent with murder and cruelty, on a foundation of ignorance and poverty and with flaming towers of ostentation and show which completely captivated the organized snobbery of the world. To be presented at the Russian Imperial Court was the last round in the ladder of ambition for every social climber in Europe and America.

The rottenness of the Czar's Government was repeatedly exposed to the liberal world. Not a finger was raised to help. On the contrary, when in desperation Russia rose in 1905 to shake off medieval despotism and establish modern democracy, Western Europe poured its treasure into the hands of the Czar to beat the wretched Revolutionists back. Now finally, when of their own strength and determination, and their own vast will to sacrifice, the Russian people have buried Czarism and tried to establish a new government that frankly faces the economic problem which the world fears to face, there is scarcely a newspaper in America that will give this experiment even decent hearing. Yet the Union of Socialist Soviet Republics is celebrating today its Tenth Anniversary, and here's hoping that this is but the first decade toward its hundred years.

FEBRUARY, 1927

WAR AND PEACE

Du Bois believed passionately that only in a world at peace could the human race approach its potential in creating the good life. He always lent his ideas and strength to opposing war and fighting for peace. Yet, paradoxically, he more than once chose to advocate the "lesser evil" of war in the face of the reality of events. He also used the history of the black American soldier to create race pride. One of his most controversial editorials consisted of only 200 words. Entitled "Close Ranks," it advocated Negro support of America in World War I. That this was only for the duration can be seen from the May 1919 editorial, which almost put him in prison as a subversive and did cause temporary suspension of mailing privileges for The Crisis. Other editorials on the subject of the Negro soldier are also included.

The Black Soldier

This number of THE CRISIS is dedicated, first, to the nearly 100,000 men of Negro descent who are today called to arms for the United States. It is dedicated, also, to the million dark men of Africa and India, who have served in the armies of Great Britain, and to the equal, if not larger, number who are fighting for France and the other Allies.

To these men we want to say above all: Have courage and determination. You are not fighting simply for Europe; you are fighting for the world, and you and your people are a part of the world.

This war is an End and, also, a Beginning. Never again

will darker people of the world occupy just the place they had before. Out of this war will rise, soon or late, an independent China; a self-governing India, and Egypt with representative institutions; an Africa for the Africans, and not merely for business exploitation. Out of this war will rise, too, an American Negro, with the right to vote and the right to work and the right to live without insult. These things may not and will not come at once; but they are written in the stars. . . .

JUNE, 1918

Close Ranks

This is the crisis of the world. For all the long years to come men will point to the year 1918 as the great Day of Decision, the day when the world decided whether it would submit to military despotism and an endless armed peace—if peace it could be called—or whether they would put down the menace of German militarism and inaugurate the United States of the World.

We of the colored race have no ordinary interest in the outcome. That which the German power represents today spells death to the aspirations of Negroes and all darker races for equality, freedom and democracy. Let us not hesitate. Let us, while this war lasts, forget our special grievances and close our ranks shoulder to shoulder with our own white fellow citizens and the allied nations that are fighting for democracy. We make no ordinary sacrifice, but we make it gladly and willingly with our eyes lifted to the hills.

JULY, 1918

Returning Soldiers

We are returning from war! THE CRISIS and tens of thousands of black men were drafted into a great struggle. For bleeding France and what she means and has meant and will mean to us and humanity and against the threat of German race arrogance, we fought gladly and to the last drop of blood; for America and her highest ideals, we fought in far-off hope; for the dominant southern oligarchy entrenched in Washington, we fought in bitter resignation.

For the America that represents and gloats in lynching, disfranchisement, caste, brutality and devilish insult—for this, in the hateful upturning and mixing of things, we were forced by vindictive fate to fight, also.

But today we return! We return from the slavery of uniform which the world's madness demanded us to don to the freedom of civil garb. We stand again to look America squarely in the face and call a spade a spade. We sing: This country of ours, despite all its better souls have done and dreamed, is yet a shameful land.

It *lynches*.

And lynching is barbarism of a degree of contemptible nastiness unparalleled in human history. Yet for fifty years we have lynched two Negroes a week, and we have kept this up right through the war.

It *disfranchises* its own citizens.

Disfranchisement is the deliberate theft and robbery of the only protection of poor against rich and black against white. The land that disfranchises its citizens and calls itself a democracy lies and knows it lies.

It encourages *ignorance*.

It has never really tried to educate the Negro. A dominant minority does not want Negroes educated. It wants servants, dogs, whores and monkeys. And when this land allows a reactionary group by its stolen political power to force as many black folk into these categories as it possibly can, it cries in contemptible hypocrisy: "They threaten us with degeneracy; they cannot be educated."

It *steals* from us.

It organizes industry to cheat us. It cheats us out of our land; it cheats us out of our labor. It confiscates our savings. It reduces our wages. It raises our rent. It steals our profit. It taxes us without representation. It keeps us consistently and universally poor, and then feeds us on charity and derides our poverty.

It *insults* us.

It has organized a nation-wide and latterly a world-wide propaganda of deliberate and continuous insult and defamation of black blood wherever found. It decrees that it shall not be possible in travel nor residence, work nor play, education nor instruction for a black man to exist without tacit or open acknowledgment of his inferiority to the dirtiest white dog. And it looks upon any attempt to question or even discuss this dogma as arrogance, unwarranted assumption and treason.

This is the country to which we Soldiers of Democracy

return. This is the fatherland for which we fought! But it is *our* fatherland. It was right for us to fight. The faults of *our* country are *our* faults. Under similar circumstances, we would fight again. But by the God of Heaven, we are cowards and jackasses if now that that war is over, we do not marshal every ounce of our brain and brawn to fight a sterner, longer, more unbending battle against the forces of hell in our own land.

We *return*.

We *return from fighting*.

We *return fighting*.

Make way for Democracy! We saved it in France, and by the Great Jehovah, we will save it in the United States of America, or know the reason why.

MAY, 1919

Rape

The charge of rape against colored Americans was invented by the white South after Reconstruction to excuse mob violence. No such wholesale charge was dreamed of in slavery days and during the war black men were often the sole protection of white women.

After the war, when murder and mob violence was the recognized method of re-enslaving blacks, it was discovered that it was only necessary to add a charge of rape to justify before the North and Europe any treatment of Negroes. The custom became widespread. In vain have Negroes and their friends protested that in less than *one-quarter* of the cases of lynching Negroes has rape been even *alleged* as an excuse. And in the alleged cases guilt has not been even probable in the vast majority of cases.

We do not for a moment deny or seek to deny that Negroes are guilty of rape and of other horrible crimes. What we do deny and what the facts overwhelmingly prove is that *as a race they are less guilty of such crimes* of violence than any other group similarly oppressed by poverty and compulsory ignorance.

Today the nasty and absolutely false charge returns to justify the outrageous treatment of Negroes by Americans in France.

What is the truth?

I have written to twenty-one Mayors of towns and cities

in all parts of France where Negro troops have been quartered asking them as to the conduct of black troops. These are some of their replies:

Montmorillon (Vienne)
> *"They have earned our high regard by their discipline and their faultless behavior."*

Le Mans (Sarthe)
> *"They have been accused of no crimes or misdemeanors."*

St. Dié (Vosges)
> *"Very excellent conduct."*

Bourbonne les Bains (Haute-Marne)
> *"Pleasant remembrances and irreproachable conduct."*

Liverdun (Meurthe-et-Moselle)
> *"Excellent conduct—no complaints."*

Rayon l'Etape (Vosges)
> *"Fine character and exquisite courtesy."*

Fresne (Haute-Marne)
> *"No complaints concerning their conduct."*

Domfront (Orne)
> *"Won the esteem and sympathy of all the population."*

Marbache (Meurthe-et-Moselle)
> *"No complaint—well disciplined."*

Bordeaux (Gironde)
> *"No unfavorable comments."*

Serqueux (Haute-Marne)
> *"Well-conducted—no crimes."*

Chamberey (Savoie)
> *"Proud to welcome them."*

Brest (Finistere)
> *"Not qualified to give information."*

St. Nazaire (Loire Inferieure)
> *"Cannot give any information."*

Docelles (Vosges)
> *"Good conduct, good discipline and fine spirit."*

Couptrain (Mayenne)
> *"Perfect propriety without complaint."*

Gezoncourt (Meurthe-et-Moselle)
> *"No complaint as to conduct or morals."*

Frouard (Meurthe-et-Moselle)
> *"Well-regulated conduct."*

We have, too, official figures covering the Ninety-second Division, consisting of Negro troops, with largely Negro company officers.

Only ONE soldier of the Ninety-second Division in

France was convicted of rape, while TWO others were convicted of intent to rape. . . .

MAY, 1919

AFRICA

It is likely that Du Bois thought and wrote more on Africa, especially evils of colonialism, than any other American of his generation. Early in his career he deliberately set himself to search out and publicize the story of Africa—its history, conditions, demands for freedom. This was one of the principal topics appearing in The Crisis *during the Du Bois years.*

Pan-Africa

The growth of a body of public opinion among peoples of Negro descent broad enough to be called Pan-Africanism is a movement belonging almost entirely to the twentieth century.

Seven hundred and fifty years before Christ the Negroes as rulers of Ethiopia and conquerors of Egypt were practically supreme in the civilized world; but the character of the African continent was such that this supremacy brought no continental unity; rather the inhabitants of the narrow Nile Valley set their faces toward the Mediterranean and Asia more than toward the western Sudan, the valley of the Congo and the Atlantic.

From that time even in the rise of the Sudanese kingdoms of the 13th, 14th and 15th centuries there was still no Pan-Africa; and after that the slave trade brought continental confusion.

In 1900 at the time of the Paris Exposition there was called on January 23, 24 and 25 a Pan-African Conference in Westminster Hall, London. A second conference was held at Tuskegee Institute about 1912.

Finally, at the time of the Peace Conference in Paris,

February, 1919, the first Pan-African Congress was called. The interest in this congress was world-wide among the darker peoples. Delegates were elected in the United States, the West Indies, South and West Africa and elsewhere. Most of them, of course, were prevented from attending as a result of war measures and physical difficulties.

However, there did assemble in Paris 57 delegates from 15 countries where over 85,000,000 Negroes and persons of African descent dwell. Resolutions were adopted taking up the question of the relation of Africa to the League of Nations, and the general questions of land, capital, labor, education, hygiene and the treatment of civilized Negroes. Blaise Diagne, Deputy from Senegal and Commissioner in charge of the French Colonial Troops, was elected president of a permanent organization, and W. E. B. Du Bois of the United States, Editor of THE CRISIS was made secretary. A second congress was called to meet in Paris in September, 1921.

Meantime, the feeling of the necessity for understanding among the Africans and their descendants has been growing throughout the world. There was held from March 11–29, 1920, the National Congress of British West Africa. This body after careful conference adopted resolutions concerning legislative reforms, the franchise, administrative changes, a West African University, commercial enterprise, judicial and sanitary programs. They also stated their opinion concerning the land question and self-determination and sent a deputation to the King. The deputation, consisting of three lawyers, two merchants, an ex-Deputy Mayor, a physician and a native ruler, went to England and presented to the King their demands, which included right to vote, local self-government, and other matters.

Other movements have gone on. In the agitation for Egyptian independence there is a large number of men of Negro descent. In South Africa, the African Political Organization and the Native Congress have had a number of conferences and have sent delegates to London, protesting against the land legislation of the Union of South Africa.

In the Canal Zone and in the West Indies have come movements looking toward union of effort among peoples of African descent and emphasizing the economic bond. In the United States there is the National Association for the Advancement of Colored People, with its 90,000 members and its very wide influence and activities.

Many of these movements will be represented in the second Pan-African Congress next fall, and out of this meeting will undoubtedly grow a larger and larger unity of thought among Negroes and through this, concerned action. At first this action will probably include a demand for political rights, for economic freedom—especially in relation to the land—for the abolition of slavery, peonage and caste, and for freer access to education. . . .

MAY, 1921

From *BLACK RECONSTRUCTION*

Black Reconstruction, *not as widely read as* The Souls of Black Folk *nor as influential in creating the militant Negro intelligentsia as Du Bois' writings in* The Crisis, *is considered by many his finest single work of scholarship. Certainly it was an extraordinary job of research, interpretation and writing, and is still the best history of the Reconstruction period. Also, it has probably had the most impact on white students and historians of all of Dr. Du Bois' writings. As Martin Luther King, Jr., said in his eulogy of Dr. Du Bois at Carnegie Hall, New York City, February 23, 1968,* Black Reconstruction *did as much for white people as for black, for in it he gave the whites truth where truth had been denied.*

Just to outline the important points on which Dr. Du Bois challenged and revised the "lost cause" defended by white historians would require a small volume. However, without any attempt to be exhaustive, some of these points are mentioned here.

Du Bois denies that Negroes were handed their freedom by whites. He documents his claim that they earned and deserved freedom because of their own struggles as Union soldiers (estimated at 200,000 strong), their services as Union spies, laborers and saboteurs. He makes a strong case that Reconstruction, instead of being a "tragic era," was actually one of the highest points reached in American democracy. It was during this period that effective effort was made to realize the promises in the Declaration of Independence. Reconstruction, he demonstrates, did not fall because of its own weakness but because of the Southern white power structure's use of official and unofficial fraud, economic pressure, and relentless violence, and because of Northern acquiescence in the betrayal of the ideals of equality. If Reconstruction failed, he says, it was a "splendid failure."

Du Bois defends the maligned "carpetbaggers" and depicts them as a kind of "peace corps." He refers to the work of the Northern schoolteachers who went South to teach the freedmen and poor whites how to exercise citizenship as being the "ninth crusade." He identifies the "scalawags" as being in the main loyal southern whites, usually veterans of the Union armies—37,000 whites had served as Union soldier volunteers from Tennessee alone! Also he defends the ability and character of Negro leaders during Reconstruction, some of whom were free men and highly educated before the War, and some of whom were quickly learning to govern by governing. Du Bois points out that the former slaveowners sabotaged government and refused to seek or to accept office. Therefore, many Negroes got into office by default.

Du Bois documents his charges that the Ku Klux Klan was a great underground army of midnight assassins under the leadership of the "chivalry" and made up almost entirely of Confederate army veterans; that post-Civil War "Black Codes" were reenacted, in substance if not always in form, to serve as a means of social control; and that the infamous Southern prison system, especially the chain gang and convict lease plan, was created mainly for the purpose of supplying forced labor.

In short, Du Bois said that even more than the armies of Grant and Sherman the democratizing movement of congressional Reconstruction, with solidarity between freedmen and poor whites—"scalawags" and "carpetbaggers"—threatened the social, political, and economic hegemony of the white Southern ruling class and this was what drove this class to seek Northern support in destroying the democratizing effort. The support was given and culminated in the final restoration of the old slave-owning class to power in the South and to a position of influence in the Federal government as part of the "arrangement" that placed Rutherford B. Hayes in the White House in 1876. From this point forward, Du Bois says, the United States could no longer use the ideals and lessons of the Civil War.

The tributes to this great history have been many. Francis L. Broderick, a recent Du Bois biographer, calls it "the scholarly book for which he will probably be remembered longest." Dr. Martin Luther King, Jr., said he had been influenced by its "towering contributions." Howard K. Beale, the historian, commented that this book presents "a mass of material, formerly ignored, that every future historian must reckon with." Professor Charles H. Wesley, in an essay praising Black Reconstruction, *wrote "This volume directed attention to the achievements of Reconstruction by Negroes after the Civil War."*

A big question that Du Bois raised in Black Reconstruction *and elsewhere is "How far in a state can a recognized moral wrong safely be compromised?"*

Two chapters from Black Reconstruction *are included here:* "The Propaganda of History", *and* "The Counter Revolution of Property".

The Propaganda of History

How the facts of American history have in the last half century been falsified because the nation was ashamed. The South was ashamed because it fought to perpetuate human slavery. The North was ashamed because it had to call in the black men to save the Union, abolish slavery and establish democracy.

What are American children taught today about Reconstruction? Helen Boardman has made a study of current textbooks and notes these three dominant theses:

1. *All Negroes were ignorant.*

"All were ignorant of public business." (Woodburn and Moran, "Elementary American History and Government," p. 397.)

"Although the Negroes were now free, they were also ignorant and unfit to govern themselves." (Everett Barnes, "American History for Grammar Grades," p. 334.)

"The Negroes got control of these states. They had been slaves all their lives, and were so ignorant they did not even know the letters of the alphabet. Yet they now sat in the state legislatures and made the laws." (D. H. Montgomery, "The Leading Facts of American History," p. 332.)

"In the South, the Negroes who had so suddenly gained their freedom did not know what to do with it." (Hubert Cornish and Thomas Hughes, "History of the United States for Schools," p. 345.)

"In the legislatures, the Negroes were so ignorant that they could only watch their white leaders—carpetbaggers, and vote aye or no as they were told." (S. E. Forman, "Advanced American History," Revised Edition, p. 452.)

"Some legislatures were made up of a few dishonest white men and several Negroes, many too ignorant to know anything about law-making." (Hubert Cornish and Thomas Hughes, "History of the United States for Schools," p. 349.)

2. *All Negroes were lazy, dishonest and extravagant.*

"These men knew not only nothing about the government, but also cared for nothing except what they could gain for themselves." (Helen F. Giles, "How the United States Became a World Power," p. 7.)

"Legislatures were often at the mercy of Negroes, childishly ignorant, who sold their votes openly, and whose 'loyalty' was gained by allowing them to eat, drink and

180

clothe themselves at the state's expense." (William J. Long, "America—A History of Our Country," p. 392.)

"Some Negroes spent their money foolishly, and were worse off than they had been before." (Carl Russell Fish, "History of America," p. 385.)

"This assistance led many freed men to believe that they need no longer work. They also ignorantly believed that the lands of their former masters were to be turned over by Congress to them, and that every Negro was to have as his allotment 'forty acres and a mule.'" (W. F. Gordy, "History of the United States," Part II, p. 336.)

"Thinking that slavery meant toil and that freedom meant only idleness, the slave after he was set free was disposed to try out his freedom by refusing to work." (S. E. Forman, "Advanced American History," Revised Edition.)

"They began to wander about, stealing and plundering. In one week, in a Georgia town, 150 Negroes were arrested for thieving." (Helen F. Giles, "How the United States Became a World Power," p. 6.)

3. *Negroes were responsible for bad government during Reconstruction.*

"Foolish laws were passed by the black law-makers, the public money was wasted terribly and thousands of dollars were stolen straight. Self-respecting Southerners chafed under the horrible régime." (Emerson David Fite, "These United States," p. 37.)

"In the exhausted states already amply 'punished' by the desolation of war, the rule of the Negro and his unscrupulous carpetbagger and scalawag patrons, was an orgy for extravagance, fraud and disgusting incompetency." (David Saville Muzzey, "History of the American People," p. 408.)

"The picture of Reconstruction which the average pupil in these sixteen States receives is limited to the South. The South found it necessary to pass Black Codes for the control of the shiftless and sometimes vicious freedmen. The Freedmen's Bureau caused the Negroes to look to the North rather than to the South for support and by giving them a false sense of equality did more harm than good. With the scalawags, the ignorant and non-propertyholding Negroes under the leadership of the carpetbaggers, engaged in a wild orgy of spending in the legislatures. The humiliation and distress of the Southern whites was in part relieved by the Ku Klux Klan, a secret organization which frightened the superstitious blacks." [1]

[1] "Racial Attitudes in American History Textbooks," *Journal of Negro History*, XIX, p. 257.

Grounded in such elementary and high school teaching, an American youth attending college today would learn from current textbooks of history that the Constitution recognized slavery; that the chance of getting rid of slavery by peaceful methods was ruined by the Abolitionists; that after the period of Andrew Jackson, the two sections of the United States "had become fully conscious of their conflicting interests. Two irreconcilable forms of civilization . . . in the North, the democratic . . . in the South, a more stationary and aristocratic civilization." He would read that Harriet Beecher Stowe brought on the Civil War; that the assault on Charles Sumner was due to his "coarse invective" against a South Carolina Senator; and that Negroes were the only people to achieve emancipation with no effort on their part. That Reconstruction was a disgraceful attempt to subject white people to ignorant Negro rule; and that, according to a Harvard professor of history (the italics are ours), "Legislative expenses were grotesquely extravagant; the *colored members in some states engaging in a saturnalia of corrupt expenditure*" (Encyclopaedia Britannica, 14th Edition, Volume 22, p. 815, by Frederick Jackson Turner).

In other words, he would in all probability complete his education without any idea of the part which the black race has played in America; of the tremendous moral problem of abolition; of the cause and meaning of the Civil War and the relation which Reconstruction had to democratic government and the labor movement today.

Herein lies more than mere omission and difference of emphasis. The treatment of the period of Reconstruction reflects small credit upon American historians as scientists. We have too often a deliberate attempt so to change the facts of history that the story will make pleasant reading for Americans. The editors of the fourteenth edition of the Encyclopaedia Britannica asked me for an article on the history of the American Negro. From my manuscript they cut out all my references to Reconstruction. I insisted on including the following statement:

"White historians have ascribed the faults and failures of Reconstruction to Negro ignorance and corruption. But the Negro insists that it was Negro loyalty and the Negro vote alone that restored the South to the Union; established the new democracy, both for white and black; and instituted the public schools."

This the editor refused to print, although he said that the article otherwise was "in my judgment, and in the judgment of others in the office, an excellent one, and one with which it seems to me we may all be well satisfied." I was not satisfied and refused to allow the article to appear.

War and especially civil strife leave terrible wounds. It is the duty of humanity to heal them. It was therefore soon conceived as neither wise nor patriotic to speak of all the causes of strife and the terrible results to which sectional differences in the United States had led. And so, first of all, we minimized the slavery controversy which convulsed the nation from the Missouri Compromise down to the Civil War. On top of that, we passed by Reconstruction with a phrase of regret or disgust.

But are these reasons of courtesy and philanthropy sufficient for denying Truth? If history is going to be scientific, if the record of human action is going to be set down with that accuracy and faithfulness of detail which will allow its use as a measuring rod and guidepost for the future of nations, there must be set some standards of ethics in research and interpretation.

If, on the other hand, we are going to use history for our pleasure and amusement, for inflating our national ego, and giving us a false but pleasurable sense of accomplishment, then we must give up the idea of history either as a science or as an art using the results of science, and admit frankly that we are using a version of historic fact in order to influence and educate the new generation along the way we wish.

It is propaganda like this that has led men in the past to insist that history is "lies agreed upon"; and to point out the danger in such misinformation. It is indeed extremely doubtful if any permanent benefit comes to the world through such action. Nations reel and stagger on their way; they make hideous mistakes; they commit frightful wrongs; they do great and beautiful things. And shall we not best guide humanity by telling the truth about all this, so far as the truth is ascertainable?

Here in the United States we have a clear example. It was morally wrong and economically retrogressive to build human slavery in the United States in the eighteenth century. We know that now, perfectly well; and there were many Americans North and South who knew this and said it in the eighteenth century. Today, in the face of new slavery established elsewhere in the world under other names and guises, we ought to emphasize this lesson of the past. Moreover, it is not well to be reticent in describing that past. Our histories tend to discuss American slavery so impartially, that in the end nobody seems to have done wrong and everybody was right. Slavery appears to have been thrust upon unwilling helpless America, while the South was blameless in becoming its center. The difference of development, North and South, is explained as a sort of working out of cosmic social and economic law.

One reads, for instance, Charles and Mary Beard's "Rise of American Civilization," with a comfortable feeling that nothing right or wrong is involved. Manufacturing and industry develop in the North; agrarian feudalism develops in the South. They clash, as winds and waters strive, and the stronger forces develop the tremendous industrial machine that governs us so magnificently and selfishly today.

Yet in this sweeping mechanistic interpretation, there is no room for the real plot of the story, for the clear mistake and guilt of rebuilding a new slavery of the working class in the midst of a fateful experiment in democracy; for the triumph of sheer moral courage and sacrifice in the abolition crusade; and for the hurt and struggle of degraded black millions in their fight for freedom and their attempt to enter democracy. Can all this be omitted or half suppressed in a treatise that calls itself scientific?

Or, to come nearer the center and climax of this fascinating history: What was slavery in the United States? Just what did it mean to the owner and the owned? Shall we accept the conventional story of the old slave plantation and its owner's fine, aristocratic life of cultured leisure? Or shall we note slave biographies, like those of Charles Ball, Sojourner Truth, Harriet Tubman and Frederick Douglass; the careful observations of Olmsted and the indictment of Hinton Helper?

No one can read that first thin autobiography of Frederick Douglass and have left many illusions about slavery. And if truth is our object, no amount of flowery romance and the personal reminiscences of its protected beneficiaries can keep the world from knowing that slavery was a cruel, dirty, costly and inexcusable anachronism, which nearly ruined the world's greatest experiment in democracy. No serious and unbiased student can be deceived by the fairy tale of a beautiful Southern slave civilization. If those who really had opportunity to know the South before the war wrote the truth, it was a center of widespread ignorance, undeveloped resources, suppressed humanity and unrestrained passions, with whatever veneer of manners and culture that could lie above these depths.

Coming now to the Civil War, how for a moment can anyone who reads the *Congressional Globe* from 1850 to

1860, the lives of contemporary statesmen and public characters, North and South, the discourses in the newspapers and accounts of meetings and speeches, doubt that Negro slavery was the cause of the Civil War? What do we gain by evading this clear fact, and talking in vague ways about "Union" and "State Rights" and differences in civilization as the cause of that catastrophe?

Of all historic facts there can be none clearer than that for four long and fearful years the South fought to perpetuate human slavery; and that the nation which "rose so bright and fair and died so pure of stain" was one that had a perfect right to be ashamed of its birth and glad of its death. Yet one monument in North Carolina achieves the impossible by recording of Confederate soldiers: "They died fighting for liberty!"

On the other hand, consider the North and the Civil War. Why should we be deliberately false, like Woodward, in "Meet General Grant," and represent the North as magnanimously freeing the slave without any effort on his part?

"The American Negroes are the only people in the history of the world, so far as I know, that ever became free without any effort of their own. . . .

"They had not started the war nor ended it. They twanged banjos around the railroad stations, sang melodious spirituals, and believed that some Yankee would soon come along and give each of them forty acres of land and a mule."[1]

The North went to war without the slightest idea of freeing the slave. The great majority of Northerners from Lincoln down pledged themselves to protect slavery, and they hated and harried Abolitionists. But on the other hand, the thesis which Beale tends to support that the whole North during and after the war was chiefly interested in making money, is only half true; it was abolition and belief in democracy that gained for a time the upper hand after the war and led the North in Reconstruction; business followed abolition in order to maintain the tariff, pay the bonds and defend the banks. To call this business program "the program of the North" and ignore abolition is unhistorical. In growing ascendancy for a calculable time was a great moral movement which turned the North from its economic defense of slavery and led it to Emancipation. Abolitionists attacked slavery because it was wrong and their moral battle cannot be truthfully minimized or forgotten. Nor does this fact deny that the majority of Northerners before the war were not abolitionists, that they attack slavery only in order

[1] W. E. Woodward, *Meet General Grant,* p. 372.

to win the war and enfranchised the Negro to secure this
result.

One has but to read the debates in Congress and state
papers from Abraham Lincoln down to know that the decisive action which ended the Civil War was the emancipation and arming of the black slave; that, as Lincoln said:
"Without the military help of black freedmen, the war
against the South could not have been won." The freedmen,
far from being the inert recipients of freedom at the hands
of philanthropists, furnished 200,000 soldiers in the Civil
War who took part in nearly 200 battles and skirmishes,
and in addition perhaps 300,000 others as effective laborers
and helpers. In proportion to population, more Negroes
than whites fought in the Civil War. These people, withdrawn from the support of the Confederacy, with threat of
the withdrawal of millions more, made the opposition of the
slaveholders useless, unless they themselves freed and armed
their own slaves. This was exactly what they started to do;
they were only restrained by realizing that such action removed the very cause for which they began fighting. Yet
one would search current American histories almost in vain
to find a clear statement or even faint recognition of these
perfectly well-authenticated facts.

All this is but preliminary to the kernel of the historic
problem with which this book deals, and that is Reconstruction. The chorus of agreement concerning the attempt to
reconstruct and organize the South after the Civil War and
emancipation is overwhelming. There is scarce a child in
the street that cannot tell you that the whole effort was a
hideous mistake and an unfortunate incident, based on ignorance, revenge and the perverse determination to attempt
the impossible; that the history of the United States from
1866 to 1876 is something of which the nation ought to be
ashamed and which did more to retard and set back the
American Negro than anything that has happened to him;
while at the same time it grievously and wantonly wounded
again a part of the nation already hurt to death.

True it is that the Northern historians writing just after
the war had scant sympathy for the South, and wrote ruthlessly of "rebels" and "slave-drivers." They had at least the
excuse of a war psychosis.

As a young labor leader, Will Herberg, writes: "The great
traditions of this period and especially of Reconstruction
are shamelessly repudiated by the official heirs of Stevens
and Sumner. In the last quarter of a century hardly a single
book has appeared consistently championing or sympatheti-

cally interpreting the great ideals of the crusade against slavery, whereas scores and hundreds have dropped from the presses in ignoble 'extenuation' of the North, in open apology for the Confederacy, in measureless abuse of the Radical figures of Reconstruction. The Reconstruction period as the logical culmination of decades of previous development, has borne the brunt of the reaction."[1]

First of all, we have James Ford Rhodes' history of the United States. Rhodes was trained not as an historian but as an Ohio business man. He had no broad formal education. When he had accumulated a fortune, he surrounded himself with a retinue of clerks and proceeded to manufacture a history of the United States by mass production. His method was simple. He gathered a vast number of authorities; he selected from these authorities those whose testimony supported his thesis, and he discarded the others. The majority report of the great Ku Klux investigation, for instance, he laid aside in favor of the minority report, simply because the latter supported his sincere belief. In the report and testimony of the Reconstruction Committee of Fifteen, he did practically the same thing.

Above all, he begins his inquiry convinced, without admitting any necessity of investigation, that Negroes are an inferior race:

"No large policy in our country has ever been so conspicuous a failure as that of forcing universal Negro suffrage upon the South. The Negroes who simply acted out their nature, were not to blame. How indeed could they acquire political honesty? What idea could barbarism thrust into slavery obtain of the rights of property? . . .

"From the Republican policy came no real good to the Negroes. Most of them developed no political capacity, and the few who raised themselves above the mass, did not reach a high order of intelligence."[2]

Rhodes was primarily the historian of property; of economic history and the labor movement, he knew nothing; of democratic government, he was contemptuous. He was trained to make profits. He used his profits to write history. He speaks again and again of the rulership of "intelligence and property" and he makes a plea that intelligent use of the ballot for the benefit of property is the only real foundation of democracy.

The real frontal attack on Reconstruction, as interpreted by the leaders of national thought in 1870 and for some

---

[1] Will Herberg, *The Heritage of the Civil War*, p. 3.
[2] Rhodes, *History of the United States*, VII, pp. 232–233.

time thereafter, came from the universities and particularly from Columbia and Johns Hopkins.

The movement began with Columbia University and with the advent of John W. Burgess of Tennessee and William A. Dunning of New Jersey as professors of political science and history.

Burgess was an ex-Confederate soldier who started to a little Southern college with a box of books, a box of tallow candles and a Negro boy; and his attitude toward the Negro race in after years was subtly colored by this early conception of Negroes as essentially property like books and candles. Dunning was a kindly and impressive professor who was deeply influenced by a growing group of young Southern students and began with them to re-write the history of the nation from 1860 to 1880, in more or less conscious opposition to the classic interpretations of New England.

Burgess was frank and determined in his anti-Negro thought. He expounded his theory of Nordic supremacy which colored all his political theories:

"The claim that there is nothing in the color of the skin from the point of view of political ethics is a great sophism. A black skin means membership in a race of men which has never of itself succeeded in subjecting passion to reason, has never, therefore, created any civilization of any kind. To put such a race of men in possession of a 'state' government in a system of federal government is to trust them with the development of political and legal civilization upon the most important subjects of human life, and to do this in communities with a large white population is simply to establish barbarism in power over civilization."

Burgess is a Tory and open apostle of reaction. He tells us that the nation now believes "that it is the white man's mission, his duty and his right, to hold the reins of political power in his own hands for the civilization of the world and the welfare of mankind."[1]

For this reason America is following "the European idea of the duty of civilized races to impose their political sovereignty upon civilized, or half civilized, or not fully civilized, races anywhere and everywhere in the world."[2]

He complacently believes that "There is something natural in the subordination of an inferior race to a superior race, even to the point of the enslavement of the inferior

[1] Burgess, *Reconstruction and the Constitution*, pp. viii, ix.
[2] Burgess, *Reconstruction and the Constitution*, p. 218.

race, but there is nothing natural in the opposite."[1] He therefore denominates Reconstruction as the rule "of the uncivilized Negroes over the whites of the South."[2] This has been the teaching of one of our greatest universities for nearly fifty years.

Dunning was less dogmatic as a writer, and his own statements are often judicious. But even Dunning can declare that "all the forces [in the South] that made for civilization were dominated by a mass of barbarous freedmen"; and that "the antithesis and antipathy of race and color were crucial and ineradicable."[3] The work of most of the students whom he taught and encouraged has been one-sided and partisan to the last degree. Johns Hopkins University has issued a series of studies similar to Columbia's; Southern teachers have been welcomed to many Northern universities, where often Negro students have been systematically discouraged, and thus a nation-wide university attitude has arisen by which propaganda against the Negro has been carried on unquestioned.

The Columbia school of historians and social investigators have issued between 1895 and the present time sixteen studies of Reconstruction in the Southern States, all based on the same thesis and all done according to the same method: first, endless sympathy with the white South; second, ridicule, contempt or silence for the Negro; third, a judicial attitude towards the North, which concludes that the North under great misapprehension did a grievous wrong, but eventually saw its mistake and retreated.

These studies vary, of course, in their methods. Dunning's own work is usually silent so far as the Negro is concerned. Burgess is more than fair in law but reactionary in matters of race and property, regarding the treatment of a Negro as a man as nothing less than a crime, and admitting that "the mainstay of property is the courts."

In the books on Reconstruction written by graduates of these universities and others, the studies of Texas, North Carolina, Florida, Virginia and Louisiana are thoroughly bad, giving no complete picture of what happened during Reconstruction, written for the most part by men and women without broad historical or social background, and all designed not to seek the truth but to prove a thesis. Hamilton reaches the climax of this school when he charac-

---

[1] Burgess, *Reconstruction and the Constitution*, pp. 244–245.
[2] Burgess, *Reconstruction and the Constitution*, p. 218.
[3] Dunning, *Reconstruction, Political and Economic*, pp. 212, 213.

terizes the black codes, which even Burgess condemned, as "not only . . . on the whole reasonable, temperate and kindly, but, in the main, necessary."[1]

Thompson's "Georgia" is another case in point. It seeks to be fair, but silly stories about Negroes indicating utter lack of even common sense are included, and every noble sentiment from white people. When two Negro workers, William and Jim, put a straightforward advertisement in a local paper, the author says that it was "evidently written by a white friend." There is not the slightest historical evidence to prove this, and there were plenty of educated Negroes in Augusta at the time who might have written this. Lonn's "Louisiana" puts Sheridan's words in Sherman's mouth to prove a petty point.

There are certain of these studies which, though influenced by the same general attitude, nevertheless have more of scientific poise and cultural background. Garner's "Reconstruction in Mississippi" conceives the Negro as an integral part of the scene and treats him as a human being. With this should be bracketed the recent study of "Reconstruction in South Carolina" by Simkins and Woody. This is not as fair as Garner's, but in the midst of conventional judgment and conclusion, and reproductions of all available caricatures of Negroes, it does not hesitate to give a fair account of the Negroes and of some of their work. It gives the impression of combining in one book two antagonistic points of view, but in the clash much truth emerges.

Ficklen's "Louisiana" and the works of Fleming are anti-Negro in spirit, but, nevertheless, they have a certain fairness and sense of historic honesty. Fleming's "Documentary History of Reconstruction" is done by a man who has a thesis to support, and his selection of documents supports the thesis. His study of Alabama is pure propaganda.

Next come a number of books which are openly and blatantly propaganda, like Herbert's "Solid South," and the books by Pike and Reynolds on South Carolina, the works by Pollard and Carpenter, and especially those by Ulrich Phillips. One of the latest and most popular of this series is "The Tragic Era" by Claude Bowers, which is an excellent and readable piece of current newspaper reporting, absolutely devoid of historical judgment or sociological knowledge. It is a classic example of historical propaganda of the cheaper sort.

We have books like Milton's "Age of Hate" and Win-

---

[1] Hamilton, "Southern Legislation in Respect to Freedmen" in *Studies in Southern History and Politics*, p. 156.

ston's "Andrew Johnson" which attempt to re-write the character of Andrew Johnson. They certainly add to our knowledge of the man and our sympathy for his weakness. But they cannot, for students, change the calm testimony of unshaken historical facts. Fuess' "Carl Schurz" paints the picture of this fine liberal, and yet goes out of its way to show that he was quite wrong in what he said he saw in the South.

The chief witness in Reconstruction, the emancipated slave himself, has been almost barred from court. His written Reconstruction record has been largely destroyed and nearly always neglected. Only three or four states have preserved the debates in the Reconstruction conventions; there are few biographies of black leaders. The Negro is refused a hearing because he was poor and ignorant. It is therefore assumed that all Negroes in Reconstruction were ignorant and silly and that therefore a history of Reconstruction in any state can quite ignore him. The result is that most unfair caricatures of Negroes have been carefully preserved; but serious speeches, successful administration and upright character are almost universally ignored and forgotten. Wherever a black head rises to historic view, it is promptly slain by an adjective—"shrewd," "notorious," "cunning"— or pilloried by a sneer; or put out of view by some quite unproven charge of bad moral character. In other words, every effort has been made to treat the Negro's part in Reconstruction with silence and contempt.

When recently a student tried to write on education in Florida, he found that the official records of the excellent administration of the colored Superintendent of Education, Gibbs, who virtually established the Florida public school, had been destroyed. Alabama has tried to obliterate all printed records of Reconstruction.

Especially noticeable is the fact that little attempt has been made to trace carefully the rise and economic development of the poor whites and their relation to the planters and to Negro labor after the war. There were five million or more non-slaveholding whites in the South in 1860 and less than two million in the families of all slaveholders. Yet one might almost gather from contemporary history that the five million left no history and had no descendants. The extraordinary history of the rise and triumph of the poor whites has been largely neglected, even by Southern white students.[1]

The whole development of Reconstruction was primarily an economic development, but no economic history or

---

[1] Interesting exceptions are Moore's and Ambler's monographs.

proper material for it has been written. It has been regarded as a purely political matter, and of politics most naturally divorced from industry.[1]

All this is reflected in the textbooks of the day and in the encyclopedias, until we have got to the place where we cannot use our experiences during and after the Civil War for the uplift and enlightenment of mankind. We have spoiled and misconceived the position of the historian. If we are going, in the future, not simply with regard to this one question, but with regard to all social problems, to be able to use human experience for the guidance of mankind, we have got clearly to distinguish between fact and desire.

In the first place, somebody in each era must make clear the facts with utter disregard to his own wish and desire and belief. What we have got to know, so far as possible, are the things that actually happened in the world. Then with that much clear and open to every reader, the philosopher and prophet has a chance to interpret these facts; but the historian has no right, posing as scientist, to conceal or distort facts; and until we distinguish between these two functions of the chronicler of human action, we are going to render it easy for a muddled world out of sheer ignorance to make the same mistake ten times over.

One is astonished in the study of history at the recurrence of the idea that evil must be forgotten, distorted, skimmed over. We must not remember that Daniel Webster got drunk but only remember that he was a splendid constitutional lawyer. We must forget that George Washington was a slave owner, or that Thomas Jefferson had mulatto children, or that Alexander Hamilton had Negro blood, and simply remember the things we regard as creditable and inspiring. The difficulty, of course, with this philosophy is that history loses its value as an incentive and example; it paints perfect men and noble nations, but it does not tell the truth.

No one reading the history of the United States during 1850–1860 can have the slightest doubt left in his mind that Negro slavery was the cause of the Civil War, and yet during and since we learn that a great nation murdered thousands and destroyed millions on account of abstract doctrines concerning the nature of the Federal Union. Since the attitude of the nation concerning state rights has been revolutionized by the development of the central government since the war, the whole argument becomes an aston-

---

[1] *The Economic History of the South* by E. Q. Hawk is merely a compilation of census reports and conventionalities.

ishing *reductio ad absurdum,* leaving us apparently with no cause for the Civil War except the recent reiteration of statements which make the great public men on one side narrow, hypocritical fanatics and liars, while the leaders on the other side were extraordinary and unexampled for their beauty, unselfishness and fairness.

Not a single great leader of the nation during the Civil War and Reconstruction has escaped attack and libel. The magnificent figures of Charles Sumner and Thaddeus Stevens have been besmirched almost beyond recognition. We have been cajoling and flattering the South and slurring the North, because the South is determined to re-write the history of slavery and the North is not interested in history but in wealth.

This, then, is the book basis upon which today we judge Reconstruction. In order to paint the South as a martyr to inescapable fate, to make the North the magnanimous emancipator, and to ridicule the Negro as the impossible joke in the whole development, we have in fifty years, by libel, innuendo and silence, so completely misstated and obliterated the history of the Negro in America and his relation to its work and government that today it is almost unknown. This may be fine romance, but it is not science. It may be inspiring, but it is certainly not the truth. And beyond this it is dangerous. It is not only part foundation of our present lawlessness and loss of democratic ideals; it has, more than that, led the world to embrace and worship the color bar as social salvation and it is helping to range mankind in ranks of mutual hatred and contempt, at the summons of a cheap and false myth.

Nearly all recent books on Reconstruction agree with each other in discarding the government reports and substituting selected diaries, letters, and gossip. Yet it happens that the government records are an historic source of wide and unrivaled authenticity. There is the report of the select Committee of Fifteen, which delved painstakingly into the situation all over the South and called all kinds and conditions of men to testify; there are the report of Carl Schurz and the twelve volumes of reports made on the Ku Klux conspiracy; and above all, the *Congressional Globe.* None who has not read page by page the *Congressional Globe,* especially the sessions of the 39th Congress, can possibly have any idea of what the problems of Reconstruction facing the United States were in 1865–1866. Then there were the reports of the Freedmen's Bureau and the executive and other documentary reports of government officials, especially in the war and treasury departments, which give the historian the only groundwork upon which he can build a real and truthful picture. There are certain historians who have not tried deliberately to falsify the picture: Southern whites like Frances Butler Leigh and Susan Smedes; Northern historians, like McPherson, Oberholtzer, and Nicolay and Hay. There are foreign travelers like Sir George Campbell, Georges Clemenceau and Robert Somers. There are the personal reminiscences of Augustus Beard, George Julian, George F. Hoar, Carl Schurz and John Sherman. There are the invaluable work of Edward McPherson and the more recent studies by Paul Haworth, A. A. Taylor, and Charles Wesley. Beale simply does not take Negroes into account in the critical year of 1866.

Certain monographs deserve all praise, like those of Hendricks and Pierce. The work of Flack is prejudiced but built on study. The defense of the carpetbag régime by Tourgée and Allen, Powell Clayton, Holden and Warmoth are worthy antidotes to the certain writers.

The lives of Stevens and Sumner are revealing even when slightly apologetic because of the Negro; while Andrew Johnson is beginning to suffer from writers who are trying to prove how seldom he got drunk, and think that important.

It will be noted that for my authority in this work I have depended very largely upon secondary material; upon state histories of Reconstruction, written in the main by those who were convinced before they began to write that the Negro was incapable of government, or of becoming a constituent part of a civilized state. The fairest of these histories have not tried to conceal facts; in other cases, the black man has been largely ignored; while in still others, he has been traduced and ridiculed. If I had had time and money and opportunity to go back to the original sources in all cases, there can be no doubt that the weight of this work would have been vastly strengthened, and as I firmly believe, the case of the Negro more convincingly set forth.

Various volumes of papers in the great libraries like the Johnson papers in the Library of Congress, the Sumner manuscripts at Harvard, the Schurz correspondence, the Wells papers, the Chase papers, the Fessenden and Greeley collections, the McCulloch, McPherson, Sherman, Stevens and Trumbull papers, all must have much of great interest to the historians of the American Negro. I have not had time nor opportunity to examine these, and most of those who have examined them had little interest in black folk.

Negroes have done some excellent work on their own history and defense. It suffers of course from natural partisanship and a desire to prove a case in the face of a chorus of unfair attacks. Its best work also suffers from the fact that Negroes with difficulty reach an audience. But this is also true of such white writers as Skaggs and Bancroft who could not get first-class publishers because they were saying something that the nation did not like.

The Negro historians began with autobiographies and reminiscences. The older historians were George W. Williams and Joseph T. Wilson; the new school of historians is led by Carter G. Woodson; and I have been greatly helped by the unpublished theses of four of the youngest Negro students. It is most unfortunate that while many young white Southerners can get funds to attack and ridicule the Negro and his friends, it is almost impossible for first-class Negro students to get a chance for research or to get finished work in print.

I write then in a field devastated by passion and belief. Naturally, as a Negro, I cannot do this writing without believing in the essential humanity of Negroes, in their ability to be educated, to do the work of the modern world, to take their place as equal citizens with others. I cannot for a moment subscribe to that bizarre doctrine of race that makes most men inferior to the few. But, too, as a student of science, I want to be fair, objective and judicial; to let no searing of the memory by intolerable insult and cruelty make me fail to sympathize with human frailties and contradiction, in the eternal paradox of good and evil. But armed and warned by all this, and fortified by long study of the facts, I stand at the end of this writing, literally aghast at what American historians have done to this field.

What is the object of writing the history of Reconstruction? Is it to wipe out the disgrace of a people which fought to make slaves of Negroes? Is it to show that the North had higher motives than freeing black men? Is it to prove that Negroes were black angels? No, it is simply to establish the Truth, on which Right in the future may be built. We shall never have a science of history until we have in our colleges men who regard the truth as more important than the defense of the white race, and who will not deliberately encourage students to gather thesis material in order to support a prejudice or buttress a lie.

Three-fourths of the testimony against the Negro in Reconstruction is on the unsupported evidence of men who hated and despised Negroes and regarded it as loyalty to blood, patriotism to country, and filial tribute to the fathers to lie, steal or kill in order to discredit these black folk. This may be a natural result when a people have been humbled and impoverished and degraded in their own life; but what is inconceivable is that another generation and another group should regard this testimony as scientific truth, when it is contradicted by logic and by fact. This chapter, therefore, which in logic should be a survey of books and sources, becomes of sheer necessity an arraignment of American historians and an indictment of their ideals. With a determination unparalleled in science, the mass of American writers have started out so to distort the facts of the greatest critical period of American history as to prove right wrong and wrong right. I am not familiar enough with the vast field of human history to pronounce on the relative guilt of these and historians of other times and fields; but I do say that if the history of the past has been written in the same fashion, it is useless as science and misleading as ethics. It simply shows that with sufficient general agreement and determination among the dominant classes, the truth of history may be utterly distorted and contradicted and changed to any convenient fairy tale that the masters of men wish.

I cannot believe that any unbiased mind, with an ideal of truth and of scientific judgment, can read the plain, authentic facts of our history, during 1860–1880, and come to conclusions essentially different from mine; and yet I stand virtually alone in this interpretation. So much so that the very cogency of my facts would make me hesitate, did I not seem to see plain reasons. Subtract from Burgess his belief that only white people can rule, and he is in essential agreement with me. Remember that Rhodes was an uneducated money-maker who hired clerks to find the facts which he needed to support his thesis, and one is convinced that the same labor and expense could easily produce quite opposite results.

One fact and one alone explains the attitude of most recent writers toward Reconstruction; they cannot conceive Negroes as men; in their minds the word "Negro" connotes "inferiority" and "stupidity" lightened only by unreasoning gayety and humor. Suppose the slaves of 1860 had been white folk. Stevens would have been a great statesman, Sumner a great democrat, and Schurz a keen prophet, in a mighty revolution of rising humanity. Ignorance and poverty would easily have been explained by history, and the demand for land and the franchise would have been justified as the birthright of natural freemen.

But Burgess was a slaveholder, Dunning a Copperhead and Rhodes an exploiter of wage labor. Not one of them apparently ever met an educated Negro of force and ability. Around such impressive thinkers gathered the young postwar students from the South. They had been born and reared in the bitterest period of Southern race hatred, fear and contempt. Their instinctive reactions were confirmed and encouraged in the best of American universities. Their scholarship, when it regarded black men, became deaf, dumb and blind. The clearest evidence of Negro ability, work, honesty, patience, learning and efficiency became distorted into cunning, brute toil, shrewd evasion, cowardice and imitation—a stupid effort to transcend nature's law.

For those seven mystic years between Johnson's "swing 'round the circle" and the panic of 1873, a majority of thinking Americans in the North believed in the equal manhood of black folk. They acted accordingly with a clear-cut decisiveness and thorough logic, utterly incomprehensible to a day like ours which does not share this human faith; and to Southern whites this period can only be explained by deliberate vengeance and hate.

The panic of 1873 brought sudden disillusion in business enterprise, economic organization, religious belief and political standards. A flood of appeal from the white South reënforced this reaction—appeal with no longer the arrogant bluster of slave oligarchy, but the simple moving annals of the plight of a conquered people. The resulting emotional and intellectual rebound of the nation made it nearly inconceivable in 1876 that ten years earlier most men had believed in human equality.

Assuming, therefore, as axiomatic the endless inferiority of the Negro race, these newer historians, mostly Southerners, some Northerners who deeply sympathized with the South, misinterpreted, distorted, even deliberately ignored any fact that challenged or contradicted this assumption. If the Negro was admittedly sub-human, what need to waste time delving into his Reconstruction history? Consequently historians of Reconstruction with a few exceptions ignore the Negro as completely as possible, leaving the reader wondering why an element apparently so insignificant filled the whole Southern picture at the time. The only real excuse for this attitude is loyalty to a lost cause, reverence for brave fathers and suffering mothers and sisters, and fidelity to the ideals of a clan and class. But in propaganda against the

Negro since emancipation in this land, we face one of the most stupendous efforts the world ever saw to discredit human beings, an effort involving universities, history, science, social life and religion.

The most magnificent drama in the last thousand years of human history is the transportation of ten million human beings out of the dark beauty of their mother continent into the new-found Eldorado of the West. They descended into Hell; and in the third century they arose from the dead, in the finest effort to achieve democracy for the working millions which this world had ever seen. It was a tragedy that beggared the Greek; it was an upheaval of humanity like the Reformation and the French Revolution. Yet we are blind and led by the blind. We discern in it no part of our labor movement; no part of our industrial triumph; no part of our religious experience. Before the dumb eyes of ten generations of ten million children, it is made mockery of and spit upon; a degradation of the eternal mother; a sneer at human effort; with aspiration and art deliberately and elaborately distorted. And why? Because in a day when the human mind aspired to a science of human action, a history and psychology of the mighty effort of the mightiest century, we fell under the leadership of those who would compromise with truth in the past in order to make peace in the present and guide policy in the future.

One reads the truer deeper facts of Reconstruction with a great despair. It is at once so simple and human, and yet so futile. There is no villain, no idiot, no saint. There are just men; men who crave ease and power, men who know want and hunger, men who have crawled. They all dream and strive with ecstasy of fear and strain of effort, balked of hope and hate. Yet the rich world is wide enough for all, wants all, needs all. So slight a gesture, a word, might set the strife in order, not with full content, but with growing dawn of fulfillment. Instead roars the crash of hell; and after its whirlwind a teacher sits in academic halls, learned in the tradition of its elms and its elders. He looks into the upturned face of youth and in him youth sees the gowned shape of wisdom and hears the voice of God. Cynically he sneers at "chinks" and "niggers." He says that the nation "has changed its views in regard to the political relation of races and has at last virtually accepted the ideas of the South upon that subject. The white men of the South need now have no further fear that the Republican party, or Republican Administrations, will ever again give themselves over to the vain imagination of the political equality of man."[1]

Counter-Revolution of Property

How, after the war, triumphant industry in the North coupled with privilege and monopoly led an orgy of theft that engulfed the nation and was the natural child of war; and how revolt against this anarchy became reaction against democracy, North and South, and delivered the land into the hands of an organized monarchy of finance while it overthrew the attempt at a dictatorship of labor in the South.

The abolition-democracy of the North had been willing to try real democracy in the South because they believed in the capabilities of the Negro race and also because they had passed through war, oligarchy, and the almost unbridled power of Andrew Johnson. Relatively few of them believed in the mass of Negroes any more than they believed in the mass of whites; but they expected that with education, economic opportunity and the protection of the ballot, there would arise the intelligent and thrifty Negro to take his part in the community, while the mass would make average labor. Perhaps they did not expect the proportion of thrift and intelligence to equal that of the whites, but they knew certain possibilities from experience and acquaintance.

The machinery they were compelled to set up, with the coöperation of Northern industry, was a dictatorship of far broader possibilities than the North had at first contemplated. It put such power in the hands of Southern labor that, with intelligent and unselfish leadership and a clarifying ideal, it could have rebuilt the economic foundations of Southern society, confiscated and redistributed wealth, and built a real democracy of industry for the masses of men. When the South realized this they emitted an exceeding great cry which was the reaction of property being de-

---

[1] Burgess, *Reconstruction and the Constitution*, p. 298.

spoiled of its legal basis of being. This bitter complaint was all the more plausible because Southern labor lacked sufficient intelligent and unselfish leadership. Some in truth it got—from black men who gave their heart's blood to make Reconstruction go; from white men who sacrificed everything to teach and guide Negroes. But for the most part their leaders were colored men of limited education, with the current honesty of the times and little experience, and Northern and Southern whites who varied from conventional and indifferent officeholders to demagogues, thieves, and scoundrels.

The next step would have been, under law and order, gradually to have replaced the wrong leaders by a better and better sort. This the Negroes and many whites sought to do from 1870 to 1876. But they failed because the military dictatorship behind labor did not function successfully in the face of the Ku Klux Klan and especially because the appeal of property in the South got the ear of property in the North.

After the war, industry in the North found itself with a vast organization for production, new supplies of raw material, a growing transportation system on land and water, and a new technical knowledge of processes. All this, with the exclusion of foreign competition through a system of import taxes, and a vast immigration of laborers, tremendously stimulated the production of goods and available services. But to whom were the new goods and the increased services to belong, and in whose hands would lie the power which that ownership gave?

An almost unprecedented scramble for this new power, new wealth and new income ensued. It broke down old standards of wealth distribution, old standards of thrift and honesty. It led to the anarchy of thieves, grafters, and highwaymen. It threatened the orderly processes of production as well as government and morals. The governments, federal, state and local, had paid three-fifths of the cost of the railroads and handed them over to individuals and corporations to use for their profit. An empire of rich land, larger than France, Belgium and Holland together, had been snatched from the hands of prospective peasant farmers and given to investors and land speculators. All of the national treasure of coal, oil, copper, gold and iron had been given away for a song to be made the monopolized basis of private fortunes with perpetual power to tax labor for the right to live and work. Speculation rose and flourished on the hard foundation of this largess. . . .

The slime of this era of theft and corruption, which engulfed the nation, did not pass by the South. Legislators and public officials were bribed. Black men and white men were eager to get rich. In every Southern state white members of the old planting aristocracy were part and parcel of the new thieving and grafting. But the South did not lay the blame of all this on war and poverty, and weak human nature, or on the wretched example of the whole nation. No. After first blaming greedy and vengeful Northerners and then holding up to public execration those Southerners who accepted Negro suffrage, THE SOUTH, FINALLY, WITH ALMOST COMPLETE UNITY, NAMED THE NEGRO AS THE MAIN CAUSE OF SOUTHERN CORRUPTION. THEY SAID, AND REITERATED THIS CHARGE, UNTIL IT BECAME HISTORY: THAT THE CAUSE OF DISHONESTY DURING RECONSTRUCTION WAS THE FACT THAT 4,000,000 DISFRANCHISED BLACK LABORERS, AFTER 250 YEARS OF EXPLOITATION, HAD BEEN GIVEN A LEGAL RIGHT TO HAVE SOME VOICE IN THEIR OWN GOVERNMENT, IN THE KINDS OF GOODS THEY WOULD MAKE AND THE SORT OF WORK THEY WOULD DO, AND IN THE DISTRIBUTION OF THE WEALTH WHICH THEY CREATED. . . .

Great corporations, through their control of new capital, began to establish a super-government. On the one hand, they crushed the robber-barons, the thieves and the grafters, and thus appeased those of the old school who demanded the old standards of personal honesty. Secondly, they made treaty with the petty bourgeoisie by guarantying them reasonable and certain income from their investments, while they gradually deprived them of real control in industry. And finally, they made treaty with labor by dealing with it as a powerful, determined unit and dividing it up into skilled union labor, with which the new industry shared profit in the shape of a higher wage and other privileges, and a great reservoir of common and foreign labor which it kept at work at low wages with the threat of starvation and with police control.

Control of super-capital and big business was being developed during the ten years of Southern Reconstruction and was dependent and consequent upon the failure of democracy in the South, just as it fattened upon the perversion of democracy in the North. And when once the control of industry by big business was certain through consolidation and manipulation that included both North and South, big business shamelessly deserted, not only the Negro, but the cause of democracy; not only in the South, but in the North. . . .

In the South universal suffrage could not function without personal freedom, land and education, and until these institutions were real and effective, only a benevolent dictatorship in the ultimate interests of labor, black and white, could establish democracy. . . .

The object of this new American industrial empire, so far as that object was conscious and normative, was not national well-being, but the individual gain of the associated and corporate monarchs through the power of vast profit on enormous capital investment; through the efficiency of an industrial machine that bought the highest managerial and engineering talent and used the latest and most effective methods and machines in a field of unequaled raw material and endless market demand. That this machine might use the profit for the general weal was possible and in cases true. But the uplift and well-being of the mass of men, of the cohorts of common labor, was not its ideal or excuse. Profit, income, uncontrolled power in My Business for My Property and for Me—this was the aim and method of the new monarchial dictatorship that displaced democracy in the United States in 1876.

Part and parcel of this system was the emancipated South. Property control especially of land and labor had always dominated politics in the South, and after the war, it set itself to put labor to work at a wage approximating as nearly as possible slavery conditions, in order to restore capital lost in the war. . . .

It had been insistently and firmly believed by the best thought of the South: (1) that the Negro could not work as a free laborer; (2) that the Negro could not really be educated, being congenitally inferior; (3) that if political power were given to Negroes it would result virtually in the overthrow of civilization.

Now, it is quite clear that during the period we are studying, the results failed to prove these assumptions. First of all, the Negro did work as a free laborer. Slowly but certainly the tremendous losses brought on by the Civil War were restored, and restoration, as compared with other great wars, was comparatively rapid. By 1870, the Cotton Kingdom was reëstablished, and by 1875, the South knew that with cheap labor and freedom from government control, it was possible for individuals to reap large profit in the old agriculture and in new industry. . . .

If we include in "morals" and "culture" the prevailing manner of holding and distributing wealth, then the sudden enfranchisement of a mass of laborers threatens fundamental and far-reaching change, no matter what their race or color. It was this that the South feared and had reason to fear. Economic revolution did not come immediately. Negro labor was ignorant, docile and conservative. But it was beginning to learn; it was beginning to assert itself. It was beginning to have radical thoughts as to the distribution of land and wealth. . . .

The bitter conflict, therefore, which followed the enfranchisement of Negro labor and of white labor, came because impoverished property holders were compelled by the votes of poor men to bear a burden which meant practically confiscation of much of that property which remained to them and were denied opportunity to exploit labor in the future as they had in the past. It was not, then, that the post-bellum South could not produce wealth with free labor; it was the far more fundamental question as to whom this wealth was to belong to and for whose interests laborers were to work. There is no doubt that the object of the black and white labor vote was gradually conceived as one which involved confiscating the property of the rich. This was a program that could not be openly avowed by intelligent men in 1870, but it has become one of the acknowledged functions of the state in 1933; and it is quite possible that long before the end of the twentieth century, the deliberate distribution of property and income by the state on an equitable and logical basis will be looked upon as the state's prime function.

Put all these facts together and one gets a clear idea, not of the failure of Negro suffrage in the South, but of the basic difficulty which it encountered; and the results are quite consistent with a clear judgment that Negro and white labor ought to have had the right to vote; that they ought to have tried to change the basis of property and redistribute income; and that their failure to do this was a disaster to democratic government in the United States.

To men like Charles Sumner, the future of democracy in America depended on bringing the Southern revolution to a successful close by accomplishing two things: the making of the black freedmen really free, and the sweeping away of the animosities due to the war.

What liberalism did not understand was that such a revolution was economic and involved force. Those who against the public weal have power cannot be expected to yield save to superior power. The North used its power in the Civil War to break the political power of the slave barons. During and after the war, it united its force with that of the workers to uproot the still vast economic power of the planters. It hoped with the high humanitarianism of Charles Sumner eventually to induce the planter to surrender his economic power peacefully, in return for complete political amnesty, and hoped that the North would use its federal police power to maintain the black man's civil rights in return for peaceful industry and increasing intelligence. But Charles Sumner did not realize, and that other Charles—Karl Marx—had not yet published *Das Kapital* to prove to men that economic power underlies politics. Abolitionists failed to see that after the momentary exaltation of war, the nation did not want Negroes to have civil rights and that national industry could get its way easier by alliance with Southern landholders than by sustaining Southern workers. They did not know that when they let the dictatorship of labor be overthrown in the South they surrendered the hope of democracy in America for all men. . . .

The basic difficulty with the South after the war was poverty, a depth of grinding poverty not easily conceivable even in these days of depression. In the first place, it goes without saying that the emancipated slave was poor; he was desperately poor, and poor in a way that we do not easily grasp today. He was, and always had been, without money and, except for his work in the Union Army, had no way of getting hold of cash. He could ordinarily get no labor contract that involved regular or certain payments of cash. He was without clothes and without a home. He had no way to rent or build a home. Food had to be begged or stolen, unless in some way he could get hold of land or go to work; and hired labor would, if he did not exercise the greatest care and get honest advice, result in something that was practically slavery. . . .

But after all, the amount of cash handled by the freedman was small and by far the most pressing of his problems as a worker was that of land. This land hunger—this absolutely fundamental and essential thing to any real emancipation of the slaves—was continually pushed by all emancipated Negroes and their representatives in every Southern state. It was met by ridicule, by anger, and by dishonest and insincere efforts to satisfy it apparently. . . .

A million acres among a million farmers meant nothing, and from the beginning there was need of from 25 to 50 million acres more if the Negroes were to be installed as peasant farmers. Against any plan of this sort was the settled determination of the planter South to keep the bulk of

Negroes as landless laborers and the deep repugnance on the part of Northerners to confiscating individual property. . . .

Surprise and ridicule has often been voiced concerning this demand of Negroes for land. It has been regarded primarily as a method of punishing rebellion. Motives of this sort may have been in the minds of some Northern whites, but so far as the Negroes were concerned, their demand for a reasonable part of the land on which they had worked for a quarter of a millennium was absolutely justified, and to give them anything less than this was an economic farce. On the other hand, to have given each one of the million Negro free families a forty-acre freehold would have made a basis of real democracy in the United States that might easily have transformed the modern world. . . .

Demand for land by government action and the increased disposition to vote public funds for the benefit of the pauperized masses incensed the planters. In every Southern state, the South from 1868 to 1876 stressed more and more the anomaly of letting people who had no property vote away the wealth of the rich. The strongest statement of the case against the black legislature of South Carolina was that they paid almost no taxes upon property, they who for the most part had only had the right to hold property since 1866.

This charge against the poor, frequent as it always is in democratic movements, is not valid. The first attempt of a democracy which includes the previously disfranchised poor is to redistribute wealth and income, and this is exactly what the black South attempted. The theory is that the wealth and the current income of the wealthy ruling class does not belong to them entirely, but is the product of the work and striving of the great millions; and that, therefore, these millions ought to have a voice in its more equitable distribution; and if this is true in modern countries, like France and England and Germany, how much more true was it in the South after the war where the poorest class represented the most extreme case of theft of labor that the world can conceive; namely, chattel slavery? . . .

Moreover, it is certain that unless the right to vote had been given the Negro by Federal law in 1867, he would never have got it in America. There never has been a time since when race propaganda in America offered the slightest chance for colored people to receive American citizenship. There would have been, therefore, perpetuated in the South and in America, a permanently disfranchised mass of laborers; and the dictatorship of capital would, under those circumstances, have been even more firmly implanted than it is today. . . .

Property involves theft by the Rich from the Poor; but there comes a grave question; given a mass of ignorance and poverty, is that mass less dangerous without the ballot? The answer to this depends upon whose danger one envisages. They are not dangerous to the mass of laboring men. If they are kept in ignorance and poverty and dominated by capital, they are certainly dangerous to capital. To escape such revolution and prolong its sway property must yield political power to the mass of laborers, and let it wield that power more intelligently by giving it public schools and higher wages. It is naturally easier for capital to do this gradually, and if there could have been a choice in 1867 between an effective public school system for black labor in the South and its gradual enfranchisement, or even beyond that, a property qualification for such laborers as through free land and higher wage had some chance to accumulate some property—if this had been possible, it would have been, without doubt, the best transition program for capital and labor, provided of course that capitalists thus tamely yielded power. But there was no such alternative. Labor, black labor, must be either enfranchised or enslaved, unless, of course, the United States government was willing to come in with a permanent Freedmen's Bureau to train Negroes toward economic freedom and against the interest of Southern capital. This was revolution. This was force and no such permanent Freedmen's Bureau backed by a strongly capitalistic Northern government could have been expected in 1867.

The essential problem of Negro enfranchisement was this: How far is the poor and ignorant electorate a permanent injury to the state, and how far does the extent of the injury make for efforts to counteract it? More than a million Negroes were enfranchised in 1867. Of these, it is possible that between 100,000 and 200,000 could read and write, and certainly not more than 25,000, including black immigrants from the North, could be called educated. It was the theory that if these people were given the right to vote, the state, first of all, would be compelled to discontinue plans of political action or industrial organization which did not accord with the general plans of the North, and secondly, in self-defense, it would have to begin the education of the freedmen and establish a system of free labor with wages and conditions of work much fairer than those in vogue during slavery.

How far was this a feasible social program? It was not possible, of course, if the South had the right to continue its industrial organization based on land monopoly and ownership of labor. Conceding the emancipation of labor, that emancipation meant nothing if land monopoly continued and the wage contract was merely nominal. If a wage system was to be installed, it must receive protection either from an outside power, like that of the Federal government, or from the worker himself. So far as the worker was concerned, the only protection feasible was the ballot in the hands of a united and intelligently led working class. Could it be assumed now that the possession of the ballot in the hands of ignorant working people, black and white, would lead to real economic emancipation, or on the other hand would it not become a menace to the state so great that its very existence would be threatened?

It had been the insistent contention of many that the basis of the state was threatened between 1867 and 1876 and, therefore, the revolution of 1876 had to take place. The known facts do not sustain this contention and it seems probable that if we had preserved a more complete story of the action of the Negro voter the facts in his favor would even be stronger. As it is, it must be remembered that the proponents of Negro suffrage did not for a moment contend that the experiment was not difficult and would not involve hardship and danger. The elections for the conventions went off, for the most part, without upheaval, with intelligence and certainly with unusual fairness. The conduct of the Negro voters, their selection of candidates, their action in conventions and early legislatures, was, on the whole, sane, thoughtful, and sincere. No one can, with any color of truth, say that civilization was threatened or the foundations of the state attacked in the South in the years from 1868 to 1876.

Then, however, came a time of decisions. Did the South want the Negro to become an intelligent voter and participant in the state under any circumstances, or on the other hand was it opposed to Negro voters no matter how intelligent and efficient?

It may be said, then, that the argument for giving the right to vote to the mass of the poor and ignorant still stands as defensible, without for a moment denying that there should not be such a class in any civilized community;

but if the class is there, the fault is the fault of the community and the community must suffer and pay for it. The South had exploited Negro labor for nearly two and one-half centuries. If in ten years or twenty years things could be so changed that this class was receiving an education, getting hold of land, exercising some control over capital, and becoming co-partners in the state, the South would be a particularly fortunate community.

If, on the other hand, there had been the moral strength in the South so that without yielding immediate political power, they could have educated and uplifted the blacks and gradually inducted them into political power and real industrial emancipation, the results undoubtedly would have been better. There was no such disposition, and under the profit ideal of a capitalist organization, there could not have been. That would have required, after the losses of war, an industrial unselfishness of which capitalist organization does not for a moment admit. Force, therefore, and outside force, had to be applied or otherwise slavery would have persisted in a but slightly modified form, and the persistence of slavery in the United States longer than it had already persisted would have been a calamity worse than any of the calamities, real or imagined, of Reconstruction.

Consequently, with Northern white leadership, the Negro voters quite confounded the planter plan; they proved apt pupils in politics. They developed their own leadership. They gained clearer and clearer conceptions of how their political power could be used for their own good. They were unselfish, too, in wishing to include in their own good the white worker and even the ex-master. Of course, all that was done in Constitution-making and legislation at this time was not entirely the work of black men, and in the same way all that was done in maladministration and corruption was not entirely the fault of the black man. But if the black man is to be blamed for the ills of Reconstruction, he must also be credited for its good, and that good is indubitable. In less than ten years, the basic structure of capitalism in the South was changed by his vote. A new modern state was erected in the place of agrarian slavery. And its foundations were so sound and its general plan so good that despite bitter effort, the South had to accept universal suffrage in theory at least, and had to accept the public school system. It had to broaden social control by adding to the landholder the industrial capitalist.

Indeed the Negro voter in Reconstruction had disappointed all the prophets. The bravest of the carpetbaggers,

Tourgée, declared concerning the Negro voters: "They instituted a public school system in a realm where public schools had been unknown. They opened the ballot-box and jury box to thousands of white men who had been debarred from them by a lack of earthly possessions. They introduced home rule in the South. They abolished the whipping post, and branding iron, the stocks and other barbarous forms of punishment which had up to that time prevailed. They reduced capital felonies from about twenty to two or three. In an age of extravagance they were extravagant in the sums appropriated for public works. In all that time no man's rights of person were invaded under the forms of laws." The Negro buttressed Southern civilization in precisely the places it was weakest, against popular ignorance, oligarchy in government, and land monopoly. His schools were more and more successful. If now he became a recognized part of the state, a larger and larger degree of social equality must be granted him. This was apparent in his demand for a single system of public schools without discrimination of race—a demand that came for obvious reasons of economy as well as for advantages of social contact. It appeared also in the demand for equal accommodations on railroads and in public places.

Ultimately, of course, a single system of public schools, and state universities without distinction of race, and equality of civil rights was going to lead to some social intermingling and attacks upon the anti-intermarriage laws which encouraged miscegenation and deliberately degraded women. This was a possibility that the planter class could not contemplate without concern and it stirred among the poor whites a blind and unreasoning fury. . . .

These facts and similar ones show that the overthrow of Reconstruction was in essence a revolution inspired by property, and not a race war. . . .

It is one of the anomalies of history that political and economic reform in the North and West after 1873 joined hands with monopoly and reaction in the South to oppress and reënslave labor.

Every effort was made by careful propaganda to induce the nation to believe that the Southern wing of the Democratic party was fighting the same kind of corruption as the North and that corruption was represented in the South solely by carpetbaggers and Negroes. This was only partly true in the South; for there labor too was fighting corruption and dishonesty, so far as land and capital, which were secretly abetting graft in order to escape taxation, would allow it to do so without disfranchisement. But the South now began to use the diplomacy so badly lacking in its previous leadership since the war. Adroitly it stopped attacking abolitionists and even carpetbaggers, and gradually transferred all the blame for post-war misgovernment to the Negroes. The Negro vote and graft were indissolubly linked in the public mind by incessant propaganda. Race repulsion, race hate, and race pride were increased by every subtle method, until the Negro and his friends were on the defensive and the Negro himself almost convinced of his own guilt. Negro haters and pseudo-scientists raised their heads and voices in triumph. Lamar of Mississippi, fraudulently elected to Congress, unctuously praised Sumner with his tongue in his cheek; and Louisiana solemnly promised to give Negroes full political and civil rights with equal education for Negro children—a deliberate lie which is absolutely proven by the revelations of the last fifty years.

The South was impelled to brute force and deliberate deception in dealing with the Negro because it had been astonished and disappointed not by the Negro's failure, but by his success and promise of greater success.

All this came at a time when the best conscience of the nation—the conscience which was heir to the enthusiasm of abolitionist-democracy—was turned against the only power which could support democracy in the South The truth of the insistence of Stevens was manifest without land and without vocation, the Negro voter could not gain that economic independence which would protect his vote. Unless, therefore, his political and civil rights were supported by the United States army, he was doomed to practical reënslavement. But the United States army became in the seventies the representative of the party of political corruption, while its political opponents represented land monopoly and capitalistic reaction in the South. When, therefore, the conscience of the United States attacked corruption, it at the same time attacked in the Republican Party the only power that could support democracy in the South . . .

Honest labor government would be more fatal to land monopoly and industrial privilege than government by bribery and graft.

The white South, therefore, quickly substituted violence and renewal of the war in order to get rid of the possibility of good government supported by black labor votes.

There was not a single honest Southerner who did not know that any reasonable political program which included a fair chance for the Negro to get an honest wage. personal protection, land to work, and schools for his children, would have received the staunch, loyal and unyielding support of the overwhelming mass of Negro voters; but this program, when ostensibly offered the Negro, concealed the determination to reduce him practically to slavery. He knew this and in his endeavor to escape floundered through bribery, corruption, and murder, seeking a path to peace, freedom, and the income of a civilized man.

The South has itself to blame. It showed no historic sign of favoring emancipation before the war, rather the contrary. It showed no disposition to yield to the offer of recompensed emancipation which Abraham Lincoln repeatedly made. It showed no desire to yield to emancipation with correspondingly curtailed political power as Congress suggested. It showed no disposition to reform democracy with the Negro vote. It relied on stubborn brute force.

Meantime, the leaders of Northern capital and finance were still afraid of the return of Southern political power after the lapse of the military dictatorship. This power was larger than before the war and it was bound to grow. If it were to be used in conjunction with Northern liberals, it might still mean the reduction of the tariff, the reduction of monopoly, and an attack upon new financial methods and upon concentrated control in industry. There was now no sentiment like "freedom" to which the Northern industrialists could appeal. It was, therefore, necessary for Northern capital to make terms with the dominant South.

Thus, both the liberal and the conservative North found themselves willing to sacrifice the interests of labor in the South to the interest of capital. The temporary dictatorship as represented by the Freedmen's Bureau was practically ended by 1870. This led to an increase of violence on the part of the Ku Klux Klan to subject black labor to strict domination by capital and to break Negro political power. The outbreak brought a temporary return of military dictatorship, but the return was unpopular in the North and aroused bitter protest in the South.

Yet the end that planters and poor whites envisaged and, as the fight went on, the end that large numbers of the Northern capitalists were fighting for, was a movement in the face of modern progress. It did not go to the length of disfranchising the whole laboring class, black and white, because it dared not do this, although this was its logical end. It did disfranchise black labor with the aid of white Southern labor and with the silent acquiescence of white Northern labor.

The white capitalist of the South saw a chance of getting rid of the necessity of treating with and yielding to the voting power of fully half the laboring class. It seized this opportunity, knowing that it thus was setting back the economic progress of the world; that the United States, instead of marching forward through the preliminary revolution by which the petty bourgeois and the laboring class armed with the vote were fighting the power of capital, was disfranchising a part of labor and on the other hand allowing great capital a chance for enormous expansion in the country. And this enormous expansion got its main chance through the thirty-three electoral votes which the counting of the full black population in the South gave to that section. It was only necessary now that this political power of the South should be used in behalf of capital and not for the strengthening of labor and universal suffrage. This was the bargain of 1876.

Reconstruction, therefore, in the South degenerated into a fight of rivals to control property and through that to control the labor vote. This rivalry between dictators led to graft and corruption as they bid against each other for the vote of the Negro, while meantime Negro labor in its ignorance and poverty was agonizing for ways of escape. Northern capital compromised, and Southern capital accepted race hate and black disfranchisement as a permanent program of exploitation. . . .

It was not, then, race and culture calling out of the South in 1876; it was property and privilege, shrieking to its kind, and privilege and property heard and recognized the voice of its own.

The bargain of 1876 was essentially an understanding by which the Federal Government ceased to sustain the right to vote of half of the laboring population of the South, and left capital as represented by the old planter class, the new Northern capitalist, and the capitalist that began to rise out of the poor whites, with a control of labor greater than in any modern industrial state in civilized lands. Out of that there has arisen in the South an exploitation of labor unparalleled in modern times, with a government in which all pretense at party alignment or regard for universal suffrage is given up. The methods of government have gone uncriticized, and elections are by secret understanding and manipulation; the dictatorship of capital in the South is complete.

The military dictatorship was withdrawn, and the representatives of Northern capital gave up all efforts to lead the Negro vote. The new dictatorship became a manipulation of the white labor vote which followed the lines of similar control in the North, while it proceeded to deprive the black voter by violence and force of any vote at all. The rivalry of these two classes of labor and their competition neutralized the labor vote in the South. The black voter struggled and appealed, but it was in vain. And the United States, reënforced by the increased political power of the South based on disfranchisement of black voters, took its place to reënforce the capitalistic dictatorship of the United States, which became the most powerful in the world, and which backed the new industrial imperialism and degraded colored labor the world over.

This meant a tremendous change in the whole intellectual and spiritual development of civilization in the South and in the United States because of the predominant political power of the South, built on disfranchised labor. The United States was turned into a reactionary force. It became the cornerstone of that new imperialism which is subjecting the labor of yellow, brown and black peoples to the dictation of capitalism organized on a world basis; and it has not only brought nearer the revolution by which the power of capitalism is to be challenged, but also it is transforming the fight to the sinister aspect of a fight on racial lines embittered by awful memories.

It is argued that Negro suffrage was bad because it failed, and at the same time that its failure was a proof of its badness. Negro suffrage failed because it was overthrown by brute force. Even if it had been the best government on earth, force, exercised by a majority of richer, more intelligent and more experienced men, could have overthrown it. It was not overthrown so long as the military dictatorship of the North sustained it. But the South proved by appropriate propaganda that Negro government was the worst ever seen and that it threatened civilization. They suited their propaganda to their audience. They had tried the accusation of laziness but that was refuted by a restoration of agriculture to the pre-war level and beyond it. They tried the accusation of ignorance but this was answered by the Negro schools.

It happened that the accusation of incompetence impressed the North not simply because of the moral revolt there against graft and dishonesty but because the North had never been thoroughly converted to the idea of Negro equality. When, therefore, the North, even granting that all the South said of the Negro was not true, contemplated possibilities, it paused. Did the nation want blacks with power sitting in the Senate and in the House of Representatives, accumulating wealth and entering the learned professions? Would this not eventually and inevitably lead to social equality and even to black sons and daughters-in-law and mulatto descendants? Was it possible to contemplate such eventualities?

Under such circumstances, it was much easier to believe the accusations of the South and to listen to the proof which biology and social science hastened to adduce of the inferiority of the Negro. . . .

Moreover, Americans saw throughout the world the shadow of the coming change of the philanthropic attitude which had dominated the early nineteenth century, with regard to the backward races. International and commercial imperialism began to get a vision. Within the very echo of that philanthropy which had abolished the slave trade was beginning a new industrial slavery of black and brown and yellow workers in Africa and Asia. Arising from this, as a result of this economic foundation, came the change in the attitude toward these darker people. They were no longer "Brothers in Black"; they were inferiors. These inferiors were to be governed for their own good. They were to be raised out of sloth and laziness by being compelled to work. The whole attitude of Europe was reflected in America and it found in America support for its own attitude.

The great republic of the West was trying an impossible experiment. They were trying to make white men out of black men. It could not be done. It was a mistake to conceive it. The North and Europe were still under the sway of individual laissez-faire in industry, and "hands off" in government. It was easy, therefore, for the North to persuade itself that whatever happened politically in the South was right. If the majority did not want Negro rule, or Negro participation in government, the majority was right, and they would not allow themselves to stop and ask how that majority was made. They knew that an organized inner group was compelling the mass of white people to act as a unit; was pounding them by false social sanctions into a false uniformity.

If that part of the white South which had a vision of democracy and was willing to grant equality to Negroes of equal standing had been sustained long enough by a standing Federal police, democracy could have been established in the South. But brute force was allowed to use its unchecked power in the actions of the whites to destroy the possibility of democracy in the South, and thereby make the transition from democracy to plutocracy all the easier and more inevitable.

Through the rift of the opposition, between votes for and against the Negro, between high and low tariff, between free land and land monopoly, plutocracy drove a silent coach and four.

What the South did in 1876 was to make good its refusal either to give up slavery or to yield the political power based on the counting of slaves.

And so the South rode the wind into the whirlwind and accomplished what it sought. Did it pay? Did it settle either the Negro's problem or any problem of wealth, labor, or human uplift? On the contrary, it made the government of the South a system of secret manipulations with lying and cheating. It made its religion fundamental hypocrisy. And the South knows today that the essential Negro problem is just as it was—how far it dare let the Negro be a modern man.

It was all so clear and right and logical. A nation could not exist half-slave and half-free. If it tried, either its mass of laborers would by force of competition sink into the depths of exploited, ignorant poverty, or rising in bloody revolt break the monopoly of land and materials and endow the mass with more equal income and more political power to maintain their freedom.

So in America came Civil War over the slavery of labor and the end was not peace, but the endeavor really and honestly to remove the cause of strife—to give the black freedman and the white laborer land and education and power to conduct the state in the interests of labor and not of landed oligarchy. Labor lurched forward after it had paid in blood for the chance. And labor, especially black labor, cried for Light and Land and Leading. The world laughed. It laughed North. It laughed West. But in the South it roared with hysterical, angry, vengeful laughter. It said: "Look at these niggers; they are black and poor and ignorant. How can they rule those of us who are white and have been rich and have at our command all wisdom and skill? Back to slavery with the dumb brutes!"

Still the brutes strove on and up with silent, fearful persistency. They restored the lost crops; they established schools; they gave votes to the poor whites; they established democracy; and they even saved a pittance of land and capital out of their still slave-bound wage.

The masters feared their former slaves' success far more than their anticipated failure. They lied about the Negroes.

They accused them of theft, crime, moral enormities and laughable grotesqueries. They forestalled the danger of a united Southern labor movement by appealing to the fear and hate of white labor and offering them alliance and leisure. They encouraged them to ridicule Negroes and beat them, kill and burn their bodies. The planters even gave the poor whites their daughters in marriage, and raised a new oligarchy on the tottering, depleted foundations of the old oligarchy, a mass of new rulers the more ignorant, intolerant and ruthless because of their inferiority complex. And thus was built a Solid South impervious to reason, justice or fact. . . .

WRITINGS FOR CHILDREN

Shortly before his death and while an exile in Ghana, Du Bois wrote that he was saddened because "The colored children have ceased to hear my name." Surely they once heard it loud and clear, for he devoted much of his writing as poet, short-story teller, essayist and editor to the education and entertainment of children. W. E. B. Du Bois loved children—all children, but he felt his "children of the sun" needed him most—and mental and physical cruelty to children aroused him as nothing else did. One of Du Bois' most moving essays is his account in The Souls of Black Folk *of the death of his small son before racism had seared the child's life.*

He realized as an educator that one had seriously to consider children in working for race pride and for eventual establishment of full citizenship for black Americans. During the 25 years he edited The Crisis, *Du Bois made an effort to win young readers. He devoted the annual October issue to topics of interest to children. He appealed for stories about children and photographs. He frequently wrote personal letters to some child who had appealed to him for advice. But nothing shows his concern more than what he said in his famous 1904* Credo:

> I believe in the training of children, black even as white; the leading out of little souls into the green pastures and the cool waters, not for self or peace, but for life lit by some large vision of beauty and goodness and truth.

Many important Negro leaders have testified about the great influence The Crisis' *children's educational material had on them when they read it so avidly in their youth. Among these were Dr. Horace Mann Bond, educator and father of Georgia legislator Julian Bond, and the poet, Langston Hughes.*

Eventually Dr. Du Bois decided that what he was doing in The Crisis *and elsewhere was not enough. Black children needed a magazine of their own. Too many of them were*

217

being insulted and hurt by exposure to several white racist publications for children, including the popular St. Nicholas magazine where the only Negro children to appear in picture or story were the Little Black Sambo or Topsy types. As was usual with Du Bois, thought led to action. Therefore he proceeded to establish a children's magazine.

It was called the Brownies' Book *and it lasted two years: January 1920 through December 1921.*

In introducing it Dr. Du Bois wrote:

This is the *Brownies' Book*, a monthly magazine for the children of the sun—designed for all children, but especially OURS. It aims to be a thing of joy and beauty, dealing in happiness, laughter and emulation, and designed especially for the kiddies from six to sixteen.

Also, he declared its aim to be:

To make colored children realize that being colored is a normal, beautiful thing, to make them familiar with the history and achievements of the Negro race . . . to teach them delicately a code of honor and action in their relations with white children.

In Dusk of Dawn, *Du Bois wrote of the* Brownies' Book:

I made one effort toward which I look back with infinite satisfaction; an attempt in the *Brownie's Book* to furnish a little magazine for Negro children . . . It was really a beautiful publication, but it did not pay its way.

A moving tribute to the magazine was made recently by Elinor Desverney Sinnette, librarian and author, in Freedomways *magazine:*

Today we all look back upon the *Brownies' Book* . . . It was a magnificent publication. Through it one of the greatest men of the twentieth century contributed unstintingly in an effort to restore a sense of self-esteem to the black child, our child of the sun. It brought satisfaction to the thousands of children who knew it.

The selections used here from his writings for children include editorials, poems and essays from The Crisis *and* the Brownies' Book *and quotations from various other sources. These include his announcements about the children's numbers of* The Crisis *and also his announcements of the beginning of the* Brownies' Book *(January 1920) and of its final issue (December 1921). One of Du Bois' contributions to the* Brownies' Book, *an industrial nature story "Honey," appeared in the August 1920 issue. He also wrote two columns, "The Judge" and "As the Crow Flies." He was the crow.*

But to know the rich material in The Crisis *and the* Brownies' Book *one must go to the original sources and read the biographies of famous Negroes, poems, stories, games, songs, and history by such authors as Langston Hughes, James Weldon Johnson, Jesse Fausett, and Nina Yolanda Du Bois.*

Of Children

This is the Children's Number, and as it has grown and developed in the editor's hesitating hands, it has in some way come to seem a typical rather than a special number. Indeed, there is a sense in which all numbers and all words of a magazine of ideas must point to the child—to that vast immortality and wide sweep and infinite possibility which the child represents. Such thought as this it was that made men say of old as they saw baby faces like these that adorn our pages this month:

"And whosoever shall offend one of these little ones * * * it is better for him that a millstone were hanged about his neck, and he were cast into the sea."

Of the Giving of Life

And yet the mothers and fathers and the men and women of our race must often pause and ask:

Is it worth while?

Ought children be born to us?

Have we a right to make human souls face what we face to-day?

The answer is clear: if the great battle of human right against poverty, against disease, against color prejudice is to be won, it must be won not in our day, but in the day of our children's children. Ours is the blood and dust of battle, theirs the rewards of victory. If then they are not there because we have not brought them to the world, then we have been the guiltiest factor in conquering ourselves. It is our duty then to accomplish the immortality of black blood in order that the day may come in this dark world when poverty shall be abolished, privilege based on individual desert, and the color of a man's skin be no bar to the outlook of his soul.

Of the Shielding Arm

If then it is our duty as honest colored men and women battling for a great principle to bring not aimless rafts of children to the world, but as many as, with reasonable sacrifice, we can train to largest manhood, what in its inner essence shall that training be, particularly in its beginning? Our first impulse is to shield our children absolutely. Look at these happy little innocent faces: for most of them there is as yet no shadow, no thought of a color line. The world is beautiful and good, and real life is joy. But we know only too well that beyond all the disillusionment and hardening that lurk for every human soul there is that extra hurting which, even when unconscious, with fiendish refinement of cruelty waits on each corner to shadow the joy of our children; if they are backward or timid, there is the sneer; if they are forward, there is repression; the problems of playmates and amusements are infinite, and street and school and church have all that extra hazard of pain and temptation that spells hell to our babies.

The first temptation then is to shield the child; to hedge it about that it may not know and will not dream. Then, when we can no longer wholly shield, to indulge and pamper and coddle, as though in this dumb way to compensate. From this attitude comes the multitude of our spoiled, wayward, disappointed children; and must we not blame ourselves? For while the motive was pure and the outer menace undoubted, is shielding and indulgence the way to meet it?

Of the Grim Thrust

Some parents, realizing this, leave their children to sink or swim in this sea of race prejudice. They neither shield nor explain, but thrust them forth grimly into school or street, and let them learn as they may from brutal fact. Out of this may come strength, poise, self-dependence, and out of it, too, may come bewilderment, cringing deception and self-distrust. It is, all said, a brutal, unfair method, and in its way as bad as shielding and indulgence. Why not rather face the facts and tell the truth? Your child is wiser than you think.

The Power and the Glory

Out of little unspoiled souls rise up wonderful resources and healing balm. Once the colored child understands the world's attitude and the shameful wrong of it, you have furnished it with a great life motive—a power and impulse toward good, which is the mightiest thing man has. How many white folks would give their own souls if they might graft into their children's souls a great, moving, guiding ideal!

With this power there comes in the transfiguring soul of childhood the glory: the vision of accomplishment—the lofty ideal. Once let the strength of the motive work, and it becomes the life task of the parent to guide and shape the ideal; to raise it from resentment and revenge, to dignity and self-respect, to breadth and accomplishment, to human service; to beat back every thought of cringing and surrender.

Here, at last, we can speak with no hesitating, with no lack of faith, for we know that as the world grows better there will be realized in our children's lives that for which we fight unfalteringly but vainly now.

The Frank Truth

The truth lies ever between extremes. It is wrong to introduce the child to race consciousness prematurely. It is dangerous to let that consciousness grow spontaneously without intelligent guidance. With every step of dawning intelligence explanation—frank, free guiding explanation—must come. The day will dawn when mother must explain gently but clearly why the little girls next door do not want to play with "Niggers"; what the real cause is of the teachers' unsympathetic attitude, and how people may ride on the backs of street cars and the smoker end of trains, and still be people, honest high-minded souls.

Remember, too, that in such frank explanation you are speaking in nine cases out of ten to a good deal clearer understanding than you think, and that the child mind has what your tired soul may have lost faith in—the power and the glory.

OCTOBER, 1912

Of the Children of Peace

Come, all my father's children and sit beside my knee, here with this child of mine, and listen:

Have you ever seen a soldier? It is a brave sight, is it not? Once upon a time, many, many years before your dear little curly heads were born, I remember seeing an army that marched because a King was visiting an Emperor. Berlin was joy mad. Houses streamed with color and music reeled and rioted. Then came the army. Tall, handsome men, all gold and silver and broadcloth, sworded, spurred and plumed, led on horses that curvetted and tossed their shining bits. (Do you not love a horse with his great, sweet eyes and quivery, shining softness!) Next came the soldiers, erect, rigid. "Eyes left!" Pit-pat, pit-pat! Clasping their little innocent guns. Next came the artillery: files of wildly prancing horses dragging long leaden things. How the crowd roared. The King bowed to the Emperor and the Emperor bowed to the King, and there rose a great cry of pride and joy and battle from the people. With that cry I seemed to awake. I somehow saw *through;* (you know sometimes how you seem to see, but are blind until something happens and you really see?)

I saw then what I see now. I saw and see the WAR that men said could not be.

Gone was all the brave tinsel, the glitter, sheen and music. The men trudged and limped, naked and dirty, with sodden, angry, distorted faces; their eyes were sunken and bloodshot, with murder in them; they staggered over corpses and severed arms and feet and dead horses and they carried—not little innocent guns, but little innocent children; they dragged, not pale and leaden guns, but pale and bounden women, and before them staggered and crept old women and grandfathers, the sick and the maimed, the weak and the half-grown boys and girls.

I heard the cry that hovered over this fearsome army: it was a wail of hunger and crime, of thirst and pain and death, and the cry rose and met an answering cry that came from beyond the forest to the West.

Two toddling children slipped from their fathers' arms and met in the gloom of the forest, where the beasts cowered and livid, disbodied hands seemed to creep in the darkness.

"Mother," they whispered.

"Mama," they cried.

"Mütterchen," they sobbed.

Wild with horror too bound mothers beat their naked hands against the gun-carriages, groping and struggling through the gloom, as death flamed through their hearts.

Then the armies met. Two fathers leapt from the two armies ahead and each seized the other's child. They strangled and crushed and maimed and murdered it, till each baby lay pale, limp and dead.

(Nay, shrink not, my children; horrible as the tale may be, the truth is worse and you must know it.)

Then War was loose. Then six million human beings left their fields of golden grain and the busy hum of their factories and taking their own children for weapons dashed them against the trees and the lampposts and the churches and wallowed and gasped in their blood!

Come, all my father's children and hear how beyond the blue mists of the Everlasting Sea, the mothers mad with hunger, grief and pain, are fronting the blood-stained heavens with bared and haunted breasts and are shrieking:

"Why?"

"Why?"

Their shriek is the booming of guns, and the booming of cannon is the shriek of mothers.

And you must answer, Children of Peace, you must answer!

You must cry: "There is no why!"

"The cause of War is Preparation for War."

"The cause of Preparation for War is the Hatred and Despising of Men, your and my Brothers."

"War is murder in a red coat."

"War is raped mothers and bleeding fathers and strangled children."

"War is Death, Hate, Hunger and Pain!"

"Hell is War!"

And when you believe this with all your little hearts;

And when you cry it across the seas and across the years with all your little voices—

Then shall the mothers of all dead children hear;

Then shall the Sisters of all dead Brothers hear; then shall the Daughters of all dead Fathers hear; then shall the Women rise and say:

"War is done."

"Henceforward and forever there shall be no organized murder of men, for the children we bear shall be the Children of Peace, else there shall be no children."

Amen!

But cry, little children, cry and cry loud and soon, for until you and the Mothers speak, the men of the world bend stupid and crazed beneath the burden of hate and death. Behold, this old and awful world is but one slaughter-pen, one tale of innocent blood and senseless hate and strife. . . .

OCTOBER, 1914

"Wait, Thou Child of Hope, for Time shall teach Thee all things."

The Immortal Children

Children give us the real immortality—the endless life concerning which there is no doubt or casuistry, no selfishness nor fear. With the children, whether they are ours or others, our life goes on renewed in its splendid youth, uplifted by its quivering, ever-glorious dreams, like to all life and yet always different because it grasps new worlds and lives in a universe continually unfolding to new possibilities.

To all this we are singularly obtuse. Our children are in our way; they hinder the settling of life's problems; they are the after-thought of things and not things themselves; they must be broken to our world and their wills enthralled. Yet now and then the thrill and glory of their meaning emerges. We see ourselves as we should—the servants of our children; the followers of their knowledge; the worshippers of their future.

To none can this be truer than to the children of the darker world who hold in their little hands so vast a destiny. They will look back some day in wonder at their files of THE CRISIS and say, can these things be true? Was not this exaggerated? Little realizing that the editor must palliate and soften the awful truth even for his darkest readers less they sicken and fail and die.

Through children's eyes, then, we look into a triumphant future and this Children's number of THE CRISIS is a sort of annual festival decorated with their flowering faces and their wonder-filled eyes and the mighty softness of their hands.

They who look at you from these pages are but a little and imperfect selection of those who might. We have chosen them out of hundreds of their fellows and we are full of apologies to the mothers of those not chosen; after all, these are not individual children; they belong to no persons and no families; they belong to a great people and in their hands is that people's future.

OCTOBER, 1916

School

This is school month. Send the children to school. Do not be tempted to keep them at work because they are earning large wages. The race is to the intelligent and not merely to the busy. Wisdom is the principal thing, therefore, GET WISDOM! Hustle the children off the farms and out of the factories and into the schools. Do not wait—do not hesitate. Our life depends uon it. Our rise is founded on the rock of knowledge. Put the children in school. Keep the children in school.

OCTOBER, 1916

The Slaughter of the Innocents

Again the rolling of the years brings us to the annual Children's Number. Attention has been called this year especially to the child and the United States Government has been spreading widely the gospel of the preservation of child life. The death of some ten million men who would have been fathers of unborn children has made the world think of the horrors of peace as well as the horrors of war. And the greatest of the horrors of peace is the unnecessary and persistent slaughter of little children. It is a crime of every civilization and of every race, but we Negroes are among the guiltiest, among us from two hundred to five hundred of every thousand of our babies born die before they reach one year of age. We have pleaded poverty, prejudice and slavery as excuse, but the time is come not to excuse but to combat with our own available weapons this murder.

The remedy is, first, care and fore-thought in bringing children into the world and, second, pure food and air for them when they come. We persist in keeping windows shut and living indoors; we persist in buying food carelessly and feeding all kinds of food indiscriminately to children. Outdoor life and simple, pure foods regularly fed would save the lives of a quarter million Negro children each year. Look on these pages. Are not these little lives worth the saving?

OCTOBER, 1918

The True Brownies

The Children's CRISIS has been published annually for nine years and is easily the most popular number of the year—that is, it makes the widest appeal to our readers. This is as it should be. Of course, we are and must be interested in our children above all else, if we love our race and humanity.

But in the problem of our children we black folk are sorely puzzled. For example, a little girl writes us—we remember her as red-bronze and black-curled, with dancing eyes—"I want to learn more about my race, so I want to begin early. . . . *I hate the white man just as much as he hates me and probably more!*"

Think of this from twelve little years! And yet, can you blame the child? To the consternation of the Editors of

THE CRISIS we have had to record some horror in nearly every Children's Number—in 1915, it was Leo Frank; in 1916, the lynching at Gainesville, Fla.; in 1917 and 1918, the riot and court martial at Houston, Tex., etc.

This was inevitable in our rôle as newspaper—but what effect must it have on our children? To educate them in human hatred is more disastrous to them than to the hated; to seek to raise them in ignorance of their racial identity and peculiar situation is inadvisable—impossible.

There seems but one alternative: We shall publish hereafter not ONE Children's Number a year, but TWELVE! Messrs. Du Bois and Dill will issue in November, in cooperation with THE CRISIS, but as an entirely separate publication, a little magazine for children—for all children, but especially for *ours*, "the Children of the Sun."

It will be called, naturally, THE BROWNIES' BOOK, and as we have advertised, "It will be a thing of Joy and Beauty, dealing in Happiness, Laughter and Emulation, and designed especially for Kiddies from Six to Sixteen.

"It will seek to teach Universal Love and Brotherhood for all little folk—black and brown and yellow and white.

"Of course, pictures, puzzles, stories, letters from little ones, clubs, games and oh—everything!"

Deftly intertwined with this mission of entertainment will go the endeavor:

(a) To make colored children realize that being "colored" is a normal, beautiful thing.

(b) To make them familiar with the history and achievements of the Negro race.

(c) To make them know that other colored children have grown into beautiful, useful and famous persons.

(d) To teach them delicately a code of honor and action in their relations with white children.

(e) To turn their little hurts and resentments into emulation, ambition and love of their own home, and companions.

(f) To point out the best amusements and joys and worth-while things of life.

(g) To inspire them to prepare for definite occupations and duties with a broad spirit of sacrifice.

This is a great program—a tremendous task. We want the advice of all mothers and fathers, of all men and women and children in helping us accomplish it. We can conceive of no more splendid duty at this critical hour.

OCTOBER, 1919

FROM THE BROWNIES' BOOK:

This is

THE BROWNIES' BOOK

A Monthly Magazine

For the Children of the Sun

DESIGNED FOR ALL CHILDREN,
BUT ESPECIALLY FOR *OURS*.

It aims to be a thing of Joy and Beauty, dealing in Happiness, Laughter and Emulation, and designed especially for Kiddies from Six to Sixteen.
It will seek to teach Universal Love and Brotherhood for all little folk—black and brown and yellow and white.
Of course, pictures, stories, letters from little ones, games and oh—everything!

ONE DOLLAR AND A HALF A YEAR

FIFTEEN CENTS A COPY

W. E. B. Du Bois.........Editor
A. G. DILL.........Business Manager

Address: THE BROWNIES' BOOK

2 West 13th Street   New York, N. Y.

JANUARY, 1920

The Grown-ups' Corner

The Brownies' Book is exactly one year old this month. We hope you have liked it and have enjoyed reading it as much as we have enjoyed publishing it.

We think you do like it and because of this we are going to ask you to assist us in various ways:

1. *Manuscripts*—We want new and interesting stories about colored children, their interests, their difficulties, the way they live and the places they live in. We are especially eager for the boys and girls of the West to know all about

their playmates in the East, and for the North to become better acquainted with the South. The easiest and quickest way to accomplish this is for you and your children to tell all about yourselves and send it to us to publish in our columns. We wish people who have friends in foreign countries where there are dark people would get information to us about those places too.

2. *Pictures*—Of course we want pictures of "Our Little Friends". Send us all you like; we cannot have too many. But, Parents, please remember that other parents are sending us pictures of their little ones too. We cannot publish them all at once. So the only fair thing to do is to publish them in the order in which they come. Then nobody has any real complaint. We should be greatly obliged too if you would not ask for the return of the photographs. Getting them back from the engraver in good condition and to you is a tedious job which consumes more of our time than we ought to give.

3. *Subscribers*—Have you any idea how extremely expensive it is to publish a magazine? Paper—and you know we use a good quality—is high; the price of cuts for reproducing photographs is soaring; the printer's bill is tremendous. Yet with 12,000 subscribers we would be able to put *The Brownies' Book* on a self-supporting basis. Will not every parent who reads this and every little boy or girl who enjoys *The Brownies' Book* constitute himself a committee of one to get three new subscribers within the next month? Will you not speak of it in Sunday School, in public school and in societies for the betterment of our children? We are trying to help children, to the best of our ability, by publishing this magazine. Will you not help us to help?

A gentleman writes us from Boston: "Your magazine is teaching one group of American children to respect themselves, and another group to show them respect." That is something to accomplish—will you not do your part toward it?

Did you know that 98% of the articles appearing in *The Brownies' Book* have been written by *colored* men, women and children? You see we are really creating modern Negro literature. And all of the original drawings—*but one*—have come from the pen of colored artists. You recognize the work by now—don't you—of Laura Wheeler, Albert Smith, Hilda Wilkinson, Marcellus Hawkins, Louise Latimer, Mary Effie Lee and others? The children contribute, too, occasionally; we are very proud of a page of their drawings which appeared in the May, 1920, issue. This is a stimulus to the expression of modern Negro art. Is not a magazine which insures such beginnings worthy of your wholehearted support? We believe you think so.

Grown-ups like *The Brownies' Book*, too.

Suppose we let it make the New Year A Happy One for All of Us.

The Editors.
JANUARY, 1921

Du Bois is the judge in the following selections.

The Judge

"My teacher wants to know which is the greatest continent," said Billikins.

"America," answered Billy promptly.

"Why?" asked the Judge.

"O, well—it just is, everybody knows that."

"I should certainly say Europe," said William.

"Why?" asked the Judge again.

"Because it's the center of the greatest civilization the world has known—the leader in Art and Science and Industry, and governs most of the world."

"Nevertheless, I should say Asia," said Wilhelmina, "because it is the oldest and wisest—the mother of all religion, the home of most men, the mother of races and the originator of human culture."

"And I," said the Judge, "would say Africa."

They all stared at him.

"Are you joking?" asked Billy.

"No."

"But you don't really mean it," protested William.

"I suppose," pouted Wilhelmina, "that you're just saying Africa because we are all of African descent. Of course—"

"Do I usually lie?" asked the Judge.

"No-o oh no!—but how on earth can you say that Africa

is the greatest continent? It is stuck way in the back of the Atlas and the geography which Billy uses devotes only a paragraph to it."

"I say it because I believe it is so. Not because I want to believe it true—not because I think it ought to be true, but because in my humble opinion it is true."

"And may we know the reasons?" said William.

"Certainly; they are seven."

("O Master, we are Seven," chanted Wilhelmina.)

"*First:* Africa was the only continent with a climate mild and salubrious enough to foster the beginnings of human culture.

"*Second:* Africa excels all other continents in the variety and luxuriance of its natural products.

"*Third:* In Africa originated probably the first, certainly the longest, most vigorous, human civilization.

"*Fourth:* Africa made the first great step in human culture by discovering the use of iron.

"*Fifth:* Art in form and rhythm, drawing and music found its earliest and most promising beginnings in Africa.

"*Sixth:* Trade in Africa was the beginning of modern world commerce.

"*Seventh:* Out of enslavement and degradation on a scale such as humanity nowhere else has suffered, Africa still stands today, with her gift of world labor that has raised the great crops of Sugar, Rice, Tobacco and Cotton and which lie at the foundation of modern industrial democracy."

"Gee!" said Billy.

"Don't understand," wailed Billikins.

"Few people do," said the Judge.

"I was just wondering," mused Wilhelmina, "who the guys are that write our histories and geographies."

"Well you can bet they're not colored," said William.

"No—not yet," said the Judge.

"Do they tell lies?" asked Billy.

"No they tell what they think is the truth."

"And I suppose," said Wilhelmina, "that what one thinks is the truth, *is* the truth."

"Certainly not," answered the Judge. "To tell what one believes is the truth, is not necessarily to lie, but it is not consequently true."

"Then one can tell falsehoods and not always lie."

"Certainly."

"I'm going to try that," said Billy.

"I wouldn't," warned the Judge. "You see it's this way: there are lots of things to be known and few to know them.

Our duty is therefore not simply to tell what we believe is true, but to remember our ignorance and be sure that we know before we speak."

JUNE, 1920

The Judge

"Come into the library," Wilhelmina whispers mysteriously to the Judge, "somebody wants to see you."

They walk in arm in arm to find William, Billy, Billikins, and two or three other children of the neighborhood waiting.

Wilhelmina strikes an attitude. "Dear children, we have with us today the distinguished visitor, Judge of *The Brownies*, who will now address you on the subject of Africa."

"I see I'm in for it," the Judge says, not at all unwillingly, "but you know there's nothing I'd rather do in all the world than talk to you about that. Now where was I to begin?"

"With books," William reminds him. "Don't you recall you were going to tell us what to read?"

"Oh, yes, it comes back to me now. I was telling you last time about three books, 'The Bantu—Past and Present', by S. M. Molema; 'Africa: Slave or Free?', by John H. Harris, and 'Songs and Tales from the Dark Continent', arranged by Natalie Curtis. Which do you want to hear of first?"

"The Bantam," says Billikins, eagerly. "I had a little rooster once. My, but he could fight!" The others stare at him in amazement.

"What in the world—" begins Billy.

"He thought I said Bantam," the Judge explains kindly, "whereas I was speaking of the Bantu, the name of a group of people."

"Of a particular tribe, isn't it?" asks William. "I know I've read a lot about them."

"No, it isn't the name of a particular tribe, although most people just like you seem to think so. It is such errors as this that Mr. Molema corrects in his book, and that is the reason why I am especially anxious to have you read it."

"I'm not sure I understand what you mean when you speak of a 'group' of people," says Gertrude, one of the neighborhood children.

"Come out on the porch and I'll explain. Now is everybody happy?"

The Judge continues solemnly, "The name 'Bantu' refers to a whole racial group of Africans, very much as the term 'Indian' refers to a whole group here in the United States, and yet we speak of the 'Choctaw,' the 'Iroquois,' the 'Sioux' and so forth.

"The man who wrote this book belongs to the Bantu group himself, so it is only reasonable to believe that he knows what he's talking about. He shows that the Bantus are a finely developed people with a culture and a civilization which, while not as far advanced as ours, is as good as ours was when we were at their stage and which certainly suits them and the country in which they live.

"Mr. Harris' book is very informing. He tells all about Liberia, the Negro Republic and about its resources. It is a very rich country—but almost every part of Africa is rich—and abounds in mahogany and gums, scented woods, wild rubber and vegetable oils."

"I really believe I'll go there when I grow up," says William, dreaming to himself. "I'm going to write to Cornell today to see about the requirements for engineering."

"What I'm always crazy to know," Wilhelmina interrupts, "is how the people live, what they have to eat, what they say to each other, what games they play, what they do at their parties and how they make love—that is if they do make love."

"As of course they do. Then what you must read is the book which Miss Curtis has compiled. You see she didn't really write it herself, she just put down the stories and legends, folk-tales and accounts which Kamba Simango of Portuguese East Africa and Madikane Qandeyana Cele of Zululand gave her. It has lots of illustrations and it is in the library on my desk. I'll show it to you when I go in. Why where are you all going?"

For all of them, including the grown-up Wilhelmina, have started off on a mad rush into the house. "All of us want the picture-book," someone's voice comes floating back, "and you know it's first come, first served."

SEPTEMBER, 1920

Honey

(Rewritten after Maeterlink)

"I think honey is the bestest thing in the world," said Boy as he added another golden spoonful to a mouth already full.

"I like Honey, too," said Mother, rearranging bib and pouring another glass of milk.

"Oho!" said Boy, "you mean me—I mean 'honey.' "

"And what does Honey know about bees?"

"O, bees—they sting—please, Mother some more bread—I got stung once."

"Is that all?"

"Course not—they make honey—stings and honey."

"No—honey and stings—shall I tell you about honey?"

"Yes, and about stings too."

"Look out the window—it all begins with the Miracle of Flowers."

"Are flowers miracles?"

"Yes—the most miraculous of miracles. After nature has dug in ugliness and slime and then risen to be practical and useful, suddenly in a wild moment it becomes merely beautiful and riots in color and perfume and lovely form."

"I don't understand all that, but I like roses and lilies and buttercups."

"And so do the bees—but what's more wonderful, the flowers love the bees."

"Can flowers love?"

"O yes—they may not know they're loving, but they love because they want to live forever."

"But they die."

"Yes, but they arise from the dead each spring and live again and again and forever. But without the bees they couldn't."

"Why?"

"On the heads of the flowers, which tremble with eagerness, is a magic powder and hidden below is a sweet mess called honey."

"Oho! the bees don't make it, they steal it."

"No, it is given them gladly in exchange for other magic powders which they bring."

"I thought you said the flowers had a powder?"

"They do—but each flower's powder is no good for the flower that grows it—it must be carried to other flowers, and the bees carry it. They come to the earliest flowers in

March and April bringing little sacks on their hips. Down into the pretty flowers they dip and fill some sacks with honey and others with the magic powder. Then they go to other flowers dropping bits of the fertilizing powder and taking more powder and honey with them. Their sacks full, home they hasten to the hive, humming a little tune. They visit often two or three hundred flowers in an hour and collect in a summer 120 pounds of honey from a hive, which is 600,000 times the weight of a single bee."

"O goody! I'd like to see a hive."

"We'll go and see one this afternoon in Uncle Abraham's backyard—we may be in time to see the Great Renunciation."

"That's an awful big word, Mother."

"And it stands for a great idea, full of awe. It means the 'Great Giving-up'. It is now June—perfect June. For three months the bees have heaped up honey. The hive is full and overflowing and then, suddenly, the bees go and leave it."

"For us?"

"No—although we may share, but for their children and children's children."

"Do they have to go?"

"No—just as you do not have to stop eating honey—but—"

"O, Mother, just a spoonful more, and a little more bread and—"

"No, Honey, this is the time for Renunciation."

"But giving up's no fun."

"Neither is tummy ache."

"O, I see, we and the bees give up because we're afraid."

"Not entirely. We are afraid of sickness which comes of overdoing anything, but we are led also by a vision of good to others which comes of sharing."

"Well, Mother, I s'pose—"

"Come quick or we'll miss the swarm."

"What's that?"

"The Great Renunciation—Uncle Abraham tells me that for days a strange unrest has stirred his bees. Most of the Foragers have stopped searching for honey and the Queen has left her palace."

"Do bees have queens?"

"Their Queen is their Mother."

"That's fine. You'se my Queen, ain't you Mother?"

"I hope so. The Queen of the bees is the mother of the hive—all the other bees are her children."

"How jolly—aren't there any other mothers?"

"There is only one mother in a hive. The Queen-Mother is now leading the swarm and we must hurry."

They hastened through the backyard and down the lane by the singing river and under the old lime tree where they came to Uncle Abraham's cabin.

"Have they swarmed yet?"

"Yas'm, one swarm done gone—but there's another—look!"

Then Boy saw a wonderful thing: Out of a little, low hive hidden beneath a plum tree, rushed two dark flying columns of 70,000 bees.

"Oooh-ooh," cried Boy, "they're colored folks, ain't they, Mother?"

"Yes, they're black and golden-brown like you. There are no white bees."

"And where are they going?"

"They do not know."

"They don't know where they're going, but they're on their way," laughed Boy.

They flew like a cloud or a magic blanket.

"And if we could see her, the Queen is in their midst, well to the front, larger and more beautiful of body than the rest, but with smaller head and 16,000 eyes."

"My, she ought to see a lot."

"Around her fly her 50,000 daughters, small and spare and plain, but with big brains and short lives because they work so hard."

"And her sons too?"

"No, they stay behind—lazy things!"

"But where are the Queen and her daughters going?"

"They are searching for a new home—see, they have hung themselves like a cluster of myriad grapes on yonder tree. If left alone they would send out scouts north, south, east and west to find a new home. But see, Uncle Abraham is going to catch them and guide them to a new hive."

"Won't he get stung?"

"No, not if he is gentle. Come! See here, they are settling in this dark empty box beneath the plain tree."

"Can we look in?"

"No, we should see nothing but darkness and there is a strange silence after the noise of the swarm."

"What are they doing?"

"I will tell you as we walk home. First, they carefully explore the home and while some clean and varnish it, others forming in columns march up the sides and attach themselves to the very top and by clinging to each other drop in long streamers. Then slowly intertwining the streamers formed on their attached bodies they make an inverted cone. Once the cone is formed there ensues a long and awful silence, twenty-four hours. It grows hotter and hotter in the hive. Suddenly from four little packets beneath the stomach of each bee appears a sort of light snow, the 'Spirit of the Flowers', which stiffens until the surface of the living cone is covered with 'ivory tablets' of wax. Then suddenly a busy woman carpenter will climb over the bodies of her fellows to the very top of the hive. She will take one of the wax scales from her stomach, fashion it and knead it and attach it securely to the roof. Then she adds the other tablets, pats them and secures them, and so the Bee city's foundation stone is laid."

"But on the roof? Upside down?"

"Yes, the city is built *upside down!* When the Carpenter-Masons have formed a sufficient block of wax, a Carver appears, a little busy woman whom the crowd of bees watches eagerly. She carries no wax but beginning at the top she scoops out deftly and surely a little six-sided hole in the wax."

"Oh, I saw it in the honey-comb, the comb's full of them."

"Yes. She excavates the hole, piling the wax up at the edge. Then she leaves and others follow, working on both sides of the wax and producing the honey-comb, that wonderful, beautiful House of the Hexagon."

"What's a Hexagon?"

"Anything six sided, and this form gives the greatest space with the fewest walls. After one comb is finished the Carpenter-Masons lay a second and third and more, leaving avenues of half an inch between. And thus they work for two or three months, through June, July and well into August.

"The finished city has 120,000 cells. If we were the size of bees, we would see their upside down city beginning in slim and silver beauty higher than the highest church steeple. Some of the cells are filled with pollen, each color in its own cell forming a yellow, red and black pile. Next come 20,000 reservoirs of the first gathered honey carefully sealed; then come open vats of later honey. In the centre, where it is warmest and safest, is the Royal Palace. Here are 10,000 cells for the Queen's eggs, 15,000 cells of larvae, and 40,000 rooms inhabited by nymphs. Then in the midst are from 30 to 12 royal cells where lie the Sleeping Princesses."

"I don't quite understand, Mother."

"All life, dear, is born from eggs. The work of the Queen is to lay eggs. These eggs grow and little live larvae emerge and after a while grow into nymphs and finally into little bees.

"No sooner is the swarm settled and building than the Foragers start out. It is the height of flower-time. The world is flowers—roses and liles and apple blossoms.

"They hurry to fill the cells while the Queen Mother begins to lay her eggs. It is solemn, unending work. She carries within her body two million eggs."

"Gee! What a lot!"

"Yes, it is a vast and prodigal horde. Of course she may not live to lay all the eggs and all may not hatch; but no sooner is her palace ready than she begins. Caressed and attended by her daughters, she moves from cell to cell, peeps in to see if all is well and then turning, lays her tiny blue eggs which the Nurses hasten to seal up. All her life save twice the Queen walks to and fro in the darkness laying her million eggs.

"Feverishly the hive works and far into the fall until the last flowers droop and die and the cold winds come down. Then the house becomes quiet. The doors are half closed and the bees gather in the centre of the hive clinging to the combs, with the Queen and Royal Guard in the centre. The first row attaches themselves to the cells, the second to them and so on till the last row forms a great envelope of all. When the bees in the outer envelope are cold they crawl in and others take their places, while those next to the cells pass out honey and feed all. All the bees slowly beat their wings to keep the air pure and temperature even, and thus they rest and eat and drowse the winter away."

Boy yawned prodigiously. "I think I'll drowse a little," he said, and off he went to bed.

Several days went by before Boy thought of bees again. Then one winter day beside the cozy fire with a book he came across a picture.

"Mother," he asked suddenly, "what do the bees do when they wake up in the spring?"

Mother was busy and had to put off answering a while. But after supper she took him in her lap.

"As early as February the Queen awakes and begins again to lay her eggs. In March the Foragers gingerly brave the wind and wet and frost and seek the earliest flowers. By April the hive seethes with feverish activity. The honey cells are replenished and sealed, the pollen is piled up and the city enlarged. By June the open honey vats are built and the city is rich and prosperous. Then comes the Great Renunciation."

"I know," said Boy—"they swarm."

"Not all of them—perhaps 70,000 go and leave 10,000 behind."

"Who tells 'em who is to go and who can't go?"

"We do not know. Perhaps they tell themselves, perhaps God tells them; but a day comes when seven-eighths of the city fly away with the Queen and leave a lonesome few, with no Queen, but with the hope of one.

"In the city there remain some 400 men—lazy but splendid, big, clad in glistening helmets and gaily colored cloaks. Then there are several thousand Foragers, who still seek the flowers, and many guards and cleaners. But most of those left are nurses."

"Nurses? How funny—are there any sick folks or babies?"

"Babies—thousands and thousands of babies and babies-to-be—10,000 eggs, 18,000 bits of life, 36,000 sleeping Baby Bees and seven or eight Sleeping Princesses."

"O me! O my! What a nest! They must yawl something awful."

"No, they are all very pale and quiet lying in their golden cradles and fed on nurses' milk. The nurses dance and hurry and wave their wings and feed the young until they are born."

"Is the whole bunch born at once?"

"Oh no—at intervals according to the time the eggs were laid. Here at a cell appears a little black head and long antennae. It gnaws at the wax. The nurses come running and help clear the wax away. Out comes the larvae and a bee is born. It is weak and shivery and pale. It is brushed and cleaned and given its first honey. After a week it takes it first flight into the air and after a second week it seeks the flowers and begins to work."

"They sure ain't babies long."

"But still the hive is incomplete—still there is no Queen; so the nurses redouble their attention to the splendid royal cradles where the Princesses sleep."

"They're a different sort of bee, ain't they?"

"No, any egg taken early enough and fed on the Royal Jelly becomes a Princess. The royal cradles rise like white tombs in the centre of the City—three or four times as large as the common cells. In here are larvae hatched after three days from eggs. About a week after the departure of the swarm, the nurses begin to thin the wax on the ripest royal cell, while the Princess gnaws within. The head appears and she thrusts herself forward. She emerges, is cleaned, fed and caressed. Almost as soon as she is born a strange restlessness seizes her."

"Why?"

"She knows that a hive can have but one Queen and that other queens are waiting to be born."

"Gee! but she's mean!"

"It is one of the puzzles of life. The world now sweet with flower and song suddenly turns and hurts and kills."

"But why, Mother?"

"We do not know. Perhaps Evil is a hard and heavy step toward Good; perhaps we shall out-grow it as we try; but now it is here and we must be brave and face it. God alone knows and perhaps some time He will tell.

"Bent on her furious errand of murder, the young Queen paces to and fro. Perhaps she knows that a hive with two queens would perish because it could not work in unison, and to save her people she must kill her rivals—at any rate she seeks them.

"Then in some mysterious way the bees take council and decide. They may decide not to let her reign and forming a wall they keep her back. They never use force, they never turn their backs on the royal person, they simply hold hands and present an immovable wall. The Queen's anger rises; her war-song rings like a far-off trumpet. The muffled answer of her rivals waiting to be born rings back but the nurses pile on wax and keep them imprisoned. Then at last the Queen understands. She summons her host and with twenty or thirty thousand followers leaps out into the air and thus a second swarm leaves the hive. But the hive must be careful—[one departing swarm] it can spare and two leave it dangerously bare of workers—three or four might ruin it. So when the second Princess is born (and sometimes when the first) there is no living wall to oppose. In fury she attacks the royal cells and destroys the unborn Princesses and the workers carry the dead bodies away. [Sometimes two princesses are born at once and they duel, drawing their unused scimitars which the queens use only then— never on workers or on men.]

"Then at last the Queen is supreme in the home—but not yet does she reign because she is not married."

"How funny! Do bees marry?!"

"Only one, the Queen. Her daughters, the workers, never marry. They are hard working, clear-witted old maids who do the work of their world, dying early after a busy life of a few months. Of her sons, one marries now and then, one in ten thousand, and with his marriage kiss, he dies."

"Good gracious, if I died every time I kissed you, Mother, I'd be awful dead already, wouldn't I?"

"Yes, darling. But love is a great and holy thing and always near to death; that is why Death is beautiful."

Mother looked thoughtfully at the picture across the room which Boy called Father, for Father was dead. A tear came to Mother's eye but Boy comforted and kissed her and she said:

"You see, Heart's Dearest, your father kissed me with his lips and life and his hard, hard work and—it killed him."

"But after a long time, Mother, after I was a big baby."

"Yes, dear; but Time is neither short nor long, it is just Deed. But now to our bees. The Virgin Queen steps to the door of the hive while the workers sing the royal hymn. For the first time and perhaps the last she looks on the sky and sun. She poises herself on the threshhold and all the men, the splendid, idle men, gather from all the neighboring hives with glittering helmets and gorgeous cloaks and shining wings to follow her. She rushes into the air, flies backward a bit in great circles to see and know [her] home and finally leaps into the blue, with 10,000 suitors, gorgeous in panoply, following her. Up, up she soars, up beyond bee and bird. Her suitors weaken, drop behind. Only the strongest follow. Then in the centre of the open heaven she turns and marries her chosen mate. With a great gasp of love and pain he falls the mighty mile to Death, while the bride dumb with happiness and trailing a part of the bridegroom's corpse, circles and swoops and drops to her hive home.

"Then she is Queen. Then she begins to lay her two million eggs and the hive quickened by a world of flowers seethes with work and happiness.

"Yet there remains a menace. It is not the robber moth, who may approach singing his bold royal song while the hive draws their stings and fights him fiercely; no, it is the *men*.

"The splendid, idle men are born hourly. They crowd the hive. They toil not neither do they spin. They swagger, they gorge, they waste. They fly and revel in the sun and then return and sleep and eat.

"At last the dread decree is sent forth. Idleness must go and with one swoop the armed working women fall on the splendid, idle men and kill them."

"Whew! But, Mother, this bee business is sort of—of cruel, ain't it?"

"Yes, but the end is honey, beautiful, sweet honey.

"After the cruel but perhaps necessary massacre, the hive works and thrives."

"I'm going to work when I grow up."

"Yes, Boy; of all crimes idleness is worst. Work is Love. Love is Life. Life is flowers and honey and work."

"Sort of circle, ain't it, Mother?"

"Yes, with bees and with men."

AUGUST, 1920

In his role of The Crow in the Brownie's column "As the Crow Flies," Dr. Du Bois never failed to remind his young readers of the beauty of their color.

Race Pride

I like my black feathers—
    don't you?
Whirl, whirl, up, whirl and fly
home to my sweet, little, black
crowlets . . . Ah, but they're black
and sweet and bonnie.

The crow is black and O so beautiful, shining with dark blues and purples, with little hints of gold in his mighty wings. He flies far above the Earth, looking downward with his sharp eyes. What a lot of things he must see and hear and if he could only talk—and lo, The Brownies' Book has made him talk for you. . . .

Du Bois, as the Crow, says Farewell to the Brownies' Book

This is the last Brownies' Book. For twenty-four months we have brought Joy and Knowledge to four thousand Brownies stretched from Oregon to Florida. But there are two million Brownies in the United States, and unless we got at least one in every hundred to read our pages and help pay printing, we knew we must at last cease to be. And now the month has come to say goodbye. We are sorry—much sorrier than any of you, for it has all been such fun. After all—who knows—perhaps we shall meet again . . .

Goodbye, dear kiddies. I do not know whom I shall tell all I see hereafter. Nobody I suppose. Besides if I do not fly I shall not see. No, I am not crying. Crows cannot cry. It's a fine thing to be able to cry—sometimes.

DECEMBER, 1921

From *DUSK OF DAWN*

Dusk of Dawn, *first published in 1940 and recently reprinted, is another of the seminal books written by Du Bois. It contains many things, but its theme can be grasped by the subtitle "An Essay Toward an Autobiography of a Race Concept." Some of the most interesting and informative writing in the book deals with Du Bois' life. However, though he had ample family pride, Du Bois devoted relatively little of his time and space to writing about himself or his family; it was always family in relation to the duality of life for a black person in America—life "within the veil."*

The autobiographical information in Dusk of Dawn *is compressed chiefly into two chapters. Called "A New England Boy and Reconstruction," the first of these deals mostly with boyhood and family—his mothers' family, the Black Burghardts—in the hills of Southern Berkshire near Great Barrington, Massachusetts. The title is significant for Du Bois was essentially a Yankee and, as one gathers from* Dusk of Dawn *and other autobiographical writings, he loved New England, its institutions and its natural features.*

Chapter Five entitled "The Concept of Race," continues the autobiography begun in Chapter Two and adds more on the Black Burghardts and on the Du Bois branch of the family which is traced back through Connecticut to the West Indies and to France. Added to the excerpts of biographical material from Dusk of Dawn *is a brief essay, "The House of the Black Burghardts," which appeared originally in* The Crisis *(April, 1928). The old cellar hole marking the site of the Black Burghardts, together with five acres of meadows and pine groves, which was the boyhood home of William Edward Burghardt Du Bois, is now owned by the Du Bois Memorial Committee.*

The other selection here is excerpted from Chapter Seven, "The Colored World Within," in which Du Bois presents his ideas on voluntary segregation as a weapon for ending all segregation.

A New England Boy and Reconstruction

As I have written elsewhere, "I was born by a golden river and in the shadow of two great hills." My birthplace was Great Barrington, a little town in western Massachusetts in the valley of the Housatonic, flanked by the Berkshire hills. Physically and socially our community belonged to the Dutch valley of the Hudson rather than to Puritan New England, and travel went south to New York more often and more easily than east to Boston. But my birthplace was less important than my birth-time. The Civil War had closed but three years earlier and 1868 was the year in which the freedmen of the South were enfranchised and for the first time as a mass took part in government. Conventions with black delegates voted new constitutions all over the South; and two groups of laborers—freed slaves and poor whites— dominated the former slave states. It was an extraordinary experiment in democracy. Thaddeus Stevens, the clearest-headed leader of this attempt at industrial democracy, made his last speech impeaching Andrew Johnson on February sixteenth and on February twenty-third [1868] I was born.

Less than a month after my birth Andrew Johnson passed from the scene and Ulysses Grant became President of the United States. The Fifteenth Amendment enfranchising the Negro as a race became law and the work of abolishing slavery and making Negroes men was accomplished, so far as law could do it. Meanwhile elsewhere in the world there were stirring and change which were to mean much in my life: in Japan the Meiji Emperors rose to power the year I was born; in China the intrepid Empress Dowager was fighting strangulation by England and France; Prussia had fought with Austria and France, and the German Empire arose in 1871. In England, Victoria opened her eighth parliament; the duel of Disraeli and Gladstone began; while in Africa came the Abyssinian expedition and opening of the Suez Canal, so fateful for all my people.

My town was shut in by its mountains and provincialism; but it was a beautiful place, a little New England town nested shyly in its valley with something of Dutch cleanliness and English reticence. The Housatonic, yellowed by the paper mills, rolled slowly through its center; while Green River, clear and beautiful, joined in to the south. Main Street was lined with ancient elms; the hills held white pines and orchards and then faded up to magnificent rocks and caves which shut out the neighboring world. The people were mainly of English descent with much Dutch blood and with a large migration of Irish and German workers to the mills as laborers.

The social classes of the town were built partly on land-holding farmers and more especially on manufacturers and merchants, whose prosperity was due in no little degree to the new and high tariff. The rich people of the town were not very rich nor many in number. The middle class were farmers, merchants and artisans; and beneath these was a small proletariat of Irish and German mill workers. They lived in slums near the woolen mills and across the river clustering about the Catholic Church. The number of colored people in the town and country was small. They were all, save directly after the war, old families, well-known to the old settlers among the whites. The color line was manifest and yet not absolutely drawn. I remember a cousin of mine who brought home a white wife. The chief objection was that he was not able to support her and nobody knew about her family; and knowledge of family history was counted as highly important. Most of the colored people had some white blood from unions several generations past. That they congregated together in their own social life was natural because that was the rule in the town: there were little social knots of people, but not much that today would be called social life, save that which centered about the churches; and there the colored folk often took part. My grandmother was Episcopalian and my mother, Congregational. I grew up in the Congregational Sunday school.

In Great Barrington there were perhaps twenty-five, certainly not more than fifty, colored folk in a population of five thousand. My family was among the oldest inhabitants of the valley. The family had spread slowly through the county intermarrying among cousins and other black folk with some but limited infiltration of white blood. . . .

My immediate family, which I remember as a young child, consisted of a very dark grandfather, Othello Burghardt, sitting beside the fireplace in a high chair, because of an injured hip. He was good-natured but not energetic. The energy was in my grandmother, Sally, a thin, tall, yellow and hawk-faced woman, certainly beautiful in her youth, and efficient and managing in her age. My mother, Mary Sylvina, was born at Great Barrington, January 14, 1831, and died there in 1885 at the age of fifty-four years. . . .

My mother was brown and rather small with smooth skin and lovely eyes, and hair that curled and crinked down each side [of] her forehead from the part in the middle. She was rather silent, but very determined and very patient. My father, a light mulatto, died in my infancy so that I do not remember him. . . .

I early began to take a direct interest in my own family as a group and became curious as to that physical descent which so long I had taken for granted quite unquestioningly. But I did not at first think of any but my Negro ancestors. I knew little and cared less of the white forebears of my father. But this chauvinism gradually changed. There is, of course, nothing more fascinating than the question of the various types of mankind and their intermixture. The whole question of heredity and human gift depends upon such knowledge; but ever since the African slave trade and before the rise of modern biology and sociology, we have been afraid in America that scientific study in this direction might lead to conclusions with which we were loath to agree; and this fear was in reality because the economic foundation of the modern world was based on the recognition and preservation of so-called racial distinctions. . . .

Of my own immediate ancestors I knew personally only four: my mother and her parents and my paternal grandfather. One other I knew at second hand—my father. I had his picture. I knew what my mother told me about him and what others who had known him, said. So that in all, five of my immediate forebears were known to me. Three others, my paternal great-grandfather and my maternal great-grandfather and great-great-grandfather, I knew about through persons who knew them and through records; and also I knew many of my collateral relatives and numbers of their descendants. My known ancestral family, therefore, consisted of eight or more persons. None of these had reached any particular distinction or were known very far beyond their own families and localities. . . .

My paternal great-grandfather, Dr. James Du Bois, was white and descended from Chrétien Du Bois who was a French Huguenot farmer and perhaps artisan and resided at Wicres near Lille in French Flanders. It is doubtful if he had any ancestors among the nobility, although his white American descendants love to think so. He had two, possibly three, sons of whom Louis and Jacques came to America to escape religious persecution. Jacques went from France first to Leiden in the Netherlands, where he was married and had several children, including a second Jacques or James. In 1674 that family came to America and settled at Kingston, New York. James Du Bois appears in the

Du Bois family genealogy as a descendant of Jacques in the fifth generation, although the exact line of descent is not clear; but my grandfather's written testimony establishes that James was a physician and a landholder along the Hudson and in the West Indies. He was born in 1750, or later. . . .

The career of Dr. James Du Bois was chiefly as a plantation proprietor and slave owner in the Bahama Islands with his headquarters at Long Cay. Cousins of his named Gilbert also had plantations near. He never married, but had one of his slaves as his common-law wife, a small brown-skinned woman born on the island. Of this couple two sons were born, Alexander and John. Alexander, my grandfather, was born in 1803. . . .

Alexander Du Bois . . . married into the colored group and his oldest son allied himself with a Negro clan but four generations removed from Africa. He himself first married Sarah Marsh Lewis in 1823 and then apparently set out to make his way in Haiti. There my father was born in 1825. . . .

Coenrod Burghardt seems to have been a shrewd pushing Dutchman and is early heard of in Kinderhook [New York], together with his son John. This family came into possession of an African Negro named Tom, who had formerly belonged to the family of Etsons (Ettens?) and had come to the Burghardts by purchase or possibly by marriage. This African has had between one hundred and fifty and two hundred descendants, a number of whom are now living and reach to the eighth generation.

Tom was probably born about 1730. His granddaughter writes me that her father told her that Tom was born in Africa and was brought to this country when he was a boy. For many years my youthful imagination painted him as certainly the son of a tribal chief, but there is no warrant for this even in family tradition. Tom was probably just a stolen black boy from the West African Coast, nameless and lost, either a war captive or a tribal pawn. He was probably sent overseas on a Dutch ship at the time when their slave trade was beginning to decline and the vast English expansion to begin. He was in the service of the Burghardts and was a soldier in the Revolutionary War, going to the front probably several times; of only one of these is there official record when he appeared with the rank of private on the muster and payroll of Colonel John Ashley's Berkshire County regiment and Captain John Spoor's company in 1780. The company marched northward by order of Brigadier-General Fellows on an alarm when Fort Anne and

Fort George were taken by the enemy. It is recorded that Tom was "reported a Negro." (Record Index of the Military Archives of Massachusetts, Vol. 23, p. 2.)

Tom appears to have been held as a servant and possibly a legal slave first by the family of Etsons or Ettens and then to have come into the possession of the Burghardts who settled at Great Barrington. Eventually, probably after the Revolutionary War, he was regarded as a freeman. There is record of only one son, Jacob Burghardt, who continued in the employ of the Burghardt family, and was born apparently about 1760. He is listed in the census of 1790 as "free" with two in his family. He married a wife named Violet [W. E. B. Du Bois' great-grandmother] who was apparently newly arrived from Africa and brought with her an African song which became traditional in the family. After her death, Jacob married Mom Bett, a rather celebrated figure in western Massachusetts history. She had been freed under the Bill of Rights of 1780 and the son of the judge who freed her wrote, "Even in her humble station, she had, when occasion required it, an air of command which conferred a degree of dignity and gave her an ascendancy over those of her rank, or color. Her determined and resolute character, which enabled her to limit the ravages of Shays's mob, was manifested in her conduct and deportment during her whole life. She claimed no distinction, but it was yielded to her from her superior experience, energy, skill and sagacity. Having known this woman as familiarly as I knew either of my parents, I cannot believe in the moral or physical inferiority of the race to which she belonged. The degradation of the African must have been otherwise caused than by natural inferiority."

Family tradition has it that her husband, Jacob, took part in suppressing this Shays's Rebellion. Jacob Burghardt had nine children, five sons of whom one was my grandfather, and four daughters. My grandfather's brothers and sisters had many children: Harlow had ten and Ira also ten; Maria had two. Descendants of Harlow and Ira still survive. Three of these sons, Othello, Ira, Harlow, and one daughter Lucinda settled on South Egremont plain near Great Barrington, where they owned small adjoining farms. A small part of one of these farms I continue to own.

Othello was my grandfather. He was born November 18, 1791, and married Sarah Lampman in 1811. Sarah was born in Hillsdale, New York, in 1793, of a mother named Lampman. There is no record of her father. She was probably the child of a Dutchman perhaps with Indian blood.

This couple had ten children, three sons and seven daughters. Othello died in 1872 at the age of eighty-one and Sarah or Sally in 1877 at the age of eighty-six. Their sons and daughters married and drifted to town as laborers and servants. I thus had innumerable cousins up and down the valley. I was brought up with the Burghardt clan and this fact determined largely my life and "race." The white relationship and connections were quite lost and indeed unknown until long years after. The black Burghardts were ordinary farmers, laborers and servants. The children usually learned to read and write. I never heard or knew of any of them of my mother's generation or later who were illiterate. I was, however, the first one of the family who finished in the local high school. Afterward, one or two others did. Most of the members of the family left Great Barrington. Parts of the family are living and are fairly prosperous in the Middle West and on the Pacific Coast. I have heard of one or two high school graduates in the Middle West branch of the family.

This, then, was my racial history and as such it was curiously complicated. With Africa I hold only one direct cultural connection and that was the African melody which my great-grandmother Violet used to sing. Where she learned it, I do not know. Perhaps she herself was born in Africa or had it of a mother or father stolen and transported. But at any rate, as I wrote years ago in the "Souls of Black Folk," "coming to the valleys of the Hudson and Housatonic, black, little, and lithe, she shivered and shrank in the harsh north winds, looked longingly at the hills, and often crooned a heathen melody to the child between her knees, thus:

> Do bana coba, gene me, gene me!
> Do bana coba, gene me, gene me!
> Ben d' nuli, nuli, nuli, nuli, ben d' le.

The child sang it to his children and they to their children's children, and so two hundred years it has traveled down to us and we sing it to our children. . . .

Living with my mother's people I absorbed their culture patterns and these were not African so much as Dutch and New England. The speech was an idiomatic New England tongue with no African dialect; the family customs were New England, and the sex mores. My African racial feeling was then purely a matter of my own later learning and reaction; my recoil from the assumptions of the whites; my experience in the South at Fisk. But it was none the less real and a large determinant of my life and character. I felt myself African by "race" and by that token was African and an integral member of the group of dark Americans who were called Negroes.

At the same time I was firm in asserting that these Negroes were Americans. For that reason and on the basis of my great-grandfather's Revolutionary record I was accepted as a member of the Massachusetts Society of the Sons of the American Revolution, in 1908. When, however, the notice of this election reached the headquarters in Washington and was emphasized by my requesting a national certificate, the secretary, A. Howard Clark of the Smithsonian Institution, wrote to Massachusetts and demanded "proof of marriage of the ancestor of Tom Burghardt and record of birth of the son." He knew, of course, that the birth record of a stolen African slave could not possibly be produced. My membership was, therefore, suspended. . . .

For several generations my people had attended schools for longer or shorter periods so most of them could read and write. I was brought up from earliest years with the idea of regular attendance at school. This was partly because the schools of Great Barrington were near at hand, simple but good, well-taught, and truant laws were enforced. I started on one school ground, which I remember vividly, at the age of five or six years, and continued there in school until I was graduated from high school at sixteen. I was seldom absent or tardy, and the school ran regularly ten months in the year with a few vacations. The curriculum was simple: reading, writing, spelling and arithmetic; grammar, geography and history. We learned the alphabet; we were drilled rigorously on the multiplication tables and we drew accurate maps. We could spell correctly and read clearly.

By the time I neared the high school, economic problems and questions of the future began to loom. These were partly settled by my own activities. My mother was then a widow with limited resources of income through boarding the barber, my uncle; supplemented infrequently by day's work, and by some kindly but unobtrusive charity. But I was keen and eager to eke out this income by various jobs: splitting kindling, mowing lawns, doing chores. My first regular wage began as I entered the high school: I went early of mornings and filled with coal one or two of the new so-called "base-burning" stoves in the millinery shop of Madame L'Hommedieu. From then on, all through my high school course, I worked after school and on Saturdays;

I sold papers, distributed tea from the new A & P stores in New York; and for a few months, through the good will of Johnny Morgan [owner of local newsstand], actually rose to be local correspondent of the *Springfield Republican*.

Meantime the town and its surroundings were a boy's paradise: there were mountains to climb and rivers to wade and swim; lakes to freeze and hills for coasting. There were orchards and caves and wide green fields; and all of it was apparently property of the children of the town. My earlier contacts with playmates and other human beings were normal and pleasant. Sometimes there was a dearth of available playmates but that was peculiar to the conventions of the town where families were small and children must go to bed early and not loaf on the streets. . . .

Later, in the high school, there came some rather puzzling distinctions which I can see now were social and racial; but the racial angle was more clearly defined against the Irish than against me. It was a matter of income and ancestry more than color. I have written elsewhere of the case of exchanging visiting cards where one girl, a stranger, did not seem to want mine to my vast surprise.

I presume I was saved evidences of a good deal of actual discrimination by my own keen sensitiveness. My companions did not have a chance to refuse me invitations; they must seek me out and urge me to come as indeed they often did. When my presence was not wanted they had only to refrain from asking. But in the ordinary social affairs of the village—the Sunday school with its picnics and festivals; the temporary skating rink in the town hall; the coasting in crowds on all the hills—in all these, I took part with no thought of discrimination on the part of my fellows, for that I would have been the first to notice.

Later, I was protected in part by the fact that there was little social activity in the high school; there were no fraternities; there were no school dances; there were no honor societies. Whatsoever of racial feeling gradually crept into my life, its effect upon me in these earlier days was rather one of exaltation and high disdain. They were the losers who did not ardently court me and not I, which seemed to be proven by the fact that I had no difficulty in outdoing them in nearly all competition, especially intellectual. In athletics I was not outstanding. I was only moderately good at baseball and football; but at running, exploring, story-telling and planning of intricate games, I was often if not always the leader. This made discrimination all the more difficult.

When, however, during my high school course the matter of my future career began to loom, there were difficulties. The colored population of the town had been increased a little by "contrabands," who on the whole were well received by the colored group; although the older group held some of its social distinctions and the newcomers astonished us by forming a little Negro Methodist Zion Church, which we sometimes attended. The work open to colored folk was limited. There was day labor; there was farming; there was house-service, particularly work in summer hotels; but for a young, educated and ambitious colored man, what were the possibilities? And the practical answer to this inquiry was: Why encourage a young colored man toward such higher training? I imagine this matter was discussed considerably among my friends, white and black, and in a way it was settled partially before I realized it.

My high school principal was Frank Hosmer, afterward president of Oahu College, Hawaii. He suggested, quite as a matter of fact, that I ought to take the college preparatory course which involved algebra, geometry, Latin and Greek. If Hosmer had been another sort of man, with definite ideas as to a Negro's "place," and had recommended agricultural "science" or domestic economy, I would doubtless have followed his advice, had such "courses' been available. I did not then realize that Hosmer was quietly opening college doors to me, for in those days they were barred with ancient tongues. . . .

Finally in the fall of 1885, the difficulty of my future education was solved. The whole subtlety of the plan was clear neither to me nor my relatives at the time. Merely I was offered through the Reverend C. C. Painter, once excellent Federal Indian Agent, a scholarship to attend Fisk University in Nashville, Tennessee; the funds were to be furnished by four Connecticut churches which Mr. Painter had formerly pastored. Disappointed though I was at not being able to go to Harvard, I merely regarded this as a temporary change of plan; I would of course go to Harvard in the end. But here and immediately was adventure. I was going into the South; the South of slavery, rebellion and black folk; and above all I was going to meet colored people of my own age and education, of my own ambitions. Once or twice already I had had swift glimpses of the colored world: at Rocky Point on Narragansett Bay, I had attended an annual picnic beside the sea, and had seen in open-mounted astonishment the whole gorgeous color gamut of the American Negro world; the swaggering men, the beautiful girls, the laughter and gaiety, the unhampered self-expression I was astonished and inspired. I became aware, once a chance to go to a group of such young people was opened up for me, of the spiritual isolation in which I was living. I heard too in these days for the first time the Negro folk songs. A Hampton Quartet had sung them in the Congregational Church. I was thrilled and moved to tears and seemed to recognize something inherently and deeply my own. I was glad to go to Fisk.

I started out and went into Tennessee at the age of seventeen to be a sophomore at Fisk University. It was to me an extraordinary experience. I was thrilled to be for the first time among so many people of my own color or rather of such various and such extraordinary colors, which I had only glimpsed before, but who it seemed were bound to me by new and exciting and eternal ties. Never before had I seen young men so self-assured and who gave themselves such airs, and colored men at that; and above all for the first time I saw beautiful girls. At my home among my white school mates there were a few pretty girls; but either they were not entrancing or because I had known them all my life I did not notice them; but at Fisk at the first dinner I saw opposite me a girl of whom I have often said, no human being could possibly have been as beautiful as she seemed to my young eyes that far-off September night of 1885.

The House of the Black Burghardts

If one slips out the northern neck of Manhattan and flies to the left of the silver Sound, one swoops in time onto the Golden River; and dodging its shining beauty, now right, now left, one comes after a hundred miles of lake, hill and mountain, in the Old Bay State. Then at the foot of high Mt. Everett one takes a solemn decision: left is sweet, old Sheffield; but pass it stolidly by and slip gently right into tiny South Egremont which always sleeps. Then wheel right again and come to Egremont Plain and the House of the Black Burghardts.

It is the first home that I remember. There my mother

was born and all her nine brothers and sisters. There perhaps my grandfather was born, although that I do not know. At any rate, on this wide and lovely plain, beneath the benediction of gray-blue mountain and the low music of rivers, lived for a hundred years the black Burghardt clan. Up and to the east on a hill of rocks was Uncle Ira; down and to the south was Uncle Harlow in a low, long, red house beside a pond—in a house of secret passages, sudden steps, low, narrow doors and unbelievable furniture. And here right in the center of the world was Uncle 'Tallow, as Grandfather Othello was called.

It was a delectable place—simple, square and low, with the great room of the fireplace, the flagged kitchen, half a step below, and the lower woodshed beyond. Steep, strong stairs led up to Sleep, while without was a brook, a well and a mighty elm. Almost was I born there myself but that Alfred Du Bois and Mary Burghardt honeymooned a year in town and then brought me as a baby back to Egremont Plain.

I left the home as a child to live in town again and go to school. But for furtive glimpses I did not see the house again for more than a quarter century. Then riding near on a chance journey I suddenly was homesick for that house. I came to the spot. There it stood, old, lonesome, empty. Its windowless eyes stared blindly on the broad, black highway to New York. It seemed to have shrunken timidly into itself. It had lost color and fence and grass and up to the left and down to the right its sister homes were gone—dead and gone with no stick nor stone to mark their burial.

From that day to this I desperately wanted to own that house for no earthly reason that sounded a bit like sense. It was 130 long miles from my work. It was decrepit almost beyond repair save that into its tough and sturdy timbers the Black Burghardts had built so much of their own dumb pluck that—

"Why the stairs don't even creak!" said She, climbing gingerly aloft.

But I fought the temptation away. Yachts and country estates and limousines are not adapted to my income. Oh, I inquired of course. The replies were discouraging. And once every year or so I drove by and stared sadly; and even more sadly and brokenly the House of the Black Burghardts stared back.

Then of a sudden Somebody whose many names and places I do not know sent secret emissaries to me on a birthday which I had firmly resolved *not* to celebrate. Sent emissaries who showed me all the Kingdoms of this World, including something in green with a cupola; and also The House; and I smiled at the House. And they said by telegram: *The House of the Black Burghardts is come home again—it is yours!*[1]

Whereat in great joy I celebrated another birthday and drew plans. And from its long hiding-place I brought out an old black pair of tongs. Once my grandfather, and mayhap his, used them in the great fireplace of the House. Long years I have carried them tenderly over all the earth. The sister shovel, worn in holes, was lost. But when the old fireplace rises again from the dead on Egremont Plain, its dead eyes shall see not only the ghosts of old Tom and his son Jack and his grandson Othello and his great grandson, me—but also the real presence of these iron tongs resting again in fire worship in the House of the Black Burghardts.

THE CRISIS APRIL, 1928

Du Bois expands his ideas of self-segregation over which he broke with the NAACP in 1934, six years earlier.

The Colored World Within

Historically, beginning with their thought in the eighteenth century and coming down to the twentieth, Negroes have tended to choose between . . . and emphasize two lines of action: the *first* is exemplified in [David] Walker's Appeal, that tremendous indictment of slavery by a colored man published in 1829, and resulting very possibly in the murder of the author; and coming down through the work of the Niagara Movement and the National Association for the Advancement of Colored People in our day. This program of organized opposition to the action and attitude of the dominant white group includes ceaseless agitation and insistent demand for equality: the equal right to work, civic

---

[1] [The Berkshire Hills and the home of his maternal ancestors, "The Black Burghardts" were dear to Du Bois. His friends knew this and in 1928 many of them, including Clarence Darrow, Jane Addams, Moorfield Storey and others bought and gave to him the "House of the Black Burghardts."]

and political equality, and social equality. It involves the use of force of every sort: moral suasion, propaganda and where possible even physical resistance.

There are, however, manifest difficulties about such a program. First of all it is not a program that envisages any direct action of Negroes themselves for the uplift of their socially depresed masses; in the very conception of the program, such work is to be attended to by the nation and Negroes are to be the subjects of uplift forces and agencies to the extent of their numbers and need. Another difficulty is that the effective organization of this plan of protest and agitation involves a large degree of inner union and agreement among Negroes. Now for obvious reasons of ignorance and poverty, and the natural envy and bickering of any disadvantaged group, this unity is difficult to achieve ... even if there were the necessary unity and resources available, there are two assumptions usually made in such a campaign, which are not quite true; and that is the assumption on one hand that most race prejudice is a matter of ignorance to be cured by information; and on the other hand that much discrimination is a matter of deliberate deviltry and unwillingness to be just. Admitting widespread ignorance concerning the guilt of American whites for the plight of the Negroes; and the undoubted existence of sheer malevolence, the present attitude of the whites is much more the result of inherited customs and of those irrational and partly subconscious actions of men which control so large a proportion of their deeds. Attitudes and habits thus built up cannot be changed by sudden assault. They call for a long, patient, well-planned and persistent campaign of propaganda. . . .

In the meantime of course the agitating group may resort to a campaign of countermoves. They may organize and collect resources and by every available means teach the white majority and appeal to their sense of justice; but at the very best this means a campaign of waiting and the colored group must be financially able to afford to wait and patient to endure without spiritual retrogression while they wait.

The *second* group effort to which Negroes have turned is more extreme and decisive. One can see it late in the eighteenth century when the Negro union of Newport, Rhode Island, in 1788 proposed to the Free African Society of Philadelphia a general exodus to Africa on the part at least of free Negroes. This "back to Africa" movement has recurred time and time again in the philosophy of American

Negroes and has commended itself not simply to the inexperienced and to demagogues, but to the prouder and more independent type of Negro; to the black man who is tired of begging for justice and recognition from folk who seem to him to have no intention of being just and do not propose to recognize Negroes as men. . . .

The hard facts which killed all these proposals were first lack of training, education and habits on the part of ex-slaves which unfitted them to be pioneers; and mainly that tremendous industrial expansion of Europe which made colonies in Africa or elsewhere about the last place where colored folk could successfully seek freedom and equality. These extreme plans tended always to fade to more moderate counsel. First came the planned inner migration of the Negro group: to Canada, to the North, to the West, to cities everywhere. This has been a vast and continuing movement, affecting millions and changing and modifying the Negro problems. One result has been a new system of racial integrations. Groups of Negroes in their own clubs and organizations, in their own neighborhoods and schools, were formed, and were not so much the result of deliberate planning as the rationalization of the segregation into which they were forced by racial prejudice. These groups became physical and spiritual cities of refuge, where sometimes the participants were inspired to efforts for social uplift, learning and ambition; and sometimes reduced to sullen wordless resentment. It is toward this sort of group effort that the thoughts and plans of Booker T. Washington led. He did not advocate a deliberate and planned segregation, but advised submission to segregation in settlement and in work, in order that this bending to the will of a powerful majority might bring from that majority gradually such sympathy and sense of justice that in the long run the best interests of the Negro group would be served; particularly as those interests were, he thought, inseparable from the best interests of the dominant group. The difficulty here was that unless the dominant group saw its best interests bound up with those of the black minority, the situation was hopeless; and in any case the danger was that if the minority ceased to agitate and resist oppression it would grow to accept it as normal and inevitable.

A *third* path of the advance which lately I have been formulating and advocating can easily be mistaken for a program of complete racial segregation and even nationalism among Negroes. Indeed it has been criticized as such. This is a misapprehension. First, ignoring other racial separations, I have stressed the economic discrimination as fundamental and advised concentration of planning here. We need sufficient income for health and home; to supplement our education and recreation; to fight our own crime problem; and above all to finance a continued, planned and intelligent agitation for political, civil and social equality. How can we Negroes in the United States gain such average income as to be able to attend to these pressing matters? The cost of this program must fall first and primarily on us, ourselves. It is silly to expect any large number of whites to finance a program which the overwhelming majority of whites today fear and reject. Setting up as a bogey-man an assumed proposal for an absolute separate Negro economy in America, it has been easy for colored philosophers and white experts to dismiss the matter with a shrug and a laugh. But this is not so easily dismissed. In the first place we have already got a partially segregated Negro economy in the United States. There can be no question about this. We not only build and finance Negro churches, but we furnish a considerable part of the funds for our segregated schools. We furnish most of our own professional services in medicine, pharmacy, dentistry and law. We furnish some part of our food and clothes, our home building and repairing and many retail services. We furnish books and newspapers; we furnish endless personal services like those of barbers, beauty shop keepers, hotels, restaurants. It may be said that this inner economy of the Negro serves but a small proportion of its total needs; but it is growing and expanding in various ways; and what I propose is to so plan and guide it as to take advantage of certain obvious facts.

It is of course impossible that a segregated economy for Negroes in the United States should be complete. It is quite possible that it could never cover more than the smaller part of the economic activities of Negroes. Nevertheless, it is also possible that this smaller part could be so important and wield so much power that its influence upon the total economy of Negroes and the total industrial organization of the United States would be decisive for the great ends toward which the Negro moves. . . .

This plan of action would have for its ultimate object, full Negro rights and Negro equality in America; and it would most certainly approve, as one method of attaining this, continued agitation, protest and propaganda to that end. On the other hand my plan would not decline frankly to face the possibility of eventual emigration from America of some considerable part of the Negro population, in case they could find a chance for free and favorable development unmolested and unthreatened, and in case the race prejudice in America persisted to such an extent that it would not permit the full development of the capacities and aspirations of the Negro race. With its eyes open to the necessity of agitation and to possible migration, this plan would start with the racial grouping that today is inevitable and proceed to use it as a method of progress along which we have worked and are now working. Instead of letting this segregation remain largely a matter of chance and unplanned development, and allowing its objects and results to rest in the hands of the white majority or in the accidents of the situation, it would make the segregation a matter of careful thought and intelligent planning on the part of Negroes.

The object of that plan would be two-fold: first to make it possible for the Negro group to await its ultimate emancipation with reasoned patience, with equitable temper and with every possible effort to raise the social status and increase the efficiency of the group. And secondly and just as important, the ultimate object of the plan is to obtain admission of the colored group to co-operation and incorporation into the white group on the best possible terms.

This planned and deliberate recognition of self-segregation on the part of colored people involves many difficulties which have got to be faced. First of all, in what lines and objects of effort should segregation come? This choice is not wide, because so much segregation is compulsory: most colored children, most colored youth, are educated in Negro schools and by Negro teachers. . . .

It is not then the theory but a fact that faces the Negro in education. He has group education in large proportion and he must organize and plan these segregated schools so that they become efficient, well-housed, well-equipped, with the best of teachers and with the best results on the children; so that the illiteracy and bad manners and criminal tendencies of young Negroes can be quickly and effectively reduced. Most Negroes would prefer a good school with properly paid colored teachers for educating their children, to forcing their children into white schools which met them with injustice and humiliation and discouraged their efforts to progress.

So too in the church, the activities for ethical teaching, character-building, and organized charity and neighborliness, which are largely concentrated in religious organizations, are segregated racially more completely than any other human activity; a curious and eloquent commentary upon modern Christianity. These are the facts and the colored church must face them. . . .

There has been a larger movement on the part of the Negro intelligentsia toward racial grouping for the advancement of art and literature. There has been a distinct plan for reviving ancient African art through an American Negro art movement; and more especially a thought to use the extremely rich and colorful life of the Negro in America and elsewhere as a basis for painting, sculpture and literature. This has been partly nullified by the fact that if these new artists expect support for their art from the Negro group itself, that group must be deliberately trained and schooled in art appreciation and in willingness to accept new canons of art and in refusal to follow the herd instinct of the nation. Instead of this artistic group following such lines, it has largely tried to get support for the Negro art movement from the white public, often with disastrous results. Most whites want Negroes to amuse them; they demand caricature; they demand jazz; and torn between these allegiances: between the extraordinary reward for entertainers of the white world, and meager encouragement to honest self-expression, the artistic movement among American Negroes has accomplished something, but it has never flourished and never will until it is deliberately planned. Perhaps its greatest single accomplishment is Carter Woodson's "Negro History Week."

In the same way there is a demand for a distinct Negro health movement. We have few Negro doctors in proportion to our population and the best training of Negro doctors has become increasingly difficult because of their exclusion from the best medical schools of America. Hospitalization among Negroes is far below their reasonable health needs and the individual medical practitioner depending upon fees is the almost universal pattern in this group. What is needed is a carefully planned and widely distributed system of Negro hospitals and socialized medicine with an adequate number of doctors on salary, with the object of social health and not individual income. "Negro Health Week," originating in Tuskegee, is a step in this direction. The whole planned political program of intelligent Negroes is deliberate segregation of their vote for Negro welfare. . . .

The same need is evident in the attitude of Negroes toward Negro crime; obsessed by the undoubted fact that crime is increased and magnified by race prejudice, we ignore the other fact that we have crime and a great deal of it and that we ourselves have got to do something about it; what we ought to do is to cover the Negro group with the services of legal defense organizations in order to counteract the injustice of the police and of the magistrate courts; and then we need positive organized effort to reclaim young and incipient malefactors. . . .

From all the foregoing, it is evident that economic planning to insure adequate income is the crying need of Negroes today. This does not involve plans that envisage a return to the old patterns of economic organization in America and the world. This is the American Negro's present danger. Most of the well-to-do with fair education do not realize the imminence of profound economic change in the modern world. They are thinking in terms of work, thrift, investment and profit. They hope with the late Booker T. Washington to secure better economic conditions for Negroes by wider chances of employment and higher wages. They believe in savings and investment in Negro and in general business, and in the gradual evolution of a Negro capitalist class which will exploit both Negro and white labor. . . .

Negro membership in labor unions has increased and is still increasing. This is an excellent development, but it has difficulties and pitfalls. The American labor movement varies from closed skilled labor groups, who are either nascent capitalists or stooges, to masses of beaten, ignorant labor outcasts, quite as helpless as the Negroes. Moreover among the working white masses the same racial repulsion persists as in the case of other cultural contacts. This is only natural. The white laborer has been trained to dislike and fear black labor; to regard the Negro as an unfair competitor, able and willing to degrade the price of labor; and even if the Negro prove a good union man, his treatment as an equal would involve equal status, which the white laborer through his long cultural training bitterly resents as a degradation of his own status. Under these circumstances the American Negro faces in the current labor movement, especially in the A F of L and also even in the CIO, the current racial patterns of America.

To counteract this, a recent study of Negro unionism suggests that like the Jews with their United Hebrew Trades, so the Negroes with a United Negro Trades should fight for equality and opportunity within the labor ranks. This illustrates exactly my plan to use the segregation technique for industrial emancipation. The Negro has but one clear path: to enter the white labor movement wherever and whenever he can; but to enter fighting still within labor ranks for recognition and equal treatment. . . .

There has come a third solution which is really a sophisticated attempt to dodge the whole problem of color in economic change; this proposal says that Negroes should join the labor movement, and also so far as possible should join themselves to capital and become capitalists and employers; and in this way, gradually the color line will dissolve into a class line between employers and employees. . . .

This plan will have inserted into the ranks of the Negro race a new cause of division, a new attempt to subject the masses of the race to an exploiting capitalist class of their own people. Negro labor will be estranged from its own intelligentsia, which represents black labor's own best blood; upper class Negroes and Negro labor will find themselves cutting each other's throats on opposite sides of a desperate economic battle, which will be but replica of the old battle which the white world is seeking to outgrow. Instead of forging ahead to a new relation of capital and labor, we would relapse into the old discredited pattern.

It seems to me that all three of these solutions are less hopeful than a fourth solution and that is a racial attempt to use the power of the Negro as a consumer not only for his economic uplift but in addition to that, for his economic education. What I propose is that into the interstices of this collapse of the industrial machine, the Negro shall search intelligently and carefully and farsightedly plan for his entrance into the new economic world, not as a continuing slave but as an intelligent free man with power in his hands.

I see this chance for planning in the role which the Negro plays as a consumer. In the future reorganization of industry the consumer as against the producer is going to become the key man. Industry is going to be guided according to his wants and needs and not exclusively with regard to the profit of the producers and transporters. Now as a consumer the Negro approaches economic equality much more nearly than he ever has as producer. Organizing then and conserving and using intelligently the power which twelve million people have through what they buy, it is possible for the American Negro to help in the rebuilding of the economic state. . . .

The fact that the number of Negro college graduates has increased from 215 between 1876 and 1880 to 10,000 between 1931 and 1935 shows that the ability is there if it can act. In addition to mental ability there is demanded an extraordinary moral strength, the strength to endure discrimination and not become discouraged; to face almost universal disparagement and keep one's soul; and to sacrifice for an ideal which the present generation will hardly see fulfilled. This is an unusual demand and no one can say off-hand whether or not the present generation of American Negroes is equal to it. But there is reason to believe that if the high emotional content of the Negro soul could once be guided into channels that promise success, the end might be accomplished.

Despite a low general level of income, Negroes probably spend at least one hundred and fifty million a month under ordinary circumstances, and they live in an era when gradually economic revolution is substituting the consumer as the decisive voice in industry rather than the all-powerful producer of the past. Already in the Negro group the consumer interest is dominant. Outside of agriculture the Negro is a producer only so far as he is an employee and usually a subordinate employee of large interests dominated almost entirely by whites. His social institutions, therefore, are almost entirely the institutions of consumers and it is precisely along the development of these institutions that he can move in general accordance with the economic development of his time and of the larger white group, and also in this way evolve unified organization for his own economic salvation.

The fact is, as the Census of 1930 shows, there is almost no need that a modern group has which Negro workers already trained and at work are not able to satisfy. Already Negroes can raise their own food, build their own homes, fashion their own clothes, mend their own shoes, do much of their repair work, and raise some raw materials like tobacco and cotton. A simple transfer of Negro workers, with only such additional skills as can easily be learned in a few months, would enable them to weave their own cloth, make their own shoes, slaughter their own meat, prepare furniture for their homes, install electrical appliances, make their own cigars and cigarettes.

Appropriate direction and easily obtainable technique and capital would enable Negroes further to take over the whole of their retail distribution, to raise, cut, mine and manufacture a considerable proportion of the basic raw material, to man their own manufacturing plants, to process foods, to import necessary raw materials, to invent and build machines. Processes and monopolized natural resources they must continue to buy, but they could buy them on just as advantageous terms as their competitors if they bought in large quantities and paid cash, instead of enslaving themselves with white usury.

Large numbers of other Negroes working as miners, laborers in industry and transportation, could without difficulty be transferred to productive industries designed to cater to Negro consumers. The matter of skill in such industries is not as important as in the past, with industrial operations massed and standardized.

Without doubt, there are difficulties in the way of this program. The Negro population is scattered. The mouths which the Negro farmers might feed might be hundreds or thousands of miles away, and carpenters and mechanics would have to be concentrated and guaranteed a sufficiency of steady employment. All this would call for careful planning and particularly for such an organization of consumers as would eliminate unemployment, risk and profit. Demand organized and certain must precede the production and transportation of goods. The waste of advertising must be eliminated. The difference between actual cost and selling price must disappear, doing away with exploitation of labor which is the source of profit.

All this would be a realization of democracy in industry led by consumers' organizations and extending to planned production. Is there any reason to believe that such democracy among American Negroes could evolve the necessary leadership in technique and the necessary social institutions which would so guide and organize the masses that a new economic foundation could be laid for a group which is today threatened with poverty and social subordination? . . .

This integration of the single consumers' co-operative into wholesales and factories will intensify the demand for selected leaders and intelligent democratic control over them —for the discovery of ability to manage, of character, of absolute honesty, of inspirational push not toward power but toward efficiency, of expert knowledge in the technique of production and distribution and of scholarship in the past and present of economic development. Nor is this enough. The eternal tendency of such leadership is, once it is established, to assume its own technocratic right to rule, to begin to despise the mass of people who do not know, who have no idea of difficulties of machinery and processes, who succumb to the blandishments of the glib talker, and are willing to select people not because they are honest and sincere but because they wield the glad hand.

Now these people must not be despised, they must be taught. They must be taught in long and lingering conference, in careful marshaling of facts, in the willingness to come to decision slowly and the determination not to tyrannize over minorities. There will be minorities that do not understand. They must patiently be taught to understand. There will be minorities who are stubborn, selfish, self-opinionated. Their real character must be so brought out and exhibited until the overwhelming mass of people who own the co-operative movement and whose votes guide and control it will be able to see just exactly the principles and persons for which they are voting.

The group can socialize most of its professional activities. Certain general and professional services they could change from a private profit to a mutual basis. They could mutualize in reality and not in name, banking and insurance, law and medicine. Health can be put upon the same compulsory basis that we have tried in the case of education, with universal service under physicians paid if possible by the state, or helped by the state, or paid entirely by the group. Hospitals can be as common as churches and used to far better advantage. The legal profession can be socialized and instead of being, as it is now, a defense of property and of the anti-social aggressions of wealth, it can become as it should be, the defense of the young, poor, ignorant and careless.

Banking should be so arranged as to furnish credit to the honest in emergencies or to put unneeded savings to useful and socially necessary work. Banking should not be simply and mainly a method of gambling, theft, tyranny, exploitation and profit-making. Our insurance business should cease to be, as it so largely is, a matter of deliberate gambling and become a co-operative service to equalize the incidence of misfortune equitably among members of the whole group without profit to anybody.

Negroes could not only furnish pupils for their own schools and colleges, but could control their teaching force and policies, their textbooks and ideals. By concentrating their demand, by group buying and by their own plants they could get Negro literature issued by the best publishers without censorship upon expression and they could evolve Negro art for its own sake and for its own beauty and not simply for the entertainment of white folk.

The American Negro must remember that he is primarily a consumer; that as he becomes a producer, it must be at the demand and under the control of organized consumers and according to their wants; that in this way he can gradually build up the absolutely needed co-operation in occupations. Today we work for others at wages pressed down to the limit of subsistence. Tomorrow we may work for ourselves, exchanging services, producing an increasing proportion of the goods which we consume and being rewarded by a living wage and by work under civilized conditions. This will call for self-control. It will eliminate the millionaire and even the rich Negro; it will put the Negro leader upon a salary which will be modest as American salaries go and yet sufficient for a life under modern standards of decency and enjoyment. It will eliminate also the pauper and the industrial derelict.

To a degree, but not completely, this is a program of segregation. The consumer group is in important aspects a self-segregated group. We are now segregated largely without reason. Let us put reason and power beneath this segregation. . . .

There are unpleasant eventualities which we must face even if we succeed. For instance, if the Negro in America is successful in welding a mass or large proportion of his people into groups working for their own betterment and uplift, they will certainly, like the Jews, be suspected of sinister designs and inner plotting; and their very success in cultural advance be held against them and used for further and perhaps fatal segregation. There is, of course, always the possibility that the plan of a minority group may be opposed to the best interests of a neighboring or enveloping or larger group; or even if it is not, the larger and more powerful group may think certain policies of a minority are inimical to the national interests. The possibility of this happening must be taken into account.

The Negro group in the United States can establish, for a large proportion of its members, a co-operative commonwealth, finding its authority in the consensus of the group and its intelligent choice of inner leadership. It can see to it that not only no action of this inner group is opposed to the real interests of the nation, but that it works for and in conjunction with the best interests of the nation.

Have we the brains to do this?

Here in the past we have easily landed into a morass of criticism, without faith in the ability of American Negroes to extricate themselves from their present plight. Our former panacea emphasized by Booker T. Washington was flight of class from mass in wealth with the idea of escaping the masses or ruling the masses through power placed by white capitalists into the hands of those with larger income. My own panacea of earlier days was flight of class from mass through the development of a Talented Tenth; but the power of this aristocracy of talent was to lie in its knowledge and character and not in its wealth. The problem which I did not then attack was that of leadership and authority within the group, which by implication left controls to wealth—a contingency of which I never dreamed. But now the whole economic trend of the world has changed. That mass and class must unite for the world's salvation is clear. . . .

American Negroes must know that the advance of the Negro people since emancipation has been the extraordinary success in education, technique and character among a small number of Negroes and that the emergence of these exceptional men has been largely a matter of chance; that their triumph proves that down among the mass, ten times their number with equal ability could be discovered and developed, if sustained effort and sacrifice and intelligence were put to this task. That, on the contrary, today poverty, sickness and crime are choking the paths to Negro uplift, and that salvation of the Negro race is to come by planned and sustained efforts to open ways of development to those who now form the unrisen mass of the Negro group. . . .

It is to be admitted this will be a real battle. There are chances of failure, but there are also splendid chances of success. In the African communal group, ties of family and blood, of mother and child, of group relationship, made the group leadership strong, even if not always toward the highest culture. In the case of the more artificial group among American Negroes, there are sources of strength in common memories of suffering in the past; in present threats of degradation and extinction; in common ambitions and ideals; in emulation and the determination to prove ability and desert. Here in subtle but real ways the communalism of the African clan can be transferred to the Negro American group, implemented by higher ideals of human accomplishment through the education and culture which have arisen and may further arise through contact of black folk with the modern world. The emotional wealth of the American Negro, the nascent art in song, dance, and drama can all be applied, not to amuse the white audience, but to inspire and direct the acting Negro group itself. I can conceive no more magnificent nor promising crusade in modern times. We have a chance here to teach industrial and cultural democracy to a world that bitterly needs it.

CREATIVE WRITINGS

Even in the midst of his efforts to deal with many other important matters, Dr. Du Bois apparently always found ample time to encourage young black men and women to concern themselves seriously with various types of creation —fiction, drama, poetry, painting. He helped establish drama groups; he encouraged the awarding of prizes for meritorious work in the cultural field; he provided space in his magazines, especially in The Crisis, for the display of the talents of young people. For 25 years under his editorship The Crisis alone used hundreds of such contributions. And many successful Negro artists have paid tribute to Du Bois both for inspiring them and for publishing their works.

Du Bois himself was a highly creative man and if he had limited himself to literature he would surely have made a distinguished name for himself as a novelist, short-story writer and dramatist. And, as a matter of fact, he did make substantial contributions as a creative writer but his historical, sociological, educational, and organizational successes were so great that his artistic work was overshadowed. He wrote five fine novels: The Quest of the Silver Fleece *(1911);* The Dark Princess *(1928); and his* The Black Flame *trilogy in the period 1959–1961. He wrote many short stories. Two of these, "Of the Coming of John" from* The Souls of Black Folk *and "Jesus Christ in Georgia" from* The Crisis, *are in this group of selections.*

Dr. Du Bois was always fascinated with drama and did some producing himself. He was an experimenter and advocated the use of outdoor symphonic-dance-drama for education and entertainment. (Later Paul Green, Kermit Hunter, and others used this form most successfully in the South and West.) He wrote and produced one such drama, The Star of Ethiopia, *which told the story of the long history of the black people in Africa and America. It was first produced in New York City before an audience of almost 30,000 people as part of a national emancipation celebration. The next production was in Philadelphia. Later it was produced in the baseball park in Washington, D.C. The last production was in the Hollywood Bowl in California.*

Charles Burroughs directed and J. Rosamond Johnson composed or selected the 50 pieces of music. Several hundred Negro actors performed and played to more than 100,000 people. Yet for Du Bois playwriting was only a sideline.

Perhaps Du Bois is best known for his poetry. His "A Litany at Atlanta" (expressing his horror over the Atlanta, Georgia, race massacre of 1906) is one of the most quoted of all his writings. Another powerful poem is "The Song of the Smoke," a paean to black beauty. Others of his poems are "The Burden of Black Women," "A Christmas Poem" (the lynching of God), "Ghana Calls," "War," and "Almighty Death."

Eugene O'Neill is one of the many artists who praised Du Bois as a writer. O'Neill wrote of him:

Ranking as he does among the foremost writers of true importance in the country, one wishes sometimes (as a writer oneself) that he could devote all of his time to the accomplishment of that fine and moving prose which distinguishes his books. But at the same time one realizes, self-reproachfully, that with Dr. Du Bois it is a cause—an ideal—that overcomes the personal egoism of the artist.

O'Neill showed rare awareness of Du Bois and one of his many conflicts. He did want to create literature; he realized that he had talent, but he hewed to the line and followed the compulsion to engage in the bigger job of education for racial and social advancement. He used his art for that purpose. And more than once he appealed to creative black men and women to use their talents also for the cause. In fact, he once said: "I don't give a damn for art that is not propaganda."

The Song of the Smoke

I am the smoke king,
I am black.
    I am swinging in the sky,
    I am ringing worlds on high;
    I am the thought of the throbbing mills,
    I am the soul of the Soul toil kills,
    I am the ripple of trading rills.
Up I'm curling from the sod,
I am whirling home to God.
I am the smoke king,
I am black.

I am the smoke king,
I am black.
    I am wreathing broken hearts,
    I am sheathing devils' darts;
    Dark inspiration of iron times,
    Wedding the toil of toiling climes,
    Shedding the blood of bloodless crimes,
Down I lower in the blue,
Up I tower toward the true.
I am the smoke king,
I am black.

I am the smoke king,
I am black.
    I am darkening with song,
    I am hearkening to wrong;
    I will be black as blackness can,
    The blacker the mantle the mightier the man,
    My purpl'ing midnights no day dawn may ban.
I am carving God in night,
I am painting Hell in white.
I am the smoke king,
I am black.

I am the smoke king,
I am black.
    I am cursing ruddy morn,
    I am hearsing hearts unborn;
    Souls unto me are as mists in 'he night,
    I whiten my black men, I blacken my white,
    What's the hue of a hide to a man in his might!
Hail, then, gritty, grimy hands,
Sweet Christ, pity toiling lands!

Hail to the smoke king,
Hail to the black!

ORIGINAL VERSION FIRST PUBLISHED IN THE HORIZON, 1899

A Litany at Atlanta

O Silent God, Thou whose voice afar in mist and mystery hath left our ears an-hungered in these fearful days—
Hear us, good Lord;
Listen to us, Thy children: our faces dark with doubt are made a mockery in Thy Sanctuary. With uplifted hands we front Thy Heaven, O God, crying:
We beseech Thee to hear us, good Lord;
We are not better than our fellows, Lord; we are but weak and human men. When our devils do deviltry, curse Thou the doer and the deed—curse them as we curse them, do to them all and more than ever they have done to innocence and weakness, to womanhood and home.
Have mercy upon us, miserable sinners;
And yet, whose is the deeper guilt? Who made these devils? Who nursed them in crime and fed them on injustice? Who ravished and debauched their mothers and their grandmothers? Who bought and sold their crime and waxed fat and rich on public iniquity?
Knowest, good God!
Is this Thy Justice, O Father, that guile be easier than innocence and the innocent be crucified for the guilt of the untouched guilty?
Justice, O Judge of men;
Wherefore do we pray? Is not the God of the Fathers dead? Have not seers seen in Heaven's halls Thine hearsed and lifeless form stark amidst the black and rolling smoke of sin, where all along bow bitter forms of endless dead?
Awake, Thou that sleepest!
Thou art not dead, but flown afar, up hills of endless light through blazing corridors of suns, where worlds do swing of good and gentle men, of women strong and free— far from the cozenage, black hypocrisy, and chaste prostitution of this shameful speck of dust!
Turn again, O Lord; leave us not to perish in our sin!
From lust of body and lust of blood—
Great God, deliver us!
From lust of power and lust of gold—
Great God, deliver us!
From the leagued lying of despot and of brute—
Great God, deliver us!

A city lay in travail, God our Lord, and from her loins sprang twin Murder and Black Hate. Red was the midnight; clang, crack, and cry of death and fury filled the air and trembled underneath the stars where church spires pointed silently to Thee. And all this was to sate the greed of greedy men who hide behind the veil of vengeance.

Bend us Thine ear, O Lord!

In the pale, still morning we looked upon the dead. We stopped our ears and held our leaping hands, but they—did they not wag their heads and leer and cry with bloody jaws: *Cease from Crime!* The word was mockery, for thus they train a hundred crimes while we do cure one.

Turn again our captivity, O Lord!

Behold this maimed and broken thing, dear God; it was an humble black man, who toiled and sweat to save a bit from the pittance paid him. They told him: *Work and Rise.* He worked. Did this man sin? Nay, but someone told how someone said another did—one whom he had never seen nor known. Yet for that man's crime this man lieth maimed and murdered, his wife naked to shame, his children to poverty and evil.

Hear us, O heavenly Father!

Doth not this justice of hell stink in Thy nostrils, O God? How long shall the mounting flood of innocent blood roar in Thine ears and pound in our hearts for vengeance? Pile the pale frenzy of blood-crazed brutes, who do such deeds, high on Thine Altar, Jehovah Jirah, and burn it in hell forever and forever!

Forgive us, Good Lord; we know not what we say!

Bewildered we are and passion-tossed, mad with the madness of a mobbed and mocked and murdered people; straining at the armposts of Thy throne, we raise our shackled hands and charge Thee, God, by the bones of our stolen fathers, by the tears of our dead mothers, by the very blood of Thy crucified Christ: What meaneth this? Tell us the plan; give us the sign!

Keep not Thou silent, O God!

Sit not longer blind, Lord God, deaf to our prayer and dumb to our dumb suffering. Surely Thou, too, art not white, O Lord, a pale, bloodless, heartless thing!

Ah, Christ of all the Pities!

Forgive the thought! Forgive these wild, blasphemous words. Thou are still the God of our black fathers and in Thy Soul's Soul sit some soft darkenings of the evening, some shadowings of the velvet night.

But whisper—speak—call, great God, for Thy silence is

white terror to our hearts! The way, O God, show us the way and point us the path!

Whither? North is greed and South is blood; within the coward, and without the liar. Whither? To death?

Amen, Welcome, dark sleep!

Whither? To life? But not this life, dear God, not this. Let the cup pass from us, tempt us not beyond our strength, for there is that clamoring and clawing within, to whose voice we would not listen, yet shudder lest we might—and it is red. Ah! God! It is red and awful shape.

Selah!

In yonder East trembles a star.

Vengeance is Mine; I will repay, saith the Lord!

Thy Will, O Lord, be done!

Kyrie Eleison!

Lord, we have done these pleading, wavering words,

We beseech Thee to hear us, good Lord!

We bow our heads and hearken soft to the sobbing of women and little children,

We beseech Thee to hear us, good Lord!

Our voices sink in silence and in night.

Hear us, good Lord,

In night, O God of a godless land!

Amen!

In silence, O Silent God.

Selah!

A Christmas Poem

Blood? Is it wet with blood?
'Tis from my brother's hands.
(I know; his hands are mine.)
It flowed for Thee, O Lord.

War? Not so, not war:
Dominion, Lord, and over black, not white.
Black, brown and fawn,
And not Thy chosen brood, O God,
We murdered.

To build Thy kingdom,
To drape our wives and little ones,
And set their souls a'glitter—

For this we killed these lesser breeds
And civilized their dead,
Raping red rubber, diamonds, cocoa, gold.

For this, too, once, and in Thy name
I lynched a Nigger—

> (He raved and writhed,
> I heard him cry,
> I felt the life light leap and lie,
> I watched him crackle there, on high,
> I saw him wither!)

     *   *   *   *   *

Thou?
Thee?
I lynched Thee?

     *   *   *   *   *

Awake me, God, I sleep!
What was that awful word Thou saidst?
That black and riven Thing—was it Thee?
That gasp—was it Thine?
This pain—is it Thine?
Are then these bullets piercing Thee?
Have all the wars of all the world,
Down all dim time, drawn blood from Thee?
Have all the lies, and thefts, and hates—
Is this Thy crucifixion, God,
And not that funny little cross,
With vinegar and thorns?

     *   *   *   *   *

Help!
I sense that low and awful cry—
Who cries?
Who weeps
With silent sob that rends and tears—
Can God sob?

Who prays?
I hear strong prayers throng by,
Like mighty winds on dusky moors—
Can God pray?

     *   *   *   *   *

Prayest Thou, Lord, and to me?
Thou needest me?
Thou *needest* me?

Thou needest *me?*
Poor wounded Soul!
Of this I never dreamed. I thought—
*Courage, God,
I come!*

THE CRISIS DECEMBER, 1914

The Burden of Black Women

Dark daughter of the lotus leaves that watch the Southern
    sea,
Wan spirit of a prisoned soul a-panting to be free;
    The muttered music of thy streams, the whispers of the
      deep
    Have kissed each other in God's name and kissed a world
      to sleep.

The will of the world is a whistling wind sweeping a cloud-
    cast sky,
And not from the east and not from the west knelled its
    soul-searing cry;
But out of the past of the Past's grey past, it yelled from the
    top of the sky;
    Crying: Awake, O ancient race! Wailing: O woman arise!
    And crying and sighing and crying again as a voice in the
      midnight cries;
    But the burden of white men bore her back, and the white
      world stifled her sighs.

The White World's vermin and filth:
    All the dirt of London,
    All the scum of New York;
    Valiant spoilers of women
    And conquerors of unarmed men;
    Shameless breeders of bastards
    Drunk with the greed of gold,
    Baiting their blood-stained hooks
    With cant for the souls of the simple,
    Bearing the White Man's Burden
    Of Liquor and Lust and Lies!
    Unthankful we wince in the East,
    Unthankful we wail from the westward,
    Unthankfully thankful we sing,
    In the un-won wastes of the wild:

I hate them, Oh!
I hate them well,
I hate them, Christ!
As I hate Hell,
If I were God
I'd sound their knell
This day!

Who raised the fools to their glory
But black men of Egypt and Ind?
Ethiopia's sons of the evening,
Chaldeans and Yellow Chinese?
The Hebrew children of Morning
And mongrels of Rome and Greece?
       Ah, well!

And they that raised the boasters
Shall drag them down again:
Down with the theft of their thieving
And murder and mocking of men,
Down with their barter of women
And laying and lying of creeds,
Down with their cheating of childhood,
And drunken orgies of war—

     down,

       down,

         deep down,

Till the Devil's strength be shorn,
Till some dim, darker David a-hoeing of his corn,
And married maiden, Mother of God,
Bid the Black Christ be born!

Then shall the burden of manhood,
Be it yellow or black or white,
And Poverty, Justice and Sorrow—
The Humble and Simple and Strong,
Shall sing with the Sons of Morning
And Daughters of Evensong:

Black mother of the iron hills that guard the blazing sea,
Wild spirit of a storm-swept soul a-struggling to be free,

Where 'neath the bloody finger marks, thy riven bosom
    quakes,
Thicken the thunders of God's voice, and lo! a world awakes!
                    THE CRISIS, NOVEMBER, 1914

On Being Crazy

It was one o'clock and I was hungry. I walked into a restaurant, seated myself and reached for the bill-of-fare. My
table companion rose.

"Sir," said he, "do you wish to force your company on
those who do not want you?"

No, said I, I wish to eat.

"Are you aware, sir, that this is social equality?"

Nothing of the sort, sir, it is hunger—and I ate.

The day's work done, I sought the theatre. As I sank into
my seat, the lady shrank and squirmed.

I beg pardon, I said.

"Do you enjoy being where you are not wanted?" she
asked coldly.

Oh no, I said.

"Well you are not wanted here."

I was surprised. I fear you are mistaken, I said. I certainly want the music and I like to think the music wants
me to listen to it.

"Usher," said the lady, "this is social equality."

No, madame, said the usher, it is the second movement
of Beethoven's Fifth Symphony.

After the theatre, I sought the hotel where I had sent my
baggage. The clerk scowled.

"What do you want?" he asked.

Rest, I said.

"This is a white hotel," he said.

I looked around. Such a color scheme requires a great
deal of cleaning, I said, but I don't know that I object.

"We object," said he.

Then why, I began, but he interrupted.

"We don't keep niggers," he said, "we don't want social
equality."

Neither do I, I replied gently, I want a bed.

I walked thoughtfully to the train. I'll take a sleeper
through Texas. I'm a bit dissatisfied with this town.

"Can't sell you one."

I only want to hire it, said I, for a couple of nights.

"Can't sell you a sleeper in Texas," he maintained. "They consider that social equality."

I consider it barbarism, I said, and I think I'll walk.

Walking, I met a wayfarer who immediately walked to the other side of the road where it was muddy. I asked his reasons.

"Niggers is dirty," he said.

So is mud, said I. Moreover I added, I am not as dirty as you—at least not yet.

"But you're a nigger, ain't you?" he asked.

My grandfather was so called.

"Well then!" he answered triumphantly.

Do you live in the South? I persisted, pleasantly.

"Sure," he growled, "and starve there."

I should think you and the Negroes might get together and vote out starvation.

"We don't let them vote."

We? Why not? I said in surprise.

"Niggers is too ignorant to vote."

But, I said, I am not so ignorant as you.

"But you're a nigger."

Yes, I'm certainly what you mean by that.

"Well then!" he returned, with that curiously inconsequential note of triumph. "Moreover," he said, "I don't want my sister to marry a nigger."

I had not seen his sister, so I merely murmured, let her say, no.

"By God you shan't marry her, even if she said yes."

But—but I don't want to marry her, I answered a little perturbed at the personal turn.

"Why not!" he yelled, angrier than ever.

Because I'm already married and I rather like my wife.

"Is she a nigger?" he asked suspiciously.

Well, I said again, her grandmother—was called that.

"Well then!" he shouted in that oddly illogical way.

I gave up.

Go on, I said, either you are crazy or I am.

"We both are," he said as he trotted along in the mud.

Mr. Paleface entered his parlor mincingly—"My dear man," he said, expressively.

"I am Brownson," said the dark man quietly.

"Of course, of course—I know you well, and your people. My father was an abolitionist, and I had a black mammy—"

Mr. Brownson looked out of the window, and said rapidly:

"I have come to ask for certain rights and privileges. My people—"

"—suffer; I know it; I know it. I have often remarked what a shame it was. Sir, it is an outrage!"

"—yes; we want to ask—"

Mr. Paleface raised a deprecating finger, "Not social equality," he murmured, "I trust you are not asking that."

"Certainly not," said Brownson. "I think the right of a man to select his friends and guests and decide with whom he will commit matrimony, is sacredly his and his alone."

"Good, good! Now, my man, we can talk openly, face to face. We can pour out our souls to each other. What can I do? I have already sent my annual check to Hampton."

"Sir, we want to vote."

"Ah! That is difficult, difficult. You see, voting has come to have a new significance. We used to confine our votes to politics, but now—bless me!—we are voting religion, work, social reform, landscape-gardening, and art. Then, too, women are in politics—you see—well, I'm sure you sense the difficulties. Moreover, what is voting? A mere form—the making and execution of the laws is the thing, and there I promise you that I—"

"Well, then; we would help in carrying out the laws."

"Commendable ambition. Very, very commendable. But this involves even greater difficulties. Administrators and executives are thrown closely together—often in the same room—at the same desk. They have to mingle and consult. Much as I deplore the fact, it is true, that a man will not sit at a desk or work at a bench with a man whose company at a theatre he would resent."

"I see," said Brownson, thoughtfully. "I presume, then, it is our business to demand this right to sit in theatres and places of popular entertainment."

"Good Lord, man, that's impossible! Civil rights like this cannot be forced. Objectionable persons must grow, develop —er wash, before—"

"Then I am sure you will help me clean and train my people. I want to join in the great movements for social uplift."

"Splendid! I will have some movements organized for your folks."

"No, I want to be part of the general movement, so as to get the training and inspiration, the wide outlook, the best plans."

"Are you crazy? Don't you know that social uplift work consists of a series of luncheons, dinners, and teas, with ladies present?"

"Um," said Brownson. "I see. I, also, see that in answering your first question, I made a mistake. In the light of your subsequent definition, I see that social equality, far from being what I don't want, is precisely what I do want."

"I knew it!" screamed Mr. Paleface. "I knew it all the time; I saw it sneaking into your eyes. You want—you dare to want to marry my sister."

"Not if she looks like you," said Brownson, "and not if she's as big a liar."

"Get out—get out—leave my house, you ungrateful—"

THE CRISIS, MARCH, 1920

Of the Coming of John

Carlisle Street runs westward from the centre of Johnstown, across a great black bridge, down a hill and up again, by little shops and meat-markets, past single-storied homes, until suddenly it stops against a wide green lawn. It is a broad, restful place, with two large buildings outlined against the west. When at evening the winds come swelling from the east, and the great pall of the city's smoke hangs wearily above the valley, then the red west glows like a dreamland down Carlisle Street, and, at the tolling of the supper-bell, throws the passing forms of students in dark silhouette against the sky. Tall and black, they move slowly by, and seem in the sinister light to flit before the city like dim warning ghosts. Perhaps they are; for this is Wells Institute, and these black students have few dealings with the white city below.

And if you will notice, night after night, there is one dark form that ever hurries last and late toward the twinkling lights of Swain Hall—for Jones is never on time. A long, straggling fellow he is, brown and hard-haired, who seems to be growing straight out of his clothes, and walks with a half-apologetic roll. He used perpetually to set the quiet dining-room into waves of merriment, as he stole to his place after the bell had tapped for prayers; he seemed so perfectly awkward. And yet one glance at his face made one forgive him much—that broad, good-natured smile in which lay no bit of art or artifice, but seemed just bubbling good-nature and genuine satisfaction with the world.

He came to us from Altamaha, away down there beneath the gnarled oaks of Southeastern Georgia, where the sea croons to the sands and the sands listen till they sink half drowned beneath the waters, rising only here and there in long, low islands. The white folk of Altamaha voted John a good boy—fine plough-hand, good in the rice-fields, handy everywhere, and always good-natured and respectful. But they shook their heads when his mother wanted to send him off to school. "It'll spoil him—ruin him," they said; and they talked as though they knew. But full half the black folk followed him proudly to the station, and carried his queer little trunk and many bundles. And there they shook and shook hands, and the girls kissed him shyly and the boys clapped him on the back. So the train came, and he pinched his little sister lovingly, and put his great arms about his mother's neck, and then was away with a puff and a roar into the great yellow world that flamed and flared about the doubtful pilgrim. Up the coast they hurried, past the squares and palmettos of Savannah, through the cotton-fields and through the weary night, to Millville, and came with the morning to the noise and bustle of Johnstown.

And they that stood behind, that morning in Altamaha, and watched the train as it noisily bore playmate and brother and son away to the world, had thereafter one ever-recurring word—"When John comes." Then what parties were to be, and what speakings in the churches; what new furniture in the front room—perhaps even a new front room; and there would be a new schoolhouse, with John as teacher; and then perhaps a big wedding; all this and more —when John comes. But the white people shook their heads.

At first he was coming at Christmas-time—but the vacation proved too short; and then, the next summer—but times were hard and schooling costly, and so, instead, he worked in Johnstown. And so it drifted to the next summer, and the next—till playmates scattered, and mother grew gray, and sister went up to the Judge's kitchen to work. And still the legend lingered—"When John comes."

Up at the Judge's they rather liked this refrain; for they too had a John—a fair-haired, smooth-faced boy, who had played many a long summer's day to its close with his darker namesake. "Yes, sir! John is at Princeton, sir," said the broad-shouldered gray-haired Judge every morning as he marched down to the post-office. "Showing the Yankees what a Southern gentleman can do," he added; and strode home again with his letters and papers. Up at the great pil-lared house they lingered long over the Princeton letter—the Judge and his frail wife, his sister and growing daugh-ters. "It'll make a man of him," said the Judge, "college is the place." And then he asked the shy little waitress, "Well, Jennie, how's your John?" and added reflectively, "Too bad, too bad your mother sent him off—it will spoil him." And the waitress wondered.

Thus in the far-away Southern village the world lay wait-ing, half consciously, the coming of two young men, and dreamed in an inarticulate way of new things that would be done and new thoughts that all would think. And yet it was singular that few thought of two Johns—for the black folk thought of one John, and he was black; and the white folk thought of another John, and he was white. And neither world thought the other world's thought, save with a vague unrest.

Up in Johnstown, at the Institute, we were long puzzled at the case of John Jones. For a long time the clay seemed unfit for any sort of moulding. He was loud and boisterous, always laughing and singing, and never able to work con-secutively at anything. He did not know how to study; he had no idea of thoroughness; and with his tardiness, care-lessness, and appalling good-humor, we were sore perplexed. One night we sat in faculty-meeting, worried and serious; for Jones was in trouble again. This last escapade was too much, and so we solemnly voted "that Jones, on account of repeated disorder and inattention to work, be suspended for the rest of the term."

It seemed to us that the first time life ever struck Jones as a really serious thing was when the Dean told him he must leave school. He stared at the gray-haired man blankly, with great eyes. "Why—why," he faltered, "but—I haven't graduated!" Then the Dean slowly and clearly explained, reminding him of the tardiness and the carelessness, of the poor lessons and neglected work, of the noise and disorder, until the fellow hung his head in confusion. Then he said quickly, "But you won't tell mammy and sister—you won't write mammy, now will you? For if you won't I'll go out into the city and work, and come back next term and show you something." So the Dean promised faithfully, and John shouldered his little trunk, giving neither word nor look to the giggling boys, and walked down Carlisle Street to the great city, with sober eyes and a set and serious face.

Perhaps we imagined it, but someway it seemed to us that the serious look that crept over his boyish face that afternoon never left it again. When he came back to us he went to work with all his rugged strength. It was a hard struggle, for things did not come easily to him—few crowding memories of early life and teaching came to help him on his new way; but all the world toward which he strove was of his own building, and he builded slow and hard. As the light dawned lingeringly on his new creations, he sat rapt and silent before the vision, or wandered alone over the green campus peering through and beyond the world of men into a world of thought. And the thoughts at times puzzled him sorely; he could not see just why the circle was not square, and carried it out fifty-six decimal places one midnight—would have gone further, indeed, had not the matron rapped for lights out. He caught terrible colds lying on his back in the meadows of nights, trying to think out the solar system; he had grave doubts as to the ethics of the Fall of Rome, and strongly suspected the Germans of being thieves and rascals, despite his text-books; he pondered long over every new Greek word, and wondered why this meant that and why it couldn't mean something else, and how it must have felt to think all things in Greek. So he thought and puzzled along for himself—pausing perplexed where others skipped merrily, and walking steadily through the difficulties where the rest stopped and surrendered.

Thus he grew in body and soul, and with him his clothes seemed to grow and arrange themselves; coat sleeves got longer, cuffs appeared, and collars got less soiled. Now and then his boots shone, and a new dignity crept into his walk. And we who saw daily a new thoughtfulness growing in his eyes began to expect something of this plodding boy. Thus he passed out of the preparatory school into college, and we who watched him felt four more years of change, which almost transformed the tall, grave man who bowed to us commencement morning. He had left his queer thought-

world and come back to a world of motion and of men. He
looked now for the first time sharply about him, and wondered he had seen so little before. He grew slowly to feel
almost for the first time the Veil that lay between him and
the white world; he first noticed now the oppression that
had not seemed oppression before, differences that erstwhile
seemed natural, restraints and slights that in his boyhood
days had gone unnoticed or been greeted with a laugh. He
felt angry now when men did not call him "Mister," he
clenched his hands at the "Jim Crow" cars, and chafed at
the color-line that hemmed in him and his. A tinge of sar-
casm crept into his speech, and a vague bitterness into his
life; and he sat long hours wondering and planning a way
around these crooked things. Daily he found himself shrinking from the choked and narrow life of his native town.
And yet he always planned to go back to Altamaha—always planned to work there. Still, more and more as the day
approached he hesitated with a nameless dread; and even
the day after graduation he seized with eagerness the offer
of the Dean to send him North with the quartette during
the summer vacation, to sing for the Institute. A breath of
air before the plunge, he said to himself in half apology.

It was a bright September afternoon, and the streets of
New York were brilliant with moving men. They reminded
John of the sea, as he sat in the square and watched them,
so changelessly changing, so bright and dark, so grave and
gay. He scanned their rich and faultless clothes, the way
they carried their hands, the shape of their hats; he peered
into the hurrying carriages. Then, leaning back with a sigh,
he said, "This is the World." The notion suddenly seized
him to see where the world was going; since many of the
richer and brighter seemed hurrying all one way. So when
a tall, light-haired young man and a little talkative lady
came by, he rose half hesitatingly and followed them. Up
the street they went, past stores and gay shops, across a
broad square, until with a hundred others they entered the
high portal of a great building.

He was pushed toward the ticket-office with the others,
and felt in his pocket for the new five-dollar bill he had
hoarded. There seemed really no time for hesitation, so he
drew it bravely out, passed it to the busy clerk, and received
simply a ticket but no change. When at last he realized that
he had paid five dollars to enter he knew not what, he stood
stockstill amazed. "Be careful," said a low voice behind
him; "you must not lynch the colored gentleman simply
because he's in your way," and a girl looked up roguishly

into the eyes of her fair-haired escort. A shade of annoyance passed over the escort's face. "You *will* not understand us at the South," he said half impatiently, as if continuing an argument. "With all your professions, one never sees in the North so cordial and intimate relations between white and black as are everyday occurrences with us. Why, I remember my closest playfellow in boyhood was a little Negro named after me, and surely no two—*well!*" The man stopped short and flushed to the roots of his hair, for there directly beside his reserved orchestra chairs sat the Negro he had stumbled over in the hallway. He hesitated and grew pale with anger, called the usher and gave him his card, with a few peremptory words, and slowly sat down. The lady deftly changed the subject.

All this John did not see, for he sat in a half-maze minding the scene about him; the delicate beauty of the hall, the faint perfume, the moving myriad of men, the rich clothing and low hum of talking seemed all a part of a world so different from his, so strangely more beautiful than anything he had known, that he sat in dreamland, and started when, after a hush, rose high and clear the music of Lohengrin's swan. The infinite beauty of the wail lingered and swept through every muscle of his frame, and put it all a-tune. He closed his eyes and grasped the elbows of the chair, touching unwittingly the lady's arm. And the lady drew away. A deep longing swelled in all his heart to rise with that clear music out of the dirt and dust of that low life that held him prisoned and befouled. If he could only live up in the free air where birds sang and setting suns had no touch of blood! Who had called him to be the slave and butt of all? And if he had called, what right had he to call when a world like this lay open before men?

Then the movement changed, and fuller, mightier harmony swelled away. He looked thoughtfully across the hall, and wondered why the beautiful gray-haired woman looked so listless, and what the little man could be whispering about. He would not like to be listless and idle, he thought, for he felt with the music the movement of power within him. If he but had some master-work, some life-service, hard—aye, bitter hard, but without the cringing and sickening servility, without the cruel hurt that hardened his heart and soul. When at last a soft sorrow crept across the violins, there came to him the vision of a far-off home—the great eyes of his sister, and the dark drawn face of his mother. And his heart sank below the waters, even as the sea-sand sinks by the shores of Altamaha, only to be lifted aloft again with that last ethereal wail of the swan that quivered and faded away into the sky.

It left John sitting so silent and rapt that he did not for some time notice the usher tapping him lightly on the shoulder and saying politely, "Will you step this way, please, sir?" A little surprised, he arose quickly at the last tap, and, turning to leave his seat, looked full into the face of the fair-haired young man. For the first time the young man recognized his dark boyhood playmate, and John knew that it was the Judge's son. The White John started, lifted his hand, and then froze into his chair; the black John smiled lightly, then grimly, and followed the usher down the aisle. The manager was sorry, very, very sorry—but he explained that some mistake had been made in selling the gentleman a seat already disposed of; he would refund the money, of course—and indeed felt the matter keenly, and so forth, and—before he had finished John was gone, walking hurriedly across the square and down the broad streets, and as he passed the park he buttoned his coat and said, "John Jones, you're a natural-born fool." Then he went to his lodgings and wrote a letter, and tore it up; he wrote another, and threw it in the fire. Then he seized a scrap of paper and wrote: "Dear Mother and Sister—I am coming—John."

"Perhaps," said John, as he settled himself on the train, "perhaps I am to blame myself in struggling against my manifest destiny simply because it looks hard and unpleasant. Here is my duty to Altamaha plain before me; perhaps they'll let me help settle the Negro problems there—perhaps they won't. 'I will go into the King, which is not according to the law; and if I perish, I perish.'" And then he mused and dreamed, and planned a life-work; and the train flew south.

Down in Altamaha, after seven long years, all the world knew John was coming. The homes were scrubbed and scoured—above all, one; the gardens and yards had an unwonted trimness, and Jennie bought a new gingham. With some finesse and negotiation, all the dark Methodist and Presbyterians were induced to join in a monster welcome at the Baptist Church; and as the day drew near, warm discussions arose on every corner as to the exact extent and nature of John's accomplishments. It was noontide on a gray and cloudy day when he came. The black town flocked to the depot, with a little of the white at the edges—a happy throng, with "Good-mawnings" and "Howdys" and laughing and joking and jostling. Mother sat yonder in the window watching; but sister Jennie stood on the platform, nervously fingering her dress, tall and lithe, with soft brown skin and loving eyes peering from out a tangled wilderness of hair. John rose gloomily as the train stopped, for he was thinking of the "Jim Crow" car; he stepped to the platform, and paused: a little dingy station, a black crowd gaudy and dirty, a half-mile of dilapidated shanties along a straggling ditch of mud. An overwhelming sense of the sordidness and narrowness of it all seized him; he looked in vain for his mother, kissed coldly the tall, strange girl who called him brother, spoke a short, dry word here and there; then, lingering neither for hand-shaking nor gossip, started silently up the street, raising his hat merely to the last eager old aunty, to her open-mouthed astonishment. The people were distinctly bewildered. This silent, cold man—was this John? Where was his smile and hearty hand-grasp? " 'Peared kind o' down in the mouf," said the Methodist preacher thoughtfully. "Seemed monstus stuck up," complained a Baptist sister. But the white postmaster from the edge of the crowd expressed the opinion of his folks plainly. "That damn Nigger," said he, as he shouldered the mail and arranged his tobacco, "has gone North and got plum full o' fool notions; but they won't work in Altamaha." And the crowd melted away.

The meeting of welcome at the Baptist Church was a failure. Rain spoiled the barbecue, and thunder turned the milk in the ice-cream. When the speaking came at night, the house was crowded to overflowing. The three preachers had especially prepared themselves, but somehow John's manner seemed to throw a blanket over everything—he seemed so cold and preoccupied, and had so strange an air of restraint that the Methodist brother could not warm up to his theme and elicited not a single "Amen"; the Presbyterian prayer was but feebly responded to, and even the Baptist preacher, though he wakened faint enthusiasm, got so mixed up in his favorite sentence that he had to close it by stopping fully fifteen minutes sooner than he meant. The people moved uneasily in their seats as John rose to reply. He spoke slowly and methodically. The age, he said, demanded new ideas; we were far different from those men of the seventeenth and eighteenth centuries—with broader ideas of human brotherhood and destiny. Then he spoke of the rise of charity and popular education, and particularly of the spread of wealth and work. The question was, then, he added reflectively, looking at the low discolored ceiling, what part the Negroes of this land would take in the striving of the new century. He sketched in vague outline the new

Industrial School that might rise among these pines, he spoke in detail of the charitable and philanthropic work that might be organized, of money that might be saved for banks and business. Finally he urged unity, and deprecated especially religious and denominational bickering. "To-day," he said, with a smile, "the world cares little whether a man be Baptist or Methodist, or indeed a churchman at all, so long as he is good and true. What difference does it make whether a man be baptized in river or washbowl, or not at all? Let's leave all that littleness, and look higher." Then, thinking of nothing else, he slowly sat down. A painful hush seized that crowded mass. Little had they understood of what he said, for he spoke an unknown tongue, save the last word about baptism; that they knew, and they sat very still while the clock ticked. Then at last a low suppressed snarl came from the Amen corner, and an old bent man arose, walked over the seats, and climbed straight up into the pulpit. He was wrinkled and black, with scant gray and tufted hair; his voice and hands shook as with palsy; but on his face lay the intense rapt look of the religious fanatic. He seized the Bible with his rough, huge hands; twice he raised it inarticulate, and then fairly burst into words, with rude and awful eloquence. He quivered, swayed, and bent; then rose aloft in perfect majesty, till the people moaned and wept, wailed and shouted, and a wild shrieking arose from the corners where all the pent-up feeling of the hour gathered itself and rushed into the air. John never knew clearly what the old man said; he only felt himself held up to scorn and scathing denunciation for trampling on the true Religion, and he realized with amazement that all unknowingly he had put rough, rude hands on something this little world held sacred. He arose silently, and passed out into the night. Down toward the sea he went, in the fitful starlight, half conscious of the girl who followed timidly after him. When at last he stood upon the bluff, he turned to his little sister and looked upon her sorrowfully, remembering with sudden pain how little thought he had given her. He put his arm about her and let her passion of tears spend itself on his shoulder.

Long they stood together, peering over the gray unresting water.

"John," she said, "does it make every one—unhappy when they study and learn lots of things?"

He paused and smiled. "I am afraid it does," he said.

"And, John, are you glad you studied?"

"Yes," came the answer, slowly but positively.

She watched the flickering lights upon the sea, and said thoughtfully, "I wish I was unhappy—and—and," putting both arms about his neck, "I think I am, a little, John."

It was several days later that John walked up to the Judge's house to ask for the privilege of teaching the Negro school. The Judge himself met him at the front door, stared a little hard at him, and said brusquely, "Go 'round to the kitchen door, John, and wait." Sitting on the kitchen steps, John stared at the corn, thoroughly perplexed. What on earth had come over him? Every step he made offended some one. He had come to save his people, and before he left the depot he had hurt them. He sought to teach them at the church, and had outraged their deepest feeling. He had schooled himself to be respectful to the Judge, and then blundered into his front door. And all the time he had meant right—and yet, and yet, somehow he found it so hard and strange to fit his old surroundings again, to find his place in the world about him. He could not remember that he used to have any difficulty in the past, when life was glad and gay. The world seemed smooth and easy then. Perhaps —but his sister came to the kitchen door just then and said the Judge awaited him.

The Judge sat in the dining-room amid his morning's mail, and he did not ask John to sit down. He plunged squarely into the business. "You've come for the school, I suppose. Well, John, I want to speak to you plainly. You know I'm a friend to your people. I've helped you and your family, and would have done more if you hadn't got the notion of going off. Now I like the colored people, and sympathize with all their reasonable aspirations; but you and I both know, John, that in this country the Negro must remain subordinate, and can never expect to be the equal of white men. In their place, your people can be honest and respectful; and God knows, I'll do what I can to help them. But when they want to reverse nature, and rule white men, and marry white women, and sit in my parlor, then, by God! we'll hold them under if we have to lynch every Nigger in the land. Now, John, the question is, are you, with your education and Northern notions, going to accept the situation and teach the darkies to be faithful servants and laborers as your fathers were—I knew your father, John, he belonged to my brother, and he was a good Nigger. Well—well, are you going to be like him, or are you going to try to put fool ideas of rising and equality into these folks' heads, and make them discontented and unhappy?"

"I am going to accept the situation, Judge Henderson,"

answered John, with a brevity that did not escape the keen old man. He hesitated a moment, and then said shortly, "Very well—we'll try you awhile. Good-morning."

It was a full month after the opening of the Negro school that the other John came home, tall, gay, and headstrong. The mother wept, the sisters sang. The whole white town was glad. A proud man was the Judge, and it was a goodly sight to see the two swinging down Main Street together. And yet all did not go smoothly between them, for the younger man could not and did not veil his contempt for the little town, and plainly had his heart set on New York. Now the one cherished ambition of the Judge was to see his son mayor of Altamaha, representative to the legislature, and—who could say?—governor of Georgia. So the argument often waxed hot between them. "Good heavens, father," the younger man would say after dinner, as he lighted a cigar and stood by the fireplace, "you surely don't expect a young fellow like me to settle down permanently in this—this God-forgotten town with nothing but mud and Negroes?" "*I* did," the Judge would answer laconically; and on this particular day it seemed from the gathering scowl that he was about to add something more emphatic, but neighbors had already begun to drop in to admire his son, and the conversation drifted.

"Heah that John is livenin' things up at the darky school," volunteered the postmaster, after a pause.

"What now?" asked the Judge, sharply.

"Oh, nothin' in particulah—just his almightly air and uppish ways. B'lieve I did heah somethin' about his givin' talks on the French Revolution, equality, and such like. He's what I call a dangerous Nigger."

"Have you heard him say anything out of the way?"

"Why, no—but Sally, our girl, told my wife a lot of rot. Then, too, I don't need to heah: a Nigger what won't say 'sir' to a white man, or—"

"Who is this John?" interrupted the son.

"Why, it's little black John, Peggy's son—your old play-fellow."

The young man's face flushed angrily, and then he laughed.

"Oh," said he, "it's the darky that tried to force himself into a seat beside the lady I was escorting—"

But Judge Henderson waited to hear no more. He had been nettled all day, and now at this he rose with a half-smothered oath, took his hat and cane, and walked straight to the schoolhouse.

For John, it had been a long, hard pull to get things started in the rickety old shanty that sheltered his school. The Negroes were rent into factions for and against him, the parents were careless, the children irregular and dirty, and books, pencils, and slates largely missing. Nevertheless, he struggled hopefully on, and seemed to see at last some glimmering of dawn. The attendance was larger and the children were a shade cleaner this week. Even the booby class in reading showed a little comforting progress. So John settled himself with renewed patience this afternoon.

"Now, Mandy," he said cheerfully, "that's better; but you mustn't chop your words up so: 'If—the—man—goes.' Why, your little brother even wouldn't tell a story that way, now would he?"

"Naw, suh, he cain't talk."

"All right; now let's try again: 'If the man—' "

"John!"

The whole school started in surprise, and the teacher half arose, as the red, angry face of the Judge appeared in the open doorway.

"John, this school is closed. You childrer can go home and get to work. The white people of Altamaha are not spending their money on black folks to have their heads crammed with impudence and lies. Clear out! I'll lock the door myself."

Up at the great pillared house the tall young son wandered aimlessly about after his father's abrupt departure. In the house there was little to interest him; the books were old and stale, the local newspaper flat, and the women had retired with headaches and sewing. He tried a nap, but it was too warm. So he sauntered out into the fields, complaining disconsolately, "Good Lord! how long will this imprisonment last!" He was not a bad fellow—just a little spoiled and self-indulgent, and as headstrong as his proud father. He seemed a young man pleasant to look upon, as he sat on the great black stump at the edge of the pines idly swinging his legs and smoking. "Why, there isn't even a girl worth getting up a respectable flirtation with," he growled. Just then his eye caught a tall, willowy figure hurrying toward him on the narrow path. He looked with interest at first, and then burst into a laugh as he said, "Well, I declare, if it isn't Jennie, the little brown kitchen-maid! Why, I never noticed before what a trim little body she is. Hello, Jennie! Why, you haven't kissed me since I came home," he said gaily. The young girl stared at him in surprise and confusion—faltered something inarticulate, and attempted to pass. But a wilful mood had seized the young idler, and he caught at her arm. Frightened, she slipped by; and half mischievously he turned and ran after her through the tall pines.

Yonder, toward the sea, at the end of the path, came John slowly, with his head down. He had turned wearily homeward from the schoolhouse; then, thinking to shield his mother from the blow, started to meet his sister as she came from work and break the news of his dismissal to her. "I'll go away," he said slowly; "I'll go away and find work, and send for them. I cannot live here longer." And then the fierce, buried anger surged up into his throat. He waved his arms and hurried wildly up the path.

The great brown sea lay silent. The air scarce breathed. The dying day bathed the twisted oaks and mighty pines in black and gold. There came from the wind no warning, not a whisper from the cloudless sky. There was only a black man hurrying on with an ache in his heart, seeing neither sun nor sea, but starting as from a dream at the frightened cry that woke the pines, to see his dark sister struggling in the arms of a tall and fair-haired man.

He said not a word, but, seizing a fallen limb, struck him with all the pent-up hatred of his great black arm; and the body lay white and still beneath the pines, all bathed in sunshine and in blood. John looked at it dreamily, then walked back to the house briskly, and said in a soft voice, "Mammy, I'm going away—I'm going to be free."

She gazed at him dimly and faltered, "No'th, honey, is yo' gwine No'th agin?"

He looked out where the North Star glistened pale above the waters, and said, "Yes, mammy, I'm going—North."

Then, without another word, he went out into the narrow lane, up by the straight pines, to the same winding path, and seated himself on the great black stump, looking at the blood where the body had lain. Yonder in the gray past he had played with that dead boy, romping together under the solemn trees. The night deepened; he thought of the boys at Johnstown. He wondered how Brown had turned out, and Carey? And Jones—Jones? Why, *he* was Jones, and he wondered what they would all say when they knew, when they knew, in that great long dining-room with its hundreds of merry eyes. Then as the sheen of the starlight stole over him, he thought of the gilded ceiling of that vast concert hall, and heard stealing toward him the faint sweet music of the swan. Hark! was it music, or the hurry and shouting of men? Yes, surely! Clear and high the faint sweet melody rose and fluttered like a living thing, so that the very earth trembled as with the tramp of horses and murmur of angry men.

He leaned back and smiled toward the sea, whence rose the strange melody, away from the dark shadows where lay the noise of horses galloping, galloping on. With an effort he roused himself, bent forward, and looked steadily down the pathway, softly humming the "Song of the Bride"—

"Freudig geführt, ziehet dahin."

Amid the trees in the dim morning twilight he watched their shadows dancing and heard their horses thundering toward him, until at last they came sweeping like a storm, and he saw in front that haggard white-haired man, whose eyes flashed red with fury. Oh, how he pitied him—pitied him— and wondered if he had the coiling twisted rope. Then, as the storm burst round him, he rose slowly to his feet and turned his closed eyes toward the Sea.

And the world whistled in his ears.

FROM THE SOULS OF BLACK FOLK

———

Jesus Christ in Georgia

The convict guard laughed.

"I don't know," he said, "I hadn't thought of that—"

He hesitated and looked at the stranger curiously. In the solemn twilight he got an impression of unusual height and soft dark eyes.

"Curious sort of acquaintance for the Colonel," he thought; then he continued aloud: "But that nigger there is bad; a born thief and ought to be sent up for life; is practically; got ten years last time—"

Here the voice of the promoter talking within interrupted; he was bending over his figures, sitting by the Colonel. He was slight, with a sharp nose.

"The convicts," he said, "would cost us $96 a year and board. Well, we can squeeze that so that it won't be over $125 apiece. Now, if these fellows are driven, they can build this line within twelve months. It will be running next

April. Freights will fall fifty per cent. Why, man, you will be a millionaire in less than ten years."

The Colonel started. He was a thick, short man, with clean-shaven face, and a certain air of breeding about the lines of his countenance; the word millionaire sounded well in his ears. He thought—he thought a great deal; he almost heard the puff of the fearfully costly automobile that was coming up the road, and he said:

"I suppose we might as well hire them."

"Of course," answered the promoter.

The voice of the tall stranger in the corner broke in here: "It will be a good thing for them?" he said, half in question.

The Colonel moved. "The guard makes strange friends," he thought to himself. "What's this man doing here, anyway?" He looked at him, or rather, looked at his eyes, and then somehow felt a warming toward him. He said:

"Well, at least it can't harm them—they're beyond that."

"It will do them good, then," said the stranger again. The promoter shrugged his shoulders.

"It will do us good," he said.

But the Colonel shook his head impatiently. He felt a desire to justify himself before those eyes, and he answered:

"Yes, it will do them good; or, at any rate, it won't make them any worse than they are."

Then he started to say something else, but here sure enough the sound of the automobile breathing at the gate stopped him and they all arose.

"It is settled, then," said the promoter.

"Yes," said the Colonel, signing his name and turning toward the stranger again.

"Are you going into town?" he asked with the Southern courtesy of white man to white man in a country town. The stranger said he was.

"Then come along in my machine. I want to talk to you about this."

They went out to the car. The stranger as he went turned again to look back at the convict. He was a tall, powerfully built black fellow. His face was sullen, with a low forehead, thick, hanging lips, and bitter eyes. There was revolt written about the mouth, and a hangdog expression. He stood bending over his pile of stones pounding listlessly.

Beside him stood a boy of twelve, yellow, with a hunted, crafty look. The convict raised his eyes, and they met the eyes of the stranger. The hammer fell from his hands.

The stranger turned slowly toward the automobile, and

the Colonel introduced him. He could not exactly catch the foreign-sounding name, but he mumbled something as he presented him to his wife and little girl, who were waiting. As they whirled away he started to talk, but the stranger had taken the little girl into his lap, and together they conversed in low tones all the way home.

In some way, they did not exactly know how, they got the impression that the man was a teacher, and of course he must be a foreigner. The long cloak-like coat told this. They rode in the twilight through the half-lighted town, and at last drew up before the Colonel's mansion, with its ghost-like pillars.

The lady in the back seat was thinking of the guests she had invited to dinner, and wondered if she ought not to ask this man to stay. He seemed cultured, and she supposed he was some acquaintance of the Colonel's. It would be rather a distinction to have him there, with the Judge's wife and daughter and the Rector. She spoke almost before she thought:

"You will enter and rest awhile?"

The Colonel and the little girl insisted. For a moment the stranger seemed about to refuse. He said he was on his way North, where he had some business for his father in Pennsylvania. Then, for the child's sake, he consented. Up the steps they went, and into the dark parlor, and there they sat and talked a long time. It was a curious conversation. Afterward they did not remember exactly what was said, and yet they all remembered a certain strange satisfaction in that long talk.

Presently the nurse came for the reluctant child, and the hostess bethought herself:

"We will have a cup of tea—you will be dry and tired."

She rang and switched on a blaze of light. With one accord they all looked at the stranger, for they had hardly seen him well in the glooming twilight. The woman started in amazement and the Colonel half rose in anger. Why, the man was a mulatto, surely—even if he did not own the Negro blood, their practised eyes knew it. He was tall and straight, and the coat looked like a Jewish gabardine. His hair hung in close curls far down the sides of his face, and his face was olive, even yellow.

A peremptory order rose to the Colonel's lips, and froze there as he caught the stranger's eyes. Those eyes, where had he seen those eyes before? He remembered them long years ago—the soft tear-filled eyes of a brown girl. He remembered many things, and his face grew drawn and white. Those eyes kept burning into him, even when they were turned half away toward the staircase, where the white figure of the child hovered with her nurse, and waved good-night. The lady sank into her chair and thought: "What will the Judge's wife say? How did the Colonel come to invite this man here? How shall we be rid of him?" She looked at the Colonel in reproachful consternation.

Just then the door opened and the old butler came in. He was an ancient black man with tufted white hair, and he held before him a large silver tray filled with a china tea service. The stranger rose slowly and stretched forth his hands as if to bless the viands. The old man paused in be-wildernment, tottered and then, with sudden gladness in his eyes, dropped to his knees as the tray crashed to the floor.

"My Lord!" he whispered, "and My God!" But the woman screamed:

"Mother's china!"

The doorbell rang.

"Heavens! Here is the dinner party!" exclaimed the lady.

She turned toward the door, but there in the hall, clad in her night clothes, was the little girl. She had stolen down the stairs to see the stranger again, and the nurse above was calling in vain. The woman felt hysterical and scolded at the nurse, but the stranger had stretched out his arms, and with a glad cry the child nestled in them. "Of such," he whispered, "is the Kingdom of Heaven," as he slowly mounted the stairs with his little burden.

The mother was glad; anything to be rid of the interloper even for a moment. The bell rang again, and she hastened toward the door, which the loitering black maid was just opening. She did not notice the shadow of the stranger as he came slowly down the stairs and paused by the newel post, dark and silent.

The Judge's wife entered. She was an old woman, frilled and powdered into a caricature of youth, and gorgeously gowned. She came forward, smiling with extended hands, but just as she was opposite the stranger, a chill from some-where seemed to strike her, and she shuddered and cried: "What a draft!" as she drew a silken shawl about her and shook hands cordially; she forgot to ask who the stranger was. The Judge strode in unseeing, thinking of a puzzling case of theft.

"Eh? What? Oh—er—yes—good-evening," he said, "good-evening."

Behind them came a young woman in the glory of youth, daintily silked, with diamonds around her fair neck, beautiful in face and form. She came in lightly, but stopped with a little gasp; then she laughed gaily and said:

"Why, I beg your pardon. Was it not curious? I thought I saw there behind your man"—she hesitated ("but he must be a servant," she argued)—"the shadow of wide white wings. It was but the light on the drapery. What a turn it gave me—so glad to be here!" And she smiled again. With her came a tall and haughty naval officer. Hearing his lady refer to the servant, he hardly looked at him, but held his gilded cap and cloak carelessly toward him; the stranger took them and placed them carefully on the rack.

Last came the Rector, a man of forty, and well clothed. He started to pass the stranger, stopped and looked at him inquiringly.

"I beg your pardon," he said, "I beg your pardon, I think I have met you?"

The stranger made no answer, and the hostess nervously hurried the guests on. But the Rector lingered and looked perplexed.

"Surely I know you; I have met you somewhere," he said, putting his hand vaguely to his head. "You—you remember me, do you not?"

The stranger quietly swept his cloak aside, and to the hostess' unspeakable relief moved toward the door.

"I never knew you," he said in low tones, as he went.

The lady murmured some faint excuse about intruders, but the Rector stood with annoyance written on his face.

"I beg a thousand pardons," he said to the hostess absently. "It is a great pleasure to be here—somehow I thought I knew that man. I am sure I knew him, once."

The stranger had passed down the steps, and as he went the nurse-maid, lingering at the top of the staircase, flew down after him, caught his cloak, trembled, hesitated, and then kneeled in the dust. He touched her lightly with his hand and said, "Go, and sin no more."

With a glad cry the maid left the house with its open door and turned north, running, while the stranger turned eastward to the night. As they parted a long low howl rose tremulously and reverberated through the town. The Colonel's wife within shuddered.

"The bloodhounds," she said. The Rector answered carelessly. "Another one of those convicts escaped, I suppose; really, they need severer measures." Then he stopped. He was trying to remember that stranger's name. The Judge's wife looked about for the draft and arranged her shawl. The girl glanced at the white drapery in the hall, but the young officer was bending over her, and the fires of life burned in her veins.

Howl after howl rose in the night, swelled and died away. The stranger strode rapidly along the highway and out into the deep forest. There he paused and stood waiting, tall and still. A mile up the road behind him a man was running, tall and powerful and black, with grime-stained face, with convict's stripes upon him and shackles on his legs. He ran and jumped in little short steps, and the chains rang. He fell and rose again, while the howl of the hounds rung harder behind him.

Into the forest he leaped and crept and jumped and ran, streaming with sweat; seeing the tall form rise before him, he stopped suddenly, dropped his hands in sullen impotence and sank panting to the earth. A bloodhound shot into the woods behind him, howled, whined and fawned before the stranger's feet. Hound after hound bayed, leapt and lay there; then silent, one by one, with bowed head, they crept backward toward the town.

The stranger made a cup of his hands and gave the man water to drink, bathed his hot head, and gently took the chains and irons from his feet. By and by the convict stood up. Day was dawning above the treetops. He looked into the stranger's face, and for a moment a gladness swept over the stains of his face.

"Why, you'se a nigger, too," he said.

Then the convict seemed anxious to justify himself.

"I never had no chance," he said furtively.

"Thou shalt not steal," said the stranger.

The man bridled.

"But how about them? Can they steal? Didn't they steal a whole year's work and then, when I stole to keep from starving—" he glanced at the stranger. "No, I didn't steal just to keep from starving. I stole to be stealing. I can't help stealing. Seems like when I sees things I just must—but, yes, I'll try!"

The convict looked down at his striped clothes, but the stranger had taken off his long coat—and put it around him, and the stripes disappeared. In the opening morning the black man started toward the low log farmhouse in the distance, and the stranger stood watching him. There was a new glory in the day. The black man's face cleared up and the farmer was glad to get him.

All day he worked as he had never worked before, and the farmer gave him some cold food toward night.

"You can sleep in the barn," he said, and turned away.

"How much do I git a day?" asked the man.

The farmer scowled:

"If you'll sign a contract for the season," he said, "I'll give you ten dollars a month."

"I won't sign no contract to be a slave," said the man doggedly.

"Yes, you will," said the farmer, threateningly, "or I'll call the convict guard." And he grinned.

The convict shrunk and slouched to the barn. As night fell he looked out and saw the farmer leave the place. Slowly he crept out and sneaked toward the house. He looked into the kitchen door. No one was there, but the supper was spread as if the mistress had laid it and gone out. He ate ravenously. Then he looked into the front room and listened. He could hear low voices on the porch. On the table lay a silver watch. He gazed at it, and in a moment was beside it, with his hand on it. Quickly he slipped out of the house and slouched toward the field. He saw his employer coming along the highway. He fled back stealthily and around to the front of the house, when suddenly he stopped. He felt the great dark eyes of the stranger and saw the same dark, cloaklike coat, where he was seated on the doorstep talking with the mistress of the house. Slowly, guiltily, he turned back, entered the kitchen and laid the watch where he had found it; and then he rushed wildly with arms outstretched back toward the stranger.

The woman had laid supper for her husband, and going down from the house had walked out toward a neighbor's. She was gone but a little while, and when she came back she started to see a dark figure on the doorsteps under the tall red oak. She thought it was the new Negro hand until he said in a soft voice:

"Will you give me bread?"

Reassured at the voice of a white man, she answered quickly in her soft Southern tones:

"Why, certainly."

She was a little woman. Once she had been handsome, but now her face was drawn with work and care. She was nervous, and was always thinking, wishing, wanting for something. She went in and got him some cornbread and a glass of cool, rich buttermilk, and then came out and sat down beside him. She began, quite unconsciously, to tell him about herself—the things she had done, and had not done, and the things she had wished. She told him of her husband, and this new farm they were trying to buy. She said it was so hard to get niggers to work. She said they ought all to be in the chain gang and made to work. Even then some ran away. Only yesterday one had escaped.

At last she gossiped of her neighbors; how good they were and how bad.

"And do you like them all?" asked the stranger.

She hesitated.

"Most of them," she said; and then, looking up into his face and putting her hand in his as though he were her father, she said:

"There are none I hate; no, none at all."

He looked away and said dreamily:

"You love your neighbor as yourself?"

She hesitated—

"I try—" she began, and then looked the way he was looking; down under the hill, where lay a little, half-ruined cabin.

"They are niggers," she said briefly.

He looked at her. Suddenly a confusion came over her, and she insisted, she knew not why—

"But they are niggers."

With a sudden impulse she rose, and hurriedly lighted the lamp that stood just within the door and held it above her head. She saw his dark face and curly hair. She shrieked in angry terror, and rushed down the path; and just as she rushed down, the black convict came running up with hands outstretched. They met in midpath, and before he could stop he had run against her, and she fell heavily to earth and lay white and still. Her husband came rushing up with cry and oath:

"I knew it," he said; "it is that runaway nigger." He held the black man struggling to the earth, and raised his voice to a yell. Down the highway came the convict guard with hound and mob and gun. They poured across the fields. The farmer motioned to them.

"He—attacked—my wife," he gasped.

The mob snarled and worked silently. Right to the limb of the red oak they hoisted the struggling, writhing black man, while others lifted the dazed woman. Right and left as she tottered to the house she searched for the stranger, with a sick yearning, but the stranger was gone. And she told none of her guest.

"No—no—I want nothing," she insisted, until they left her, as they thought, asleep. For a time she lay still listening to the departure of the mob. Then she rose. She shuddered as she heard the creaking of the limb where the body hung. But resolutely she crawled to the window and peered out into the moonlight; she saw the dead man writhe. He stretched his arms out like a cross, looking upward. She gasped and clung to the window sill. Behind the swaying body, and down where the little, half-ruined cabin lay, a single flame flashed up amid the far-off shout and cry of the mob. A fierce joy sobbed up through the terror in her soul and then sank abashed as she watched the flame rise. Suddenly whirling into one great crimson column it shot to the top of the sky and threw great arms athwart the gloom until above the world and behind the roped and swaying form below hung quivering and burning a great crimson cross.

She hid her dizzy, aching head in an agony of tears, and dared not look, for she knew. Her dry lips moved:

"Despised and rejected of men."

She knew, and the very horror of it lifted her dull and shrinking eyelids. There, heaven-tall, earth-wide, hung the stranger on the crimson cross, riven and bloodstained with thorn-crowned head and pierced hands. She stretched her arms and shrieked.

He did not hear. He did not see. His calm dark eyes all sorrowful were fastened on the writhing, twisting body of the thief, and a voice came out of the winds of the night, saying:

"This day thou shalt be with me in Paradise!"

THE CRISIS, DECEMBER, 1911

POLICY STATEMENTS

As we try to assess Du Bois' great influence on his race, on America, and the world, one often ignored phase of his activities will have to be carefully studied: his influence— even domination—of many groups, organizations, and world conferences. Almost invariably he went to these meetings with a program and was able to gain acceptance of that program. Surely many of the splendid statements or blueprints for action he wrote for groups during this century, beginning with the London Pan African Congress in 1900 and extending to the Appeal to the United Nations which he wrote for the NAACP in 1947, will eventually find their way into many collections of important American documents.

The following was written for the 1900 London Pan-African Conference. This early meeting against colonialism used the term "Pan-Africanism" for the first time. Here also Du Bois made his most famous prophecy: "The problem of the twentieth century is the problem of the color line." He next used it in The Souls of Black Folk.

An Appeal to the World

Let the world take no backward step in that slow but sure progress which has successively refused to let the spirit of class, of caste, of privilege, or of birth, debar from life liberty and the pursuit of happiness a striving human soul.

Let not color or race be a feature of distinction between white and black man, regardless of worth or ability.

Let not the natives of Africa be sacrificed to the greed of gold, their liberties taken away, their family life debauched, their just aspirations repressed, and avenues of advancement and culture taken from them.

Let not the cloak of Christian missionary enterprise be allowed in the future, as so often in the past, to hide the ruthless economic exploitation and political downfall of less developed nations, whose chief fault has been reliance on the plighted faith of the Christian church.

Let the British nation, the first modern champion of Negro freedom, hasten to crown the work of Wilberforce, and Clarkson, and Buxton, and Sharpe, Bishop Colenso, and Livingstone, and give, as soon as practicable, the rights of responsible government to the black colonies of Africa and the West Indies.

Let not the spirit of Garrison, Phillips, and Douglass wholly die out in America; may the conscience of a great nation rise and rebuke all dishonesty and unrighteous oppression toward the American Negro, and grant to him the right of franchise, security of person and property, and generous recognition of the great work he has accomplished in a generation toward raising nine millions of human beings from slavery to manhood.

Let the German Empire, and the French Republic, true to their great past, remember that the true worth of colonies lies in their prosperity and progress, and that justice, impartial alike to black and white, is the first element of prosperity.

Let the Congo Free State become a great central Negro State of the world, and let its prosperity be counted not simply in cash and commerce, but in the happiness and true advancement of its black people.

Let the nations of the World respect the integrity and independence of the free Negro States of Abyssinia, Liberia, Haiti, and the rest, and let the inhabitants of these States, the independent tribes of Africa, the Negroes of the West Indies and America, and the black subjects of all nations take courage, strive ceaselessly, and fight bravely, that they may prove to the world their incontestible right to be counted among the great brotherhood of mankind.

Thus we appeal with boldness and confidence to the Great Powers of the civilized world, trusting in the wide spirit of humanity, and the deep sense of justice of our age, for a generous recognition of the righteousness of our cause.

ALEXANDER WALTERS (Bishop)
President Pan-African Association

HENRY B. BROWN
Vice-President

H. SYLVESTER-WILLIAMS
General Secretary

W. E. BURGHARDT DU BOIS
Chairman Committee on Address
From the address: TO THE NATIONS OF THE WORLD, 1900

THE NIAGARA MOVEMENT

Eventually it is almost certain that the Niagara Movement statements formulated and written by Dr. Du Bois will take their rightful place among the great documents of

American history. For, as Elliot Rudwick, a recent Du Bois biographer, wrote, "The Niagara addresses were masterpieces." It is likely that when the definitive history of the modern civil rights movement is written the Niagara movement statements will be credited as providing the founding philosophy. Du Bois recounts how they came into being and presents the text of the 1906 convention:

. . . I sent out from Atlanta in June, 1905, a call to a few selected persons "for organized determination and aggressive action on the part of men who believe in Negro freedom and growth." I proposed a conference during the summer "to oppose firmly present methods of strangling honest criticism; to organize intelligent and honest Negroes; and to support organs of news and public opinion."

Fifty-nine colored men from seventeen different states signed a call for a meeting near Buffalo, New York, during the week of July 9, 1905. I went to Buffalo and hired a little hotel on the Canada side of the river at Fort Erie, and waited for the men to attend the meeting. If sufficient men had not come to pay for the hotel, I should certainly have been in bankruptcy and perhaps in jail; but as a matter of fact, twenty-nine men, representing fourteen states, came. The "Niagara Movement" was organized January 31, 1906, and was incorporated in the District of Columbia.

Its particular business and objects are to advocate and promote the following principles:

1. Freedom of speech and criticism.
2. Unfettered and unsubsidized press.
3. Manhood suffrage.
4. The abolition of all caste distinctions based simply on race and color.
5. The recognition of the principles of human brotherhood as a practical present creed.
6. The recognition of the highest and best human training as the monopoly of no class or race.
7. A belief in the dignity of labor.
8. United effort to realize these ideals under wise and courageous leadership.

The Niagara Movement raised a furor of the most disconcerting criticism. I was accused of acting from motives of envy of a great leader and being ashamed of the fact that I was a member of the Negro race. The leading weekly of the land, the New York *Outlook*, pilloried me with scathing articles. But the movement went on. The next year, 1906, instead of meeting in secret, we met openly at Harper's Ferry, the scene of John Brown's raid, and had in significance if not numbers one of the greatest meetings that American Negroes have ever held. We made pilgrimage at dawn bare-footed to the scene of Brown's martyrdom and we talked some of the plainest English that has been given voice to by black men in America. The resolutions which I wrote expressed with tumult of emotion my creed of 1906:

"The men of the Niagara Movement, coming from the toil of the year's hard work, and pausing a moment from the earning of their daily bread, turn toward the nation and again ask in the name of ten million the privilege of a hearing. In the past year the work of the Negro hater has flourished in the land. Step by step the defenders of the rights of American citizens have retreated. The work of stealing the black man's ballot has progressed and the fifty and more representatives of stolen votes still sit in the nation's capital. Discrimination in travel and public accommodation has so spread that some of our weaker brethren are actually afraid to thunder against color discrimination as such and are simply whispering for ordinary decencies.

"Against this the Niagara Movement eternally protests. We will not be satisfied to take one jot or title less than our full manhood rights. We claim for ourselves every single right that belongs to a freeborn American, political, civil, and social; and until we get these rights we will never cease to protest and assail the ears of America. The battle we wage is not for ourselves alone, but for all true Americans. It is a fight for ideals, lest this, our common fatherland, false to its founding, become in truth the land of the Thief and the home of the Slave—a by-word and a hissing among the nations for its sounding pretensions and pitiful accomplishment.

"Never before in the modern age has a great and civilized folk threatened to adopt so cowardly a creed in the treatment of its fellow-citizens, born and bred on its soil. Stripped of verbiage and subterfuge and in its naked nastiness, the new American creed says: fear to let black men even try to rise lest they become the equals of the white. And this is the land that professes to follow Jesus Christ. The blasphemy of such a course is only matched by its cowardice.

"In detail our demands are clear and unequivocal. First,

we would vote; with the right to vote goes everything: freedom, manhood, the honor of your wives, the chastity of your daughters, the right to work, and the chance to rise, and let no man listen to those who deny this.

"We want full manhood suffrage, and we want it now, henceforth and forever.

"Second. We want discrimination in public accommodation to cease. Separation in railway and street cars, based simply on race and color, is un-American, undemocratic, and silly. We protest against all such discrimination.

"Third. We claim the right of freemen to walk, talk, and be with them that wish to be with us. No man has a right to choose another man's friends, and to attempt to do so is an impudent interference with the most fundamental human privilege.

"Fourth. We want the laws enforced against rich as well as poor; against Capitalist as well as Laborer; against white as well as black. We are not more lawless than the white race, we are more often arrested, convicted and mobbed. We want justice even for criminals and outlaws. We want the Constitution of the country enforced. We want Congress to take charge of the Congressional elections. We want the Fourteenth Amendment carried out to the letter and every State disfranchised in Congress which attempts to disfranchise its rightful voters. We want the Fifteenth Amendment enforced and no State allowed to base its franchise simply on color.

"The failure of the Republican Party in Congress at the session just closed to redeem its pledge of 1904 with reference to suffrage conditions at the South seems a plain, deliberate, and premeditated breach of promise, and stamps that party as guilty of obtaining votes under false pretense.

"Fifth. We want our children educated. The school system in the country districts of the South is a disgrace and in few towns and cities are the Negro schools what they ought to be. We want the national government to step in and wipe out illiteracy in the South. Either the United States will destroy ignorance, or ignorance will destroy the United States.

"And when we call for education, we mean real education. We believe in work. We ourselves are workers, but work is not necessarily education. Education is the development of power and ideal. We want our children trained as intelligent human beings should be, and we will fight for all time against any proposal to educate black boys and girls simply as servants and underlings, or simply for the use of other people. They have a right to know, to think, to aspire.

"These are some of the chief things which we want. How shall we get them? By voting where we may vote; by persistent, unceasing agitation; by hammering at the truth; by sacrifice and work.

"We do not believe in violence, neither in the despised violence of the raid nor the lauded violence of the soldier, nor the barbarous violence of the mob; but we do believe in John Brown, in that incarnate spirit of justice, that hatred of a lie, that willingness to sacrifice money, reputation, and life itself on the altar of right. And here on the scene of John Brown's martyrdom, we reconsecrate ourselves, our honor, our property to the final emancipation of the race which John Brown died to make free."

FROM THE AUTOBIOGRAPHY OF W. E. B. DU BOIS

THE GEORGIA EQUAL RIGHTS CONVENTION, 1906

The following statement was Du Bois' summation of the program of the Georgia Equal Rights Convention which he attended in Macon, Georgia, February 13–14, 1906. Five hundred delegates—blacks and whites—were there from all parts of the state.

We, colored men of Georgia, representing every district in the State and speaking for more than a million human souls, send this statement and plea to the world:

Two races came to Georgia in the early eighteenth century and lived as master and slave. In that long hard apprenticeship we learned to work, to speak the tongue of the land, and better to know God. We learned this but we learned it at the cost of self-respect, self-reliance, knowledge, and the honor of our women.

This training left us above all ignorant. We are still ignorant, partly by our own fault in not striving more doggedly after knowledge, but chiefly because of the wretched educational opportunities given us in this state. The white and black school populations are nearly equal and yet out of every dollar of the state school money eighty cents go to the white child and twenty cents to the Negro child; each white child receives $5.92 a year, while the Negro child receives $2.27; white teachers receive over a million dollars a year, Negro teachers less than three hundred thousand. Less than half our children have school facilities furnished them and not a cent is given by the state to the higher training of Negro teachers and professional men. Of more than a million dollars given by the United States government for agricultural training, we who are preeminently the farmers of the state have received only $264,000, and the fund is at present being divided at the rate of $34,000 to the whites and $8,000 to the Negroes. We are a poor people. Poor in wealth and habit. We are not as efficient laborers as we might be. Yet the accumulated wealth of this great state has been built upon our bowed backs, and its present prosperity depends largely upon us. No portion of the community is giving more of its labor and money to support the public burdens than we; and yet we are not receiving just wages for our toil; we are too often cheated out of our scanty earnings; while the laws that govern our economic life and the rules of their administration are cunning with injustice toward us.

Especially true is this in the freedom of labor contracts; so much so that farm labor is almost reduced to slavery in many parts of the state. . . .

We do not deny that some of us are not yet fit for the ballot; but we do affirm that the majority of us are fit—fit by our growing intelligence, our ownership of property and our conservative, law-abiding tendencies—and in any case certainly disfranchisement and oppression will not increase our fitness, nor will they settle the race problem. The right to vote is in itself an education; and if Georgia had taken as much time and trouble to fit us for political responsibility as she has denying us our rights, she would have a safer and saner electorate than that which is today swaying her by appeals to her worst passions. Voteless workingmen are slaves; without the defense of the ballot we stand naked to our enemies, the helpless victims of jealousy and hate, subjected to, and humiliated by an unreasoning caste spirit, which grows by what it feeds upon. If we are good enough to be represented by five Georgia congressmen in the Councils of the nation, we are surely good enough to choose those representatives; and if we are not good enough to be represented, at least, as human beings, we are too good to be misrepresented by our enemies. We ask of this nation therefore the enforcement of the 14th and 15th amendments.

We do not desire association with any one who does not wish our company, but we do expect in a Christian, civilized land, to live under a system of law and order, to be secure in life, limb and property, to travel in comfort and decency and to receive a just equivalent for our money, and yet we are the victims of the most unreasoning sort of caste legislation. . . .

We ask for an abolition of Jim Crow cars on railroads and the substitution of first and second class cars, which would separate men according to condition, and not according to color.

The menace of the drunken unreasoning mob hangs ever above us. Since 1885, 260 Georgia Negroes have been lynched and burned without the semblance of a legal trial not to mention hundreds of unaccused persons who have been murdered.

We ask the right to enter the militia of Georgia. We have fought for this country in four wars and if we are good enough to fight we are good enough to be trained for fighting.

We ask, further, representation on the juries of the state. Trial by one's peers is one of the fundamental rights of common law and this is systematically denied in Georgia.

Far be it from us to claim any great and especial righteousness of our own. We are a sinful people who have not lived up to the fullness of our narrow opportunity. The sense of our shortcomings is heavy upon us, and there are those among us whose wicked ways shame us bitterly. We are not however as bad as the wilfully distorted and criminally unfair press reports picture us; on the contrary we can take honest comfort in the fact that we are growing daily in honesty, sobriety, industry and chastity; and God alone knows how much faster we might grow were it not for the open traffic in Negro crime which flourishes in this state, and were it not for the defenseless condition of our daughters. As long as public and private wealth in Georgia fattens on the sale of black criminals, so long will crime be encouraged and the outcry against it will ring with hypocrisy.

Colored men are punished in this state without intelligent discrimination; old and young, thug and mischief-maker and often men and women are herded together after unfair trials before juries who would rather convict ten innocent Negroes than let one guilty one escape. The sentences inflicted are cruel and excessive. Twenty-five per cent of the convicts are condemned for life and sixty per cent for ten years or more. White men escape conviction entirely or are promptly pardoned. These slaves of the state are then sold body and soul to private capitalists for the sake of gain, without the shadow of an attempt at reformation, and are thrown into relentless competition with free Negro laborers.

The fortune of many a prominent white Georgia family is red with the blood and sweat of black men justly and unjustly held to labor in Georgia prison camps; the state today is receiving $225,000 a year of this blood money and boasting of her ability to make crime pay.

As long as any white man is openly taught disrespect for black womanhood so long will her degradation be the damnation of some black man's daughter. Let us black men then look to the care and protection of our wives and daughters. Let us, as far as possible, keep them at home and support them there, and defend their honor with our lives.

To stand up thus in our own defense, we must earn a decent living. We must work hard. We must buy land and homes. We must encourage Negro business men. And at the same time we must agitate, complain, protest and keep protesting.

MORE ON BOOKER T. WASHINGTON

Du Bois' famous essay of 1903 in The Souls of Black Folk *(see pp. 29–40) attacked the compromise policy of Booker T. Washington. In the statement below Du Bois answers a lecture given by Booker T. Washington in England in 1910 praising race relations in the United States. A number of distinguished race leaders including J. Max Barber, Archibald H. Grimke, William Monroe Trotter, and Bishop Alexander Walters, signed Du Bois' forthright answer to Washington.*

The National Negro Committee on
Mr. Washington, 1910

To the People of Great Britain and Europe—

The undersigned Negro-Americans have heard, with great regret, the recent attempt to assure England and Europe that their condition in America is satisfactory. They sincerely wish that such were the case, but it becomes their plain duty to say that if Mr. Booker T. Washington, or any other person, is giving the impression abroad that the Negro problem in America is in process of satisfactory solution, he is giving an impression which is not true.

We say this without personal bitterness toward Mr. Washington. He is a distinguished American and has a perfect right to his opinions. But we are compelled to point out that Mr. Washington's large financial responsibilities have made him dependent on the rich charitable public and that, for this reason, he has for years been compelled to tell, not the whole truth, but that part of it which certain powerful interests in America wish to appear as the whole truth. . . .

Our people were emancipated in a whirl of passion, and then left naked to the mercies of their enraged and impoverished ex-masters. As our sole means of defence we were given the ballot, and we used it so as to secure the real fruits of the War. Without it we would have returned to slavery; with it we struggled toward freedom. No sooner, however, had we rid ourselves of nearly two-thirds of our illiteracy, and accumulated $600,000,000 worth of property in a generation, than this ballot, which had become increasingly necessary to the defence of our civil and property rights, was taken from us by force and fraud.

Today in eight States where the bulk of the Negroes live, Black men of property and university training can be, and usually are, by law denied the ballot, while the most ignorant White man votes. This attempt to put the personal and property rights of the best of the Blacks at the absolute political mercy of the worst of the Whites is spreading each day.

Along with this has gone a systematic attempt to curtail the education of the Black race. Under a widely advertised system of "universal" education, not one Black boy in three today has in the United States a chance to learn to read and write. The proportion of school funds due to Black

children are often spent on Whites, and the burden on
private charity to support education, which is a public duty,
has become almost intolerable.

In every walk of life we meet discrimination based solely
on race and color, but continually and persistently misrepresented to the world as the natural difference due to
condition.

We are, for instance, usually forced to live in the worst
quarters, and our consequent death rate is noted as a race
trait, and reason for further discrimination. When we seek
to buy property in better quarters we are sometimes in
danger of mob violence, or, as now in Baltimore, of actual
legislation to prevent.

We are forced to take lower wages for equal work, and
our standard of living is then criticised. Fully half the labor
unions refuse us admittance, and then claim that as "scabs"
we lower the price of labor.

A persistent caste proscription seeks to force us and
confine us to menial occupations where the conditions of
work are worst.

Our women in the South are without protection in law
and custom, and are then derided as lewd. A widespread
system of deliberate public insult is customary, which makes
it difficult, if not impossible, to secure decent accommodation in hotels, railway trains, restaurants and theatres, and
even in the Christian Church we are in most cases given
to understand that we are unwelcome unless segregated.

Worse than all this is the wilful miscarriage of justice in
the courts. Not only have 3,500 Black men been lynched
publicly by mobs in the last twenty-five years without semblance or pretence of trial, but regularly every day throughout the South the machinery of the courts is used, not to
prevent crime and correct the wayward among Negroes, but
to wreak public dislike and vengeance, and to raise public
funds. This dealing in crime as a means of public revenue
is a system well-nigh universal in the South, and while its
glaring brutality through private lease has been checked,
the underlying principle is still unchanged.

Everywhere in the United States the old democratic doctrine of recognising fitness wherever it occurs is losing
ground before a reactionary policy of denying preferment
in political or industrial life to competent men if they have
a trace of Negro blood, and of using the weapons of public insult and humiliation to keep such men down. It is
today a universal demand in the South that on all occasions
social courtesies shall be denied any person of known

Negro descent, even to the extent of refusing to apply the titles of "Mr.," "Mrs.," and "Miss."

Against this dominant tendency strong and brave Americans, White and Black, are fighting, but they need, and need sadly, the moral support of England and of Europe in this crusade for the recognition of manhood, despite adventitious differences of race, and it is like a blow in the face to have one, who himself suffers daily insult and humiliation in America, give the impression that all is well. It is one thing to be optimistic, self-forgetful and forgiving, but it is quite a different thing, consciously or unconsciously, to misrepresent the truth.

ECONOMIC PROGRAM

In 1936, two years after his break with the NAACP over the issue of expedient voluntary race separation, Du Bois came out with a formula for black economic self-sufficiency. Here, as in many other instances, the current militant movement has to acknowledge its debt to W. E. B. Du Bois. Many of Du Bois' own ideas on Negro business, Negro co-ops, and economic separatism came out of his monumental researches at Atlanta University from 1897 to 1912. The following statement was widely quoted and was reprinted in Dusk of Dawn *in 1940.*

Basic American Negro Creed

... I naturally turned my thought toward putting into permanent form that economic program of the Negro which I believed should succeed, and implement the long fight for political and civil rights and social equality which it was my privilege for a quarter of a century to champion. I tried to do this in a preliminary way, through a little study of the "Negro and the New Deal" which I was asked to undertake in 1936 by the colored "Associates in Negro Folk Education," working under the American Association for Adult Education. The editor of this series, Alain

Locke, pressed me for the manuscript and by working hard I finished it and was paid for it just before my trip abroad in 1936. I think I made a fair and pretty exhaustive study of the experience of the Negro from 1933 to 1936 and by way of summing up I appended a statement and credo which I had worked out through correspondence with a number of the younger Negro scholars. It was this:

1. We American Negroes are threatened today with lack of opportunity to work according to gifts and training and lack of income sufficient to support healthy families according to standards demanded by modern culture.

2. In industry, we are a labor reservoir, fitfully employed and paid a wage below subsistence; in agriculture, we are largely disfranchised peons; in public education, we tend to be disinherited illiterates; in higher education, we are the parasites of reluctant and hesitant philanthropy.

3. In the current reorganization of industry, there is no adequate effort to secure us a place in industry, to open opportunity for Negro ability, or to give us security in age or unemployment.

4. Not by the development of upper classes anxious to exploit the workers, nor by the escape of individual genius into the white world, can we effect the salvation of our group in America. And the salvation of this group carries with it the emancipation not only of the darker races of men who make the vast majority of mankind, but of all men of all races. We, therefore, propose this:

A. As American Negroes, we believe in unity of racial effort, so far as this is necessary for self-defense and self-expression, leading ultimately to the goal of a united humanity and the abolition of all racial distinctions.

B. We repudiate all artificial and hate-engendering deification of race separation as such; but just as sternly, we repudiate an ennervating philosophy of Negro escape into an artificially privileged white race which has long sought to enslave, exploit and tyrannize over all mankind.

C. We believe that the Talented Tenth among American Negroes, fitted by education and character to think and do, should find primary employment in determining by study and measurement the present field and demand for racial action and the method by which the masses may be guided along this path.

D. We believe that the problems which now call for such racial planning are Employment, Education and Health; these three; but the greatest of these is Employment.

E. We believe that the labor force and intelligence of twelve million people is more than sufficient to supply their own wants and make their advancement secure. Therefore, we believe that, if carefully and intelligently planned, a co-operative Negro industrial system in America can be established in the midst of and in conjunction with the surrounding national industrial organization and in intelligent accord with that reconstruction of the economic basis of the nation which must sooner or later be accomplished.

F. We believe that Negro workers should join the labor movement and affiliate with such trade unions as welcome them and treat them fairly. We believe that Workers' Councils organized by Negroes for interracial understanding should strive to fight race prejudice in the working class.

G. We believe in the ultimate triumph of some form of Socialism the world over; that is, common ownership and control of the means of production and equality of income.

H. We do not believe in lynching as a cure for crime; nor in war as a necessary defense of culture; nor in violence as the only path to economic revolution. Whatever may have been true in other times and places, we believe that today in America we can abolish poverty by reason and the intelligent use of the ballot, and above all by that dynamic discipline of soul and sacrifice of comfort which, revolution or no revolution, must ever be the only real path to economic justice and world peace.

I. We conceive this matter of work and equality of adequate income as not the end of our effort, but the beginning of the rise of the Negro race in this land and the world over, in power, learning and accomplishment.

J. We believe in the use of our vote for equalizing wealth through taxation, for vesting the ultimate power of the state in the hands of the workers; and as an integral part of the working class, we demand our proportionate share in administration and public expenditure.

K. This is and is designed to be a program of racial effort and this narrowed goal is forced upon us today by the unyielding determination of the mass of the white race to enslave, exploit and insult Negroes; but to this vision of work, organization and service, we welcome all men of all colors so long as their subscription to this basic creed is sincere and is proven by their deeds.

AN APPEAL TO THE WORLD, 1947

Acting as an official representative of the NAACP to the United Nations in 1947 Du Bois wrote an appeal to the new body calling for the protection of America's black minority—which he calls "a nation within a nation" and "one of the considerable nations of the world."

There were in the United States of America, 1940, 12,8 5,518 citizens and residents, something less than a tenth of the nation, who form largely a segregated caste, with restricted legal rights, and many illegal disabilities. They are descendants of the Africans brought to America during the sixteenth, seventeenth, eighteenth and nineteenth centuries and reduced to slave labor. This group has no complete biological unity, but varies in color from white to black, and comprises a great variety of physical characteristics, since many are the offspring of white European-Americans as well as of Africans and American Indians. There are a large number of white Americans who also descend from Negroes but who are not counted in the colored group nor subjected to caste restrictions because the preponderance of white blood conceals their descent.

The so-called American Negro group, therefore, while it is in no sense absolutely set off physically from its fellow Americans, has nevertheless a strong, hereditary cultural unity, born of slavery, of common suffering, prolonged proscription and curtailment of political and civil rights; and especially because of economic and social disabilities. Largely from this fact, have arisen their cultural gifts to America—their rhythm, music and folk-song; their religious faith and customs; their contribution to American art and literature; their defense of their country in every war, on land, sea and in the air; and especially the hard, continuous toil upon which the prosperity and wealth of this continent has largely been built.

The group has long been internally divided by dilemma as to whether its striving upward should be aimed at strenghening its inner cultural and group bonds, both for intrinsic progress and for offensive power against caste; or whether it should seek escape wherever and however possible into the surrounding American culture. Decision in this matter has been largely determined by outer compulsion rather than inner plan; for prolonged policies of segregation and discrimination have involuntarily welded the mass almost into a nation within a nation with its own schools, churches, hospitals, newspapers and many business enterprises.

The result has been to make American Negroes to a wide extent provincial, introvertive, self-conscious and narrowly race-loyal; but it has also inspired them to frantic and often successful effort to achieve, to deserve, to show the world their capacity to share modern civilization. As a result there is almost no area of American civilization in which the Negro has not made creditable showing in the face of all his handicaps.

If, however, the effect of the color caste system on the North American Negro has been both good and bad, its effect on white America has been disastrous. It has repeatedly led the greatest modern attempt at democratic government to deny its political ideas, to falsify its philanthropic assertions and to make its religion to a great extent hypocritical. A nation which boldly declared "That all men are created equal," proceeded to build its economy on chattel slavery; masters who declared race-mixture impossible, sold their own children into slavery and left a mulatto progeny which neither law nor science can today disentangle; churches which excused slavery as calling the heathen to God, refused to recognize the freedom of converts or admit them to equal communion. Sectional strife over the profits of slave labor and conscientious revolt against making human beings real estate led to bloody civil war, and to a partial emancipation of slaves which nevertheless even to this day is not complete. Poverty, ignorance, disease and crime have been forced on these unfortunate victims of greed to an extent far beyond any social necessity; and a great nation, which today ought to be in the forefront of the march toward peace and democracy, finds itself continuously making common cause with race-hate, prejudiced exploitation and oppression of the common man. Its high and noble words are turned against it, because they are contradicted in every syllable by the treatment of the American Negro for three hundred and twenty-eight years.

Let us examine these facts more carefully. The United States has always professed to be a Democracy. She has never wholly attained her ideal, but slowly she has approached it. The privilege of voting has in time been widened by abolishing limitations of birth, religion and lack of property. After the Civil War, which abolished slavery, the nation in gratitude to the black soldiers and laborers who helped win that war, sought to admit to the suffrage all persons without distinction of "race, color or previous condition of servitude." They were warned by the great leaders of abolition, like Sumner, Stevens and Douglass, that this could only be effective, if the Freedmen were given schools, land and some minimum of capital. A Freedmen's Bureau to furnish these prerequisites to effective citizenship was planned and put into partial operation. But Congress and the nation, weary of the costs of war and eager to get back to profitable industry, refused the necessary funds. The effort died, but in order to restore friendly civil government in the South the enfranchised Freedmen, seventy-five per cent illiterate, without land or tools, were thrown into competitive industry with a ballot in their hands. By herculean effort, helped by philanthropy and their own hard work, Negroes built a school system, bought land and cooperated in starting a new economic order in the South. In a generation they had reduced their illiteracy by half and had become wage-earning laborers and share-croppers. They still were handicapped by poverty, disease and crime, but nevertheless the rise of American Negroes from slavery in 1860 to freedom in 1880, has few parallels in modern history.

Opposition to any democracy which included the Negro race on any terms was so strong in the former slave-holding South, and found so much sympathy in large parts of the rest of the nation, that despite notable improvement in the condition of the Negro by every standard of social measurement, the effort to deprive him of the right to vote succeeded. At first he was driven from the polls in the South by mobs and violence; and then he was openly cheated; finally by a "Gentlemen's agreement" with the North, the Negro was disfranchised in the South by a series of laws, methods of administration, court decisions and general public policy, so that today three-fourths of the Negro population of the nation is deprived of the right to vote by open and declared policy.

Most persons seem to regard this as simply unfortunate for Negroes, as depriving a modern working class of the minimum rights for self-protection and opportunity for progress. This is true as has been shown in poor educational opportunities, discrimination in work, health and protection and in the courts. But the situation is far more serious than this: the disfranchisement of the American Negro makes the functioning of all democracy in the nation difficult; and as democracy fails to function in the leading democracy in the world, it fails in the world. . . .

Let us face the facts: the representation of the people in the Congress of the United States is based on population; members of the House of Representatives are elected by groups of approximately 275,000 to 300,000 persons living in 435 Congressional Districts. Naturally difficulties of division within state boundaries, unequal growth of population, migration from year to year, and slow adjustment to these and other changes, make equal population of these districts only approximate; but unless by and large, and in the long run, essential equality is maintained, the whole basis of democratic representation is marred and as in the celebrated "rotten borough" cases in England in the nineteenth century, representation must be eventually equalized or democracy relapses into oligarchy or even fascism.

This is exactly what threatens the United States today because of the unjust disfranchisement of the Negro and the use of his numerical presence to increase the political power of his enemies and of the enemies of democracy. The nation has not the courage to eliminate from citizenship all persons of Negro descent and thus try to restore slavery. It therefore makes its democracy unworkable by paradox and contradiction.

Let us see what effect the disfranchisement of Negroes has upon democracy in the United States. In 1944, five hundred and thirty-one electoral votes were cast for the president of the United States. Of these, one hundred and twenty-nine came from Alabama, Arkansas, Georgia, Louisiana, Oklahoma, North and South Carolina, Texas, Virginia, Florida and Mississippi. The number of these votes and the party for which they were cast, depended principally upon the disfranchisement of the Negro and were not subject to public opinion or democratic control. They represented nearly a fourth of the power of the electoral college and yet they represented only a tenth of the actual voters.

In other words while this nation is trying to carry on the government of the United States by democratic methods, it is not succeeding because of the premium which we put on the disfranchisement of the voters of the South. Moreover, by the political power based on this disfranchised vote the rulers of this nation are chosen and policies of the country determined. The number of congressmen is determined by the population of a state. The larger the number of that population which is disfranchised means greater power for the few who cast the vote. As one national Republican committeeman from Illinois declared, "The Southern states can block any amendment to the United States Constitution and nullify the desires of double their total of Northern and Western states." . . .

When the two main political parties in the United States become unacceptable to the mass of voters, it is practically impossible to replace either of them by a third party movement because of the rotten borough system based on disfranchised voters.

Not only this but who is interested in this disfranchisement and who gains power by it?

It must be remembered that the South has the largest percentage of ignorance, of poverty, of disease in the nation. At the same time, and partly on account of this, it is the place where the labor movement has made the least progress; there are fewer unions and the unions are less effectively organized than in the North. Besides this, the fiercest and most successful fight against democracy in industry is centering in the South, in just that region where medieval caste conditions based mainly on color, and partly on poverty and ignorance, are more prevalent and most successful. And just because labor is so completely deprived of political and industrial power, investors and monopolists are today being attracted there in greater number and with more intensive organization than anywhere else in the United States.

Southern climate has made labor cheaper in the past. Slavery influenced and still influences the conditions under which Southern labor works. There is in the South a reservoir of labor, more laborers than jobs, and competing groups eager for the jobs. Industry encourages the culture patterns which make these groups hate and fear each other. Company towns with control over education and religion are common. Machines displace many workers and increase the demand for jobs at any wage. The United States government economists declare that the dominant characteristics of the Southern labor force are: (1) greater potential labor growth in the nation; (2) relatively larger number of nonwhite workers (which means cheaper workers); (3) predominance of rural workers (which means predominance of ignorant labor); (4) greater working year span (which means child labor and the labor of old people); (5) relatively fewer women in industrial employment. Whole industries are moving South toward this cheaper labor. The recent concentration of investment and monopoly in the South is tremendous.

If concentrated wealth wished to control congressmen or senators, it is far easier to influence voters in South Carolina, Mississippi or Georgia where it requires only from four thousand to sixteen thousand votes to elect a congressman, than to try this in Illinois, New York or Minnesota, where one hundred to one hundred and fifty thousand votes must be persuaded. This spells danger: danger to the American way of life, and danger not simply to the Negro, but to white folk all over the nation, and to the nations of the world.

The federal government has for these reasons continually cast its influence with imperial aggression throughout the world and withdrawn its sympathy from the colored peoples and from the small nations. It has become through private investment a part of the imperialistic bloc which is controlling the colonies of the world.

This paradox and contradiction enters into our actions, thoughts and plan. After the First World War, we were alienated from the proposed League of Nations because of sympathy for imperialism and because of race antipathy to Japan, and because we objected to the compulsory protection of minorities in Europe, which might lead to similar demands upon the United States. We joined Great Britain in determined refusal to recognize equality of races and nations; our tendency was toward isolation until we saw a chance to make inflated profits from the want which came upon the world. This effort of America to make profit out of the disaster in Europe was one of the causes of the depression of the thirties.

As the Second World War loomed the federal government, despite the feelings of the mass of people, followed the captains of industry into attitudes of sympathy toward both fascism in Italy and nazism in Germany. When the utter unreasonableness of fascist demands forced the United States in self-defense to enter the war, then at last the real feelings of the people were loosed and we again found ourselves in the forefront of democratic progress.

But today the paradox again looms after the Second World War. We have recrudescence of race hate and caste restrictions in the United States and of these dangerous tendencies not simply for the United States itself but for all nations. When will nations learn that their enemies are quite as often within their own country as without? It is not Russia that threatens the United States so much as Mississippi; not Stalin and Molotov but Bilbo and Rankin; internal injustice done to one's brothers is far more dangerous than the aggression of strangers from abroad.

Finally it must be stressed that the discrimination of which we complain is not simply discrimination against poverty and ignorance which the world by long custom is used to see: the discrimination practiced in the United States is practiced against American Negroes in spite of wealth, training and character. One of the contributors of this statement happens to be a white man, but the other three and the editor himself are subject to "Jim Crow" laws, and to denial of the right to vote, of an equal chance to earn a living, of the right to enter many places of public entertainment supported by their taxes. In other words, our complaint is mainly against a discrimination based mainly on color of skin, and it is that that we denounce as not only indefensible but barbaric.

It may be quite properly asked at this point, to whom a petition and statement such as this should be addressed? Many persons say that this represents a domestic question which is purely a matter of internal concern; and that therefore it should be addressed to the people and government of the United States and the various states.

It must not be thought that this procedure has not already been taken. From the very beginning of this nation, in the late eighteenth century, and even before, in the colonies, decade by decade and indeed year by year, the Negroes of the United States have appealed for redress of grievances, and have given facts and figures to support their contention.

It must also be admitted that this continuous hammering upon the gates of opportunity in the United States has had effect, and that because of this, and with the help of his white fellow-citizens, the American Negro has emerged from slavery and attained emancipation from chattel slavery, considerable economic independence, social security and advance in culture.

But manifestly this is not enough; no large group of a nation can lag behind the average culture of that nation, as the American Negro still does, without suffering not only itself but becoming a menace to the nation.

In addition to this, in its international relations, the United States owes something to the world; to the United Nations of which it is a part, and to the ideals which it professes to advocate. Especially is this true since the United Nations has made its headquaters in New York. The United States is in honor bound not only to protect its own people and its own interests, but to guard and respect the various people of the world who are its guests and allies. Because of caste custom and legislation along the color line, the United States is today in danger of encroaching upon the rights and privileges of its fellow nations. Most people of the world are more or less colored in skin; their presence at the meetings of the United Nations as participants and as visitors, renders them always liable to insult and to discrimination; because they may be mistaken for Americans of Negro descent.

Not very long ago the nephew of the ruler of a neighboring American state, was killed by policemen in Florida, because he was mistaken for a Negro and thought to be demanding rights which a Negro in Florida is not legally permitted to demand. Again and more recently in Illinois, the personal physician of Mahatma Gandhi, one of the great men of the world and an ardent supporter of the United Nations, was with his friends refused food in a restaurant, again because they were mistaken for Negroes. In a third case, a great insurance society in the United States in its development of a residential area, which would serve for housing the employees of the United Nations, is insisting and reserving the right to discriminate against the persons received as residents for reasons of race and color.

All these are but passing incidents; but they show clearly that a discrimination practiced in the United States against her own citizens and to a large extent a contravention of her own laws, cannot be persisted in, without infringing upon the rights of the peoples of the world and especially upon the ideals and the work of the United Nations.

This question then, which is without doubt primarily an internal and national question, becomes inevitably an international question and will in the future become more and more international, as the nations draw together. In this great attempt to find common ground and to maintain peace, it is, therefore, fitting and proper that the thirteen million American citizens of Negro descent should appeal to the United Nations and ask that organization in the proper way to take cognizance of a situation which deprives this group of their rights as men and citizens, and by so doing makes the functioning of the United States more difficult, if not in many cases impossible.

The United Nations surely will not forget that the population of this group makes it in size one of the considerable nations of the world. We number as many as the inhabitants of the Argentine or Czechoslovakia, or the whole of Scandinavia including Sweden, Norway and Denmark. We are very nearly the size of Egypt, Rumania and Yugoslavia. We are larger than Canada, Saudi Arabia, Ethiopia, Hungary or the Netherlands. We have twice as many persons as Australia or Switzerland, and more than the whole Union of South Africa. We have more people than Portugal or Peru; twice as many as Greece and nearly as many as Turkey. We have more people by far than Belgium and half as many as Spain. In sheer numbers then we are a group which has a right to be heard; and while we rejoice that other smaller nations can stand and make their wants known in the United Nations, we maintain equally that our voice should not be suppressed or ignored.

It is for this reason that American Negroes are appealing to the United Nations, and for the purposes of this appeal they have naturally turned toward the National Association for the Advancement of Colored People. This Association is not the only organization of American Negroes; there are other and worthy organizations. Some of these have already made similar appeals and others doubtless will in the future. But probably no organization has a better right to express the wishes of this vast group of people than the National Association for the Advancement of Colored People.

The National Association for the Advancement of Colored People, incorporated in 1910, is the oldest and largest organization among American Negroes designed to fight for their political, civil and social rights. It has grown from a small body of interested persons into an organization which had enrolled, at the close of 1946, four hundred fifty-two thousand two hundred eighty-nine members, in one thousand four hundred seventeen branches. At present it has over a half million members throughout the United States. The Board of Directors of this organization, composed of leading colored and white citizens of the United

States, has ordered this statement to be made and presented to the Commission on Human Rights of the Economic and Social Council of the United Nations, and to the General Assembly of the United Nations.

THE LATER YEARS

An oft-asked question of himself by the neophyte Christian is "What must I do to be saved?". George Bernard Shaw considered this question in Androcles and the Lion, *where he has the vile Spintho—who for all his life has done evil and no good—now courting martyrdom in Nero's arena, because he has learned that all he has to do as a Christian to get a quick free pass to Heaven is to confess, make last-minute repentance, and become a martyr. The brief, fleeting good would wipe out the long evil past.*

How should this work in reverse? A man gives his best years for humanity, never in his life performing a mean, criminal, violent act. For half a century he loves, succors and educates children; he eases the mental agony of the dispossessed by telling them they are beautiful and that they are to inherit the earth; he creates beauty and protects it; he visits those in prison and tries to secure their release, and he keeps many from going there; in short, he performs countless unselfish and thankless tasks and good deeds. And now suppose that this man, near the end of his life, decides to devote the remainder of his few precious years to working for so-called "unpopular" causes, such as world peace, internationalism and even communism. What standards ought now to be used in assessing him?

W. E. B. Du Bois spent more than fifty years of his long, productive life in doing deeds of valor and goodness, which were recognized as such even by large segments of the "White Establishment." Then for a relatively short period he became "bad"—he accused America of being the buttress of war, colonialism, and reaction; at the age of 93 he joined the Communist Party; he amended his early prophecy that the "problem of the twentieth century is the problem of the color line" and now said that the problem was the class-caste-color line; he became a citizen of Ghana, a country he helped greatly to create and which offered to subsidize his great Encyclopedia Africana project—first planned in 1909 but never financed in the United States. He said that in Ghana he could now be a man and "not a nigger" as he was in his native land. Another contributing factor in caus-

ing him to move to Ghana may have been his bitterness that in his 84th year the American government had placed him in handcuffs for his advocacy of peace.

Du Bois' enemies and detractors say that when he became a Communist and citizen of Ghana he became a pariah and cancelled out his long "good" years as great prophet and educator. His admirers, many of whom justify his later years or pass no judgment, feel that the place of Dr. W. E. B. Du Bois in American and world history is unalterably secure and that he was one of the most useful and influential men of his time.

The selections included here are from his writings in his later radical years—books, essays, articles. A large part of this is autobiographical in that it deals with his personal credo toward the end of his life as contrasted with his early Credo essay of 1904.

———————

The following quote is from a speech at the Paris Peace Conference, April 1949. It also appears in The Autobiography of W. E. B. Du Bois.

On Colonialism

Let us not be misled. The real cause of the differences which threaten world war is not the spread of socialism or even of the complete socialism which communism envisages. Socialism is spreading all over the world and even in the United States.... Against this spread of socialism, one modern institution is working desperately and that is colonialism, and colonialism has been and is and ever will be one of the chief causes of war.... Leading this new colonial imperialism comes my own native land, built by my father's toil and blood, the United States. The United States is a great nation; rich by grace of God and prosperous by the hard work of its humblest citizens.... Drunk with power we are leading the world to hell in a new colonialism with the same old human slavery which once ruined us; and to a Third World War which will ruin the world....

On Colonialism

The present war has made it clear that we can no longer regard Western Europe and North America as the world for which civilization exists; nor can we look upon European culture as the norm for all peoples. Henceforth the majority of the inhabitants of earth, who happen for the most part to be colored, must be regarded as having the right and the capacity to share in human progress and to become copartners in that democracy which alone can ensure peace among men, by the abolition of poverty, the education of the masses, protection from disease, and the scientific treatment of crime.

From these premises I have written this book, to examine our current efforts to ensure peace through the united action of men of goodwill. I have sought to say that insofar as such efforts leave practically untouched the present imperial ownership of disfranchised colonies, and in this and other ways proceed as if the majority of men can be regarded mainly as sources of profit for Europe and North America, in just so far we are planning not peace but war, not democracy but the continued oligarchical control of civilization by the white race. . . .

From PREFACE TO COLOR AND DEMOCRACY, 1945

On Colonialism and an International Bill of Rights

. . . In 1945, as consultant to the American delegation to the UNO in San Francisco, I tried to stress the colonial question. I wrote May 16, 1945:

"The attempt to write an International Bill of Rights into the San Francisco Conference without any specific mention of the people living in colonies seems to me a most unfortunate procedure. If it were clearly understood that freedom of speech, freedom from want and freedom from fear, which the nations are asked to guarantee, would without question be extended to the 750 million people who live in colonial areas, this would be a great and fateful step. But the very fact that these people, forming the most depressed peoples in the world, with 90 per cent illiteracy, extreme poverty and a prey to disease, who hitherto for the most part have been considered as sources of profit and not included in the democratic development of the world; and whose exploitation for three centuries has been a prime cause of war, turmoil, and suffering—the omission of specific reference to these peoples is almost advertisement of their tacit exclusion as not citizens of free states, and that their welfare and freedom would be considered only at the will of the countries owning them and not at the demand of enlightened world public opinion."

From THE AUTOBIOGRAPHY OF W. E. B. DU BOIS

On Colonialism: Missions and Mandates

FAILURE OF THE UNITED NATIONS TO COME IMME-
DIATELY TO GRIPS WITH THE PROBLEM OF COLONIES
WILL INVITE CATASTROPHE; EFFECTIVE ACTION CALLS
FOR A NEW MANDATES COMMISSION IMPLEMENTED BY
THAT UNSELFISH DEVOTION TO THE WELL-BEING OF
MANKIND WHICH HAS OFTEN, IF NOT ALWAYS, INSPIRED
THE MISSIONARY CRUSADE.

It is clear that in this world, as manifested by these terrible wars and by the suffering of mankind and the sacrifice
of peoples, there is a tremendous available amount of goodwill and desire for the uplift of mankind. This has been
shown in the past in all sorts of ways: in China's love
of peace, in the charity of the medieval Christian Church,
in the missionary crusades of Buddhists, Christians, and
Mohammedans; especially in the Christian missions of the
eighteenth and nineteenth centuries; in the suppression of
slavery and the slave trade; and in the various attempts
to alleviate, if not abolish, poverty and to do away with
ignorance.

The difficulty in this particular era is that this goodwill
must be organized and canalized. It must not aid and abet
reaction in social progress, nor be used like the missionary
effort in Africa to exploit and subdue peoples in the name
of Jesus Christ for the use of profit-making industry. It
must, on the contrary, become organized as missions of
culture to carry to backward peoples, minority groups, and
lower economic classes the cultures and education which
they are capable of absorbing and using. It must narrow
the frightful and dangerous differences between current
custom and the scientific knowledge that there are no races
and great groups incapable of the same kind of advance
that has been made by the most cultured peoples; and that
what is needed is opportunity; that we can have democracy
and peace only if the menace of poverty, ignorance, and
crime are met by positive and organized human action—
Poverty, Ignorance and Crime—these three—but the greatest of these is Poverty.

Poverty can be attacked and abolished by government
action and social organization. The way to make this clear

333

to the world is to attack the economic illiteracy, the ignorance of economic facts and developments, now deliberately encouraged in our schools and colleges, in our press and periodicals and in our books. Here is the field for the Great Crusade which will lead to democracy and peace.

The Atlantic Charter brought a new examination of the colonial question. The second point declared that the United Nations "desire to see no territorial changes that do not accord with the freely expressed wishes of the peoples concerned."

The third point was: that "they respect the right of all peoples to choose the form of government under which they will live; and they wish to see sovereign rights and self-government restored to those who have been forcibly deprived of them."

The sixth said: that "after the final destruction of the Nazi tyranny, they hope to see established a peace which will afford to all nations the means of dwelling in safety within their own boundaries, and which will afford assurance that all the men in all the lands may live out their lives in freedom from fear and want." . . .

The General Assembly of the United Nations should begin by insisting that there sit in the Assembly not simply representatives of the free nations, but with them representatives of all colonial peoples over whom they claim control. The matter of the number of such colonial delegates can well wait on time and experience. The method of their choice and the fair representation of all angles of opinion can be gradually adjusted as the Economic and Social Council gains power to investigate. But it is absolutely essential that, at the beginning, the voices of all peoples that on earth do dwell be raised fearlessly and openly in the parliament of man, to seek justice, complain of oppression, and demand equality. Difficult as this program will doubtless prove, it will not be nearly so difficult, horrible, and utterly devastating as two world wars in a single generation.

Evidently there is indicated here the necessity of earnest effort to avoid the nondemocratic and race-inferiority philosophy involved. There should be consultation among colonial peoples and their friends as to just what measures ought to be taken. This consultation should look toward asking for the following successive steps:

One, representation of the colonial peoples alongside the master peoples in the Assembly.

Two, the organization of a Mandates Commission under the Economic and Social Council, with definite power to investigate complaints and conditions in colonies and make public their findings and to hear oral petitions.

Three, a clear statement of the intentions of each imperial power to take, gradually but definitely, all measures designed to raise the peoples of colonies to a condition of complete political and economic equality with the peoples of the master nations, and eventually either to incorporate them into the polity of the master nations or to allow them to become independent free peoples.

From COLOR AND DEMOCRACY

On Democracy

. . . The mounting pressure of popular demand for democratic methods must be counted on throughout the world as popular intelligence rises. Its greatest successful opponent today is not Fascism, whose extravagance has brought its own overthrow, but rather imperial colonialism, where the disfranchisement of the mass of people has reduced millions to tyrannical control without any vestige of democracy.

It happens, not for biological or historical reasons, that most of the inhabitants of colonies today have colored skins. This does not make them one group or race or even allied biological groups or races. In fact these colored people vary vastly in physique, history, and cultural experience. The one thing that unites them today in the world's thought is their poverty, ignorance, and disease, which renders them all, in different degrees, unresisting victims of modern capitalistic exploitation. On this foundation the modern "Color Line" has been built, with all its superstitions and pseudo-science. And it is this complex today which more than anything else excuses the suppression of democracy, not only in Asia and Africa, but in Europe and the Americas. Hitler seized on "negroid" characteristics to accuse the French of inferiority. Britain points to miscegenation with colored races to prove democracy impossible in South America. But it is left to the greatest modern democracy, the United States, to defend human slavery and caste, and even defeat democratic government in its own boundaries, ostensibly because of an inferior race, but really in order to make profits out of cheap labor, both black and white.

The attitude of the United States in this development puzzles the observing world of liberalism. Intelligence and high wages in this land are linked with an extraordinary development of the rule of wealth and sympathy with imperial ambition in other lands, as well as steps toward greater American imperialism. . . .

From COLOR AND DEMOCRACY

On Revolution

So long as the colonial system perists and expands, theories of race inferiority will help to continue it. Right here lies the great danger of the future. One of the vast paradoxes of human nature is that no matter how degraded people become, it is impossible to keep them down on a large scale and forever. Rebellion will certainly ensue. If this is true of Europe, it is just as true and just as significant for Asia and Africa. The continents which have withstood the European exploitation of the nineteenth century are for that very reason not going to remain quiescent under a new order—unless that new order has a distinct place for them which allows their progress, development, and self-determination. . . . The will to revolt on the part of the colored people is immeasurably greater today than yesterday. . . .

There will return one day to all nations another group with which the world must reckon; young, disillusioned, bitter voters, disillusioned because they realize the futility of war as a settlement of human problems, because they saw its glory in mud, pain, and torn flesh. They will return maimed inevitably in body and mind and ripe for extremity in thought and action. Propaganda, as in the last war, may make them reactionary, anti-labor, anti-Negro, anti-Semitic, anti-foreign-born; counterpropaganda may make them food for revolution and violence of every kind.

From COLOR AND DEMOCRACY

On Vietnam

The nest of grafters, whoremongers and gamblers at Saigon, helped by Americans, have broken the Geneva treaty which closed the French Indo-Chinese War, and are attacking the Communists. That is called "communist aggression." It is the attempt of American business and the American Navy to supplant France as colonial ruler in Southeast Asia.

From THE AUTOBIOGRAPHY OF W. E. B. DU BOIS

The "Father of Pan Africa" speaks to his children. This Du Bois paper was read by Mrs. Du Bois at the Accra, Ghana, All-African Conference in 1958. Reprinted in the enlarged edition of The World and Africa *(International Publishers, 1965).*

On the Future of Africa

Fellow Africans: About 1735, my great-great-grandfather was kidnapped on this coast of West Africa and taken by the Dutch to the colony of New York in America, where he was sold in slavery. About the same time a French Huguenot, Jacques Du Bois, migrated from France to America, and his great-grandson, born in the West Indies and with Negro blood, married the great-great-granddaughter of my black ancestor. I am the son of this couple, born in 1868, hence my French name and my African loyalty.

As a boy I knew little of Africa save legends and some music in my family. The books which we studied in the public school had almost no information about Africa, save of Egypt, which we were told was not Negroid. I heard of few great men of Negro blood, but I built up in my mind a dream of what Negroes would do in the future even though they had no past.

Then happened a series of events: In the last decade of the 19th century, I studied two years in Europe, and often heard Africa mentioned with respect. Then, as a teacher in

337

America, I had a few African students. Later at Atlanta University a visiting professor, Franz Boaz, addressed the students and told them of the history of the Black Sudan. I was utterly amazed and began to study Africa for myself. I attended the Paris Exposition in 1900, and met with West Indians in London in a Pan-African Conference. This movement died, but in 1911 I attended a Races Congress in London which tried to bring together representatives from all races of the world. I met distinguished Africans and was thrilled. However, World War [I] killed this movement.

We held a small meeting in 1919 in Paris. After peace was declared, in 1921, we called a much larger Pan-African Congress in London, Paris and Brussels. The 200 delegates at this congress aroused the fury of the colonial powers and all our efforts for third, fourth and fifth congresses were only partially successful because of their opposition. We tried in vain to convene a congress in Africa itself.

The great depression of the 'thirties then stopped our efforts for 15 years. Finally in 1945 black trade union delegates to the Paris meeting of trade unions called for another Pan-African Congress. This George Padmore organized and, at his request, I came from America to attend the meeting at Manchester, England. Here I met Kwame Nkrumah, Jomo Kenyatta, Johnson of Liberia and a dozen other young leaders.

The program of Pan-Africa as I have outlined it was not a plan of action, but of periodical conferences and free discussion. And this was a necessary preliminary to any future plan of united or separate action. However, in the resolutions adopted by the successive Congresses were many statements urging united action, particularly in the matter of race discrimination. Also, there were other men and movements urging specific work.

World financial depression interfered with all these efforts and suspended the Pan-African Congresses until the meeting in Manchester in 1945. Then, it was reborn and this meeting now in Accra is the sixth effort to bring this great movement before the world and to translate its experience into action.

My only role in this meeting is one of advice from one who has lived long, who has studied Africa and has seen the modern world.

In this great crisis of the world's history, when standing on the highest peaks of human accomplishment we look forward to Peace and backward to War, when we look up to Heaven and down to Hell, let us mince no words. We face triumph or tragedy without alternative.

Africa, ancient Africa, has been called by the world and has lifted up her hands! Africa has no choice between private capitalism and socialism. The whole world, including capitalist countries, is moving toward socialism, inevitably, inexorably. You can choose between blocs of military alliance, you can choose between groups of political union; you cannot choose between socialism and private capitalism because private capitalism is doomed!

But what is socialism? It is a disciplined economy and political organization to which the first duty of a citizen is to serve the state; and the state is not a selected aristocracy, or a group of self-seeking oligarchs who have seized wealth and power. No! The mass of workers with hand and brain are the ones whose collective destiny is the chief object of all effort.

Gradually, every state is coming to this concept of its aim. The great Communist states like the Soviet Union and China have surrendered completely to this idea. The Scandinavian states have yielded partially; Britain has yielded in some respects, France in part, and even the United States adopted the New Deal which was largely socialism; though today further American socialism is held at bay by 60 great groups of corporations who control individual capitalists and the trade union leaders.

On the other hand, the African tribe, whence all of you sprung, was communistic in its very beginnings. No tribesman was free. All were servants of the tribe of whom the chief was father and voice.

When now, with a certain suddenness, Africa is whirled by the bitter struggle of dying private capitalism into the last great battleground of its death throes, you are being tempted to adopt at least a passing private capitalism as a step to some partial socialism. This would be a grave mistake.

For 400 years Europe and North America have built their civilization and comfort on theft of colored labor and the land and materials which rightfully belong to these colonial peoples.

The dominant exploiting nations are willing to yield more to the demands of the mass of men than were their fathers. But their yielding takes the form of sharing the loot—not of stopping the looting. It takes the form of stopping socialism by force and not of surrendering the fatal mistakes of private capitalism. Either capital belongs to all or power is denied all.

Here then, my Brothers, you face your great decision: Will you for temporary advantage—for automobiles, refrigerators and Paris gowns—spend your income in paying interest on borrowed funds; or will you sacrifice your present comfort and the chance to shine before your neighbors, in order to educate your children, develop such industry as best serves the great mass of people and make your country strong in ability, self-support and self-defense? Such union of effort for strength calls for sacrifice and self-denial, while the capital offered you at high price by the colonial powers like France, Britain, Holland, Belgium and the United States, will prolong fatal colonial imperialism, from which you have suffered slavery, serfdom and colonialism.

You are not helpless. You are the buyers, and to continue existence as sellers of capital, these great nations, former owners of the world, must sell or face bankruptcy. You are not compelled to buy all they offer now. You can wait. You can starve a while longer rather than sell your great heritage for a mess of Western capitalist pottage. You can not only beat down the price of capital as offered by the united and monopolized Western private capitalists, but at last today you can compare their offers with those of socialist countries like the Soviet Union and China, which with infinite sacrifice and pouring out of blood and tears, are at last able to offer weak nations needed capital on better terms than the West.

The supply which socialist nations can at present spare is small as compared with that of the bloated monopolies of the West, but it is large and rapidly growing. Its acceptance involves no bonds which a free Africa may not safely assume. It certainly does not involve slavery and colonial control which the West has demanded and still demands. Today she offers a compromise, but one of which you must beware:

She offers to let some of your smarter and less scrupulous leaders become fellow capitalists with the white exploiters if in turn they induce the nation's masses to pay the awful costs. This happened in the West Indies and in South America. This may yet happen in the Middle East and Eastern Asia. Strive against it with every fibre of your bodies and souls. A body of local private capitalists, even if they are black, can never free Africa; they will simply sell it into new slavery to old masters overseas.

As I have said, this is a call for sacrifice. Great Goethe sang, *"Entbehren sollst du, sollst entbehren"*—"Thou shalt forego, shalt do without." If Africa unites, it will be because each part, each nation, each tribe gives up a part of its heritage for the good of the whole. That is what union means; that is what Pan-Africa means: When the child is born into the tribe the price of his growing up is giving a part of his freedom to the tribe. This he soon learns or dies. When the tribe becomes a union of tribes, the individual tribe surrenders some part of its freedom to the paramount tribe.

When the nation arises, the constituent tribes, clans and groups must each yield power and some freedom to the demands of the nation or the nation dies before it is born. Your local tribal, much-loved languages must yield to the few world tongues which serve the largest number of people and promote understanding and world literature.

This is the great dilemma which faces Africans today, faces one and all: Give up individual rights for the needs of Mother Africa; give up tribal independence for the needs of the nation.

Forget nothing, but set everything in its rightful place; the glory of the six Ashanti wars against Britain; the wisdom of the Fanti Confederation; the growth of Nigeria; the song of the Songhay and Hausa; the rebellion of the Mahdi and the hands of Ethiopia; the greatness of the Basuto and the fighting of Chaka; the revenge of Mutessi, and many other happenings and men; but above all—Africa, Mother of Men.

Your nearest friends and neighbors are the colored people of China and India, the rest of Asia, the Middle East and the sea isles, once close bound to the heart of Africa and now long severed by the greed of Europe. Your bond is not mere color of skin but the deeper experience of wage slavery and contempt. So too, your bond with the white world is closest to those who support and defend China and help India and not those who exploit the Middle East and South America.

Awake, awake, put on thy strength, O Zion! Reject the weakness of missionaries who teach neither love nor brotherhood, but chiefly the virtues of private profit from capital, stolen from your land and labor. Africa, awake! Put on the beautiful robes of Pan-African socialism.

You have nothing to lose but your chains! You have a continent to regain! You have freedom and human dignity to attain!

Speech in Peking on his 91st birthday. It also appears in
The Autobiography of W. E. B. Du Bois.

On China and Africa

By courtesy of the government of the 600 million people
of the Chinese Republic, I am permitted on my 91st birthday to speak to the people of China and Africa and through
them to the world. Hail, then, and farewell, dwelling places
of the yellow and black races. Hail human kind!

I speak with no authority; no assumption of age nor rank;
I hold no position, I have no wealth. One thing alone I
own and that is my own soul. Ownership of that I have even
while in my own country for near a century I have been
nothing but a "nigger." On this basis and this alone I dare
speak, I dare advise.

China after long centuries has arisen to her feet and leapt
forward. Africa, arise, and stand straight, speak and think!
Act! Turn from the West and your slavery and humiliation
for the last 500 years and face the rising sun.

Behold a people, the most populous nation on this
ancient earth, which has burst its shackles, not by boasting
and strutting, not by lying about its history and its con-
quests, but by patience and long suffering, by blind struggle,
moved up and on toward the crimson sky. She aims to
"make men holy; to make men free."

But what men? Not simply the mandarins but including
mandarins; not simply the rich, but not excluding the rich.
Not simply the learned, but led by knowledge to the end
that no man shall be poor, nor sick, nor ignorant; but that
the humblest worker as well as the sons of emperors shall
be fed and taught and healed and that there emerge on
earth a single unified people, free, well and educated.

You have been told, my Africa: My Africa in Africa and
all your children's children overseas; you have been told
and the telling so beaten into you by rods and whips, that
you believe it yourselves, that this is impossible; that mankind can rise only by walking on men; by cheating them
and killing them; that only on a doormat of the despised
and dying, the dead and rotten, can a British aristocracy, a
French cultural elite or an American millionaire be nur-
tured and grown.

This is a lie. It is an ancient lie spread by church and
state, spread by priest and historian, and believed in by

fools and cowards, as well as by the downtrodden and the children of despair.

Speak, China, and tell your truth to Africa and the world. What people have been despised as you have? Who more than you have been rejected of men? Recall when lordly Britishers threw the rickshaw money on the ground to avoid touching a filthy hand. Forget not the time when in Shanghai no Chinese man dared set foot in a park which he paid for. Tell this to Africa, for today Africa stands on new feet, with new eyesight, with new brains and asks: Where am I and why?

The Western sirens answer: Britain wheedles; France cajoles; while America, my America, where my ancestors and descendants for eight generations have lived and toiled; America loudest of all, yells and promises freedom. If only Africa allows American investment!

Beware Africa, America bargains for your soul. America would have you believe that they freed your grandchildren; that Afro-Americans are full American citizens, treated like equals, paid fair wages as workers, promoted for desert and free to learn and travel across the world.

This is not true. Some are near freedom; some approach equality with whites; some have achieved education; but the price for this has too often been slavery of mind, distortion of truth and oppression of our own people.

Of 18 million Afro-Americans, 12 million are still second-class citizens of the United States, serfs in farming, low-paid laborers in industry, and repressed members of union labor. Most American Negroes do not vote. Even the rising six million are liable to insult and discrimination at any time.

But this, Africa, relates to your descendants, not to you. Once I thought of you Africans as children, whom we educated Afro-Americans would lead to liberty. I was wrong. We could not even lead ourselves, much less you. Today I see you rising under your own leadership, guided by your own brains.

Africa does not ask alms from China nor from the Soviet Union nor from France, Britain, nor the United States. It asks friendship and sympathy and no nation better than China can offer this to the Dark Continent. Let it be freely given and generously. Let Chinese visit Africa, send their scientists there and their artists and writers. Let Africa send its students to China and its seekers after knowledge. It will not find on earth a richer goal, a more promising mine of information.

On the other hand, watch the West. The new British West Indian Federation is not a form of democratic progress but a cunning attempt to reduce these islands to the control of British and American investors. Haiti is dying under rich Haitian investors who with American money are enslaving the peasantry. Cuba is showing what the West Indies, Central and South America are suffering under American big business.

The American worker himself does not always realize this. He has high wages and many comforts. Rather than lose these, he keeps in office by his vote the servants of industrial exploitation so long as they maintain his wage. His labor leaders represent exploitation and not the fight against the exploitation of labor by private capital. These two sets of exploiters fall out only when one demands too large a share of the loot.

This China knows. This Africa must learn. This the American Negro has failed so far to learn. I am frightened by the so-called friends who are flocking to Africa. Negro Americans trying to make money from your toil, white Americans who seek by investment and high interest to bind you in serfdom to business as the Near East is bound and as South America is struggling with. For this America is tempting your leaders, bribing your young scholars, and arming your soldiers. What shall you do?

First, understand! Realize that the great mass of mankind is freeing itself from wage slavery, while private capital in Britain, France, and now in America, is still trying to maintain civilization and comfort for a few on the toil, disease and ignorance of the mass of men. Understand this, and understanding comes from direct knowledge. You know America and France, and Britain to your sorrow. Now know the Soviet Union, but particularly know China.

China is flesh of your flesh, and blood of your blood. China is colored and knows to what a colored skin in this modern world subjects its owner. But China knows more, much more than this she knows what to do about it. She can take the insults of the United States and still hold her head high. She can make her own machines, when America refuses to sell her American manufactures, even though it hurts American industry, and throws her workers out of jobs. China does not need American nor British missionaries to teach her religion and scare her with tales of hell. China has been in hell too long, not to believe in a heaven of her own making. This she is doing.

Come to China, Africa, and look around. Invite Africa to

come, China, and see what you can teach by just pointing. Yonder old woman is working on the street. But she is happy. She has no fear. Her children are in school and a good school. If she is ill, there is a hospital where she is cared for free of charge. She has a vacation with pay each year. She can die and be buried without taxing her family to make some undertaker rich.

Africa can answer: but some of this we have done; our tribes undertake public service like this. Very well, let your tribes continue and expand this work. What Africa must realize is what China knows; that it is worse than stupid to allow a people's education to be under the control of those who seek not the progress of the people but their use as means of making themselves rich and powerful. It is wrong for the University of London to control the University of Ghana. It is wrong for the Catholic church to direct the education of the black Congolese. It was wrong for Protestant churches supported by British and American wealth to control higher education in China.

The Soviet Union is surpassing the world in popular and higher education, because from the beginning it started its own complete educational system. The essence of the revolution in the Soviet Union and China and in all the "iron curtain" nations, is not the violence that accompanied the change; no more than starvation at Valley Forge was the essence of the American revolution against Britain. The real revolution is the acceptance on the part of the nation of the fact that hereafter the main object of the nation is the welfare of the mass of the people and not of the lucky few.

Government is for the people's progress and not for the comfort of an artistocracy. The object of industry is the welfare of the workers and not the wealth of the owners. The object of civilization is the cultural progress of the mass of workers and not merely of an intellectual elite. And in return for all this, communist lands believe that the cultivation of the mass of people will discover more talent and genius to serve the state than any closed aristocracy ever furnished. This belief the current history of the Soviet Union and China is proving true each day. Therefore don't let the West invest when you can avoid it. Don't buy capital from Britain, France and the United States if you can get it on reasonable terms from the Soviet Union and China. This is not politics; it is common sense. It is learning from experience. It is trusting your friends and watching your enemies. Refuse to be cajoled or to change your way of life, so as to make a few of your fellows rich at the expense of a mass of workers growing poor and sick and remaining without schools so that a few black men can have automobiles.

Africa, here is a real danger which you must avoid or return to the slavery from which you are emerging. All I ask from you is the courage to know; to look about you and see what is happening in this old and tired world; to realize the extent and depth of its rebirth and the promise which glows on your hills.

Visit the Soviet Union and visit China. Let your youth learn the Russian and Chinese languages. Stand together in this new world and let the old world perish in its greed or be born again in new hope and promise. Listen to the Hebrew prophet of communism:

Ho! every one that thirsteth; come ye to the waters; come, buy and eat, without money and price!

Again, China and Africa, hail and farewell!

On China

Fifteen times I have crossed the Atlantic and once the Pacific. I have seen the world. But never so vast and glorious a miracle as China. This monster is a nation with a dark-tinted billion born at the beginning of time, and facing its end; this struggle from starved degradation and murder and suffering to the triumph of that Long March to world leadership. Oh beautiful, patient, self-sacrificing China, despised and unforgettable, victorious and forgiving, crucified and risen from the dead. . . .

I used to weep for American Negroes, as I saw what indignities and repressions and cruelties they had passed; but as I read Chinese history in these last months and had it explained to me stripped of Anglo-Saxon lies, I know that no depths of Negro slavery in America have plumbed such abysses as the Chinese have seen for 2,000 years and more. They have seen starvation and murder; rape and prostitution; sale and slavery of children; and religion cloaked in opium and gin, for converting the "heathen." . . .

My birthday was given national notice in China, and celebrated as never before; and we who all our lives have been liable to insult and discrimination on account of our race and color, in China have met universal goodwill and love, such as we never expected. . . .

China has no rank or classes; her universities grant no degrees; her government awards no medals. She has no blue book of "society." But she has leaders of learning and genius, scientists of renown, artisans of skill and millions who know and believe this and follow where these men lead. This is the joy of this nation, its high belief and its unfaltering hope.

China is no utopia. Fifth Avenue has better shops where the rich can buy and the whores parade. Detroit has more and better cars. The best American housing outstrips the Chinese, and Chinese women are not nearly as well-dressed as the guests of the Waldorf-Astoria. But the Chinese worker is happy. He has exorcised the Great Fear that haunts the West; the fear of losing his job; the fear of falling sick; the fear of accident; the fear of inability to educate his children; the fear of daring to take a vacation. To guard against such catastrophe Americans skimp and save, cheat and steal, gamble and arm for murder. The Soviet citizen, the Czech, the Pole, the Hungarian have kicked out the stooges of America and the hoodlums set to exploit the peasants. They and the East Germans no longer fear these disasters; and above all the Chinese sit high above these fears and laugh with joy. They will not be rich in old age, but they will eat. They will not enjoy sickness but they will be given care. They will not starve as thousands of Chinese did only a generation ago. They fear neither flood nor epidemic. They do not even fear war. . . .

From THE AUTOBIOGRAPHY OF W. E. B. DU BOIS

On the Soviet Union

I have in a sense seen the Union of Soviet Socialist Republics grow, not as a casual visitor, nor hurried tourist. In 1926, I saw a Russia just emerging from war with the world. The people were poor and ill-clothed; food was scarce, and long lines stood hours to get their share. Orphan children, ragged and dirty, crawled in and out of sewers. The nation faced foreign force, and Russian traitors. Yet, despite this, I saw a land of hope and hard work. . . .

What amazed and uplifted me in 1926,[1] was to see a nation stoutly facing a problem which most other modern nations did not dare even to admit was real: the abolition of poverty. Taking inspiration directly out of the mouths and dreams of the world's savants and prophets, who had inveighed against modern industrial methods and against the co-existence of progress and poverty, this new Russia founded by Lenin and inspired by Marx and Engels, proposed to build a socialist state with production for use and not for private profit; with ownership of land and capital goods by the state, and with state control of public services, including education and health. It was enough for me to see this mighty attempt. It might fail, I knew, but the effort in itself was social progress and neither foolishness nor crime. . . .

It is by its economic progress that the Soviet Union must primarily be judged. Russia had established a socialistic state. The world had long been veering toward socialism. We had made essays toward socialism; but when the socialist state appeared full-fledged, most of us called it by other names and refused to judge it by its socialism; but rather we insisted on investigating the ethics of the methods accompanying its establishment. . . .

What I saw in the Soviet Union was . . . the growth of a nation's soul, the confidence of a great people in its plan and future. And beyond that the realization around the world that the Seven Year Plan was not boasting, but knowledge shared by 200 million people. Around these millions were gathered even greater millions in China, Vietnam and Korea, who believed in socialism, and sought communism.

---

[1] [His first visit.]

Is it possible to conduct a great modern government without autocratic leadership of the rich? The answer is: this is exactly what the Soviet Union is doing today. But can she continue to do this? This is not a question of ethics or economics; it is a question of psychology. Can Russia continue to think of the state in terms of the workers? This can happen only if the Russian people believe and idealize the workingman as the chief citizen. In America we do not. The ideal of every American is the millionaire—or at least the man of "independent" means of income. We regard the laborers as the unfortunate part of the community, and even liberal thought is directed toward "emancipating" the workingman by relieving him in part, if not entirely, of the necessity for work. The Soviet Union, on the contrary, is seeking to make a nation believe that work, and work that is hard and in some respects even disagreeable, and to a large extent physical, is a necessity of human life at present and likely to be in any conceivable future world; that the people who do this work are the ones who should determine how the national income from their combined efforts should be distributed. . . .

The Russian question is: Can you make the worker and not the millionaire the center of modern power and culture? If you can, the Russian Revolution will sweep the world. . . .

The Soviet Union seems to me the only European country where people are not more or less taught and encouraged to despise and look down on some class, group or race. I know countries where race and color prejudice show only slight manifestations, but no white country where race and color prejudice seems so absolutely absent. In Paris, I attract some attention; in London I meet elaborate blankness; anywhere in America I get anything from complete ignoring to curiosity, and often insult. In Moscow, I pass unheeded. Russians quite naturally ask me information; women sit beside me quite confidently and unconsciously. Children are uniformly courteous. . . .

. . . The United States has moved from the hysteria of calling all Soviet women prostitutes, all Russian workers slaves and the whole Russian people ready for revolt; of regarding all Soviet rulers as criminals conspiring to conquer the United States and rule the world; of breaking every treaty they made. From this false and utterly ridiculous position, we have begun to recognize the Soviet Socialist Republic as giving its people the best education of any in the world, of excelling in science, and organizing industry to its highest levels. Our increasing number of visitors to Russia see a contented people who do not hate the United States, but fear its war-making, and are eager to cooperate with us. From such a nation we can learn.

From THE AUTOBIOGRAPHY OF W. E. B. DU BOIS

On Communism

I have studied socialism and communism long and carefully in lands where they are practiced and in conversation with their adherents, and with wide reading. I now state my conclusion frankly and clearly: I believe in communism. I mean by communism, a planned way of life in the production of wealth and work designed for building a state whose object is the highest welfare of its people and not merely the profit of a part. I believe that all men should be employed according to their ability and that wealth and services should be distributed according to need. Once I thought that these ends could be attained under capitalism, means of production privately owned, and used in accord with free individual initiative. After earnest observation I now believe that private ownership of capital and free enterprise are leading the world to disaster. I do not believe that so-called "people's capitalism" has in the United States or anywhere replaced the ills of private capitalism and shown an answer to socialism. The corporation is but the legal mask behind which the individual owner of wealth hides. Democratic government in the United States has almost ceased to function. A fourth of the adults are disfranchised, half of the legal voters do not go to the polls. We are ruled by those who control wealth and who by that power buy or coerce public opinion.

I resent the charge that communism is a conspiracy: Communists often conspire as do capitalists. But it is false that all Communists are criminals and that communism speaks and exists mainly by means of force and fraud. I shall therefore hereafter help the triumph of communism in every honest way that I can: without deceit or hurt; and in any way possible, without war; and with goodwill to all men of all colors, classes and creeds. If, because of this belief and such action, I become the victim of attack and calumny, I will react in the way that seems to me best for the world in which I live and which I have tried earnestly to serve. I know well that the triumph of communism will be a slow and difficult task, involving mistakes of every sort. It will call for progressive change in human nature and a better type of manhood than is common today. I believe this possible, or otherwise we will continue to lie, steal and kill as we are doing today.

Who now am I to have come to these conclusions? And of what if any significance are my deductions? What has been my life and work and of what meaning to mankind? The final answer to these questions, time and posterity must make. But perhaps it is my duty to contribute whatever enlightenment I can.

From THE AUTOBIOGRAPHY OF W. E. B. DU BOIS

A talk given on Paul Robeson's sixtieth birthday. It also appeared in The Autobiography of W. E. B. Du Bois.

On Paul Robeson

The persecution of Paul Robeson by the government and people of the United States during the last nine years has been one of the most contemptible happenings in modern history. Robeson has done nothing to hurt or defame this nation. He is, as all know, one of the most charming, charitable and loving of men. There is no person on earth who ever heard Robeson slander or even attack the land of his birth. Yet he had reason to despise America. He was a black man; the son of black folk whom Americans had stolen and enslaved. Even after his people's hard won and justly earned freedom, America made their lot as near a hell on earth as was possible. They discouraged, starved and insulted them. They sneered at helpless black children. Someone once said that the best punishment for Hitler would be to paint him black and send him to the United States. This was no joke. To struggle up as a black boy in America; to meet jeers and blows; to meet insult with silence and discrimination with a smile; to sit with fellow students who hated you and work and play for the honor of a college that disowned you—all this was America for Paul Robeson. Yet he fought the good fight; he was despised and rejected of men; a man of sorrows and acquainted with grief and we hid as it were our faces from him; he was despised and we esteemed him not.

Why? Why? Not because he attacked this country. Search Britain and France, the Soviet Union and Scandinavia for a word of his against America. What then was his crime? It was that while he did not rail at America he did praise the Soviet Union; and he did that because it treated him like a man and not like a dog; because he and his family for the first time in life were welcomed like human beings and he was honored as a great man. The children of Russia clung to him, the women kissed him; the workers greeted him; the state named mountains after him. He loved their homage. His eyes were filled with tears and his heart with thanks. Never before had he received such treatment. In America he was a "nigger"; in Britain he was tolerated; in France he was cheered; in the Soviet Union he was loved for the great artist that he is. He loved the Soviet Union in turn. He believed that every black man with blood in his veins would with him love the nation which first outlawed the color line.

I saw him when he voiced this. It was in Paris in 1949 at the greatest rally for world peace this world ever witnessed. Thousands of persons from all the world filled the Salle Playel from floor to rafters. Robeson hurried in, magnificent in height and breadth, weary from circling Europe with song. The audience rose to a man and the walls thundered. Robeson said that his people wanted Peace and "would never fight the Soviet Union." I joined with the thousands in wild acclaim.

This, for America, was his crime. He might hate anybody. He might join in murder around the world. But for him to declare that he loved the Soviet Union and would not join in war against it—that was the highest crime that the United States recognized. For that, they slandered Robeson; they tried to kill him at Peekskill; they prevented him from hiring halls in which to sing; they prevented him from travel and refused him a passport. His college, Rutgers, lied about him and dishonored him. And above all, his own people, American Negroes, joined in hounding one of their greatest artists—not all, but even men like Langston Hughes, who wrote of Negro musicians and deliberately omitted Robeson's name—Robeson who more than any living man has spread the pure Negro folk song over the civilized world. Yet has Paul Robeson kept his soul and stood his ground. Still he loves and honors the Soviet Union. Still he has hope for America. Still he asserts his faith in God. But we—what can we say or do; nothing but hang our heads in endless shame.

————

Dr. Du Bois' address on his 90th birthday. It also appeared in The Autobiography of W. E. B. Du Bois.

To His Newborn Great-Grandson

The most distinguished guest of this festive occasion is none other than my great-grandson, Arthur Edward McFarlane II, who was born this last Christmas Day. He had kindly consented to permit me to read to you a bit of advice which, as he remarked with a sigh of resignation, great-grandparents are supposed usually to inflict on the helpless young. This then is my word of advice.

As men go, I have had a reasonably happy and successful life, I have had enough to eat and drink, have been suitably clothed and, as you see, have had many friends. But the thing which has been the secret of whatever I have done is the fact that I have been able to earn a living by doing the work which I wanted to do and work that the world needed done.

I want to stress this. You will soon learn, my dear young man, that most human beings spend their lives doing work which they hate and work which the world does not need. It is therefore of prime importance that you early learn what you want to do; how you are fit to do it and whether or not the world needs this service. Here, in the next 20 years, your parents can be of use to you. You will soon begin to wonder just what parents are for besides interfering with your natural wishes. Let me therefore tell you: parents and their parents are inflicted upon you in order to show what kind of person you are; what sort of world you live in and what the persons who dwell here need for their happiness and well-being.

Right here, my esteemed great-grandson, may I ask you to stick a pin. You will find it the fashion in the America where eventually you will live and work to judge that life's work by the amount of money it brings you. This is a grave mistake. The return from your work must be the satisfaction which that work brings you and the world's need of that work. With this, life is heaven, or as near heaven as you can get. Without this—with work which you despise, which bores you and which the world does not need—this life is hell. And believe me, many a $25,000-a-year executive is living in just such a hell today.

Income is not greenbacks, it is satisfaction; it is creation; it is beauty. It is the supreme sense of a world of men going forward, lurch and stagger though it may, but slowly, inevitably going forward, and you, you yourself with your hand on the wheels. Make this choice, then, my son. Never hesitate, never falter.

And now comes the word of warning: the satisfaction with your work even at best will never be complete, since nothing on earth can be perfect. The forward pace of the world which you are pushing will be painfully slow. But what of that: the difference between a hundred and a thousand years is less than you now think. But doing what must be done, that is eternal even when it walks with poverty.

On Modern America

Perhaps the most extraordinary characteristic of current America is the attempt to reduce life to buying and selling. Life is not love unless love is sex and bought and sold. Life is not knowledge save knowledge of technique, of science for destruction. Life is not beauty except beauty for sale. Life is not art unless its price is high and it is sold for profit. All life is production for profit, and for what is profit but for buying and selling again?

Even today the contradictions of American civilization are tremendous. Freedom of political discussion is difficult; elections are not free and fair. Democracy is for us to a large extent unworkable. In business there is a tremendous amount of cheating and stealing; gambling in card games, on television and on the stock exchange is widely practiced. It is common custom for distinguished persons to sign books, articles, and speeches that they did not write; for men of brains to compose and sell opinions which they do not believe. Ghost writing is a profession. The greatest power in the land is not thought or ethics, but wealth, and the persons who exercise the power of wealth are not necessarily its owners, but those who direct its use, and the truth about this direction is so far as possible kept a secret. We do not know who owns our vast property and resources, so that most of our argument concerning wealth and its use must be based on guess work. Those responsible for the misuse of wealth escape responsibility, and even the owners of capital often do not know for what it is being used and how. The criterion of industry and trade is the profit that it accrues, not the good which it does either its owners or the public. Present profit is valued higher than future need. We waste materials. We refuse to make repairs. We cheat and deceive in manufacturing goods. . .

From THE AUTOBIOGRAPHY OF W. E. B. DU BOIS

More on the State of the Nation

The world is astonished at recent developments in the United States. Our actions and attitudes are discussed with puzzled wonder on the streets of every city in the world. Reluctantly the world is coming to believe that we actually want war; that we must have war; that in no other way can we keep our workers employed and maintain huge profits save by spending 70 thousand million dollars a year for war preparations and adding to the vast debt of 218 thousand millions which we already owe chiefly for war in the past. . . .

If tomorrow Russia disappeared from the face of the earth, the basic problem facing the modern world would remain; and that is: Why is it, with the earth's abundance and our mastery of natural forces, and miraculous technique; with our commerce belting the earth; and goods and services pouring from our stores, factories, ships and warehouses; why is it that nevertheless most human beings are starving to death, dying of preventable disease, and too ignorant to know what is the matter, while a small minority are so rich that they cannot spend their income?

That is the problem which faces the world, and Russia was not the first to pose it, nor will she be the last to ask and demand answer. . . .

It does not answer this worldwide demand to say that we of America have these things in greater abundance than the rest of the world, if our prosperity is based on or seeks to base itself on, the exploitation and degradation of the rest of mankind. Remember, it is American money that owns more and more of South African mines worked by slave labor; it is American enterprise that fattens off Central African copper; it is American investors that seek to dominate China, India, Korea, and Burma, and who are throttling the starved workers of the Near East, the Caribbean and South America. . . .

Today, in this free country, no man can be sure of earning a living, of escaping slander and personal violence, or even of keeping out of jail—unless publicly and repeatedly he proclaims that:

He hates Russia.

He opposes socialism and communism.

He supports wholeheartedly the war in Korea.

He is ready to spend any amount for further war, anywhere or anytime.

He is ready to fight the Soviet Union, China and any other country, or all countries together.

He believes in the use of the atom bomb or any other weapon of mass destruction, and regards anyone opposed as a traitor. . . .

Big business in the United States is forcing this nation into war, transforming our administration into a military dictatorship, paralyzing all democratic controls and depriving us of knowledge we need. The United States is ruled today by great industrial corporations controlling vast aggregations of capital and wealth. The acts and aims of this unprecedented integration of power, employing some of the best brain and ability of the land, are not and never have been under democratic control. . . .

If sincere dislike of this state of affairs is communism, then by the living God, no force of arms, nor power of wealth, nor smartness of intellect will ever stop it. Denial of this right to think will manufacture Communists faster than you can jail or kill them. Nothing will stop such communism but something better than communism. . . .

There is no way in the world for us to preserve the ideals of a democratic America, save by drastically curbing the present power of concentrated wealth; by assuming ownership of some natural resources, by administering many of our key industries, and by socializing our services for public welfare. This need not mean the adoption of the communism of the Soviet Union, nor the socialism of Britain, nor even of the near-socialism of France, Italy, or Scandinavia; but either in some way or to some degree we socialize our economy, restore the New Deal, and inaugurate the welfare state, or we descend into military fascism which will kill all dreams of democracy; of the abolition of poverty, disease and ignorance; or of peace instead of war.

There must come vast social change in the United States; a change not violent, but by the will of the people certain and inexorable, carried out "with malice toward none but charity for all"; with meticulous justice to the rich and thrifty, and complete sympathy for the poor, the sick and the ignorant; with Freedom and Democracy for America, and on earth, Peace, Goodwill toward men.

From THE AUTOBIOGRAPHY OF W. E. B. DU BOIS

From an address to the Southern Youth Legislature at Columbia, S.C. in 1946. 861 delegates, white and black, heard Du Bois.

Program for the South

The future of American Negroes is in the South. Here three hundred and twenty-seven years ago, they began to enter what is now the United States of America; here they have suffered the damnation of slavery, the frustration of reconstruction and the lynching of emancipation. I trust then that an organization like yours is going to regard the South as the battleground of a great crusade. Here is the magnificent climate; here is the fruitful earth under the beauty of the Southern sun; and here if anywhere on earth, is the need of the thinker, the worker and the dreamer. This is the firing line not simply for the emancipation of the American Negro but for the emancipation of the African Negro and the Negroes of the West Indies; for the emancipation of the colored races; and for the emancipation of the white slaves of modern capitalistic monopoly.

White youth in the South is peculiarly frustrated. There is not a single great ideal which they can express or aspire to, that does not bring them into flat contradiction with the Negro problem. The more they try to escape it, the more they land into hypocrisy, lying and double-dealing; the more they become, what they least wish to become, the oppressors and despisers of human beings. Some of them, in larger and larger numbers, are bound to turn toward the truth and to recognize you as brothers and as sisters, and as fellow travelers toward the new dawn.

Nevertheless reason can and will prevail; but of course it can only prevail with publicity—pitiless, blatant publicity. You have got to make the people of the United States and of the world know what is going on in the South. You have got to use every field of publicity to force the truth into their ears, and before their eyes. You have got to make it impossible for any human being to live in the South and not realize the barbarities that prevail here. You may be condemned for flamboyant methods; for calling a congress like this; for waving your grievances under the noses and in the faces of men. That makes no difference; it is your duty to do it. It is your duty to do more of this sort of thing than you have done in the past. As a result of this you are going to be called upon for sacrifice. It is no easy thing for a young black man or a young black woman to live in the South today and to plan to continue to live here; to marry and raise children; to establish a home. They are in the midst of legal caste and customary insults; they are in continuous danger of mob violence; they are mistreated by the officers of the law and they have no hearing before the courts and the churches and public opinion commensurate with the attention which they ought to receive. But that sacrifice is only the Beginning of Battle. You must rebuild this South.

There are enormous opportunities here for a new nation, a new economy, a new culture in a South really new and not a mere renewal of an old South of slavery, monopoly and race hatred. There is a chance for a new co-operative agriculture on renewed land owned by the State with capital furnished by the State, mechanized and co-ordinated with city life. There is a chance for strong, virile trade unions without race discrimination, with high wage, closed shop and decent conditions of work, to beat back and hold in check the swarm of landlords, monopolists and profiteers who are today sucking the blood out of this land. There is a chance for co-operative industry, built on the cheap power of T.V.A. and its future extensions. There is opportunity to organize and mechanize domestic service with decent hours, and high wages and dignified training.

————

A BLUEPRINT FOR US

Last Chance

If the United States really wishes to seize leadership in the present world, it will attempt to make the beneficiaries of the new economic order not simply a group, a race, or any form of oligarchy but, taking advantage of its own wealth and intelligence, will try to put democracy in control of the new economy. This will call for vital, gigantic effort; real education for the broadest intelligence and for evoking talent and genius on a scale never before attempted in the world, and putting to shame our present educational camouflage. With that program the sympathy and interest of the majority of the people of the world, particularly of the emerging darker peoples, will make the triumph of American industrial democracy over the oligarchical technocracy of Neuropa inevitable.

Democracy has failed because so many fear it. They believe that wealth and happiness are so limited that a world full of intelligent, healthy, and free people is impossible, if not undesirable. So the world stews in blood, hunger, and shame. . . .

From DEMOCRACY AND COLOR

Despite his criticism Du Bois loved America and probably was not as pessimistic about its future as he professed to be, especially in his later years. But he had asked himself "not what your country can do for you but what you can do for your country" and he knew that his contribution was in education, criticism, and prophecy.

Rebuild America

I know the United States. It is my country and the land of my fathers. It is still a land of magnificent possibilities. It is still the home of noble souls and generous people. But it is selling its birthright. It is betraying its mighty destiny. I was born on its soil and educated in its schools. I have served my country to the best of my ability. I have never knowingly broken its laws or unjustly attacked its reputation. At the same time I have pointed out its injustices and crimes and blamed it, rightly as I believe, for its mistakes. . . .

Today the United States is the leading nation in the world, which apparently believes that war is the only way to settle present disputes and difficulties. For this reason it is spending fantastic sums of money, and wasting wealth and energy on the preparation for war, which is nothing less than criminal. Yet the United States dare not stop spending money for war. If she did her whole economy, which is today based on preparation for war, might collapse. Therefore, we prepare for a Third World War; we spread our soldiers and arms over the earth and we bribe every nation we can to become our allies. We are taxing our citizens into poverty, crime and unemployment, and systematically distorting the truth about socialism. . . .

This is a beautiful world; this is a wonderful America, which the founding fathers dreamed until their sons drowned it in the blood of slavery and devoured it in greed. Our children must rebuild it.

From THE AUTOBIOGRAPHY OF W. E. B. DU BOIS

On Religion

My religious development has been slow and uncertain. I grew up in a liberal Congregational Sunday School and listened once a week to a sermon on doing good as a reasonable duty Theology played a minor part and our teachers had to face some searching questions. At 17 I was in a missionary college where religious orthodoxy was stressed; but I was more developed to meet it with argument, which I did. My "morals" were sound, even a bit puritanic, but when a hidebound old deacon inveighed against dancing I rebelled. By the time of graduation I was still a "believer" in orthodox religion, but had strong questions which were encouraged at Harvard. In Germany I became a freethinker and when I came to teach at an orthodox Methodist Negro school I was soon regarded with suspicion, especially when I refused to lead the students in public prayer. When I became head of a department at Atlanta, the engagement was held up because again I balked at leading in prayer, but the liberal president let me substitute the Episcopal prayer book on most occasions. Later I improvised prayers on my own. Finally I faced a crisis: I was using Crapsey's *Religion and Politics* as a Sunday School text. When Crapsey was hauled up for heresy, I refused further to teach Sunday School.

When Archdeacon Henry Phillips, my last rector, died, I flatly refused again to join any church or sign any church creed. From my 30th year on I have increasingly regarded the church as an institution which defended such evils as slavery, color caste, exploitation of labor and war. I think the greatest gift of the Soviet Union to modern civilization was the dethronement of the clergy and the refusal to let religion be taught in the public schools.

Religion helped and hindered my artistic sense. I know the old English and German hymns by heart. I loved their music but ignored their silly words with studied inattention. . . . I worshipped Cathedral and ceremony which I saw in Europe but I knew what I was looking at when in New York a Cardinal became a strike-breaker and the Church of Christ fought the Communism of Christianity.

From THE AUTOBIOGRAPHY OF W. E. B. DU BOIS

On Growing Old

I have been favored among the majority of men in never being compelled to earn my bread and butter by doing work that was uninteresting or which I did not enjoy or of the sort in which I did not find my greatest life interest. This rendered me so content in my vocation that I seldom thought about salary or haggled over it. My first job paid me eight hundred dollars a year and to take it I refused one which offered ten hundred and fifty. I served over a year at the University of Pennsylvania for the munificent sum of six hundred dollars and never railed at fate. I taught and worked at Atlanta University for twelve hundred a year during thirteen effective and happy years. I never once asked for an increase. I went to New York for the salary offered and only asked for an increase there when an efficient new white secretary was hired at a wage above mine. I then asked equal salary. I did not want the shadow of racial discrimination to creep into our salary schedule.

I realize now that this rather specious monetary independence may in the end cost me dearly, and land me in time upon some convenient street corner with a tin cup. For I have saved nearly nothing and lost my life insurance in the depression. Nevertheless, I insist that regardless of income, work worth while which one wants to do as compared with highly paid drudgery is exactly the difference between heaven and hell.

I am especially glad of the divine gift of laughter; it has made the world human and lovable, despite all its pain and wrong. I am glad that the partial Puritanism of my upbringing has never made me afraid of life. I have lived completely, testing every normal appetite, feasting on sunset, sea and hill, and enjoying wine, women, and song. I have seen the face of beauty from the Grand Canyon to the great Wall of China; from the Alps to Lake Baikal; from the African bush to the Venus of Milo.

Perhaps above all I am proud of a straightforward clearness of reason, in part a gift of the gods, but also to no little degree due to scientific training and inner discipline. By means of this I have met life face to face, I have loved a fight and I have realized that Love is God and Work is His prophet; that His ministers are Age and Death.

This makes it the more incomprehensible for me to see persons quite panic-stricken at the approach of their thirtieth birthday and prepared for dissolution at forty. Few of my friends have openly celebrated their fiftieth birthdays, and near none their sixtieth. Of course, one sees some reasons: the disappointment at meager accomplishment which all of us to some extent share; the haunting shadow of possible decline; the fear of death. I have been fortunate in having health and wise in keeping it. I have never shared what seems to me the essentially childish desire to live forever. Life has its pain and evil—its bitter disappointments; but I like a good novel and in healthful length of days, there is infinite joy in seeing the World, the most interesting of continued stories, unfold, even though one misses *the end*.

From DUSK OF DAWN

Last Message of Dr. Du Bois to the World

The body of Dr. W. E. B. Du Bois was laid to final rest with full military honors on the afternoon of August 29th at a spot some fifty yards from the pounding surf, beside the wall of The Castle, residence of the President of Ghana. Immediately following the interment, a last message to the world written by Dr. Du Bois was read to the thousands of assembled mourners. It was dated June 26, 1957, and had been given to his wife, Shirley Graham Du Bois, for safe-keeping until the hour of his death.

This is the Message:

It is much more difficult in theory than actually to say the last good-bye to one's loved ones and friends and to all the familiar things of this life.

I am going to take a long, deep and endless sleep. This is not a punishment but a privilege to which I have looked forward for years.

I have loved my work, I have loved people and my play, but always I have been uplifted by the thought that what I have done well will live long and justify my life; that what I have done ill or never finished can now be handed on to others for endless days to be finished, perhaps better than I could have done.

And that peace will be my applause.

One thing alone I charge you. As you live, believe in life! Always human beings will live and progress to greater, broader and fuller life.

The only possible death is to lose belief in this truth simply because the great end comes slowly, because time is long.

Good-bye.

From FREEDOMWAYS MAGAZINE, DU BOIS MEMORIAL
ISSUE, Winter 1965

CHRONOLOGY

1868	February 23. Born in Great Barrington, Mass. Son of Mary Silvina (nee Burghardt) Du Bois and Alfred Du Bois.
1875–1884	Attended public school in Great Barrington, Mass.
1885–1888	Attended Fisk University at Nashville, Tenn. Editor of the *Fisk Herald*.
1890	Graduated from Harvard with a B.A.
1892–1894	Student at University of Berlin on a Slater Fund grant.
1896	Awarded a Ph.D. from Harvard. His thesis "The Suppression of the Slave Trade in the United States" was printed as Vol. 1 in the Harvard University Historical Series.
1894–1896	Served as a professor of Greek and Latin at Wilberforce College in Ohio. Married Nina Gomer of Cedar Rapids, Iowa.
1897	Instructor at University of Pennsylvania. In 1899 he published his famous sociological study *The Philadelphia Negro: A Social Study*.
1900	Addressed the Pan-African Congress in London and wrote its report.
1897–1912	Professor of economics and history at Atlanta University. Supervised research and wrote reports for the "Atlanta Studies," printed as 16 monographs on many phases of Southern race relations—among the first important sociological studies made in America.
1903	Wrote *The Souls of Black Folk*.
1906	Founded *The Moon*, a magazine published in Memphis. In 1907 founded *Horizon*, a magazine published in Washington, D.C. These publications can be considered the forerunners of *The Crisis* which Du Bois founded in 1910.
1905–1909	Organized the Niagara Movement, the militant civil rights body that later merged with the NAACP—which Du Bois also helped to create.

1909   Published *John Brown*.
                Completed elaborate plans and outlines—with international sponsors of scholars—for the comprehensive *Encyclopedia Africana*. Du Bois was unable to finance the research until the Republic of Ghana invited him to that country in his 91st year.

1910   Founded *The Crisis,* one of the most influential journals ever published in the United States, which he edited continuously until 1934 when he resigned from the NAACP over a policy dispute.

1911   Wrote the sociological novel *The Quest of the Golden Fleece.*
                Joined Socialist Party. Became an editor of the radical magazine *The New Review.*

1913   Wrote and produced *The Star of Ethiopia,* an outdoor historical drama, in New York City.

1917–1919   Wrote controversial editorial "Close Ranks" for *The Crisis.* Involved in the Pan-African Congress in Paris in 1919.
                May 1919, wrote controversial editorial in *The Crisis* demanding equal rights for all colored peoples at home and abroad. The issue was temporarily denied mailing privileges. Worked with Mandates Commission of League of Nations but was disappointed that the League did not assume an anti-colonial position.

1920   Wrote *Darkwater,* a book of essays and creative writing which reveals Du Bois as the master propagandist for racial justice.
                Won coveted Spingarn Medal, awarded annually to the most effective fighter for civil rights, for his work in the Pan-African Congresses.

1920–1921   Founded and helped to edit and write *The Brownies' Book,* a publication aimed at the education of "our children of the sun." Its objective was to instill race pride and the idea that "Black is Beautiful."

1923   Represented the United States at inauguration of President Tubman of Liberia.

1924   Wrote *The Gift of Black Folk.*

1926   Made first visit to the Soviet Union.

1927   Became involved in the Harlem Renaissance, using his own influence and the pages of *The*

	Crisis to publish many of the writers and artists in the movement. Founded Krigwa Players.
	Helped organize Fourth Pan-African Congress in New York City.
1928	Wrote novel *The Dark Princess*.
1934	Resigned from *The Crisis* and NAACP over two issues: (1) pluralism or black self-segregation and (2) independence of *The Crisis*.
1934–1944	Appointed head of Department of Sociology at Atlanta University.
1935	Wrote *Black Reconstruction*.
1939	Published *Black Folk, Then and Now*.
1940	Published *Dusk of Dawn*.
	Founded influential opinion and literary journal, *Phylon*.
1945	Along with Walter White and Ralph Bunche, Du Bois served as official NAACP consultant at founding of United Nations. Using his experience obtained in 1919 working with the League of Nations and Mandates Commission, Du Bois asked the U.N to take a first stand against colonialism and racial injustice in the United States.
	Presided at Fifth Pan-African Congress at Manchester, England.
	Co-author with Dr. Guy B. Johnson of *Encyclopedia of the Negro,* a preliminary, detailed outline of his *Encyclopedia Africana* which he had first proposed as early as 1909.
	Published *Color and Democracy*.
1947	Wrote "An Appeal to the World" for the NAACP and presented it as a proposed program to the United Nations. Argued that the persecuted Negro minority, which Du Bois called a "nation within a nation," should have international protection.
	Published *The World and Africa*.
1948	Final break with the NAACP over policy and personality clash with Secretary Walter White.
1949	Attended various international peace conferences organized with the co-operation of left-wing groups in Paris, Moscow, and New York City. Peace was to be one of Du Bois' chief concerns for the rest of his life.
1950	Candidate for U.S. Senator from New York

on Progressive Party ticket.
Wife Nina Gomer Du Bois died.

1950–1951   Indictment on Federal charge of being an "unregistered foreign agent," because of his activities in circulating so-called Stockholm Peace Petition. Judge McGuire dismissed the indictment.

1951   Married writer Shirley Graham.

1952   Wrote *In Battle for Peace*.

1957–1960   Published *The Black Flame*, trilogy of novels.

1960   Wrote his long autobiography (published posthumously in 1968).

1961   At age of 93, Du Bois joined the Communist Party.

1963   Became a citizen of Ghana. Began work on the Encyclopedia Africana. Died on August 27. Accorded state funeral in Accra, Ghana.

BIBLIOGRAPHY

Selected Books by Du Bois

Suppression of the Slave Trade to The United States of America. New York: Longmans, Green and Co., 1896.

The Philadelphia Negro. Philadelphia: University of Pennsylvania Press, 1899.

The Souls of Black Folk. Chicago: A. C. McClurg and Co., 1903.

John Brown. Philadelphia: George W. Jacobs and Co., 1909.

The Quest of the Silver Fleece. Chicago: A. C. McClurg and Co., 1911.

The Negro. New York: Henry Holt and Co., 1915.

Darkwater. Washington, D.C.: A. Jenkins Co., 1920.

Gift of Black Folk in the making of America. Boston: The Stratford Co., 1924.

Dark Princess. New York: Harcourt, Brace, 1928.

Black Reconstruction. New York: Harcourt, Brace, 1935.

Black Folk, Then and Now. New York: Henry Holt and Co., 1939.

Dusk of Dawn. New York: Harcourt, Brace, 1940.

Encyclopedia of the Negro. New York: Phelps-Stokes Fund, Inc., 1945.

Color and Democracy. New York: Harcourt, Brace, 1945.

The World and Africa. New York: The Viking Press, 1947.

In Battle for Peace. New York: *Masses & Mainstream,* 1952.

The Black Flame (trilogy). New York: *Masses & Mainstream. The Ordeal of Mansart,* 1957. *Mansart Builds a School,* 1959. *Worlds of Color,* 1960.

An ABC of Color. Berlin: Seven Seas Publishers, 1963.

The Autobiography of W. E. B. Du Bois. New York: International Publishers, 1968.

Atlanta Studies (Sociological monographs written in the main and edited by Du Bois.) Atlanta University, 1899–1912. Reprinted one volume by *The New York Times* (Arno Press), 1969.

Magazine Articles by Du Bois, A Partial Listing

"Enforcement of the Slave-Trade Laws," *Annual Report of the American Historical Association* (1891).

"The Conservation of Races," *American Negro Academy* (Occasional Papers II, 1897).

"The Study of Negro Problems," *Annals of the American Academy of Political and Social Science* (1898).

"A Negro Schoolmaster in the New South," *The Atlantic Monthly* (Jan., 1899).

"The Negro and Crime," *Independent Magazine* (May 18, 1899).

"The Suffrage Fight in Georgia," *Independent Magazine* (Nov. 30, 1899).

"American Negro at Paris," *American Monthly Review of Reviews* (Nov., 1900).

"The Religion of the American Negro," *New World* (Dec., 1900).

"The Problem of the Twentieth Century Is the Problem of the Color Line," *The Atlantic Monthly* (1901).

"Results of the Ten Tuskegee Conferences," *Harper's Weekly* (Jan. 22, 1901).

"The Freedmen's Bureau," *The Atlantic Monthly* (March, 1901).

"The Storm and Stress in the Black World," *Dial* (April 16, 1901).

"The Negro As He Really Is," *The World's Work* (June, 1901).

"The Relation of the Negroes to the Whites in the South," *Annals of the American Academy of Political and Social Sciences* (July, 1901).

"The Burden of Negro Schooling," *Independent Magazine* (July 18, 1901).

"The Spawn of Slavery," *Missionary Review of the World* (Oct., 1901).

"The Freedmen and Their Sons," *Independent Magazine* (Nov. 14, 1901).

"The Black North," *The New York Times* (Nov. 17, 24; Dec. 1, 8, 15, 1901).

"The Opening of the Library," *Independent Magazine* (April 3, 1902).

"Of the Training of Black Men," *The Atlantic Monthly* (Sept., 1902).

"The Laboratory in Sociology at Atlanta," *Annals of the American Academy of Political and Social Sciences* (May, 1903).

"Possibilities of the Negro," *Booklover's Magazine* (July, 1903).

"The Training of Negroes for Social Power," *Outlook* (Oct. 17, 1903).

"The Negro Problem from the Negro Point of View," *The World Today* (April, 1904).

"The Development of a People," *International Journal of Ethics* (April, 1904).

"Credo," *Independent Magazine* (Oct. 6, 1904).

"The Southerner's Problem," *Dial* (May 1, 1905).

"The Niagara Movement," *The Voice of the Negro* (Sept., 1905).

"Garrison and the Negro," *Independent Magazine* (Dec. 7, 1905).

"The Economic Future of the Negro," *Publications of the American Economic Association* (Feb., 1906).

"A Litany at Atlanta," *Independent Magazine* (Oct. 11, 1906).

"The Color Line Belts the World," *Colliers* (Oct. 20, 1906).

"The Tragedy of Atlanta," *The World Today* (Nov., 1906).

"The Negro and Socialism," *Horizon* (Feb., 1907).

"The Value of Agitation," *The Voice of the Negro* (IV, March, 1907).

"Race Friction Between Black and White," *American Journal of Sociology* (May, 1908).

"National Committee on the Negro," *Survey* (June 12, 1909).

"The Negro and the YMCA," *Horizon* (March, 1910).

"Reconstruction and Its Benefits," *American Historical Review* (July, 1910).

"The Souls of White Folk," *Independent Magazine* (Aug. 18, 1910).

"Marrying of Black Folk," *Independent Magazine* (Oct. 13, 1910).

"Socialism and the Negro Problem," *New Review* (Feb. 1, 1913).

"The Negro in Literature and Art," *Annals of the Ameri-*

can Academy of Political and Social Sciences (Sept., 1913).

"The African Roots of War," *The Atlantic Monthly* (May, 1915).

"The Economic Aspects of Race Prejudice," *Editorial Review* (May, 1916).

"Of the Culture of White Folk," *Journal of Race Development* (April, 1917).

"On Being Black," *The New Republic* (Feb. 18, 1920).

"The Republicans and the Black Voter," *The Nation* (June 5, 1920).

"The South and a Third Party," *The New Republic* (Jan. 3, 1923).

"Back to Africa," *Century* (Feb., 1923). (Marcus Garvey Essay)

"The Hosts of Black Labor," *The Nation* (May 9, 1923).

"The Negro Takes Stock," *The New Republic* (Jan. 2, 1924).

"The Dilemma of the Negro," *American Mercury* (Oct., 1924).

"The Primitive Black Man," *The Nation* (Dec. 17, 1924).

"What Is Civilization? Africa's Answer," *Forum* (Feb., 1925).

"Worlds of Color," *Foreign Affairs* (April, 1925).

"France's Black Citizens in West Africa," *Current History* (July, 1925).

"Liberia and Rubber," *The New Republic* (Nov. 18, 1925).

"The Shape of Fear," *North American Review* (June, 1926).

"The Hampton Strike," *The Nation* (Nov. 2, 1927).

"Race Relations in the United States," *Annals of the American Academy of Political and Social Sciences* (Nov., 1928).

"Education and Work," *Howard University Bulletin* (Jan., 1931).

"Will the Church Remove the Color Line?" *Christian Century* (Dec. 9, 1931).

"A Negro Nation Within the Nation," *Current History* (June, 1935).

"Inter-Racial Implications of the Ethiopian Crisis," *Foreign Affairs* (Oct., 1935).

"Social Planning for the Negro: Past and Present," *Journal of Negro Education* (Jan., 1936).

"Black Africa Tomorrow," *Foreign Affairs* (Oct., 1938).

"Where Do We Go from Here," *Journal of Negro Education* (Jan., 1939).

"Chronicle of Race Relations," *Phylon* (1942).

"The Realities in Africa," *Foreign Affairs* (July, 1943).

"Reconstruction; Seventy-five Years After," *Phylon* (1943).

"Prospects of a World Without Race Conflicts," *American Journal of Sociology* (March, 1944).

"What He Meant to the Negro," *New Masses* (April 24, 1945). (On FDR)

"Colonies and Moral Responsibility," *Journal of Negro Education* (Summer, 1946).

"Common Objectives," *Soviet Russia Today* (Aug., 1946).

"Behold the Land," *New Masses* (Jan. 14, 1947).

"Can the Negro Expect Freedom by 1965?," *Negro Digest* (April, 1947).

"The Most Hopeful State in the World," *Soviet Russia Today* (Nov., 1947).

"From McKinley to Wallace: My Fifty Years as a Political Independent," *Masses & Mainstream* (Aug., 1948).

"Race Relations in the United States, 1917–1947," *Phylon* (1948).

"The Negro Since 1900: A Progress Report," *The New York Times Magazine* (Nov. 21, 1948).

"Negroes and the Crisis of Capitalism in the United States," *Monthly Review* (April, 1950).

"American Negroes and Africa," *The National Guardian* (Feb. 14, 1955).

"Pan-Africa: A Mission in My Life," *United Asia* (April, 1955).

"China and Africa," *New World Review* (April, 1959).

"The Negro People and the United States," *Freedomways* (Spring, 1961).

Suggestions for Further Reading About Du Bois

Aptheker, Dr. Herbert, "W. E. B. Du Bois: The First Eighty Years." *Phylon* (First quarter, 1948).

Bond, Dr. Horace Mann. "Negro Leadership Since Washington." *South Atlantic Quarterly* (April, 1925).

Braithwaite, William Stanley. "A Tribute to W. E. Burghardt Du Bois." *Phylon* (Fourth quarter, 1949).

Broderick, Francis L. *W. E. B. Du Bois: Negro Leader in a Time of Crisis.* Stanford, California: Stanford University Press, 1959.

Freedomways, W. E. B. Du Bois Memorial Issue (Winter, 1965).

Harding, Dr. Vincent. "W. E. B. Du Bois and the Black Messianic Vision." *Freedomways* (Winter, 1969).

Kaiser, Dr. Ernest. "A Selected Bibliography of the Published Writings of W. E. B. Du Bois." *Freedomways* (Winter, 1965).

King, Dr. Martin Luther, Jr. Centennial address at Carnegie Hall, New York City, Feb. 23, 1968. Reprinted in *Freedomways* (Spring, 1968). Also a pamphlet by the W. E. B. Du Bois Memorial Committee (1968).

Nelson, Truman. "A Prophet in Limbo." *The Nation* (January 25, 1958).

Redding, J. Saunders. "Portrait: W. E. Burghardt Du Bois." *American Scholar* (January, 1949).

Rudwick, Elliott, M. *W. E. B. Du Bois: Propagandist of the Negro Protest.* New York: Atheneum, 1968.

The Crisis, Du Bois memorial issue (Feb. 1968).

Graduate Theses About W. E. B. Du Bois

Abramowitz, Jack. *Accommodation and Military in Negro Life 1870–1915*. Doctoral dissertation. Columbia Univ., 1931.

Brisbane, Robert H. *The Rise of Protest Movements Among Negroes Since 1900*. Doctoral dissertation. Harvard Univ., 1949.

Broderick, Francis. *W. E. B. Du Bois: The Trail of His Ideas*. Doctoral dissertation. Harvard Univ., 1955.

Collins, L. M. *W. E. B. Du Bois's Views on Education*. M.A. thesis. Fisk Univ., 1937.

Franklin, B. J. *Politico-Economic Theories of Three Negro Leaders*. M.A. thesis. Howard Univ., 1936.

Johnson, Arthur L. *The Social Theories of W. E. B. Du Bois*. M.A. thesis. Atlanta Univ., 1949.

Jones, Dewey R. *The Effect of the Negro Press on Race Relationships in the South*. M.A. thesis. Columbia Univ., 1931.

Owens, Dorothy E. *W. E. Burghardt Du Bois: A Case Study of a Marginal Man*. M.A. thesis. Fisk Univ., 1944.

Pierce, James E. *The N.A.A.C.P.—A Study in Social Pressure*. M.A. thesis. Ohio State Univ., 1933.

Robinson, Carrie C. *A Study of the Literary Subject-Matter of the Crisis*. M.A. thesis. Fisk Univ., 1934.

Rudwick, Elliot M. *W. E. B. Du Bois: A Study in Minority Group Leadership*. Doctoral dissertation. Univ. of Pa., 1956.

INDEX